THEORIES OF SURPLUS
AND TRANSFER

THEORIES OF SURPLUS AND TRANSFER
Parasites and Producers in Economic Thought

HELEN BOSS

*Fellow, Harvard University
Russian Research Center*

Boston
UNWIN HYMAN
London   Sydney   Wellington

© Helen Boss 1990
This book is copyright under the Berne Convention. No
reproduction without permission. All rights reserved.

Unwin Hyman, Inc.,
8 Winchester Place, Winchester, Mass. 01890, USA

Published by the Academic Division of
Unwin Hyman Ltd
15/17 Broadwick Street, London W1V 1FP, UK

Allen & Unwin (Australia) Ltd,
8 Napier Street, North Sydney, NSW 2060, Australia

Allen & Unwin (New Zealand) Ltd in association with the
Port Nicholson Press Ltd,
Compusales Building, 75 Ghuznee Street, Wellington 1, New Zealand

First published in 1990

Library of Congress Cataloging-in-Publication Data
Boss, Helen
 Theories of surplus and transfer : parasites and producers in
economic thought / Helen Boss.
 p.   cm.
 Bibliography: p.
 Includes index.
 ISBN 0-04-330371-4.
 ISBN 0-04-330372-2 (pbk.)
 1. Economics—History. I. Title.
HB75.B726 1989
330'.09—dc20   89-9122
                                                             CIP

British Library Cataloguing in Publication Data
 Boss, Helen
  Theories of surplus and transfer : parasites and
  producers in economic thought.
  1. Economics. Theories, history
  I. Title
  330.1

 ISBN 0-04-330371-4

Typeset in 10 on 12 point Bembo
Printed in Great Britain by the University Press, Cambridge

Contents

Preface by Samuel Hollander   page xiii

Acknowledgements   xvii

1 *Introduction: Productive labor and its product*   1

Part One   RISE AND DECLINE OF THE CLASSICAL–MARXIAN SURPLUS AND TRANSFER THEORY   13

2 *Early views of production, surplus-generation, and transfer*   15

1 Kuznets's triad
2 Producers in Petty and King
      Figure 2.1 Petty's welfare economics
      Table 2.2 King's Scheme
3 Mandeville's paradox
4 Luxury and necessity in Boisguilbert and Cantillon
5 Demand and capital in Physiocracy
6 Sterility challenged, Forbonnais to Condillac
7 The boundary of the economy in 1776

3 *Division of labor and unproductive labor in a system of natural liberty: Adam Smith's dilemma*   42

1 Two sorts of unproductive labor
2 What is capital, that it be accumulated?
3 Servants in the household: consumers sovereignty, and natural liberty in the *Wealth of Nations*
4 Materiality dominant?
5 Servants of the public
6 Division of labor with unproductive laborers – a hopeless contradiction?

4 *Immaterial production from Garnier to Mill*   63

1 Physiocracy after 1789
2 'French' Classical microeconomics and the Smithian polarities
3 Ricardo avoids input-output error
4 Malthus's cure for gluts

5 Goods and services, McCulloch to Mill
6 Classicism, marginalism, and materiality

5 *Mode and matter in Marx: the factory paradigm and the scope of the base*   89

1 The productive-labor theory of value and its corollaries
2 Capitalism or materiality?
3 The factory paradigm and the production–circulation dichotomy
4 Beyond the capitalist mode: the petty producer
    Figure 5.1 Marx's economy
5 Mental labor and the 'living production machine'
6 Can immaterial services be constant-capital inputs?
7 The 'most efficacious proportion', a positive fraction
8 Marx as welfare economist
9 Inputs, outputs and epochs

Part Two   IN A NEW MODE   119

6 *Materiality and non-productivity under mixed socialism in the USSR*   121

1 Labor theorists and Austrians
2 Golden-Age Marxism from Kautsky to Lenin
3 Bukharin's economics of revolution
4 Output under incomplete socialism from Prokopovich to the Stalin textbook: the theoretical options
5 The materiality of Soviet 'material production'
6 Effects on the service share?
7 *Perestroika* and Soviet economics

Part Three   REVISIONS AND EXTENSIONS   187

7 *Old Left and New Right on government as parasite*   189

1 Post-Keynesian Marxism: capitalism spared by an unproductive war sector
2 Post-Keynesian Classicism: capitalism starved by an unproductive state sector
3 Public goods, rent-seeking, and the neoclassical economics of mode

8 *Drawing the boundary: the main variants*   227

1 From producers to products
2 Intermediate and final in the System of National Accounts and the International Comparison Project
3 Matter and mode in the Material Product System
4 New measures of final supply: towards an economics of use-values

9 Necessity without materiality, materiality without fallacy   258
1 Necessity without materiality: 'basic needs' in development economics
2 Materiality without fallacy: Polanyi–Pearson economic anthropology

10 Results, not inputs   271
1 On Sombart's torment turnpike
2 Review of the parts
3 Finality, sovereignty, and the efficacy of policy
4 Styles of dictatorship
5 Von Neumann systems
6 Intermediates, bads, and the 'most efficacious proportion'
7 The 'sole end and purpose of all production'

Note on notes, terms and translations   287

Bibliography   288

Index   333

*To four wise men,
one darling little girl
and in memory of J. C. Weldon*

Preface

In *Theories of Surplus and Transfer* Helen Boss subjects to close analysis and with remarkable liveliness the logic and history of the celebrated productive-unproductive dichotomy in its various senses – surplus-generating vs. surplus-absorbing; material vs. immaterial; marketable vs. non-marketable; final vs. intermediate. The coverage is ambitious, extending from the late 17th century national income accountancy of Petty and King to the Physiocrats, Adam Smith, the British and the French classics, the marginalists and early neo-classicists, nearly the whole range of modern orthodox literature, and also Marx, Marxist and Soviet writings. As such it constitutes a veritable *tour de force* dealing with the central issue at the foundation of all economic reasoning: who are the producers and what do they produce?

Sir John Hicks emphasises a too often neglected contrast between the history of the natural sciences and the history of economics. For the working natural scientist the history of his subject is typically of no practical significance: 'Old ideas are worked out; old controversies are dead and buried.' Not so in economics: 'we cannot escape in the same way from our own past. We may pretend to escape; but the past crowds in on us all the same.' ('Revolutions in Economics', in S. Latsis ed., *Method and Appraisal in Economics*, Cambridge, 1976, p. 207.) The themes of this book provide a case in point. Far from constituting the dusty museum piece of Schumpeterian legend, the controversies relating to the boundaries of the economic domain – within which income-generating activity occurs and upon which 'non-producers' (the author's 'parasites') are dependent – yield a range of perspectives on the nature of output and therefore on appropriate national income accounting which are of abiding theoretical and practical significance. Students would do well to become familiar with the struggles of the mind surrounding these issues, both to develop their understanding of the bases of economic logic and as a means of avoiding the arrogant provincialism in space and time which is encouraged by *Principles* texts which imply that past debates reflect nothing but confusion at last settled to everyone's satisfaction, at least to every right-thinking person's satisfaction.

The source of this narrowness of perspective seems to derive from the exclusion of history from courses and training in economics. I have long held that logic and history should be co-requirements in any self-respecting program for the training of economists. The great economists of the past did not approach their subject solely as a matter of 'pure' theory but had particular visions of the environment in mind as requiring explication. The point was made by J. S. Mill: 'The deductive Science of Society will not lay down a theorem, asserting in an universal manner the effect of any cause, but will teach us to frame the proper theorem for the circumstances of any given case. It will not give the laws of society in general, but the means of determining the phenomena of a given society from the particular elements or data of that society.' (*System of Logic*, in *Collected Works*, VIII, pp. 899–900.) E. Phelps Brown has urged that a 'clinical commitment' be made to resist 'the temptation to seek the job for the tools instead of the tool for the job'. (*Economic Journal*, 1972, p. 8.) For teachers and students of modern economics who welcome this orientation and are curious to see the effects of extending it broadly to matters of definition and classification as well as to mechanisms and mathematical tools narrowly perceived, the present work will be a boon. It is illuminating to look at changes in fashion regarding such central concepts as 'production', 'capital formation', 'consumption' and 'surplus' with an eye to the relative influences of the theoretical, ideological, computational and historical context.

That the productive-unproductive dichotomy is indeed far from a dust-covered relic is manifestly apparent in that aspects of it continually reemerge with changes in the economic situation and therefore in the focus of our attention. It is disconcerting to see that our own concern with improving the performance of Western mixed economies characterised by high levels of public expenditure raises issues in some respects identical to those debated in the 18th century.

The book charts with pleasing impartiality the shifting emphases economists and social thinkers have placed on markets and on 'mode' of production generally in their quest for an optimal mix of institutions. Dr Boss relates concern over declining proportions of 'material production' and growing service shares in Western and socialist economies to the sovereignties (producer, consumer, dictator) which drive economic outcomes. A study of this book would I suspect prove particularly illuminating to Soviet, East bloc and Chinese reformers.

In its full development of the implications of the productive-unproductive dichotomy, Helen Boss's *Theories of Surplus and Transfer* is a unique contribution so far as I am aware. It provides a fine balance of history of economic thought, economic history, welfare theory and policy, growth economics and economic systems. The quality of the scholarship is impressive; whether or not one accepts all of its provocative interpretations or indeed its agenda for an economics of the future is of secondary importance.

Samuel Hollander
University Professor and
  Professor of Economics,
  University of Toronto
Fellow of the Royal Society
  of Canada
November 1988

Acknowledgements

Friends, teachers, and colleagues helped me write *Theories of Surplus and Transfer*. It is impossible to weight the material and immaterial inputs that yielded this artefact of intellectual and manual labor. Several governments protected me while I read, ate, and wrote. Dr J. P. Manson, onetime Assistant Professor at Harvard University, launched me by an act of kindness into the study of Russia and the Soviet Union. Dr I. Tuominen, a real scientist, piqued my curiosity about Marxism. Messrs Brunt and Glowacki of London persuaded me that, even when inflation stands at 32 per cent, economics can be a fascinating and worthy subject. Professor A. Vicas of McGill introduced me to the *Wealth of Nations*, not skipping the digression on silver.

Of those kind enough to examine parts or drafts of the manuscript or to respond to queries, I would like to thank A. Asimakopulos, D. Bell, J. Berliner, M. Blaug, V. Boss, J. Chapman, J. Cohen, P. Davenport, R. Dehem, R. Dorfman, W. Eltis, P. Gregory, A. O. Hirschman, the late S. Kuznets, H. Leibenstein, W. Leontief, D. L'vov, N. Makasheva, V. Mau, P. Mirowski, K. Osband, M.-T. Pontbriand, S. Resnick, G. Schroeder, A. Sharpe, N. Shukhov, R. Skurski, L. Smolinski, A. Ulam, P. Wiles, and E. Zhil'tsov. Their responsibility for the end result is, however, not even dialectical. I ask Professors Hirschman and Goldhagen's forgiveness for not having written a promised section on Nazism Left and Right, and Professor Bakker's for omitting the latest Marxian feminists. Many other people shaped my views on subjects directly and incidentally related to economics. A. McIlhenny, A. McIlhenny, Jr, F. Lutz, S. Orcutt, B. Rumer, G. Baum, M. Frankman, P. Aaron, D. Henrion, Z. Sochor, R. Fletcher, R. Pipes, A. Gleason, B. Schwalberg, C. Meyer, E. Stubbs, M. Beissinger, M. Prell, R. Miller, H. Zeisel, and M. Mendell all helped with particular points.

Deepest thanks go to Alec Nove, who read whole sections of the manuscript and argued them with me on many an occasion, and to Abram Bergson, whose lifelong commitment to the *mot juste* and to the highest intellectual clarity set a standard I can only aspire to. Samuel Hollander left an indelible imprint on the book through action at a distance, encouraging the project from the start and setting an extraordinary example of scholarly *Fleiss* and care. W. Allan, Carolyn White and John Fraser of Unwin Hyman got the book to press as fast as I could write it. To my former colleagues at the Université du Québec à Montréal – Vély Leroy, Claude Fluet, Gilles Dostaler, Diane Bellemare, John McCallum, and Louis Gill – *grand merci*.

Most of *Theories of Surplus and Transfer* was written during my fellowship at Harvard University's Russian Research Center. I stand in deep gratitude to Professors Bergson, Berliner, and Ulam and their colleagues and staff for giving me the opportunity to work in the company of so many interested people. I would also like to thank the International Research and Exchange Board of the American Council of Learned Societies for sending me to the USSR at the height of *glasnost'* on the exchange with the Soviet Academy of Sciences. Though funds for my research were provided by the National Endowment for the Humanities and the United States Information Agencies, none of these organizations bears responsibility for the views expressed.

Theories of Surplus and Transfer owes its inception to a seminar in economic theory given by my late master, J. C. Weldon. That complex and brilliant man left much important work unfinished at his death in 1987, not least an analysis of the principal systems in economic thought. A mode-neutral Walrasian Christian, Professor Weldon was poised to develop what economists have been waiting for for most of this century: a coherent public-goods-augmented welfare economics. The task of the economist he likened to the sculptor's: within the block of marble lurks the true form of our would-be science; the pattern emerges as the errors are cleared. Though we had our disagreements, they were always fruitful, and never affected our friendship. Those who knew Jack Weldon will see his mark on every page.

CHAPTER 1

Introduction: Productive Labor and its Product

An extraordinary feature of economics has been the durability and complexity of ideas associated with the terms 'productive' and 'unproductive labor'. 'Productive' and 'unproductive', as adjectives, have served as a shorthand for concepts reaching into major areas of economic thought. The shorthand was to have provided a clear binary formula for distinguishing goods from bads, outputs from inputs, economies from societies. It was never very good at the job. Improving the clarity and comprehensiveness of the transcriptions has not been easy; as this book shows, a large part of the scientific research program of general economics since the time of Adam Smith has been taken up with this challenge; the difficulty of transcribing the shorthand accounts for the longevity of the terms 'productive' and 'unproductive' in economic discourse – and their capacity to sow confusion.

Theories of Surplus and Transfer takes as its subject the fundamental and imperfectly resolved issues of who is a producer and of what. It looks at how the great and not-so-great minds of economic science have answered economics' basic questions: what is output? which citizens produce it? is more always better than less? does 'mode' matter?

The book is organized around the distinction, articulated here for the first time, between *theories of surplus-generation and its transfer* from productives to non-productives on the one hand, and *theories of interdependence* on the other. The distinction is basic to the growth economics written for Western, socialist, and underdeveloped economies, from the seventeenth century to the present. Disagreement over which laborers are productive is at issue in a surprising number of controversies in the history of economics, from its declaration of independence from politics in the eighteenth century to its late-twentieth-century reannexation of government and the family.

The aim of the book is to trace the historical and logical connections between early political economy's 'productive/unproductive' dichotomy and modern views about the scope of 'the economy', the relevance of 'mode' of production, the sources of 'output' growth, and the nature of the links between output and 'welfare'. The new terms I introduce – 'surplus and transfer theory', 'input-output error', the 'productive-labor theory of value', the 'single-person firm', 'lexicographic modism', the 'most efficacious proportion' – should prove useful additions to the lexicon of social science.

Physiocratic and Smithian 'productive/unproductive labor' dichotomies were found to be inconsistent and incomplete by the first years of the nineteenth century, but they survived ever more sophisticated attacks for good reason. Delimiting the scope of some economy, drawing a boundary between it and what is exogenous to it, is part of the economist's fundamental declaration of faith in the subject. From Sir William Petty to Gary S. Becker, economist-observers have of necessity prefaced their inquiry into the sources of society's economic welfare by a delimitation of its scope. It was realized by the mid-eighteenth century that *any restrictive definition of the economy and the economic implies a boundary with a non-economic world* raising the question of mutual interaction.

On the boundary's economic side, activities designated as 'productive' were supposed to yield 'produce', 'products', 'output' that had positive utility. Output increased the welfare of those members of society whose welfare counts. More was better than less.

Careful boundary-drawing, a preoccupation of Chapters 8 to 10, is found to be useful in keeping ambiguities from creeping into the relation between work and ultimate welfare. If the outputs that raise welfare are all produced within 'the economy', and none are produced outside its limits, then, barring Pareto problems, the volume and mix of the economy's total output can by hypothesis be left to self-interested suppliers and demanders without paradoxical effects on social happiness.

A difficulty with having unproductive laborers in the first place is that the transfers to them that such a category implies are rarely fully motivated. Most economic systems make allowance for consumers who are not producers in the ordinary (non-Beckerian) sense: infants, students, invalids. Most economic systems allow for imperfectly equivalent exchange when there are imperfections of competition and information in marketed and other resources. But a surprisingly long list of writers postulated (a few still do) a class of 'unproductive laborers' who despite their handicap managed to survive and even prosper in a competitive social marketplace.

Central to the debate over 'productive' and 'unproductive' is the question of whether the economy is producing a 'surplus'. Depending on how the productive domain is cordoned off in a given model, some products or their inputs may be or may appear to be 'in surplus to' the consumption or disposition of designated producers. These surplus products or their money equivalent can then be syphoned over the fence into the non-economy, if there is one. *A true surplus is free for the tapping*. The tale of surplus-generation and its transfer from designated producers to consumers is told in many variations by economists in the course of the 300-year history of modern economics, but I think it is always essentially the same story.

Once the boundary of the economy is drawn and ingredients of the output maximand are listed, economist-observers are free in principle to concentrate on what Kuznets called 'valuation' (price formation). Value theory, the stuff of standard and even Marxian histories of economic thought, plays a secondary rôle in the story told in succeeding chapters. Relative prices enter in for the reason that *prices are the weights* that permit aggregation from some disparate collection of goods and services produced within a given boundary to a summary measure of individual or social product or consumption. It is of keen interest, though, whether an observer stipulates that the prices used for aggregation be set on price-making *markets*, or whether for example cost or opportunity cost will do. Restricting 'the economy' to the monetized market economy of course begs the question of how to account for the income and product of members of society whose activities are mediated by other, non-market mechanisms or 'modes'.

The present work interprets the history of general economics as a cumulative attempt to transcribe the archaic *binary* 'productive/unproductive' shorthand onto a set of concepts that are more accurate descriptors of socioeconomic phenomena. It updates those parts of Schumpeter's *History* overshadowed by recent work in public, comparative and general economics and in the history of Classical thought. Modern economics is found to differ from the Classical and Marxian by the extent to which the old dichotomous 'productive/unproductive' distinction is replaced by continuous distinctions having clearer implications for boundaries, value, and welfare. The Smithian 'productive/unproductive' dichotomy, originally convenient and telling, has been known since the first decades of the nineteenth century to be a notoriously poor guide to human action constrained by availability of time and resources. But its heady simplicity and apparent welfare-relatedness still seduce the uninitiated.

'Productive' and 'unproductive', as adjectives, have stood in for myriad qualities of economic virtue and vice. Among the most popular duos: 'surplus-generating' vs. 'surplus-absorbing', 'material' vs. 'immaterial', 'long-lasting' vs. 'short-lasting', 'necessary' vs. 'luxury', 'marketed' vs. 'non-marketed', 'final' vs. 'intermediate', 'efficient' vs. 'inefficient', 'profit-seeking' vs. 'rent-seeking', 'private' vs. 'public', 'poor' vs. 'rich in external effects'.

Unfortunately for 'productive' and 'unproductive' as shorthand, correlations between these pairwise categories are far from perfect. Worse, they vary over time and across ownership régimes and institutional arrangements. Indeed, the *contrasts that show up when the facts of everyday* life are passed through such pairwise filters constitute the primary subject-matter of both economic history and comparative systems. A surprising finding of the book is the ease with which the major socioeconomic systems can be classified according to whether they have surpluses, how surpluses get transferred from producers to non-producers, and indeed according to who is said to be a producer and who is not.

If the 'productive/unproductive' dichotomy is an unfortunate error from the past, why honor it with full-scale treatment? Should it not be consigned to the rubbish-bin of intellectual history, as Garnier and Gray proposed at the dawn of the nineteenth century? The brief first answer is that the issues raised by the 'productive/unproductive' dichotomy are both fundamental and imperfectly resolved. The surplus and transfer paradigm, far from disappearing during the Classical period, underlies all but Beckerian economics as the twentieth century approaches its final decade.

From a growth-of-knowledge perspective, criticism of what I call the Classical–Marxian theory of surplus-generation and transfer has been exceptionally fruitful. On my reading it is *the objections and exceptions to the Classical–Marxian theory that have provided the principal raw material for the Walrasian, Keynesian, public-choice and Beckerian scientific research programs*. Twentieth-century economics since Keynes can be read as a search for a more consistent and convincing way of dealing with the special problems of *public, private, and household services*. Services fall outside economics' traditional microeconomic capitalist factory paradigm and fit somewhat clumsily into the surplus and transfer models which, with a few memorable exceptions, go with it.

A third reason for the study is the opportunity it affords to write the first history of non-obvious professions in economic thought. Artisans and advocates, singing teachers and singers, dictators and domestics, teens and babushkas, speculators and surrogates are economic subjects of some intrinsic interest. As non-traditional economic citizens, they serve as Popperian anomalies that challenge the agro-industrial factory paradigms of Classical, Marxian and pre-public-choice neoclassical value theory. How such agents manage to add or otherwise acquire command over value under different sovereignties is a large part of what modern political economics is about.

Exposing the logic underlying surplus and transfer theory is socially useful for a fourth reason. Highly-trained economic theorists and practitioners presently eschew the Manichaean terminology of 'productive' and 'unproductive' as being too value-laden and crude for scientific discourse. For journalists, politicians and voters, though, such simplifications save time and worry, ranging issues for easy decision. The price-making market as society's only genuine allocation mechanism; private, material, even industrial production as the economy's only self-regenerating 'base'– wage workers in manufacturing-goods industries as the economy's 'only' or 'best' producers – such views are still heard every day, on the stump and in the street. They underlie the repeated calls for 'privatization' and 'reindustrialization'. An implication is that the degree of 'mixedness' of the mixed economy is not voted for or otherwise chosen but rather, as Marx put it bitterly, 'forced on us'.

The 'productive/unproductive' dichotomy turns out to be more than a trivial error of right-wing politicians, left-wing revolutionaries or journalists insufficiently versed in the theory of comparative advantage. To repeat, the boundary problem must be faced by all commentators, except for those who are prepared to deny the existence of either economics or non-economics. Deciding who is a producer and who, implicitly or explicitly, is a mere consumer of the fruits, is the fundamental starting point for all who would model socioeconomic action.

How and where is an observer to trace his or her economic boundary? Around the fields cultivated by horse-drawn plows à la Quesnay and Mirabeau? Around firms waiting out a period of temporarily negative profits at the bottom of the cycle at the edge of some capitalist 'mode'? The sovereign researcher can pick to suit. Are schools and armies productive? Do corporate raiders add values that are welfare-related? Is the household a firm in the manner of a peasant smallholding or a doctor's office? Surplus and transfer theories illuminate positions staked out for and against. The profession's lingering reluctance to join in the wholesale invasions of non-market territory under Lionel Robbins, James M. Buchanan and Gary S. Becker suggests that the 'productive/unproductive' dichotomy still holds its charms for economists, notwithstanding the beauty of its Walrasian rival.

Historically, economists and social scientists have been loath to accept the world-view of Voltaire's character Dr Pangloss, who maintained in *Candide* that, however outrageous the outcome of personal or socioeconomic action, things could not have been otherwise: 'all is for the best in the best of all possible worlds.' Resistance to the Panglossian argument suggests the intellectual route by which the much-denigrated Classical–Marxian unproductive-labor theory, with its narrow capitalist factory paradigm and poorly-motivated transfers to alleged socioeconomic parasites, managed to survive both the Walrasian and the Keynesian revolutions.

Surplus and transfer theories yield policy implications for welfare-related economic growth. A common conclusion is that society would enjoy more output and therefore more welfare if surplus presently accruing to unproductives could be returned to true production. Persuading parasites to take up true production can take a variety of forms: taxation and subsidy, expropriation, slavery. Arrovian dictators who tend to go for such policies may, to get good numbers, ask their statisticians to measure not levels or rates of increase of consumers' goods. Rather they may be interested in levels or rates of increase of producers' goods (including military), even though such goods do not immediately raise the welfare of the policy's target beneficiaries, non-parasites. When growth of capital is given such priority that consumption is actually minimized, consumers' sovereignty may be presumed flouted, in favor of a system of production for production's sake, a 'von Neumann system'. It comes as a shock to recall that rivers of blood have flowed in our century in the name of such systems.

The present study is predicated on the belief that surplus and transfer theory illuminates not only ancient but some contemporary economics. It goes to explain long-standing continuities of subject matter at the sectoral level. What were problem professions to eighteenth-century writers are still viewed as productivity troublemakers two centuries later. 'Immaterial' service industries yet feel the sting of Adam Smith's 'humiliating appellation of barren or unproductive'. Political candidates debate the worth of 'industrial policy' in staving off the dreadful fate that is 'tertiarization'.

As observers choose an economic boundary and fill in the vector of truly final, welfare-related goods and services, both ancient and modern writers consciously or unconsciously address the question of 'netness'. Scope, valuation and netness are facets of the problem: what is output? Simon Kuznets pointed out that the sovereign boundary-drawer could relabel as *productive yet intermediate* goods and services that would otherwise appear either as final product or as transfer out of final product. Some sort of regrettable but necessary 'social framework' may, for instance, be a *sine qua non* in order that a given net flow of consumption goods be forthcoming, even though it itself does not enter utility functions. If so, summary output measures are arguably more welfare-related when the social framework counts as gross, not net – as input, not output, as cost, not product.

Transcription of the 'productive/unproductive' shorthand into useful detail requires, it transpires, some idea of the nature of the *de facto* production functions that 'in fact' relate socially necessary inputs – including most probably some volume of 'externality-rich' public or state-sector inputs – to the outputs which raise the economic welfare of citizens who count. More satisfactory transcription of the shorthand thus holds out the distant promise of a 'full' input-output analysis worthy of political economy.

A primary source of difficulty with the 'productive/unproductive' vocabulary is confusion over input–output logic. *Labor or activities cannot in logic be both 'necessary' intermediate inputs and 'unproductive' superfluous outputs at the same time.* It took even the great economists a long time to concede this elementary point. Only 'final' outputs, by hypothesis, yield utility; inputs, material or immaterial, are forever lost to us. But the efficiency requirement that inputs be minimized for a given output does not by the same token make them 'bads'!

Reference to intermediate activities as simultaneously 'economically necessary' and 'economically unproductive' involves the error of production-function logic which I christen 'input–output error'. Input-output error comes in two kinds, labelled with some hesitation 'unproductiveness fallacy' and 'materialist fallacy'. The distinction turns on whether the economist-observer allows 'immaterial services' into the designated final-goods basket in the first place, alongside 'material goods'. For instance, if final output is defined generously enough to include at least some, e.g. marketed, services while others, e.g. state services, are described as being highly useful, nay, quite necessary to society and the economy but alas unproductive, the input–output error is said to be one of unproductiveness rather than materialist fallacy.

The historical sweep of *Theories of Surplus and Transfer* may be briefly sketched. In the century before the publication of the *Wealth of Nations* in 1776, political economy was separated off from politics and established as an independent field of inquiry into the nature and causes of 'wealth'. The new independence was grounded in the belief that only a subset of human activity contributed to the production of 'economic' goods of which 'wealth' was said to consist. But which subset? Which goods? On what reasoning? Part One looks at the answers early economists provided to the Kuznetsian questions of scope, valuation and netness.

Pre-Adamite writers can be usefully studied according to their views on scope and netness alone. Indeed, before the focus of economics shifted to exchange, scope and netness were more problematic and hotly disputed topics in political economy than was value theory itself, and were considered to be in some sense independent of it.

Inevitably the eighteenth-century division of intellectual labor between political economy and statecraft begged a number of basic questions. The ones most relevant to this history turn on the *degree of equivalence* presumed for exchanges of different types of goods on markets, and between market and non-market 'modes'. Answering them involves writers explicitly or implicitly in boundary-drawing. Boundaries, in logic, should be drawn between behavior or output that is 'economic' and behavior or output that by difference is not. If proportions are variable, some proportions will be 'more efficacious' than others. What constitutes and determines the 'most efficacious proportion' of state to private-sector activity has been practically the basic theme of social science since the time of Adam Smith's celebrated critique of mercantilism.

Strange as it may seem to students raised on modern neoclassical theories, Classical and Marxian surplus and transfer theories postulate non-equivalent exchange *even when markets are competitive*.

Neoclassical micro theory of course allows for imperfect equivalence when markets are monopolized. Most pre-Keynesian Classical and pre-public-choice neoclassical writers allow for imperfect equivalence in transactions linking households or firms and the state.

When exchanges are alleged to be non-equivalent, *some mechanism must be found* (love, terror, mutual advantage) that permits the non-economy to *transfer* to itself the 'surpluses' generated in the economy. Selfish economic agents must be persuaded to part with them.

Histories of economic thought that focus on revolutions or evolutions in value theory tend to follow Walrasian neoclassical logic in treating scope, and particularly netness, as mere corollaries of valuation. The boundary of the economy is, for example, the market boundary for the reason that *behavior is presumed to be different* depending on which side of the boundary one is on. Homogenization (equalization of rates of reward for the different factors, establishment of unique prices for products) occurs 'within the economy' but not without.

Real markets are however rarely perfect in the sense of guaranteeing rentless *quid pro quo* nor exclusive in the sense of being the only allocation mechanisms employed by societies. Only in G. S. Becker is the economy presented as a closed system. Classical–Marxian and older-fashioned neoclassical observers invariably have some producer sphere delivering its fruits across a boundary to a different, user sphere and being subjected to reciprocal influences from it; decisions about present and future 'consumption', reproduction and 'work' (to which Hirschman has felicitously added 'voice') are made in that region with claims to both sides of the border: the household.

Sovereign economist-observers are free in principle to define the limits of their inquiries as they find convenient. They may therefore choose to restrict their analyses to sets of activities that other observers disagree with, for reasons that merit study. Treating scope and netness as potentially subject to economist's sovereignty yields striking insights into the discipline as it developed up until the private-goods 'declaration of interdependence' of the 1870s (Chs 2–4).

Classical–Marxian microeconomic unproductive-labor theory is widely thought to have perished in the general-equilibrium fires of the marginal revolution. But owing to the continuing and contested expansion of economics and economies into non-market territory, and to distaste for Dr Pangloss, surplus and transfer theories have a rich present as well as a past. The archaic view of the state and of immaterial service industries as in some sense parasitic lives on. It provides a distressingly good first approximation to some current debates in macro and public economics, where all is not thought to be for the best in the best of all possible worlds: social welfare could be raised if unproductives could be set to honest work (chs 7–9).

Part One of the book charts the rise and decline of Classical–Marxian surplus and transfer theory. Early political economists are found to use variations of the 'productive/unproductive' dichotomy principally to render the distinction between necessities and luxuries, which is relevant to the issue of growth by capital accumulation at the least painful current sacrifice. The earliest writers are found to be somewhat more liberal than later in refraining from wholesale discrimination against non-material goods and non-market 'modes'.

The first full-fledged economic systems, however, and notably those of François Quesnay, Adam Smith and Karl Marx, are theories of surplus-generation and its non-equivalent transfer beyond a narrowly-defined productive domain. Serious difficulties of input–output logic and ultimately of relevance attend these core Classical paradigms.

The early nineteenth-century economists Garnier, Say, Gray and Malthus expose the inconsistencies of Adam Smith's treatment of marketed services, and of single-person firms as distinct from farms. Senior and Rossi make wry note of the fact that it is Smith's very principle of division of labor that leads unproductive state authorities to specialize in defense and harbors.

The Marx of Chapter 5 raises strong objection to the late Classics' picture of peaceful specialization. However unsatisfactory the reasoning, it is unresolved tension between 'matter' and 'mode' that helps Marxian economics to survive both the marginal and the Russian revolutions, to provide the central themes of Soviet and radical economics in our century. Soviet economists are now embarked on the hard road leading away from Bolshevik 'socialist–materialist' market- and service-bashing. Into the fourth year of *perestroika*, the idea seems to be to use 'socialist-utilitarian' elements from the 1920s as a 'modal' icing on an otherwise quite recognizable set of micro and macroeconomic concepts (Part Two).

Part Three of the book examines postwar revisions and extensions of the factory paradigm in the West, again in light of the basic contrast between surplus and transfer theories and theories of interdependence. The focus is on debates over theory and measurement of government, private and household services. As the Keynesian system is seen to lose face, commentators dissatisfied with the progress of growth and equity in mixed capitalist economies revive elements of the archaic, supposedly discredited Smitho–Marxian unproductive-labor doctrine. In an irony of intellectual history, both *laissez-faire* new Right conservatives and Marxian radicals apply surplus and transfer models to troubles in the mainstream. The public-goods-augmented conservative update is more sophisticated in that it allows for the special problems of public goods and public choices, but its conclusions remain directly Classical, with unclouded appreciation of Adam Smith's views on parsimony, industry and the incompetence of state authorities.

To judge from the prevalence of input–output error in new Classical economics and even in so-called neoclassical political economy, economics may feel increasing pressure to incorporate into its next formal synthesis some of the ideas and concerns of authors featured here. Among them are Smith, Say, Senior, Marx, Leontief, Keynes, Kuznets, von Neumann, Rawls, Arrow, Kornai, Leibenstein, Hirschman and G. S. Becker, writers not trivially reconcilable.

Without providing a formal synthesis, *Theories of Surplus and Transfer* suggests a number of areas that model-builders of the future might wish to explore. Greater care might be taken in the future to avoid input–output error, now that it has been identified. Keeping economics free of input–output error is facilitated by careful specification of the sovereignties that underlie choices. For example, the capacity in which agents vote for or buy sidewalks, raw lentils, math tutorials, or vacuum cleaners, final by convention in GNP, has implications for all economic theories of growth and welfare.

It may become *de rigueur* after the new synthesis to take account, when estimating production functions and input–output coefficients, of all inputs irrespective of 'mode'. Recommendations in favor of one or another set of legal or institutional arrangements ('modes') may have to be more demonstrably welfare-related. The debate on success indicators may be reopened. GNP (not to speak of NMP) is an imperfect index of welfare; it contains a high proportion of intermediates and bads. A renewed commitment to welfare-relatedness may mean that public-sector activities that improve 'animal spirits' will be accounted, à la Keynes-*cum*-Kuznets, together with military roads and bridges, as belonging to the economy's necessary-but-intermediate 'social framework'. Incorporation of Marx's, Say's and Becker's insights into producer utility may imply adding the fun had while 'at work' to production as a jointness; by the same token arduous 'work after market work' may be counted as the disutility that it is. Evidently, political economists and metricians of the next century have their work cut out for them.

The rest of this book traces the history of dubious professions in economic thought, West, East and South, from Petty to the present. The focus is on the sources of incomes earned by a herd of unusual and anomalous 'laborers', the black sheep of economic science: handmaidens and handymen, opera singers and opera dancers, priests and bureaucrats, kings and ministers, doctors and lawyers, leveraged buyout specialists, entrepreneurs and managers, rentiers and retirees, the self-employed. Such unpopular economic citizens fit uneasily into the agricultural or factory paradigms of Classical, Marxian and pre-public-choice neoclassical value theory. The exercise yields a nice range of views as to the scope of production, the importance of 'mode' and the nature of 'work'.

As mentioned, a main line of contrast in the book is the counterpoint maintained between theories of surplus-generation and transfer, on the one hand, and theories of interdependence, on the other. Surplus and transfer theories portray selected members of society in the above group as *de facto* economic parasites, 'maintained' without due recompense by society's true producers. Reasons are given why surplus and transfer theories tend heavily to input–output error, and how on certain rare and fascinating occasions they manage to avoid it.

Theories of interdependence by contrast postulate sovereign contracting and exchange of equivalents, *quid pro quo*, between services rendered and incomes received – across a plurality of institutions and modes. Theories of interdependence are often theories of equilibrium, though they need not be. Modern disequilibrium and Marshallian partial-equilibrium analyses, and indeed the new Hollanderian Classical economics of competitive processes, allow for temporary rents while postulating what is essentially a self-leveling, unified playing field on which all citizens meet to haggle over division of labor and spoils.

The next chapter investigates some important pre-Adamite analyses of the questions of scope, valuation and netness which all economists must face. It looks at how certain concepts of output came to prevail over a host of alternatives, some wider, some more restrictive than the materialist-*cum*-capitalist production boundary that we associate with those immortal if misguided Classics, Adam Smith and Karl Marx.

Part One

RISE AND DECLINE OF THE CLASSICAL–MARXIAN SURPLUS AND TRANSFER THEORY

CHAPTER 2

Early Views of Production, Surplus-Generation, and Transfer

> Determinatio est Negatio.
> (Spinoza, in Marx, 1867, p. 559 n.)

2.1 Kuznets's triad

In the century before the publication of the *Wealth of Nations* in 1776, political economy was separated off from politics and established as a distinct field of inquiry devoted to studying the nature and causes of 'wealth'. The new independence came grounded in the belief that only a subset of human activity contributed to the production of 'economic' goods of which 'wealth' was said to consist. But which subset? The present chapter looks at the tentative answers early economists gave to Kuznets's fundamental questions of scope, valuation, and netness.

Pre-Adamite writers may be usefully studied according to their views on scope and netness alone. Before the focus of economics shifted to exchange, scope and netness were more problematic and controversial topics in political economy than was value theory itself, and were thought to be in some degree independent of it.

2.2 Producers in Petty and King

That the Physiocrats' doctrine of agricultural productiveness and industrial sterility represented a narrowing of the economic horizon as compared with some versions of mercantilist economics is not always appreciated. Sir William Petty (1623–1687) has the honor among economists of being the first to try to quantify the total money income and expenditure of a nation, so what he saw fit to include is of interest. Despite some characteristically mercantilist notions ('There is more to be gained by Manufacture than Husbandry, and by Merchandize than Manufacture' – Petty, 1671–6, p. 256), a sharp distinction drawn between foreign and domestic commerce, and a clear bias in favor of durables, Petty treats many service-producing income earners, such as rentiers, professionals, and officers of the government, as producers of output, albeit inefficient ones.

As befitted a charter member of the Royal Society, Petty is interested in rigor of concept and measurement:

> Instead of using only comparative and superlative Words, and intellectual Arguments, I have taken the course ... to express my self in Terms of *Number, Weight*, or *Measure*; to use only Arguments of Sense, and to consider only such Causes, as have visible Foundations in Nature; leaving those that depend upon the mutable Minds, Opinions, Appetites, and Passions of particular Men, to the Considerations of others...
>
> (Petty, 1671–6, p. 244)

The aim is to capture the sum of expenditure on marketed consumption goods, which Petty does by 'adopting the basic assumption that the annual income of a country is equivalent to its "annual expence"' (1664, p. 108). In chapter VIII of the *Political Arithmetick*, accumulation is treated as a possibility that, being alas no more than that, needs no separate analysis (Petty, 1671–6, p. 308).

Petty ranges the different occupations into a hierarchy based on mercantilist reasoning as to the durability of goods capable of serving as stores of value.

> The great and ultimate effect of Trade is not Wealth at large, but particularly abundance of Silver, Gold and Jewels, which are not perishable, nor so mutable as other Commodities, but are Wealth at all times, and all places: Whereas abundance of Wine, Corn, Fowls, Flesh, &c. are Riches but *hic & nunc*, so as the raising of such Commodities, and the following of such Trade, which does store the Country with Gold, Silver, Jewels, &c. is profitable before others...
>
> (Petty, 1671–6, pp. 259–60)

Although net inflows of gold and silver are most highly ranked, Petty's classification is in other respects more satisfactory than those of his Physiocrat and Classical–Marxian successors in that it is continuous rather than binary. Petty's continuum goes from '*Meats* and *Drinks*, ... which 24 hours ... doth wholly annihilate' to 'Commodities of greater duration' (1671–6, p. 271). If we overlook the confusion of bullion as store of value with gold as value in use, Petty's formulation is consistent with utilitarian principle. If work is a bad and resources fully employed, then clearly the more durable the object upon which resources are spent, the more advantageous both to the individual and to the society, since long-lasting goods yield flows of useful and exchangeable services over many periods of time. Scarce resources need not be wasted in replacement until and in so far as goods begin to depreciate. This is fine so long as there is no problem of unemployment.

Classical–Marxians might think to find support for a binary materiality criterion for final output in Petty's formulation. However, his awareness that durability is a matter of degree leads naturally to an appreciation of *other* characteristics for which materiality may be a rather imperfect *substitute*: slow depreciation, low income elasticity, tradability, etc. These criteria admit goods and services on an equal footing, other things equal.

In Petty's arithmetic, aggregate annual expenditure or 'expence' fully corresponds to income, which is given to be the sum of revenues accruing to two factors, non-homogeneous land and labor. The former is the 'annual Proceed of [a] Stock, [the] Wealth of the Nation'; the value of the annual 'labour of the people' is then computed as the difference between the total 'expence' = income and the yields of the stock of land and buildings. In the estimate presented in the *Verbum Sapienti* for England and Wales in 1665, labor receives and expends £25 m. or 62 per cent of a total 'expence' estimated at £40 m. (Petty, 1665, p. 108).

Total 'expence' is calculated by multiplying what is taken to be average household expenditure on 'Food, Housing, Cloaths, and all other necessities' (1665, p. 105) by a population of 6 million. It includes current imputed services of long-lived assets. The idea is to capitalize a flow into a stock, which incidentally produces a more impressive *Number*.

Despite the final-consumption origin of Petty's maximand and the flashes of 'Keynesian mercantilism' (see below), not all remunerated activity is consistently productive. The two-factor labor-and-land value theory might have given him pause before he launched an attack on the rentier. However, conflating consumption and production of immaterial services, Petty castigates those who 'do nothing at all, but *eat* and *drink*, *sing*, *play* and *dance*; nay to such as study the *Metaphysicks*, or other needless *Speculation*' (1671–6, p. 270) and deplores any transfer to such men as 'produce no material thing, or [*sic*] things of real use and value in the Commonwealth' (Petty, 1671–6, p. 270). The welfare alternative to a material standard is tacked on as an afterthought, but is rich in non-materialist possibilities.

In Petty's view, too many people are engaged in inefficient production of immaterial luxury services:

> Now if the numerous Offices and Fees relating to the Government, Law, and Church, and if the number of Divines, Lawyers, Physicians, Merchants, and Retailers were also lessened, all which do receive

great wages for little work done to the Publick, with how much greater ease would common expences be defrayed? and with how much more equality would the same be assessed?

(Petty, 1662, pp. 28–9)

The implied welfare-augmenting retrenchment is to be partial, not total.

Petty touches on a problem that has greatly exercised Classical and Marxian economists of both past and present vintage. The phrase that summarizes it has, happily, a dual ancestry, having seen the light of reason in a French edition of Nassau Senior before being taken up by Karl Marx. The 'most efficacious proportion' problem (as it will be referred to in this work) tries to capture in a phrase a complex and contentious problem of economic theory in its relation to policy. The problem is that of determining the optimal weight and rôle of the 'state', viewed as both a typical and as a particular sort of non-market institution, in the affairs of the private economy.

Despite the assumption implicit in his defense of long service lives for durables, Petty harbors no illusion that the economic resources of the Commonwealth are in fact fully employed. Actual 'expence' does not reflect potential on account of numerous misallocations and disproportions, many of which may be laid at the door of feudal holdovers among the professional class. Translated into a diagram such as Figure 2.1, society is not only inside a necessity–luxury production-possibility frontier, but a northeastward move would be dominated in social welfare terms by moves east or southeast. That is to say, Petty's economy is characterized by both underemployment and an output mix that, since it is overly skewed against the production of necessities, fails to reach its potential in terms of social welfare.

Petty's view of the inefficiency of self-employed professionals and public servants does not altogether jibe with his analysis of the causes and remedies for unemployment, which Keynes rightly construed as ancestral to his own (Keynes, 1936, p. 359). A few lines after castigating 'Divines, Lawyers, Physicians, Merchants, and Retailers', Petty turns round and justifies 'Entertainments, magnificent Shews, triumphal Arches, &c.', for the reason that their costs 'refund presently to the most useful': brewers, bakers, tailors, shoemakers, and so forth, with expansionary effects on employment and income. What is more, over and above their multiplier effects, princely entertainments are valued in their own right by people who, 'for all their grumbling, . . . travel many miles to be spectators of these mistaken and distasted vanities' (Petty, 1662, p. 33). Evanescent public extravagances have simultaneous utility, therefore, as intermediate 'macroeconomic' public goods and as final

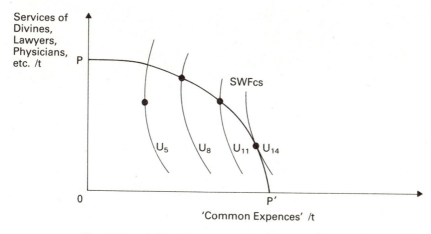

Figure 2.1 Petty's welfare economics

U_i = Social welfare functions
PP^1 = Society's production-possibility frontier

private goods – a jointness that complicates analysis of their costs and benefits (Wallace, 1983–4, pp. 295–302).

Another large output and occupational category, the transportation and distribution services performed by local and international merchants, also gives Petty analytical difficulty. The problem is input–output error, the logical error of designating activities as necessary and superfluous at the same time. Petty has the dubious honor of sharing confusion over necessary inputs and superfluous outputs with a long list of 'unproductiveness fallacists' in the history of economics, from the Schoolmen to Pol Pot. Local merchants, while excessive in number and 'yielding of themselves no fruit at all', are at the same time 'needful . . . to make subdistributions into every Village . . . and to receive back their superfluities' (Petty, 1662, p. 28). Such statements imply dissatisfaction with the structure of the monetized economy, a sort of 'most efficacious proportion' problem afflicting the private sector. Fewer merchants could do the same job; a 'large proportion of [them might] be retrenched'; yet those few remaining perform an altogether legitimate economic function which would by no means disappear in a more efficient economic universe.

Classicists of the 'French' school and post-Walrasian neoclassicists (section 4.4 below) will inquire how it is that the forces of competition do not drive redundant local merchants into bankruptcy – assuming they *are* redundant. Responses invariably stress market imperfections, interference from laws, monopoly, ignorance, inertia, and so on – just the factors that neoclassical theorists have historically shrugged off with

A SCHEME of the Income, and Expence, of the several FAMILIES of *England*; calculated for the Year 1688.

Number of Families.	RANKS, DEGREES, TITLES, AND QUALIFICATIONS.	Heads per Family.	Number of persons.	Yearly Income per Family. £. s.	Total of the Estates or Income. £.	Yearly Income per Head. £. s.	Expence per Head. £. s.	Increase per Head. £. s. d.	Total Increase per Annum. £.
160	Temporal Lords	40	6,400	2,800 —	448,000	70 —	60 —	10 — —	64,000
26	Spiritual Lords	20	520	1,300 —	33,800	65 —	55 —	10 — —	5,200
800	Baronets	16	12,800	880 —	704,000	55 —	51 —	4 — —	51,000
600	Knights	13	7,800	650 —	390,000	50 —	46 —	4 — —	31,200
3,000	Esquires	10	30,000	450 —	1,200,000	45 —	42 —	3 — —	90,000
12,000	Gentlemen	8	96,000	280 —	2,880,000	35 —	32 10	2 10 —	240,000
5,000	Persons in Offices	8	40,000	240 —	1,200,000	30 —	27 —	3 — —	120,000
5,000	Persons in Offices	6	30,000	120 —	600,000	20 —	18 —	2 — —	60,000
2,000	Merchants and Traders by Sea	8	16,000	400 —	800,000	50 —	40 —	10 — —	160,000
8,000	Merchants and Traders by Land	6	48,000	200 —	1,600,000	33 —	28 —	5 — —	240,000
10,000	Persons in the Law	7	70,000	140 —	1,400,000	20 —	17 —	3 — —	210,000
2,000	Clergymen	6	12,000	60 —	120,000	10 —	9 —	1 — —	12,000
8,000	Clergymen	5	40,000	45 —	360,000	9 —	8 —	1 — —	40,000
40,000	Freeholders	7	280,000	84 —	3,360,000	12 —	11 —	1 — —	280,000
140,000	Freeholders	5	700,000	50 —	7,000,000	10 —	9 10	— 10 —	350,000
150,000	Farmers	5	750,000	44 —	6,600,000	8 15	8 10	— 5 —	187,000
16,000	Persons in Sciences and Liberal Arts	5	80,000	60 —	960,000	12 —	11 10	1 10 —	40,000
40,000	Shop-keepers and Tradesmen	4½	180,000	45 —	1,800,000	10 —	9 10	— 10 —	90,000
60,000	Artizans and Handicrafts	4	240,000	40 —	2,400,000	10 —	9 10	— 10 —	120,000
5,000	Naval Officers	4	20,000	80 —	400,000	20 —	18 —	2 — —	40,000
4,000	Military Officers	4	16,000	60 —	240,000	15 —	14 —	1 — —	16,000
511,586 Families.		5½	2,675,520	67 —	34,495,800	12 18	12 —	— 18 —	2,447,100

Number of Families	Ranks, Degrees, Titles, and Qualifications	Heads per Family	Number of Persons	Yearly Income per Family		Yearly Income in general	Yearly Income per Head		Yearly Expence per Head		Increase or Decrease per Head			Decrease
50,000	Common Seamen	3	150,000	20	—	1,000,000	7	—	7	10	—	10	—	75,000
364,000	Labouring People and Out Servants	3½	1,275,000	15	—	5,460,000	4	10	4	12	—	2	—	127,500
400,000	Cottagers and Paupers	3¼	1,300,000	6	10	2,000,000	2	—	2	5	—	5	—	325,000
35,000	Common Soldiers	2	70,000	14	—	490,000	7	—	7	10	—	10	—	35,000
349,000 Families.		3¼	2,795,000	10	10	8,950,000	3	5	3	9	—	4	—	562,000
	Vagrants		30,000	—	—	60,000	2	—	3	—	—	1	—	60,000
849,000		3¼	2,825,000	10	10	9,010,000	3	3	3	7	6	—	4 6	622,000

So the GENERAL ACCOUNT is:

511,586 Families;	Increasing the Wealth of the Kingdom	5¼	2,675,520	67	—	34,495,800	12	18	12	—	—	—	18 —	2,447,000
849,000 Families.	Decreasing the Wealth of the Kingdom	3¼	2,825,000	10	10	9,010,000	3	3	3	7	6	—	4 6	622,000
1,360,586 Families.	Nett Total	1 1/20	5,500,520	32	—	43,505,800	7	18	7	11	3	—	6 9	1,825,100

Figure 2.2 Kings's Scheme of the Income, and Expence, of the several families of England, calculated for the year 1688

Source: G. King (1696), reprinted in P. Laslett (ed.), *The Earliest Classics* (Farnborough, Hants: Gregg International Publishers, 1973), pp. 48–9.

a disappointing glibness, in the manner of Voltaire's Dr Pangloss (e.g. Coase, 1960; see Samuels and Mercuro, 1984, p. 58; Blaug, 1980a, pp. 179 ff.).

Aspersions are not cast on all merchants. On the contrary, *international* merchants are most usefully employed, Petty avers, in exchanging England's 'superfluous Commodities' with those of other countries. In a statement at variance with previously expressed views on necessities, foreign trade – 'which does store the Country with Gold, Silver, Jewels, &c.' – is said to be 'profitable before others' (Petty, 1662, p. 28; 1671–6, p. 260).

The total output of the nation is arrived at by multiplying what Petty takes to be average *per capita* expenditure on 'necessities' times population. Proof that Petty's 'necessities' are not uniquely 'material' comes from the reluctant admission (a) that the distribution services of *some* merchants are 'needful'; (b) that some 'things of real use and value in the Commonwealth' are not material; and (c) that the services of a properly retrenched population of lawyers, physicians, and divines indeed fall into that useful category.

Compared with those of his contemporary Gregory King (1648–1712), Petty's writings are rather more concerned with *mal*distribution of current fruits than with misallocations assumed to affect rates of change over time. As an empiricist, King broke new ground, being 'the first man to study the structure of a pre-industrial society' (Laslett, 1973, p. 5). None of his remarkable estimates were published for nearly a century after his death, but his *Scheme of the Income and Expence of the Several Families of England Calculated for the Year 1688* was known for having been included in a work by Charles Davenant (King, 1696, pp. 48–9).

The great interest of King's scheme is its level of detail. The population is divided into twenty-six occupational and social groups, with estimates for the number of families in each and of average family size. Building up, for example, from tons of meat consumed, King calculates average income, expense, and net saving (negative or positive) per class of household. These times the number of members give the group subtotals, which are then summed into total income, expenditure, and net saving for the economy as a whole. Figure 2.2 reproduces the *Scheme*.

The extent to which economic waters were uncharted in late seventeenth-century England comes out in the differences between King's classification of occupations and Petty's. King groups together income from rent of land, dwellings, and other 'hereditaments'; in a second category he places income from profits and from wage labor without distinction. By modern lights the underlying value theory is less satisfactory than Petty's, no line being drawn between human and 'other' capital.

Because the subtotals are given separately, we may study not only aggregate income and its annual increment, but the distribution of income and saving between the twenty-six 'ranks, degrees, titles, and qualifications' of Englishmen. King's *Scheme* makes a further great subdivision based on whether or not a given rank's 'Expence per Head' is reckoned to be less than or greater than its 'Yearly Income per Head': 511,586 families of savers are said to be 'increasing the Wealth of the kingdom', while 849,000 families of poor 'decrease' it. The much greater individual incomes of the former mean the nation as a whole is accumulating, albeit very slowly. Development economists looking for the original statement of the conflict between equity and growth will find it here (Lewis, 1954; Chenery et al., 1974; section 9.1 below).

King places no particular emphasis on any of the goods/services dichotomies so popular with later writers. The ranks of the kingdom's net savers swell with rentiers, temporal and spiritual lords, persons in offices, 'persons in sciences and liberal arts', merchants, and traders by land and sea. The legitimacy of their revenue is not put in doubt; by implication it has not been 'transferred' rather than 'earned'. Social intercourse exhibits a 'feudal' *quid pro quo* (see Hirschman, 1982; Hicks, 1969, ch. II).

Evidence for interdependence in King is implicit and arithmetical rather than explicit. In rating the war-worthiness of England, France and Holland, total 'General Expence' is said to be made up of expenditures on food ('diet'), 'apparel', and the omnibus item 'incident charges'. These latter must in the case of England include the services of lords, office-holders, soldiers, professionals, and merchants, for the totals add up: 'expence' plus saving equals receipts (King, 1696, p. 68).

2.3 Mandeville's paradox

The brilliant Anglo-Dutch physician and satirist Bernard de Mandeville (1670–1733) builds his fascinating poem *The Fable of the Bees* (Mandeville, 1705,) around a conceit that is one of the great paradoxes in the history of ideas. It is that 'Private Vices' may yield 'Publick Benefits' (1705, subtitle). Though the *Fable* is not cited by name in the *Wealth of Nations*, Adam Smith's Invisible Hand theorem of the beneficent economic effects of unimpeded self-interest is an elaboration and, as Hirschman has charmingly shown, a softening of Mandeville's naughty paradox (Hirschman, 1977, pp. 18–19, 56–66).

The Fable of the Bees is based on the notion of fallacies of composition. These distort efforts to generalize from the experience of the individual to that of his society. Individual truth is not collective truth;

private Christian virtue in the *Fable* creates political, social, even aesthetic 'bads' as well as 'goods'. In particular, the rigorist virtues of individual modesty and thrift, the renunciation of prodigality, vanity, greed, ostentation, and luxury, may have ruinous effects on a collectivity's economic welfare (Munro, 1975, p. 269). These paradoxical consequences bear upon unproductive-labor doctrine in three ways, which may be christened the 'Crusoe', 'Kuznets', and 'Keynes' connections.

The first illustrates Mandeville's view that, in society, the whole is very different from the sum of its parts. To imagine that a hypothetical isolated individual, a Robinson Crusoe, an anchorite in the desert, is a reliable if microscopic portrait of what must go on in the macroeconomy or the happy society is certain to mislead (Hirschman, 1977, p. 119; Moore, 1975; Speck, 1975).

Art and religion, politics and economics are concerned with the mainsprings of individual human action and with the consequences of each 'rational' or 'irrational' individual act. That consequences may be paradoxically different as between Robinson Crusoe alone on his island and a whole nation of Crusoe-like economic men – for example, that unChristian, selfish behavior on the part of each citizen may work to the economic benefit of all – was current wisdom among enlightened men of the eighteenth century and by no means original with the Adam Smith of the Invisible Hand theorem. In helping to divorce ethics from politics, such views worked a shift of attention from reforming the human soul to designing institutions that made their peace with individuals' moral failings.

As we shall see in Chapter 5, the temptation to view as 'contradictions' or 'paradoxes' fallacies of composition that stem from the existence of human institutions such as 'money' or 'the labor market' reaches fullest expression in Marx. Marx has 'economy-wide' behavior so different from that of a sum of its component parts that, along with the individualism, he rejects the 'economizing' core of the Robinson Crusoe analogy, namely the Robbinsian view that scarcity of means can make any choice economic, however small the 'society', whatever the 'mode'.

The 'Kuznets' connection suggests ways to avoid the input–output error 'unproductiveness fallacy', according to which activities are labelled 'unproductive' even as they are said to be intermediate prerequisites for the production of desirable final goods. As Simon Kuznets suggested in numerous writings (Kuznets, 1941, 1946, 1948, 1973), input–output relationships may be such that resources may have to be applied to production of public goods or services that are not desired as final goods in themselves but that are none the less necessary for truly final goods to be efficiently forthcoming. That is, state goods and services may provide a regrettable but indispensable 'social framework' within which production of final goods and services takes place (section 8.4.1 below). Kuznets's reasoning puts an Emperor's-new-clothes' coloring on many sacred texts of unproductive-labor theory from Quesnay to Stalin. In the course of satirizing philosophical opponents, Mandeville identifies categories of intermediate public goods in 1705.

Mandeville's appreciation of the working of self-interest, though it implies a broad view of the direct and indirect sources of prosperity, by no means turns him into an apostle of *laissez-faire*. It is to be by the 'skilful management of the clever Politician' that private vices are made to serve the public weal. The job of creating the 'social framework' that is a prerequisite to increasing the production of goods that people want thus falls within the purview of state action (Viner, 1958, p. 341; Hirschman, 1977, p. 18).

J. M. Keynes saw in Mandeville, like the Petty of 'magnificent Shews', a forerunner of his own thinking on the rôle of aggregate demand in maintaining employment and output (1936, pp. 359 ff.). The 'Keynes' connection can be phrased as a question. If, in a given state of the world, frivolous or morally reprehensible activities generate incomes that go to support other, worthier economic goods and services, and thereby maintain demand, employment, and animal spirits *which would otherwise be deficient*, in what sense are they *economically* 'unproductive'? (Section 7.1 below.) Keynes's *General Theory* on this reasoning can come to the defense of activities both inane and offensive, of any income elasticity, and no matter how repugnant to standard-bearers of religious morality (Kaye, 1924), Rawlsian justice (Rawls, 1967), Marxian class analysis (ch. 5 below), or to bourgeois, conservationist, or do-gooder canons of taste (Mishan, 1973; Musgrave, 1959; Bowles *et al.*, 1984).

The Fable of the Bees does not consider the possibility that it may not be luxury demand in particular that 'Employ'[s] a Million of the Poor' (1705, p. 25), but rather 'demand in general'. Redistributions of original endowments are dismissed as unrealistic, though they might lead to the employment of just as many Bees, albeit in different, humbler pursuits. Mandeville has in mind worlds where 'Peace and plenty reign, And every Thing is cheap, tho' plain...' (1705, p. 34).

The *Fable* describes the effects on a bustling society of a sudden shrinkage in demand caused by the spontaneous abandonment of what to Christian rigorists are sinful wants. Its *problématique* sounds an unusual note to readers brought up on twentieth-century welfare economics, which focuses on implications of redistribution with tastes assumed constant. The poem satirizes what is now sometimes referred to as 'Buddhist' economics; 275 years ago such low-need nirvanas still were important religious models in post-Reformation Christianity.

In Keynes, people are not afraid to prefer more to less, especially when labor and capital lie idle on account of consumer and investor pessimism (section 7.1 below). The alternatives of attempting to repress wants or to redistribute income are unrealistic as compared with the social welfare benefits to be had by raising demand to bring forth supply. Given the unlikelihood of sufficient private charitable asset transfer, and given the public's unfamiliarity with government interventions designed to transfer benefits to the poor at the same time as they stimulate the macroeconomy, state expenditure on luxuries or even on nonsense activities is better than nothing:

> Two pyramids, two masses for the dead, are twice as good as one...
> To dig holes in the ground,... will increase, not only employment, but the real national dividend of useful goods and services. It is not reasonable, however, that a sensible community should be content to remain dependent on such *fortuitous and often wasteful mitigations* when once we understand the influences upon which effective demand depends.
> (Keynes, 1936, pp. 131, 220; emphasis added)

The Fable of the Bees was tried and condemned as a public nuisance by the Grand Jury of Middlesex in 1723 (Kaye, 1924, p. xxxiv) and over a century and a half later it could still be described as 'the wickedest cleverest book in the English language' (Kaye, 1924, p. i). What shocked religious morality in 1705 later looked more like economic blasphemy – an outrage against the Classical duty of high parsimony in a Say's-Law world. Before Keynes, to tout luxury, venality, and vice as the engines of prosperity was thought to make sense only with respect to the underemployed, capital-poor artisan economies of a pre-industrial age (Heckscher, 1931).

Adam Smith's 'system of natural liberty', as is shown in Chapter 3, relies on a well of human desires equally selfish as, but more parsimonious in their tastes than, those of Mandeville's licentious Bees. The *Fable* ends with a cautionary rhyme for economist-dictators who not only would reassign unproductive laborers but would tamper with their preferences:

> ... Fools only strive
> To make a Great an Honest Hive.
> T'enjoy the World's Conveniencies,
> Be fam'd in War, yet live in Ease,
> Without great Vices, is a vain
> EUTOPIA seated in the Brain.
> (Mandeville, 1705, p. 36)

2.4 Luxury and necessity in Boisguilbert and Cantillon

Boisguilbert and Vauban have been ranked with Petty and King as the first proponents of the 'comprehensive' concept of output (Studenski, 1961, p. 12). By this Studenski meant the 'Keynesian' view of output as made up of the subaggregates $C + I + G + (X - M)$. That is, Y is the sum of 'final' marketed consumer goods and services (C), marketed investment goods and services destined for but not yet put to intermediate use (I), non-marketed government expenditures on goods and services, which are final by assumption (G), and net exports ($X - M$). Just how comprehensive is the Keynesian view is discussed in Chapter 8.

It requires some interpreting to see the Keynesian comprehensive view of output in the *oeuvre* of Pierre le Pesant de Boisguilbert (1646–1714). True, in some passages Boisguilbert takes a generous view of the constituents of the nation's wealth, clearly including some immaterial services and many varieties of 'luxury' good. On the other hand, like Petty and a number of unproductive-labor theorists who succeed him, Boisguilbert compares the economy of Louis XIV's France with a hypothetical one imagined after an infinite regress, in logical time, back from our world of 'superfluous' activities to a state that has time and energy only for 'necessities'. Mapping an imagined 'early and rude state' onto a complex present, contrasting the post-lapsarian labors of our first parents with those of the inhabitants of Versailles and Paris, is an exercise guaranteed to make the former appear 'more basic' than the latter. It is a short step from this 'Garden-of-Eden' argument to Classical-Marxian unproductiveness theory, in which the producers of 'superfluous' goods and services are conceived as mere transfer recipients living off the bounty of the economy's true producers.

The fact that observers can look at an economy as an interdependent system *at a given moment* and can also deduce, by analogy with simple and poor economies, a hierarchical pattern presumed to describe growth *over time*, leaves room for more than one interpretation of Boisguilbert's pronouncements on scope, valuation, and netness. The first turns him into a proto-Physiocrat and Classic; the second has him a forerunner of J.-B. Say and the post-Classical moderns.

In his *Dissertation de la nature des richesses* (1707), Boisguilbert's aim is to refute the bullionist view that the wealth of the kingdom consists of metallic money available to the Prince. The effect is to democratize that medieval notion, in suggesting we examine the wealth (*richesse*) of the state 'as much with respect to the king as to the people', the wealth of the king being only a fraction of the wealth of his subjects. Real wealth consists not in an amassing of money but 'in full enjoyment not only of the necessities of life, but also of all the superfluities, plus all that gives pleasure to the senses which our corrupt hearts are every day inventing more refined ways to entice' (Boisguilbert, 1707a, p. 240). Thus utility, as determined by the individual's sinful but free will, is what sets the bounds of *richesse*.

That possibility is no sooner opened up than Boisguilbert reverts to Garden-of-Eden mode, ranking *richesses* according to the three kinds of wants they satisfy: 'necessaries, conveniencies, and superfluities'. The latter two can only exist 'insofar as an excess of necessaries makes possible the acquisition of that which is far from necessary' (Boisguilbert, 1707a, p. 240). In *Traité des grains*, the categories of goods that satisfy wants are further reduced to a Physiocratic two: 'the fruits of the earth, which were the only [*richesses*] at the birth or rather the infancy of the world, and man-made goods [*les biens d'industrie*] which . . . draw their origin and their sustenance from the fruits of the earth' (Boisguilbert, 1707b, pp. 189–90).

Boisguilbert's total of *fruits de la terre* and *biens d'industrie* is made up of (1) 'free Gifts of the earth' (*Mannes de la terre*) (2) the proto-Physiocratic category 'ownership of estates (*la propriété des fonds*) which engender [the *mannes*] and whose profit is shared between Master and Farmers', (3) 'the rental of Town Houses, hypothecary rents, Ecclesiastical, Military and Financial Levies, money and Bills of Exchange', and (4) 'manual labor, & Commerce both wholesale and retail'. '[The] last three take first their origins and [then] their sustenance from the fruits of the earth' (1707b, pp. 189–90). Boisguilbert's confounding of stocks of capital and flows of inputs and of outputs need not detain us.

Of greater interest is Boisguilbert's somewhat broad vision of the economic universe. Government administrative and military services, private legal and financial services are included in his domain under (3) and/or (4); other sorts of professional and domestic services are passed over in silence. No special weight is given to markets as distinct from other modes of production and distribution. Innocent of the Classical–Marxian concern with 'materiality', Boisguilbert in his fourth category lumps artisanal and agricultural activities together with those of merchants and retailers.

Boisguilbert's attitude toward well-populated service occupations suggests a liberal view of scope. A large number of actors and actresses is proof of the prosperity of a state rather than a portent of its decadence. A modern-sounding income-elasticity criterion is used in preference to a Classical–Marxian material one:

[The] two hundred professions which make up the perfection of the most polished and best-endowed states are all the progeny of the fruits of the earth, and whatever she is able to produce with abundance and to have [that produce] consumed (failing which the

surplus becomes useless and even harmful), gives them their origin; beginning with the most necessary, such as the Baker and the Tailor, and finishing with the Actor, who is the last word in luxury . . . [proof] that one is so far beyond the fear of having to do without necessities that one is happy to pay for the staging of fictions.
(Boisguilbert, 1707a, pp. 245–6)

It is a short step from a necessity–luxury distinction based on income elasticity to one grounded in photosynthesis. Despite dim awareness that agricultural surpluses must be *bought* in order for there to be incentive to produce them, agriculture appears as the self-sufficient progenitor of the 'two hundred professions' (lawyers, doctors, '*les spectacles*' and the lesser artisans of whatever métier) (Boisguilbert, 1707a, p. 245; 1696, p. 5). Feedback, interdependence, is described only to be denied.

The sketch of a theory of surplus generation and transfer in Boisguilbert is enriched by the observation that 'men are entirely divided into two classes, viz., one who does nothing and enjoys all the pleasures, and the other who labors from morning till night but has barely the necessary [minimum] and often is deprived of it entirely' (Boisguilbert, 1707a, p. 256). His list of occupations productive of *richesse* is further evidence that the Physiocrats whittled down an existing conceptual apparatus that was wider in scope, if less clear as to netness, to arrive at their own.

Other Physiocratic elements are introduced by Richard Cantillon in an *Essai sur la nature du commerce en général* (1755). This work, published only two years before Quesnay's first articles, circulated widely in manuscript following its author's mysterious death by violence in 1734 (Fox-Genovese, 1976, pp. 95–6).

While Cantillon (b. 1680?) has a high regard for agriculture, it is not yet the Physiocratic single-factor theory but a two-factor one. The *Essai* opens with the statement that 'Land is the source or the matter from which wealth is derived; human labor is the means which produces it. . .' (Cantillon, 1755, p. 1).

Cantillon does not immediately discriminate against non-agricultural labor, as Quesnay will do. Exchanges among producers of goods and services take place on something like an equivalent basis: 'farmers, artisans of all sorts, merchants, officers, soldiers and sailors, domestics and all the other orders which work or are employed in the state . . . serve not only the Prince and the proprietors but also each other' (1755, p. 28).

Nevertheless, like Boisguilbert, Cantillon is impressed by the fact that non-agricultural laborers must eat. Using Garden-of-Eden logic, he jumps from the observation that some surplus food is required to ensure the survival of non-food producers to the conclusion that 'those who do not work directly for the proprietors' are in effect '[living] at the [proprietors'] expense' (1755, p. 28).

Agricultural productivity is such that twenty-five persons can feed a hundred, a third of whom are either too old, too young or simply unfit for other work. Another sixth of the population consists of 'landed proprietors, the sick and the various kinds of entrepreneurs [wholesalers, retailers, bakers, butchers, manufacturers, who] contribute nothing [*sic*], by the labor of their hands, to the various needs of men'. Of the remaining quarter, some find work as soldiers and as domestics in well-off families, and the rest can be employed 'in the refinement by an additional labor, of the necessities of life' (1755, pp. 29, 48–9).

Though the extra processing will cause the state to be 'considered rich', it in fact 'adds nothing to the quantity of things necessary to the subsistence and maintenance of men' (1755 p. 49). Here economic science gets its first taste of the Physiocratic view of manufacturing as mere transformation of the goods making up *richesse*. Also introduced is a binary either/or reasoning which will become a staple of Classical–Marxian surplus and transfer theory, with its unproductive laborers and subsistence wage. In Classical–Marxian wage theory at its simplest what counts are not the myriad qualitative characteristics of goods, which reflect differing real costs of production and meet divergent effective demands (coarse vs. fine food or clothing), but whether 'clothing' in meters, food in pounds or calories, is available, yes or no.

In Cantillon, the proposition about the sterility of laborers outside agriculture is not insisted upon with any dogmatism. Though less unequivocally than Boisguilbert, Cantillon finds a flourishing state of manufactures and the arts to be a sign of prosperity rather than evidence of bad conduct on the part of consumers, producers or the architects of state policy.

2.5 Demand and capital in Physiocracy

Physiocracy is the first true system in the history of economic thought, second only to Marxism in the ambitiousness of its attempt to provide a full theory of economic and social man in nature. The views of François Quesnay and his disciples mark a minimum point in our history of scope, and a qualitative shift in the conceptualization of the netness of outputs over inputs. Neither before nor since has the boundary of the productive domain been made a function of so short a list of (material) goods. This radical constriction, deemed artificial in its own day, had the Popperian benefit of provoking immediate further inquiry into the mechanism of surplus-generation and transfer and the meaning of equivalence in exchange.

The *économistes'* achievements were considerable. They were the first to emphasize the relationship between capital advances and growth of goods that count (Spengler, 1960a; Vaggi, 1987). Quesnay's *Tableau* contains the original representation of the circular flow of income (Schumpeter, 1954, ch. 4; Studenski, 1961, ch. 1). His attempts to distinguish advances from net products make him Leontief's acknowledged forerunner in input–output analysis (Leontief, 1941, p. 9). After correcting for the sterility of non-agriculture, the *Tableau* could be represented as a simple Leontief system (Phillips, 1955).

2.5.1 The sterility doctrine

However, the most notable aspect of Physiocratic thought is by all accounts the doctrine of the sterility of non-agricultural, or, more precisely, non-primary economic activity.[1] The sterility doctrine has been called the 'cardinal feature of physiocratic theory', its 'fundamental proposition' (Weulersse, 1910a, I, p. 245; Herlitz, 1961, p. 44). It is defined in Quesnay's earliest zigzag *tableaux* of 1758–9 in connection with expenditure on a class of goods, *les dépenses stériles* (Quesnay, 1758–9, p. 667). By the definitive 1766 *Tableau* it is elaborated with reference to the occupations of *la classe stérile* (Quesnay, 1766, p. 793).

In drawing the boundary of the productive domain in which Nature adds her free gifts to man's efforts (1757b, p. 583), Quesnay's starting point is agriculture in the literal sense of cultivation of field crops on the land, the *bien-fonds*. Men's labor on the land generates the raw materials that sustain life (1757a, p. 548). Materials consist first and foremost of edible fruits of the soil: grains, vegetables, hay and forage for animals (1756, pp. 435, 438). Viticulture and wine-making, though labor- rather than land-intensive, are more fruitful than crops since vineyards need no fallow (1757a, pp. 547, 550). In second place are the fruits of animal husbandry: manure, wool, dairy products, butcher's meat, honey, silk; cattle- and horse-power for plowing. Third, the earth gives useful inedibles: textiles (flax, cotton) and fuels (wood and peat).

So far the only question is whether it is land alone, or labor and land together, that account for agriculture's net product. The Physiocrats' (though not Turgot's-Turgot, 1766, p. 49) strict answer is that it is land by itself. On that reasoning fishing is the first case to require exegesis.

In his early *Encyclopédie* article 'Hommes' (1757a), Quesnay writes that

> Men engaged in fishing ought to be included in the class of those who produce. Although fishing is not comparable with agriculture, it ought to be regarded as a very profitable pursuit.
> (1757a, p. 553; Meek, 1963, p. 96)

Since some manufactures are also financially profitable, this is not properly a Physiocratic argument.

Eventually Quesnay reverts to the notion that it is the food plants on the sea-bed rather than sea water *per se* that enable fishermen to bring home abundant catches of *fruits de mer*: 'without the land the seas would produce nothing' (Quesnay, 1766a, p. 764). As Dupont puts it, 'the land is the *mère nourrice* of all living things. This holds for *poissons voraces* just as it does for wolves who eat sheep, that is, who live on the grasses that the sheep have grazed upon' (Dupont de Nemours, 1765, p. xx).

Mining is more of a challenge. Though minerals without doubt come from the ground, they are not *fruits*: the Creator's bounty has been of a one-shot variety, permitting a unique, not an annual, harvest (Morellet, 1770, p. 56). Nevertheless, some members of the sect think mining generates new values over and above the salary and profit of entrepreneurs. In this restrictive sense, it is productive. Others are skeptical: Saint-Péravy for example thinks mine profits contain no pure surplus, only interest on funds advanced (Weulersse, 1910a, I, p. 277, citing Saint-Péravy, 1768, p. 153 n.).

Quesnay apparently had a change of heart about mines and fisheries early in his career as an *économiste*. Omitted from the first edition, by the second edition of the *Tableau* mines and fisheries are listed as objects of productive expenditure. The *Explication* appended to the third edition of the *Tableau* (1759) defines categories as follows:

> *Productive expenditure* is employed in agriculture, grasslands, pastures, forests, mines, fishing, etc., in order to perpetuate wealth in the form of grain, beverages, wood, live-stock, raw materials for manufactured goods, etc.
>
> *Sterile expenditure* is on manufactured commodities, house-room, clothing, interest on money, servants, commercial costs, foreign produce, etc. . .
>
> The *annual advances* of the sterile expenditure class . . . are employed for stocks and costs of trade, for the purchase of raw materials for manufactured goods, for the subsistence and other needs of the artisan until he has completed and sold his goods.
>
> (Quesnay, 1759, p. 675; Meek, 1963, p. 128)

What is the logic of applying the 'humiliating appellation of barren or unproductive' (Smith, 1776, p. 628) to France's well-developed *artisanat*? Quesnay's reply is that artisans are unable to produce a surplus over and above their expenses in food for themselves and raw materials for their trade.

Human labor in itself cannot create – even agricultural labor is sterile. As the elder Mirabeau put it, 'agriculture is a manufactory of divine institution in which the worker has as his associate the Author of Nature, the Producer of all goods and all wealth himself' (Mirabeau,

1763, p. 332; Weulersse, 1910a, I, p. 275). The implication is that God has not been so generous in His physics and chemistry as in His biology. He does not assist the worker in metal or glass to such negentropic good effect as He does the farmer, watering crops from His heavens and making them grow in the earth. It is a pre-industrial vision: the idea that non-agriculture might harness the laws of nature 'shines by its absence'.

Quesnay acknowledges the existence of rural craftsmen such as wheelwrights and blacksmiths; food in his France needs carters to transport it. Yet interestingly there is no reference to the miller, who appears in European folklore and music as an archetypical non-farmer, but one to whose aid Nature comes continuously with her wind and water.

Strictly speaking, Quesnay's artisans require flax but no looms. In Physiocratic capital theory they require *avances annuelles* (advances of materials), but neither *avances primitives* (advances of fixed capital), *avances foncières* (major improvements such as ditches and canals paid for by landlords), nor *avances souveraines* (major projects such as roads and bridges financed by state authorities). As the sterile class has no long-lasting capital equipment, no depreciation allowance need be made for its replacement. Unlike the farmers, artisans do not demand a return of 10 per cent on funds invested for over a year, since none are (Quesnay, 1763, p. 706; Spengler, 1960a; Vaggi, 1987). Similarly, neither do steriles profit from a good network of roads and bridges, as farmers do (to the extent permitted by mercantilist barriers to the free movement of grain).

According to the Physiocratic doctrine of sterility, artisans produce no surplus. Mirabeau is troubled by the fact that highly skilled craftsmen earn what appears to be a comfortable excedent over the cost of raw materials and subsistence. The third element he calls the '*price of esteem*'; it is 'just as real and [a] much more important' component of price than materials costs in works by masters such as the jeweller Lempereur, the goldsmith Germain, or the clockmaker Leroy. Neither talent nor arduous training fully explain their revenue, which corresponds in his words to the net product of agriculture (Mirabeau, 1763, pp. 321–2, in Weulersse, 1910a, I, p. 292). Quesnay acknowledges the implications of Mirabeau's concern and makes much of the costs of apprenticeship incurred in training skilled artists. The effect is to admit that their small number allows them to earn monopoly rents (Quesnay, 1766b, p. 893).

So far the sterile class is a population of capital-poor but hardworking artisans. The *Philosophie rurale* (1763) acknowledges the existence of other income-earning occupations, finding in addition to the artisan *classe stérile industrieuse* a *classe stérile soudoyée*, which is further broken down into *libre* and *dépendante* (Mirabeau, 1763, p. 55). The 'free subsidized sterile class' consists of those engaged in foreign and domestic commerce, from water-carriers to the richest merchants (Mirabeau,

1767, p. 90). The 'dependent subsidized sterile class' is composed of ministers, generals, drummer-boys and valets who live on 'fixed attributions'.

The difference between freedom and dependence turns on whether the steriles' products are to be sold on markets: pails of water in the streets of Paris are so destined, as is coffee from Arabia; not so the output of generals, drummer-boys or domestic cooks. Like the sovereign and the clergy, generals figure in the *Tableau* in so far as they are also members of the class of proprietors. The remainder of the subsidized sterile class, free and dependent, does not appear in it.

In the 1766 *Tableau* the proprietors are portrayed as in direct barter trade with the productive farmer class, as if to highlight the alleged *quid pro quo* of farmers' produce for the landlords' *avances foncières*. Middlemen and retailers play no rôle in this virtuous circular flow. If they did, proprietors would be seen to expend the entirety of their incomes on the sterile side of the Table (Molinier, 1958, pp. 60–1 and n.).

So far it is a logic of unidirectional technical causality: industry requires food and raw materials from agriculture but the reverse is not the case. Agriculture produces basics; industry, Sraffian luxuries. Surplus generation and transfer proceed unencumbered by positive feedback from recipients to donors. Exchange of equivalents and mutually beneficial interdependence characterize relations between proprietor and farmer, but not their intercourse with the steriles.

2.5.2 *Agricultural capital goods and the artisans who make them*

On Quesnay's own description of the world, there are two things wrong with that picture. The first is that artisans do not produce final urban luxuries alone; they also manufacture intermediate agricultural capital goods. Improved plows, more horseshoes for more horses, carts to speed produce to the ports – these improved 'original advances' form the backbone of the Physiocrats' technical program. Widespread adoption of superior techniques is a prerequisite of the shift from *petite* to *grande culture* which is to restore France to greatness. Secondly, if urban–rural trade does not involve exchange of equivalents, as the *Tableau* implies it does not, the sterile class must get something for nothing, for reasons unknown. Let us consider the blacksmiths first.

The initial response to the observation that artisans produce intermediate (capital) goods that are required by the productive sector is an appeal to vertical integration. 'Agriculture' becomes for a moment a 'rural sector' internalizing the local production costs of vehicles, plows, tools and other implements of long and short duration. The way out is paved for Quesnay by Mirabeau, who in 1759 described a potentially beneficent complementarity between field crops and industry.

Mirabeau came out in favor of activities that bring urban-type *savoir faire* to the villages, provided they take place in the wintry off-season so as not to interfere with field crops (Mirabeau, 1759, in Weulersse, 1910b, p. 48 and n. 3).

In describing *la grande culture* in their joint work *Philosophie rurale* (Quesnay and Mirabeau, 1763), Mirabeau presents the farm as an integrated enterprise fabricating its own capital goods. It has seven heads of household – the farmer plus an assortment of cartwrights, yard hands, threshers, harvesters, farriers, harness-makers, wheelwrights and day-laborers who together amount to six full-time workers (Mirabeau, 1763, p. 131). The countryside also harbors various other masters or entrepreneurs, such as those who buy and exploit forests, deal wholesale in manure and livestock, and transport produce and raw materials. All these rural entrepreneurs are included 'in the estate of Farmers' (Mirabeau, 1763, p. 134).

By 1766 Quesnay has all but abandoned vertical integration. In the *Second Dialogue on the Work of Artisans*, after reiterating a view of the economy as a perfectly hierarchical technical structure (a proto-'corn model' in which only agricultural inputs are required for agricultural outputs), it is conceded that artisans can 'contribute by fashioning the several instruments necessary to work the soil, [but] should [such] artisans be lacking, the cultivator would make [the instruments] himself'. There is then reversion to Garden of Eden mode: 'no matter who produces [the agricultural implements], the soil must have produced [the artisan's] subsistence in advance; it is therefore not his labor which has produced this' (Quesnay, 1766b, p. 892). Note the conjugation of 'necessary though intermediate' and 'sterile' (hallmark of input–output error) – in this case, since net product consists of agricultural produce alone, the input–output error of materialist fallacy.

Quesnay's argument did not convert the heathen. The liberal mercantilist de Forbonnais, later joined by Lauraguais, remarked that if the soil produces no revenue without labor, and that labor requires implements and animals, then land is not wealth unless assisted by other sorts of goods (Forbonnais, 1767, pp. 171, 177; Forbonnais, 1766, pp. 61, 103; Lauraguais, 1769, p. 92, cited in Weulersse, 1910a, I, p. 274, n. 2). The editor of the Physiocrat journal *Ephémérides du citoyen*, Abbé Nicolas Baudeau (1730–1792), tried his hand at the problem of artisan blacksmiths in *Explication du Tableau économique à Madame de ★★★* (Baudeau, 1776, sec. IX). Instead of an *ad hoc* appeal to vertical integration, Baudeau attempts a strictly Physiocratic explanation according to which the rural capital-goods sector is free-standing yet sterile. He is however unable to improve upon Quesnay's limited regress.

Even the *Worker* most necessary to [*foncières*] repairs, for start-up advances, for *annual* running *advances*, ... works at the *expense* of the *Cultivator*... *Workers* who are engaged in fabricating the necessary [*sic*] instruments have their materials and labor *paid* by the Cultivators and Proprietors... The entire sterile class, *even* that fraction of Workers engaged in the manufacture of implements for ploughing, is paid indirectly ... by the Cultivator or Proprietor.

(Baudeau, 1776, pp. 99–101)

The school's adamant supply-sidedness perplexed the unconvinced. To critics who objected that industry serves as *la cause occasionelle* of agriculture by buying three-quarters of its products, Baudeau replied that, while industry can make agriculture *want* to increase its production, industry is not *able* to do so without a *prior* increase in food and primary materials (Baudeau, 1776, pp. 103 ff.).

2.5.3 The nature of intersectoral exchange

Quesnay went to some lengths to defend the fundamental proposition of the sterility of non-primary activity. So confident was he of victory that he expounded the arguments of his mercantilist and Encyclopédiste adversaries in order to have the pleasure of refuting them himself. In the *Second Dialogue on the Work of Artisans*, Quesnay's pseudo-adversary is made to say that 'it is the expenditure [of artisans] which procures the sale of the products of the land and which maintains their prices' (Quesnay, 1766b, p. 891; Meek, 1963, p. 209).

A more threatening opponent would have had to add that the sterile class would not have the cash with which to maintain the exchange value of agricultural produce unless it was able to earn it by selling things of value in return. That is, there must have been something like exchange of equivalents in the fully monetized and competitive entrepreneurial economy that the *tableaux* describe.

However, this *quid pro quo* is steadfastly denied by Quesnay, in Herlitz's view in order to salvage the idiosyncratic monetary theory of the 1766 *Tableau*, according to which the sterile class 'seems to live on the "velocity of circulation" of the money' (Herlitz, 1962, p. 118). The special rôle of expenditure implies that farmers 'buy back their own products by a roundabout and expensive route in which transport costs, the wages and food consumption of the sterile class, constitute an unavoidable loss' (Herlitz, 1961, p. 38). Artisans receive cash assets every year 'not as a result of [their] own production, but as a gift!' (Herlitz, 1961, p. 40).

That something approaching free trade in grain was actually tried in France led to the downfall of the Physiocratic school as a policy influence. The Edict of 1764, plus a run of poor harvests, had the effect so sought after by Quesnay: *le bon prix* in Physiocratic parlance, 'dearness' or 'famine' in the opinion of buyers, including rioters in the streets of Paris and Rouen who made themselves increasingly visible after 1766 (Weulersse, 1910a, I, pp. 234 ff.; Fox-Genovese, 1976; Rogers, 1971).

2.6 Sterility challenged, Forbonnais to Condillac

Quesnay's contemporaries, de Forbonnais, Lauraguais, Voltaire, Galiani, Graslin, Condillac and Turgot, either rejected or qualified beyond recognition the Physiocratic view on scope and netness. Their objections turn on interdependence and the equivalence of market exchange. Like Quesnay's pseudo-adversary, the liberal mercantilist François Véron de Forbonnais (1722–1800) emphasizes the rôle demand plays in calling forth increases of agricultural output.

Though he fails to exploit its implications, it is de Forbonnais again who with Lauraguais makes the devastating point that artisans produce not just luxuries but also intermediate capital goods for agriculture (Forbonnais, 1767, pp. 171, 177; Forbonnais, 1766, pp. 61, 103; Lauraguais, 1769, p. 92, cited in Weulersse, 1910a, I, p. 274 n. 2). To the extent that agriculture has managed to achieve *la grande culture*, the Physiocratic sterility doctrine that recommends it is riddled with input–output error.

Voltaire is in our history if only for having invented the immortal Dr Pangloss, unwitting thorn in the self-congratulatory side of general-interdependence and natural-law theorists since the time of *Candide* (1759). In the spirit of the satire on Leibnitz in *Candide* ('all is for the best in the best of all possible worlds' – Voltaire, 1759, p. 210), Voltaire is offended by the Panglossian smugness of the Physiocrats' theory of taxation. *L'Homme aux quarante écus* (Voltaire, 1767) pours somewhat heavy-handed ridicule on a work of the Physiocrat official Le Mercier de la Rivière, who had the temerity to allow that the French monarchy, the single tax, and free trade in grain were part of the 'natural and essential order' of things (Le Mercier de la Rivière, 1767). An interesting analytical criticism of Voltaire's concerns the physiocrats' functional, as opposed to personal, concept of taxation and income; that will come up again in Ricardo and Marx. Voltaire finds it absurd that landlords, however impoverished, should bear the entire burden of financing a profligate and bellicose state, while millionaire merchants are exempted for the reason that commerce produces no net product. Moreover, acres of land, on which the single tax is to be levied, are homogeneously fertile only in Physiocrat abstraction. In lieu of free trade, Voltaire defends mercantilistic interventions of the sort that would restrict outflows of specie destined to purchase colonial luxury goods (1767, p. 415).

The Abbé Ferdinando Galiani (1728–1787) is similarly concerned with the social welfare and political coherence of a doctrine that applauds rises in the prices of wage goods when laborers are on the edge of starvation (Galiani, 1770a). He makes fun of the *secte*'s methodological naïveté in thinking impoverished reality can easily imitate the idealized model of a capital-rich agricultural paradise (Galiani, 1770b, quoted in Ganzoni, 1938, p. 129).

A. R. J. Turgot (1727–81), while nominally a member of the *secte*, effectively abandons its sterility doctrine in his duly celebrated *Reflections on the Formation and Distribution of Wealth* (1766). Turgot eschews the term 'sterile' altogether in favor of 'stipendiary' (*stipendié*) (Turgot, 1766, no. 8, p. 46). More emphatically than Mirabeau, Turgot maintains that 'the soil produces nothing without labor' – an idea that Béardé de l'Abbaye, for example, is able to read as the proposition that proprietors are society's most useless and idle members (Turgot, 1766, no. 17, p. 49; criticized by Baudeau, 1770, p. 111).

Moreover, at least some artisans in Turgot use capital, including acquired skills. Artisans' capital is accumulated by saving out of hard-won but perfectly net profits over wage and materials' costs – out of surplus that Quesnay denies that sterile activities can yield. Turgot thus goes a step on the way to the non-Physiocratic, non-Marxian, Smithian and 'neoclassical' proposition that 'anyone can save' (Turgot, 1766, no. 16, p. 49; see sections 3.2.1, 4.2.1, and 5.4.1 below).

Though artisans can save in theory, the reality of class distinctions in Turgot is Classical not to say Marxist. Cultivators and poor artisans 'resemble each other in many respects', among them elastic labor supply at the same, subsistence wage. The stipendiary class is differentiated. On the one hand there are 'Entrepreneurs, Manufacturers and Mastercraftsmen, all owners of large capitals' which yield returns, and on the other 'simple Artisans, who have no other property than their arms, who advance only their daily labor and receive no profit but their wages' (Turgot, 1766, no. 61, p. 71).

Reflection 60 contains a strong hint that capital mobility between agriculture and industry should produce an equalized rate of return after allowing for the heavier risks and supervisory duties of management in manufacturing (Turgot, 1766, no. 60, p. 70). The reach of this money-profit-equalization mechanism is what describes the boundary of the economy in the more coherent passages of Adam Smith's *Wealth of Nations* (ch. 3 below).

Like Petty, Turgot conceives of wealth (*richesses*) as the value of the stock of land (net revenue times the rate at which land is sold) plus the value of all the 'moveable capitals employed in the enterprises of agriculture, industry, and commerce [*sic*]: ... cattle, utensils and seed...; raw materials, tools, furniture and merchandise of every kind which fill the workhouses, shops and warehouses of all Manufacturers, Merchants and Traders ...' (Turgot, 1766, no. 91, pp. 88–9). The income flows that aliment this stock come from industry and commerce as well as from agriculture.

The upshot is that, eleven years before the publication of the *Wealth of Nations*, Turgot, in agreement with the Physiocrats on matters of tax reform and free trade in grain, quietly abandons their 'fundamental proposition' of binary productiveness and sterility. In place of Quesnay's uniquely productive agriculture, Turgot sketches a productive domain whose limits are those of the competitive economy of all goods and factors bought and sold for money.

Graslin's and Condillac's criticisms of Physiocratic sterility doctrine go past questions of boundaries and netness into valuation itself. Graslin's idea is that 'need is the sole principle of value' (Graslin, 1767, cited in Desmars, 1900, p. 105). Agricultural goods are important 'not because they are the products of the soil, but because they are the objects of our most pressing needs' (Desmars, 1900, pp. 110–11).

Prices fetched by a grandfather clock are compared to those of a bushel of wheat. A Physiocrat would think to prove the clock inferior by evoking a city under siege, during which the wheat would command more than the most precious luxury. *Au contraire*, retorts Graslin,

> that violent state fits my principles even better, since the bushel of wheat combines to the most eminent degree the two qualities of need and rarety which I have established as the measure of all wealth.
> (in Desmars, 1900, p. 110)

Schumpeter notes approvingly that Graslin's is 'a theory of total income rather than of income net of all producers' expenses including wages – a not inconsiderable improvement considering the rôle the latter was to play later on' (in Ricardo) (Schumpeter, 1954, p. 175).

E. B. de Condillac carries on the tradition of Petty and Boisguilbert in maintaining that all income-earning services, even money-lending, belong to production. A country should favor neither agriculture nor industry, but 'occupy itself with everything' (in Studenski, 1961, p. 66). Though Condillac lacks Smith's concept of the division of labor being limited by 'the extent of the market', efficiency gains are to be had when members of society specialize in trade and transport, which are 'the channels of communication, the outlet through which the surplus flows' (Condillac, 1776, p. 45).

Part of Condillac's fame as an economist comes from his analysis of the paradox of exchange of equivalents, which laid the basis of the

1870 marginalists' explanation of the link between subjective utility and contracted exchange-value (price).

> [It] is false that in exchanges one gives equal value for equal value. On the contrary, each of the contracting parties always gives a lesser one for a greater... Why? It is because, since things have no value except in relation to our needs, what is more for one is less for the other and *vice versa*.
>
> (Condillac, 1776, pp. 42–3)

Conceivably that argument was so far ahead of its time that it actually retarded the advance of general-equilibrium thinking by confusing Walras's predecessors among the exchange-of-equivalents but production- and supply-oriented 'French' *courant* within the Classical school (cf. Jevons, 1879, xxvii, xliv–xlv). The 'French' school of post-Smith Classical political economists understood division of labor and *laissez-faire* minimalism decades before there was scientific appreciation of the relationship between marginal utility and price (ch. 4 below).

Condillac's gains-from-exchange idea was, as might have been expected, completely lost on that radical supply-sider Karl Marx. In *Das Kapital* Condillac is blamed for the much-execrated argument that value is created in the very *moment* of 'exchange' (by demand) rather than during the *process* of 'production' (which culminates in supply) (Marx, 1867, ch. V). True, Condillac illustrates the point about mutual gains from trade with examples of individual acts of demand *and* offer in situations of pure exchange with tradable supplies given. But dissatisfaction with the realism of those examples does not of course imply that, when production is arduous or on a large scale, the wishes of buyers are no long relevant or, worse, that individuals no longer 'choose'.

2.7 The boundary of the economy in 1776

In the roughly hundred years separating Petty's *Political Arithmetick* from Smith's *Wealth of Nations*, several types of boundary were put forward as constituting the logical limits of the economy's productive domain. The narrower views on scope came with sometimes explicit but mostly implicit notions about the *mechanisms* by which alleged superfluities were 'transferred' to unproductive laborers in areas beyond the pale. Antedating the sterility doctrine of Quesnay's *Tableaux* by up to a century, some of the more generous schemes, such as those of Petty, King, Mandeville, and Boisguilbert, even made grudging inclusion, in their totals of the economy's revenue and expense, of the non-marketed services of a (retrenched) state sector.

The Physiocrats' emphasis on netness, on the accumulable surplus of 'products' over 'advances', laid the foundations of Classical growth theory. Physiocratic sterility doctrine contained, however, the contradictory proposition that agriculture-enhancing investments in capital goods and infrastructure were simultaneously necessary and the work of sterile artisans and state authorities.

By the 1760s both the more sophisticated mercantilists and the non-Physiocrat liberals had zeroed in upon the weaknesses of the Physiocrat explanation of monetized intersectoral exchange of final goods. They asked why such exchanges would be entered into at all if non-agricultural goods and services were not in some sense the economic *quid pro quo*s of the produce of the land. As will be seen in the next chapter, Adam Smith subjected the Physiocratic sterility doctrine to a withering critique, but omitted to apply its logic to his own unproductive-labor doctrine. Deeper understanding of the input–output error in the Physiocrats' analysis of sterile intermediate goods came only in the second decade of the nineteenth century, when Smith's own losing battle with the category 'necessary yet unproductive' was refought in the debates over immaterial production and Say's Law.

The capitalist or market boundary usually identified with Smith and the Classics had a rich pre-Adamite history. The more generous versions of the limits of the productive domain were under an agrarian cloud at mid-eighteenth century, when criticisms of 'unproductive' state meddling – which indeed precipitated the divorce between political economy and statecraft – threatened to extend to all urban pursuits, private as well as public. By the time of Turgot, Graslin, and Condillac, a production boundary circumscribing an interdependent economy of private, marketed goods and services was rapidly gaining ground, all the stronger for its encounter with the Physiocratic doctrine of the exclusive net physical productivity of the soil.

Note

1 Non-primary = non-agricultural, non-pescatorial, non-sylvicultural, non-mining. But see *variorum* discussion in Weulersse (1910a), I, pp. 277 ff. and in Vaggi (1987), ch. 2.

CHAPTER 3

Division of Labor and Unproductive Labor in a System of Natural Liberty: Adam Smith's Dilemma

3.1 Two sorts of unproductive labor

The *Wealth of Nations* contains the classic and Classical statement of the idea that 'labor' may be 'unproductive'. In Book II, chapter iii, of that immortal work, Adam Smith describes as 'productive' on the one hand 'labourers' who produce material products, on the other, those whose products earn money profits when sold.

Smith himself treats the material and money-profit definitions as perfect substitutes. That turns out to be a major error, and one of some significance for the development of political economy. Economists have devoted a good deal of time and energy since 1776 to mapping and analyzing the *non-intersections* of Smith's two sets. At first glance, in the *Wealth of Nations* domestic servants and state authorities seem to meet both of Smith's criteria for unproductiveness; the work is *locus classicus* for the doctrine of the state as economic parasite. Both that doctrine and the qualifications that will eventually explode it are set out in *An Inquiry into the Nature and Causes of the Wealth of Nations* (Smith, 1776).

The 'productive–unproductive' distinction is given an important rôle in Smith's overall scheme. It is set out on page 1 of the 'Introduction and Plan of the Work' and serves as a building block of the theory of economic growth that is the main object of the exercise.

3.1.1 Unproductive of what? – 'annual produce'

Smith's first step is to single out the annual sum of 'necessaries and conveniencies of life' as society's economic maximand (Smith, 1776, p. lvii). The relationship between total 'annual produce' and population determines the standard of living per head. The total is 'regulated by two different circumstances; first, by the skill, dexterity, and judgment with which its labour is generally applied; and, secondly, by the *proportion* between the number of those who are employed in *useful labour*, and that of those who are not so employed' (1776, p. lvii; emphasis added).

In the famous chapter iii 'Of the accumulation of capital, or of productive and unproductive labour' of Book II, it is argued that next year's plus or minus of annual produce depends on the manner in which annual produce is distributed between consumption and investment this year.

> Both productive and unproductive labourers, and those who do not labour at all, are all equally maintained by the annual produce of the land and labour of the country ... According, therefore, as a smaller or greater proportion of it is in any one year employed in maintaining unproductive hands, the more in the one case and the less in the other will remain for the productive, and the next year's produce will be greater or smaller accordingly; the whole annual produce, if we except the spontaneous productions of the earth, being the effect of productive labour.
> (Smith, 1776, p. 315)

Annual output per head is a function of 'technology' or 'knowledge', on the one hand, and of (productive) 'effort' or 'labour' on the other. Both terms we know to be problematic. Determining which citizens contribute, if only indirectly, to the production of annual produce is scarcely less difficult than identifying the secrets of firms' or societies' ability to generate outputs from given inputs. One such input is 'capital stock': '[The] number of *useful and productive* labourers ... is every where in proportion to the quantity of capital stock which is employed in setting them to work ...' (1776, p. lviii; emphasis added). The effectiveness of 'laborers' in producing 'annual produce' is directly related to their making use of 'capital stock'. So it becomes important to know of what this stock consists and how it may be increased.

3.1.2 *The value version or profitability criterion*

Smith's two versions of productive and unproductive labor are elaborated in adjacent paragraphs of Book II, chapter iii. According to the first, 'money-profit' or 'value version' (Myint, 1948, ch. V), laborers are 'productive' if their products upon market sale earn profits over and above 'real costs' of production.

> The labour of a manufacturer adds, generally, to the [money] value of the materials which he works upon, that of his own maintenance, and of his master's profit.
> (Smith, 1776, p. 314)

Aside from the implication that capital itself is material, nothing is said yet about the physical nature of the profitable activity, about the 'materiality' of the use-values that result. Laborers in private-sector service establishments earn profits for their employers over and above their wages. Such money profits may be reinvested in the same, or some other line of business.

The logic of generating and accumulating a net surplus is analogous to the Physiocratic one, with an important improvement. Smith's theory of money profits, set forth in Book I, chapter vi, has rates proportional to total capital advanced. Differences in rates in different trades tend to be evened out by competition, by entry and exit, after due allowance for risk. Since, in Smith's economy, money profits are earned on capital advanced in foreign and domestic commerce and manufacturing as well as in agriculture, the assumption of exchange of equivalents absolves him at a stroke of the need for a mechanism to transfer surplus from agriculture to the other monetized branches, such as had been required in Quesnay's *Tableau*. Smith's problems with surplus generation and transfer occur in another context, in transactions between market and non-market spheres.

Smith does not restrict, as Marx is to do, the logic of accumulation of money profits to ('capitalist') enterprises that employ specifically wage labor. *The self-employed whose goods are sold on markets are inferior in neither parsimony nor economic purposefulness to owners of capitals large enough to set many unrelated individuals to work.* In the *Wealth of Nations*, self-employed small proprietors change trades, save, and accumulate in exactly the same manner as do owners of great manufactories, even while they employ only their own labor or that of their families (1776, p. 359). Accumulation out of small surpluses, whether in money or in kind, is indeed (together with improvements in technique) the source of the progress of society from an 'early and rude state' to 'opulence'.

3.1.3 *The material version or materiality criterion*

In that same inaugural paragraph of Book II, chapter iii, Adam Smith provides a second definition of 'productive' and 'unproductive' that is in its implications and ramifications quite different from the first.

> The labour of the manufacturer fixes and realizes itself in some particular subject or vendible commodity, which lasts for some time at least after that labour is past. It is, as it were, a certain quantity of labour stocked and stored up to be employed, if necessary, upon some other occasion. That subject . . . can afterwards, if necessary, put into motion a quantity of labour equal to that which had

originally produced it. The labour of the menial servant, on the contrary, does not fix or realize itself in any particular subject or vendible commodity. His services generally perish in the very instant of their performance, and seldom leave any trace or value behind them, for which an equal quantity of service could afterwards be procured.

(Smith, 1776, pp. 314–5).

According to this material or 'storage version' (Myint, 1948; ch. 5 below), a certain durability is required of economic goods for them to be around long enough to 'command' 'an equal quantity of labor' at some future time. It is apparently assumed that only 'material' goods trade against 'wage goods' that will sustain laborers who make new items of fixed or circulating capital.

The profitability criterion and the materiality criterion are treated as perfect substitutes. The analysis of accumulation in Book II, chapter iii, deals in effect with the intersection of the two sets: those profitable activities that result in material goods lasting 'for some time at least' after their production (Anspach, 1976; Eltis, 1975c). Loss-making material-goods production would be discontinued if capital were mobile between firms and trades. Less easily justified on Smith's own description of the world are the implied corollaries that (i) profit-earning, marketed but 'immaterial' services are an empty set and that (ii) non-marketed, public-sector activities are final luxuries that in no way influence or affect the volume of annual produce that productive laborers produce.

Adam Smith's supposition that the two criteria produce identical lists of productive and unproductive activities does work in part: manufacturing and agriculture are productive on either criterion, and domestic service (of which more below) unproductive (Eltis, 1975c). Profitable production may include production of alienable, storable, material goods, and even production of wage goods destined to support workers who will thereby be able further to divide their labor. But are the two criteria interchangeable?

3.2 What is capital, that it be accumulated?

To the extent that capital is taken to be what Smith calls 'circulating' capital – that is, capital that consists mainly of wage goods used to sustain additional labor in a future period (but also of money and materials) – money profits earned in sectors 'productive' on the first criterion will require a material counterpart in 'corn' for those profits to employ additional 'productive labor'. That labor will again by the first definition yield profits, which can be invested in the employment of additional laborers, and so on in a virtuous spiral. Given the large reserve of citizens who are 'unproductive or do not labor at all', it is unlikely that extensive growth of that kind will be constrained by availability of productive laborers or their means of sustenance.

The problem is the difficulty of finding a counterpart to money profits not in the form of additional wage goods but in the form of *other* raw materials and means of labor (Hollander, 1973, p. 154). Unproductive laborers eat and sleep already, so, assuming their consumption does not change, reallocation to more worthy tasks will not in itself require an immediate increase in the availability of their consumption goods.

The creation of fixed capital in the form of 'machinery to abridge labour' in some future period, involves present outlay on subsistence and materials. Whether the item of fixed or circulation capital is purchased with profits generated in a successful opera house or a successful pin factory makes no difference once the item is ready for use. The production of the machine (or new theatre) has meant expenditure on workers' and projectors' consumption (largely if not entirely in the form of 'goods' in 1776) and on tangible raw materials. The flow of resources into the new item of fixed capital 'extends the period of time' required to produce operas or pins.

The description of growth through accumulation given in Book II, chapter iii, makes no mention of capital 'fixed and realized' in human beings as a result of their 'education, study, or apprenticeship' (1776, p. 265). The omission is somewhat startling in view of the fact that chapter i of that same Book treats 'the acquired and useful abilities of all the inhabitants or members of the society' as one of the four basic types of fixed capital, which '[afford] a revenue or profit without circulating or changing masters' (1776, p. 265).

The decision to exclude human capital from the model of growth sets a precedent to endure for nearly two centuries. It may be a holdover from the analysis of wage determination set forth in Book I. There, acquired and natural differences in human capital ('ingenuity') are given as one cause of variations in the price of 'labour' (the other being 'hardship'). The observed wage structure for individuals and trades is treated as the outcome of 'higgling and bargaining of the market' (1776, pp. 30-1), not something calculable with any precision as a return on a known, accumulated stock of skills.

Supposing subsistence to consist exclusively of material goods, an apprentice-turned-master may still be said to have accumulated only part of his 'improved dexterity' by consuming such goods. The other part of his apprenticeship consists of 'doing', 'learning', 'observing', and so on. The master's dexterity, once acquired, is inalienable; it is injured and dies with him, but cannot be transferred *en bloc* except under slavery (where it remains none the less 'embodied' in the tenor) (Hill, 1977). In the usual circumstance of wage labor, such characteristics are 'rented'. The master artisan, having acquired them purposefully, may expect a return on his investment, even if those possessed of natural human capital in the form of 'genius or superior talents' must content themselves with 'public admiration' for a considerable fraction of their reward (1776, p. 107).

3.3 Servants in the household: consumers' sovereignty and natural liberty in the *Wealth of Nations*

3.3.1 Two kinds of expenditure, of revenue and of capital

Adam Smith's Scottish soul is particularly troubled by the 'unproductiveness' of menial servants, who are said to be paid not out of 'capital' but out of the consumption category 'revenue'. Servants perform 'immaterial services', which must be continually repeated because the results do not last; a servant's work is never done. Like yeoman farmers, they perform a variety of tasks, washing clothes one day, patching them the next. We will never know whether Smith would have granted that clean clothes command a higher price *ceteris paribus* than dirty ones. The recognition problem stems from mode-mindedness: neither the washing nor the mending has been carried out with a view to immediate resale, as is the case with industry, handicrafts, or commerce. The servant's labor and the soap, thread, etc. make improvements in the clothes in both cases, though the durability of improvement associated with an hour's mending, for example, is normally greater (assuming average skill with a needle) than for an hour's washing.

That Smith did on occasion reason in terms of time rates of value-addition and -subtraction is evidenced by his analysis of the resale of second-hand furniture and clothing of the rich. '[Though they] might not be worth all that [they] cost, [such goods] would always be worth something . . . to the inferior and middling ranks of people [who] purchase them when their superiors grow weary of them. . .' (1776, p. 330).

Had it occurred to him, Smith would have been hard-pressed to disallow as increase of potential capital so obviously concrete and important a transformation as a servant adding a wing to a house or building a barn or shed (example from Eltis, 1975c). Arguably a proprietor would expect some return on his investment should the building ever be sold. It remains stored up as a potential return until such time as he should sell it. The fact that wood was sawn or bricks laid by someone *in the regular employ* of the master, rather than by an outsider specially contracted for, is wholly incidental, as is the fact that the owner is probably not a hôtelier by trade.

Further evidence of Smith's disinclination to recognize non-market accumulation of potentially marketable assets comes in the discussion of dwelling-houses, whether occupied by their owners or rented out. Housing is the most long-lasting portion of 'the general stock of any country or society' 'reserved for immediate consumption'. It is argued, pretty unconvincingly, that the housing stock 'itself can produce nothing' that is worthy of inclusion in annual produce, even when it affords a money rent. Rent of houses is portrayed as a transaction without *quid pro quo*; it is a transfer, an 'expence' of revenue analogous to that on servants (1776, pp. 264–5).

Modern economics interprets assignment of servants to builders' work in terms of Coase's (1937) argument that there may be 'costs to using the market'. These *transactions costs* of finding the right specialist may be so large as to make it worthwhile to stick to the unskilled labor on hand despite the fact that the menial's 'dexterity', and probably his efficiency too, is likely to be inferior to that of a professional carpenter or bricklayer.

Adam Smith's image of the menial servant is confined to the servant who makes small and very temporary improvements in the cleanliness of clothes. Smith was probably not misled in assuming that the lion's share of domestic man-hours were devoted to 'prevention of value subtraction' – to 'maintenance' rather than net additions to proprietors' assets. However, that is irrelevant. Furthermore, the spurious distinction fits his portrait of the independent master a good deal less well.

Appreciation of a shirt in the laundry is by a small amount soon depreciated away by renewed wear. Even the imperfectly rational proprietor may allocate his servant's time so that use-value added in a day's work on the new outbuilding is not too far out of line with his contributions in the laundry.

The distinction between 'payment out of capital' and 'out of revenue' appears on closer inspection to be less than perfectly neat. What looks like expenditure of 'revenue' on 'consumption' may contain elements of asset accumulation. It is not necessary to treat human beings as capital goods to derive this result (section 10.2 below). As already recognized by Sir William Petty, and by Smith himself in many other places (e.g. 1776, pp. 265, 330), durability is most fruitfully viewed as a continuum, from treasures stored up in heaven where neither moth nor rust doth corrupt, to the most evanescent of magic moments.

3.3.2 *Prodigality and rationality*

More than this turns on the 'revenue' – 'capital' distinction in the *Wealth of Nations*. While it might have been allowed that only an arbitrary line separates maintenance from 'production' and that domestics are occasionally assigned work of some permanence, Smith would have been quite sure to reject the notion that proprietors are as calculating when assigning domestic servants to their various tasks as they are when organizing the activities of workers in their manufactories. It is to become an axiom of Classical economics that proportions between, for example, meat roasted and socks mended, and food and clothing newly produced do not result from decisions made with similar degrees of calculation and care.

Conscious economic calculation, as we saw, plays a rôle in the choice of certain professions and in the acquisition of 'dexterity'. Domestics, on the other hand, are 'common labour' assumed not to possess any special talents, acquired or innate. They are in the labor market, though, since unlike medieval retainers they earn money wages. Their status as unproductives derives from the fact that the 'products' of their efforts are only incidentally subject to resale.

With the statement that expenditure on servants is 'out of revenue', a line is drawn between the sphere of production for sale on private markets and the consumption sphere in which private persons dispose of their income. 'Common workmen' ordinarily weigh carefully each purchase, even though 'if their wages are considerable [they] may maintain a menial servant [or] sometimes go to a play or a puppet-show...' (1776, p. 317). In contrast, consumers who employ a 'multitude' of menial servants, since they do so with imperfect rationality, are guilty of 'profusion', of passion for present enjoyment.

The interesting implication is that *private 'prodigals' may not fully deserve the sovereign freedom they have to dispose of their own money*. This is in spite of the fact that 'it is the highest impertinence and presumption ... in kings and ministers, to pretend to watch over the oeconomy of private people' (1776, pp. 324, 329). Notwithstanding the famous kind words about 'consumption' being 'the sole end and purpose of all production' (p. 625), Adam Smith has reservations when propensities incline to 'prodigality', 'profusion' or 'misconduct' (pp. 322, 324).

Tastes that favor activities other than those he approves of are branded and degraded with 'humiliating' appellations. Only 'misconduct' refers to misfortunes like bankruptcy that have no wasteful intent, only poor result. It might be thought, and not only by libertarians, that to apply the 'humiliating appellation of barren or unproductive' to remunerative professions jibes ill with Smith's analysis of the economic benefits to be had from the free play of economic self-interest. In a system of 'natural liberty', division of labor should rule out unproductive labor.

Fortunately for Great Britain, the system of natural liberty in that country is expected to be not only 'natural' and 'just', but 'productive'. The great majority of people, including the sober and industrious poor, are blessed with the right sorts of preferences. Profligates are not the norm. The strength of the desire for self-betterment means little inducement is required to get them to refrain from present enjoyment (but see Anspach, 1976, p. 504). Under natural liberty, therefore, accumulation, freed from interference from an incompetent state, may be expected to be rapid.

Despite fundamental insight into benefits deriving from the division of labor (the famous pin factory) and from the unfettered movement of labor and capital stock between trades, allocation of the labor of domestic servants is decided on a different, less 'economic' basis. There is grudging acknowledgment of private individuals' sovereign right to dispose of their revenue as they see fit. But it is qualified by disapproval of those preferences that permit the immaterial services of 'unproductive' menials to account for so large a fraction of human effort.

'A man must be perfectly crazy', writes Adam Smith, in 'countries where there is tolerable security', to fail to employ all his stock in either immediate consumption or as fixed or circulating capital (1776, p. 268). The analysis of 'the accumulation of capital, or of productive and unproductive labour' leaves the impression that not just hoarding, but 'profligacy and profusion' too are forms of madness.

3.3.3 Consumption boundaries and intermediatization

Analysis of the economic activities of domestic servants and of members of the liberal professions proceeds from a vision of when and how final goods are 'consumed' by individuals. The location of the boundary between 'production' and 'consumption' is obviously an important piece of information for the economist. There are various possibilities. The typical 'final' or 'consumer' good may be conceived as a commodity sold on a price-making market – what G. S. Becker (1965) describes as an 'X-good' (section 8.4.2 below). Beckerian X-goods are no doubt what Adam Smith has in mind: material goods sold on markets with a view to profit, irrespective of whether they require (as would 'corn') considerable additional preparation (milling, baking) before being rendered fit for human consumption.

Alternatively, if less attention is paid to markets and money prices, goods may be thought of as having achieved 'finality' when they reach the point of yielding up 'utility' to consumers. In Becker, such 'Z-goods' are produced by X-goods and 'time'. 'Bread on the table' can be a Z-good only once; the table itself yields a time-flow of Z-goods over its useful lifetime.

If adding vs. subtraction of potential market value is the criterion, domestic servants who bake bread 'produce' in the same manner as do farm laborers, wholesalers, carriers, millers, tradesmen, etc. – to mention only one round of roundaboutness – who grow corn and bring it to market. Critics of both Smith's materialist and his money-profit definitions, from Garnier, Say, and Senior to G. S. Becker, observe that neither materiality nor marketedness are synonymous with the potential to add value; they are imperfect guides to real, opportunity cost.

3.4 Materiality dominant?

The usefulness of the labor of domestic servants does not find easy expression in measurable units, whether of pounds *avoirdupois* or pounds sterling. Difficulty of measurement of the value of their products on anything but a labor-cost basis appears at the root of the assertion that its true measure is zero (sections 8.2 and 8.4.3 below). The 'humiliating appellation of the barren or unproductive class' (Smith, 1776, p. 628) indeed would be fully deserved if there were no *quid pro quo*. Despite payment of labor services in money and the presumption of a low degree of acquired dexterity (which would facilitate imputation using something like labor units), servants' output is not one of the 'conveniencies of life' included in annual produce in Adam Smith's growth model.

3.4.1 Transfers, models, and modes

When a process having positive input and zero output manages to survive in a competitive framework, it is because the system of which it is a part allows for transfers in addition to production; it is a system of surplus generation and transfer. The assertion that the exchange of money for unproductive services is not equivalent and uniformly motivated underlies Smith's 'revenue'–'capital' distinction and indeed all but the most careful applications of the 'productive–unproductive' vocabulary in economics. 'Unproductive labourers', though they 'work', are 'maintained by the annual produce of the land and labour of the country'. They are technically no better than 'those who do not labour at all'.

Menials are in this manner relegated to the supply side of a 'non-economic' household mode. They might alternatively have been kept as single-person service mini-firms in the monetized, private, for-profit sector of the economy. That is where mainly final, externality-poor, 'personal' services are provided for a fee by lawyers, physicians, teachers, barbers, and other self-employed professionals and tradesmen. The activities of self-employed producers of *marketed* services are after all described as 'regulated by the very same principles which regulate that of every other sort of labour' (1776, p. 315).

Given the emphasis some interpreters have placed on 'capitalist conditions' in the *Wealth of Nations*, it is interesting that no special attention is paid to whether firms are single- or multi-person ones, provided the outputs are material and resold. The revenue of the self-employed is simply less easily divisible into wages, profits, and rent (1776, pp. 53–4; see section 5.4 below).

Agents in Smith are assumed universally to want to better their condition. That they attempt to maximize, and succeed in earning normal, returns on human and physical assets might conceivably have won them membership in Smith's exclusive set of 'productive labourers', irrespective of the long-lastingness of the good or service sold. The possibility is not far-fetched; Smith already includes both wage workers and 'undertakers' so long as the outputs are of the right sort; it is not inconsistent with the wage theory of Book I. But it is ruled out once Smith makes his materialist declaration of faith in the sentences succeeding the ambiguous opening of the chapter 'Of the accumulation of capital, or of productive and unproductive labour'.

3.4.2 *The full list of unproductive laborers*

The full list of 'unproductive labourers' presented in chapter iii of Book II is a long and heterogeneous one. In addition to paid domestics, it contains members of the noble and some less noble professions, who sell 'immaterial' services, as well as those in the employ or service of non-profit organizations and the state. Whether the 'firm' or organization consists of one or several individuals appears not to matter. What sets Smith's unproductive laborers apart is the alleged 'immateriality', not the non-marketedness or unprofitability, of their products. The set of unproductives, while heterogeneous, is presented by Smith as complete; the passage is the source of the nineteenth-century notion that Smith subscribed to an unadulterated 'materialist concept' rather than to some confused hybrid of the two (ch. 4).

> The labour of some of the most respectable orders in the society is, like that of menial servants, unproductive of any value, and does not fix or realize itself in any permanent subject or vendible commodity, which endures after that labour is past, and for which an equal

quantity of labour could afterwards be procured. The sovereign, for example, with all the officers both of justice and war who serve under him, the whole army and navy, are unproductive labourers. They are the servants of the public, and are maintained by a part of the annual produce and of the industry of other people. Their service, how honourable, *how useful, or how necessary soever*, produces nothing for which an equal quantity of service can afterwards be procured. The protection, security, and defence of the commonwealth, the effect of their labour this year, will not purchase its protection, security, and defence for the year to come. In the same class must be ranked, some both of the gravest and most important, and some of the most frivolous professions: churchmen, lawyers, buffoons, musicians, opera-singers, opera-dancers, &c. The labour of the meanest of these has a certain value, *regulated by the very same principles which regulate that of every other sort of labour*; and that of the noblest and most useful, produces nothing which could afterwards purchase or procure an equal quantity of labour . . .

(Smith, 1776, p. 315; emphasis added)

3.4.3 *Adam Smith's input–output error*

That seductively written passage is to make a nearly indelible imprint on everyday, 'commonsense' economics, persuading serious theorists from Ricardo to Friedman. The grand cadences have the ring of truth. However, Smith's argument is not only incomplete but inconsistent. In it is altered the meaning of the word 'useful', which in the 'Introduction and Plan of the Work' had been synonymous with 'productive'. Now a 'labourer' may be economically 'useful', even 'necessary', and simultaneously 'unproductive' of annual produce.

That proposition is illogical if production functions admit of even sketchy definition. If technical and social requirements can be specified (whether proportions be fixed or variable) at some set of input prices, the volume of labor and capital services required to obtain a given flow of product can be determined. Subtract a unit of an input that is 'necessary' in this sense and *output will go down*. If coefficients are truly and irrevocably fixed, *sine qua non*, output will fall to zero. If producers are sovereign, in what sense can inputs be 'unproductive'?

Scholars are free to define the object of their inquiry as they see fit. Smith as a supplier of scholarship is 'sovereign' in this way, and is free for instance to define annual produce so as to include or exclude 'conveniencies and luxuries', whether 'material' or 'immaterial'. The economics of the production and consumption of all marketed goods and services may however be more interesting to consumers of economic scholarship than, say, the economics of iron or corn. One reason to favor the more general economics would be a belief that consumers apportion their incomes and producers their efforts, between corn X-goods, cooking pots, services of caterers and servants, tavern meals, etc. with something like uniform care.

(It is later explained that '[under] necessaries ... I comprehend not only those things which nature, but those things which the established rules of decency have rendered necessary to the lowest rank of people. All other things I call luxuries; without meaning by this appellation, to throw the smallest degree of reproach upon the temperate use of them' (1776, p. 822)).)

The upshot here is that 'produce' in the last analysis is defined according to technical and physical rather than economic criteria. It is an approach that jars in the work of the philosopher who made such headway with the diamond–water paradox (1776, p. 28; see Schumpeter, 1954, p. 309). Alas, as J.-B. Say was to put it (1819, p. 62), there is 'confusion of matter and value'.

In an analysis of the growth model of Book II, chapter iii, Sir John Hicks (1965, p. 36) observes that there can be 'little doubt that Smith intended this chapter to be regarded as the centrepiece of his whole work'. A pronounced bias towards material goods permeates the chapter. For that reason Smith's input–output error is said to be in the main one of 'materialist fallacy' rather than in the more general 'unproductiveness fallacy', though the two views of who is a productive laborer leave the question somewhat open.

3.5 Servants of the public

> The division of labour [is] the principle upon which all government is founded.
>
> (N. Senior, 1836a, p. 76)

Input–output error there is, however. The 'greatest spendthrifts in the society' and those most dangerous to the prosperity of the commonwealth are 'always, and without any exception', not employers of hapless menials or occasional circus- or opera-goers, but kings, ministers, and similar 'servants of the public' (1776, p. 329). It is in discussion of the economic rôle of such agents that Smith relaxes, albeit only slightly, the rigid assumptions of *unidirectional* flow of his theory of surplus generation and transfer. Admission that 'unproductives' may supply goods or services that 'productives' must have is the giveaway.

The qualifications made by Smith to his own statements about government economic parasitism represent the thin end of a thick wedge. Senior, Mill, and a host of twentieth-century writers will transform Smith's observations (although not beyond recognition) into the modern theory of public choice (sections 4.4 and 7.3 below). They are the intellectual foundation of Simon Kuznets's attempt to make national income a better measure of human welfare (section 8.4.1).

The pro-market *courant* in contemporary economics (sections 7.2 and 7.3 below) is a direct development of Adam Smith's 'sophisticated' case against the state. The goods market's allegedly superior accuracy of valuation as compared with other modes should, if Smith were consistent, be what disqualifies the unresold 'products' of paid domestics and public servants from inclusion in annual produce. Non-marketedness, not immateriality, is the source of weak performance. Why is this so? Special powers enable public servants to shirk the discipline of cost minimization. It is their lack of discipline as much as their ignorance that deprives them of the right to intervene in 'the oeconomy of private people'.

Input–output error in the treatment of servants of the public stems from the fact that, on Smith's own logic, not all public services end up as unmistakably final *luxuries*. In Book II, chapter iii, the 'sovereign ... with all the officers both of justice and war ..., the whole army and navy, are unproductive labourers', however 'honourable', 'useful', or 'necessary' they may be. Smith in effect affirms (at the same time that he denies it) that, despite some inefficiencies, at least some public services are prerequisites, intermediates, to the production of the goods making up annual produce. Reverting momentarily to the profitability criterion, he asserts that '[the] protection, security, and defence of the commonwealth, the effect of their labour this year, will not purchase its protection, security, and defence for the year to come' (1776, p. 315).

That is, however, a specious argument, since defense is 'necessary', and annual produce is greater this year *than it would have been* without the peace and security conferred by the activities of the sovereign, his ministers, and their executants. Correct behaviour on the part of public 'officers of justice' promotes economic growth by creating the legal and social framework conducive to it. In a 1755 essay, Smith had waxed more effusive:

> Little else is required to carry a state to the highest degree of opulence from the lowest barbarism but peace, easy taxes, and a tolerable administration of justice...
>
> (in 1776, p. xliii)

3.5.1 *Smith's critique of Physiocracy*

His brilliant exposé of Physiocrat sterility doctrine provides the key to understanding Smith's own difficulty with activities simultaneously unproductive and necessary. The reader watches with incredulity as Adam Smith the materialist fallacist is hoist by his own petard. The famous pin factory described in chapter i of Book I celebrated the gains in output per man-hour consequent upon division of labor within a multi-person firm. The chapter on the 'origin and use of money' analysed similar benefits from the perspective of social or occupational division of labor between one-person specialist firms of butchers, bakers, and so on.

The chapter on 'agricultural systems' (Book IV, chapter ix) turns the Physiocrats' admission that benefits accrue to societies that divide labor occupationally into a device for exploding their theory of the sterility of trade and manufactures. Exchanges of the products of specialization must involve a *quid pro quo*: '[A]rtificers, manufacturers, and merchants ... [whom the Physiocrats] endeavour to degrade by the humiliating appellation of the barren or unproductive class' are said by them to be none the less 'greatly useful to the other two classes. By means of the unproductive class, the cultivators are delivered from many cares which would otherwise distract their attention from the cultivation of land' (1776, pp. 628, 633).

> The superiority of produce, which, in consequence of this undivided attention, they are enabled to raise, is fully sufficient to pay the whole expense [of] the maintenance and employment of the unproductive class ... The industry of merchants, artificers and manufacturers ... contributes in this manner *indirectly* to increase the produce of the land. It increases the productive powers of productive labour, by leaving it at liberty to confine itself to its proper employment ... [The] plough goes frequently the easier and the better by means of the labour of the man who is far from the plough.
> (Smith, 1776, pp. 633–4; emphasis added)

3.5.2 *Intermediatization of government*
'PEACE, EASY TAXES, AND A TOLERABLE ADMINISTRATION OF JUSTICE'

The admission of intermediate production in Physiocracy suggests a way to rescue Smith's own unproductiveness theory from analytical disgrace, at least as far as the Sovereign is concerned. A disciple of Leontief or Kuznets, or even J. S. Mill, would have no trouble with the proposition that a materiality criterion for final output may yet leave room for the possibility that 'immaterial' services serve as intermediates. In a given economy, the types and quantities of intermediate goods 'necessary' to the production of a given final bill of, for instance, marketed material goods depend on 'technology' or 'production coefficients'. Laborers 'necessary' or 'useful' but 'unproductive' of final material produce (as *per* p. 315) may simply be producers of intermediate inputs rather than of final outputs. As noted, an intermediate good is not a bad!

Inventors and fabricators of accumulable capital goods, which 'facilitate and abridge labour' and thereby raise output per man, may in similar fashion be indirect producers of those final goods whose consumption is the 'sole end and purpose of all production' (1776, p. 625).

3.5.3 Production-function logic

Using production-function logic to rescue servants of the public from economic limbo is somewhat difficult in practice. Hopes of easy measurability are false. Estimating what volume of (retrenched) expenditures on intermediate 'peace and security' is truly socially and technically necessary for a given volume of corn to be forthcoming is fraught with difficulty, not least because there *are* no *pure* public goods. Agricultural enterprises benefit unequally from a standing army or navy, not to speak of a network of roads and bridges. Some farms are closer to the frontier, or to the naval base or the arms factory, a fact recognized by every pork-barrel politician.

The 'impureness' of goods rich in externalities has not only a spatial but an input–output dimension. The army and navy protect consumers and producers more or less simultaneously and equally. That complicates the problem of isolating flows of protection intermediate to *production*.

Estimation of intermediate requirements for peace and security, by observation of real effects of induced variations in 'supply', is not possible with any precision. For example, even if the free-rider problem could be ignored by assuming that felt demands for peace and security are naïvely revealed, and holding other things like enemy behavior constant, discontinuities on the supply side might still be on a 'near-dialectical' scale. Tinkering in the manner of engineers with a view to determining the reaction thresholds of farmers' 'animal spirits' might cause wide swings in agricultural production. Farmers might be forgiven for perceiving changes in their environment occasioned by civil or international strife as qualitative 'catastrophes' rather than as incremental changes in the state of the world.

A production-function approach would permit reclassification of some non-marketed public-sector services as 'intermediate' rather than 'final' and would then look for input–output coefficients. However thrilling the thought experiments, few clues are provided *ex ante* as to the likely value of the 'most efficacious proportion' or its structure.

Even in the special case of economic systems that are technically perfectly hierarchical, with no circular loops (Blaug, 1980b, p. 15), all but Ur-primary inputs have inputs themselves. In such systems, some level of 'peace and security' may be envisaged as necessary *at each stage of production* if in its absence the desired volume of production of private, externality-poor private intermediate capital goods would not be forthcoming.

Finding how much 'peace and security' and therefore how many 'constables and soldiers' are 'necessary but intermediate' to the production of goods that count is – though that is not saying much – perhaps scarcely more mysterious than the estimation of full production coefficients for *private* goods that also have significant external effects. The point is that, whether or not the true, socially necessary labor coefficients of 'peace and security' are *lower* (as Smith and the majority of Classical and neoconservative economists would have it), the same, or higher than in observable practice, is basically a question of *fact*.

Thomas Carlyle's description of the Smithian economy as 'anarchy plus a constable' rings false to the modern reader of Book V. The *Wealth of Nations* is riddled with implicit and explicit qualifications of the *laissez-faire* ideal. Not least of these is the implication, not alluded to by Smith, that only the state is empowered to dismantle the laws and privileges of the commercial or mercantile system and to institute the system of natural liberty (Samuels and Mercuro, 1984). Laws and institutions favorable to business, exports, and demography, which Smith does not entirely take for granted, have been credited with the 'miracle' of modern European economic growth (Jones, 1981; Hartwell, 1973).

Incidentally, it is allowed that some quite pure public goods may require well-above-subsistence 'productive consumption' in order for the beneficent result to be forthcoming in the requisite 'volume'. The 'dignity of the Sovereign' is such a good.

'[The] maintenance of good roads and communications' likewise affects 'the whole society' and for this reason merits being paid out of general tax revenue. In addition to defense, the courts, and so on, other public goods extend their benefits to narrower sections of the population. An example is the protection afforded by the police of a particular town. In the case of purely local benefits, only the locals should be taxed to cover costs (1776, p. 767).

With a view to extending the *reciprocity* characteristic of barter and market transactions as far as possible into the non-market realm, Smith recommends that payment for goods supplied by public authorities should be direct, by result, wherever circumstances allow. The expense of maintaining roads and canals should be defrayed by sellers of transported products, and indirectly by their buyers, in order to 'discharge the general revenue of the society from a very considerable burden' (1776, p. 768).

3.5.4 Education

A certain level of education is 'likewise, no doubt, beneficial to the whole society, and may, therefore, without injustice, be defrayed by the general contribution of the whole society', that is, by the state out of tax revenue (1776, p. 768). Some controversy attaches to how Smith envisaged the effects of the various types of education, among them primary education subsidized by the state purse, on the rate of increase of annual produce.

> Though the state was to derive no advantage from the instruction of the inferior ranks of people, it would still deserve its attention that they should not be altogether uninstructed. The state, however, derives no inconsiderable advantage from their instruction . . . [because] an instructed and intelligent people . . . are always more decent and orderly than an ignorant and stupid one. . .
> (Smith, 1776, p. 740)

On this basis it is argued by Blaug (1975, pp. 592–4) that Smith (and his nineteenth-century successors; West, 1975b, ch. 10) supported state education for its utility in preserving law and order rather than for its influence on technical inventiveness and the acquisition of skills of immediate economic benefit.

That 'political' interpretation neglects Smith's analysis of the sources of invention. Sufficient 'extent of the market' provides the inducement further to subdivide labor. New tools are paid for out of reinvested profits. Aside from organizational improvements, it is capital equipment that enables 'the same quantity of industry [to produce] a much greater quantity of work' (1766, p. 260). The responsibilities of the entrepreneur are thus twofold – to 'make among his workmen the most proper distribution of employment, and to furnish them with the best machines which he can either invent or afford to purchase' (1766, p. 260).

What or who are the sources of invention? One is, as noted, the 'undertaker' himself. A second is the 'philosopher or man of speculation', whose superiority over the 'common street porter' '[arises] not so much from nature, as from habit, custom and education' (1776, p. 15). Philosophers, who specialize in 'combining together the powers of the most distant and dissimilar objects', are responsible for 'some' of the improvements in machinery. 'Many' improvements have been made by artisans for whom the manufacture of capital goods has become a special trade – division of labor working its wisdom here as elsewhere (1776, p. 10). However, the greatest single source of improved machinery is the user, 'the common workman', a 'great part of the machines made use of in those manufactures in which labour is most subdivided, [being originally their] inventions' (1776, p. 9).

A society whose 'common people' are 'instructed in the elementary parts of geometry and mechanics' would therefore, on Smith's own logic, enjoy a faster rate of technical advance than one in which intra-firm division of labor had been allowed to 'benumb the understanding of almost all the inferior ranks of people', causing their 'almost entire corruption and degeneracy'. There is after all 'scarce a common trade which does not afford some opportunities of applying to it the principles of geometry and mechanics...' (1776, pp. 734–7).

3.5.5 Exchange of equivalents?

Adam Smith's account of production and exchange allows for nonequivalent exchange. Transfers go from 'productive labourers' engaged in the fabrication of material goods for market sale, to members of society occupied in different ways. One group of non-producers consists of 'those who do not labour at all': infants, children, invalids, beggars, who are 'not in the labour force'. The amount of housework or farm work carried out by this group is probably truly zero in only rare cases, to judge from how busy family members appear to be in the households and fields of Smith's independent master farmers (1776, p. 359).

It is worth repeating that the psychological propensity to which Smith attributes the division of labor and thus the 'progress of opulence' does not require a fully monetized, 'capitalist' market economy to perform its good works. People of all cultures and levels of economic development exhibit the universal propensity to 'truck, barter, and exchange one thing for another' (1776, p. 13).

Smith's second group of economic parasites perform immaterial services for money, sometimes on their own account (lawyers, physicians, domestics, clowns), sometimes as employees of larger-scale enterprises (opera-singers, opera-dancers). There is some question about how Smith understands the survival of professionals in the marketplace if they do not give customers and employers satisfaction for the wages and honoraria they receive. Their rewards are even described as 'exhorbitant' if talents be of sufficient 'rarity and beauty' (1776, p. 107).

Marketed services, Smith says, are paid for out of 'revenue' rather than from 'capital'. But this means no more than that they are bought by consumers for their own personal, albeit luxury, use. Since even Smith's working-class consumers establish their budgets with some care (Hollander, 1973, pp. 138–41), it might be thought that payment out of 'revenue' would tend to *ensure* rather than rule out equivalence in exchange. Here again, the hypothesis of surplus generation and transfer is undermined by the rationality postulate. The notion that professional services might be regularly paid for out of 'capital' because of their usefulness to 'production' Smith would likely have dismissed as sophistry.

What about the third set, 'unproductive' servants of the public? Government employees, since they do not charge specific fees for each service rendered to each citizen, earn no money profits from which the public's general level of satisfaction with their performance might be assayed.

The special powers of the state enable funds to be removed from the pockets of citizens and placed in the various coffers of national and local authorities. The question of transfer vs. equivalence in exchange turns on whether there are mechanisms in the *Wealth of Nations* that constrain kings and ministers to give 'value for money' in return for the contributions they exact from ordinary citizens (see Hicks, 1969).

A major asymmetry between private–public and private–private transactions is that state sovereignty legalizes compulsion on a scale never available to individuals. Ordinary citizens, however rich, cannot as private persons make laws and regulations that are binding on all others, though they may join the government, are individually free to bend or break laws, and may sign contracts among themselves.

Smith in fact distinguishes between (a) provision of 'certain public works and certain public institutions' in which efficiency gains may be expected from the division of labor between public and private spheres; and (b) attempts by government functionaries to 'superintend', by virtue of legally instituted 'systems ... of preference or ... restraint', the 'industry of private people' (1776, p. 651). In the former case, 'it can never be for the interest of the individual, or small number of individuals, to erect and maintain [good roads, bridges, navigable canals, harbours], because the profit could never repay the expence...' (1776, pp. 651, 682). Producers and consumers all benefit, though unequally, from the existence of such public goods.

With respect to the second case, the 'insolence of office' is without just foundation, for kings and ministers can boast neither superior knowledge nor special administrative ability. '[No] human wisdom or knowledge could ever be sufficient' to run the business affairs of private people better than they can do it themselves. 'Systems of preference or restraint', such as the mercantile system, should with few exceptions be abolished, their barriers and impediments dismantled.

The incompetence of state meddling in industrial and commercial affairs is not only due to low-quality information. The Sovereign and his ministers are by virtue of their special privileges society's 'greatest spendthrifts'. High rank and personal fortune make them strangers to thrift. Physical, legal, and informational remove, the isolation of the court, insulate king from people, weakening any imaginable link between services and policies demanded by the people and supplied by the state. The state's power to gain command over funds 'softens' its budget constraint (Kornai, 1980) to a degree unknown to private firms, which must give value for money or face the humiliation of bankruptcy. Servants of the public are disqualified from organizing production of goods that are externality-poor because they cannot help being spoiled by their special revenue-raising powers; pressure to minimize costs for given levels of performance is weak or absent. Moreover, the bad examples of princes are readily aped by their social inferiors.

> The agents of a prince regard the wealth of their master as inexhaustible; are careless at which price they buy; are careless at what price they sell; are careless at what expence they transport his goods from one place to another.
>
> (Smith, 1776, p. 771)

3.6 Division of labor with unproductive laborers – a hopeless contradiction?

In the model of capital accumulation that set the tone for growth economics until the 1950s, Adam Smith abstracts from the passages in the *Wealth of Nations* in which the productive and unproductive sectors are treated as essentially interdependent. Given the importance of division of labor in Smith's overall *Weltanschauung*, it is an irony of intellectual history that he is prevented by materialist bias from applying his own great principle to the allocation of remunerated labor between 'productive' and 'unproductive' pursuits.

Defending a narrow conception of the boundary of the economy, Smith seems scarcely aware of that contradiction, particularly as it touches the divided labors of the Sovereign and his minions in a potentially dangerous and unruly world. It is not too difficult for either internalists or externalists to think up reasons why this may have been so. But it is perhaps a source of disappointment that the brilliant Dr Smith, fresh from a devastating raid on Physiocracy and possessing such a wealth of knowledge of the world, should fail to see the extent of his input–output problem. Though in the *Wealth of Nations* he constructs the basic edifice of economic thought, much labor on it remained to be divided among his successors.

CHAPTER 4

Immaterial Production from Garnier to Mill

> Political economy, which seemed to have as its object material goods alone, finds itself embracing the social system in its entirety.
>
> (J.-B. Say, *Cours complet*, 1828–9)

The Smithian doctrine that branded some paid laborers with 'the humiliating appellation of barren or unproductive' did not go long without challenge. As the fame of the *Wealth of Nations* spread from England to the Continent, so awareness grew of the deficiencies of the Smithian theory of surplus generation and transfer. Abetted by the demise of Physiocracy, it led to one of the more durable accomplishments of post-Smithian Classical political economy: the extirpation of materialist fallacy from *laissez faire*.

Through to the end of the Napoleonic period, the great excitement caused by the *Wealth of Nations* retarded criticism of Adam Smith's unproductive-labor theory more effectively in Great Britain than in France. French writers, notably Germain Garnier and J.-B. Say, held an advantage over James Mill, Ricardo, and Malthus in that the French criticized Physiocracy with the same seriousness that the British, including Smith, reserved for mercantilism. Habits of mind acquired thinking about Quesnay lent themselves to a re-examination of Smith's theory of surplus generation and transfer, particularly its treatment of private marketed services. The result by the first decade of the nineteenth century was an economics of general interdependence worthy of 1870 in everything but its margins. Questions of scope, valuation, and netness, it was realized ever more clearly, had to be posed and resolved together.

The economics of immaterial inputs and outputs took a generation to form after 1776, but, remarkably, no longer. It is seldom realized that the basics of the modern 'microeconomic' objection to Smithian materialist surplus and transfer theory had been worked out by 1803, more than a decade before the famous names of post-Smithian British Classical political economy did their work on rent. Section 4.2 of this chapter examines the contributions to 'Classical microeconomics' of Garnier, Say, Lauderdale, Storch, and Gray. Section 4.4 looks at the implications for unproductive-labor doctrine of an idea new to Classical, if familiar to modern economists: Malthus's idea that a class of 'unproductive labourers' could, by 'consuming' more than it 'produced', alter the course of a general glut. Section 4.5 attempts to explain the survival of the material output concept for so many decades after its logical basis had been undermined. The chapter ends with a summary of the status of immaterial production *circa* 1870.

4.1 Physiocracy after 1789

Though physiocracy held a particular appeal in France, the British were not immune to the attractions of what Smith called 'agricultural systems'. Smith himself had once allowed that agriculture was exceptionally productive, yielding rent in addition to profits (1776, p. 344). Britain had her own small company of Physiocrats, of whom the most notable was William Spence (Spence, 1807; Meek, 1963). But by the post-revolutionary, post-Napoleonic period, when Classical economics came into its own in Britain, Physiocracy had long since receded as a theoretical and policy influence.

To his death in America in 1817, Dupont de Nemours *père* remained a faithful disciple of the sterility doctrine of Mirabeau and Quesnay. Dupont reproached the upstart J.-B. Say for being so harsh as to repudiate his spiritual wet-nurse; Smith, he thought, had had the gallantry to say 'Grand merci, Maman' (Say, 1848, p. 362). Except for Spence and a few unrepentant Germans (Palyi, 1928, pp. 186–97; Tribe, 1988), after 1810 Dupont was virtually alone in finding Adam Smith's unproductive-labor doctrine to err on the side of liberality.

4.2 French Classical microeconomics and the Smithian polarities

4.2.1 *Garnier rejects materiality*

The Smithian doctrine of the unproductiveness of all services ran into trouble from the start (Cannan, 1917, pp. 14–21; Allix, 1912). In a remarkable series of notes appended to his translation of the *Wealth of Nations*, Germain Garnier (1754–1821), self-proclaimed but Smith-leaning Physiocrat, made fundamental objections to the materialist approach to productive labor and its product. Garnier's brief contribution (1802, V) marks the beginning of an explicit microeconomics of immaterial services.

Garnier's criticism of Smith stems from a view of the consumer as rational and self-interested. *All* paid laborers must be productive in the manner in which Smith thinks only 'productive labourers' are; otherwise employers could have no interest in hiring them (Garnier, 1802, p. 171). The Smithian requirement that products be resold if 'labourers' are to count as 'productive' is not fundamental. It is illogical to treat the (varied) work performed by servants differently from that of specialized tradespeople. The domestic servant 'who . . . does my hair, who cleans and maintains my clothes and furniture, who prepares my food, etc. renders services of absolutely the same type' as the laundress, the tradesman who stores furs or furniture, the caterer, the tavern-keeper, the barber, the coiffeur, even the mason, the glazier, the nightman, chimney-sweep, etc. (1802, pp. 171–2). Value-addition and prevention of value-subtraction belong on the same continuum. 'Repair and maintenance' and 'new construction', 'conservation', and 'production' (p. 172) differ only in the success with which net new values are added.

Similarly Garnier disputes Smith's view of the economic parasitism of state authorities. 'Production' occurs both within and beyond the market domain, and it is not so that one mode has unequivocal efficiency advantage over the others. Why should 'clerk-inspectors' or 'entrepreneurs' be 'productive' when public 'administrators' who look after roads, canals, ports, the currency, and 'other great instruments . . . of commerce, the safety of transportation and communications, [and] the carrying out of contracts' are not? 'The work is of absolutely the same genre, albeit on a larger scale' (1802, pp. 172–3).

Moreover, whatever the mode of production, materiality is a poor and misleading guide to 'necessity'. The solution is not limitation of 'production' to necessary material goods, but rather enlargement of the economic domain to include all services whose labor inputs earn monetary rewards.

Garnier's *Notes* launch a tradition of counterexample in Classical political economy that is to cast Adam Smith's materiality criterion in a dubious and ultimately unacceptable light. In the *Wealth of Nations*, materiality is made the decisive factor, even though many material goods are far from necessary. In what way do the *pâtissier*, the *confiseur*, or the *parfumeur* deserve productive status, asks Garnier, when it is denied the musician and actor?

Further, if musicians and actors are unproductive, how can the violin-maker, the organ-builder, the seller of sheet music, the set designer, be productive laborers, when they merely set the stage for the activities of non-producers (1802, p. 175)? What is the sense of having productive inputs for unproductive outputs? The implied response is that there can be none, and that the economic boundary should be redrawn to prevent that sort of 'input–output error in reverse'.

An offshoot of Garnier's defense of live performers is the observation that one person's consumption of a good or service need not rule out its simultaneous consumption by others. The same good may be enjoyed by two or more people at the same time, thereby multiplying total utility for a given expenditure of effort and materials. Great actors provide, 'for the same expenditure, a product incomparably greater [than do producers of most goods, since] they furnish precious enjoyment to several thousand consumers [sic] at a time', with few inputs other than their talent (Garnier, 1802, p. 179).

Examination of the economics of the arts leads Garnier to note that immaterial services may be exported (see Viner, 1937, pp. 13–15). Tourists flock to a country to hear performers of renown, and bring in with them foreign currency, which ends up in the pockets of the local population, stimulating 'national opulence'. How can famous artists be '*non productif*' if their talents attract 'a crowd of rich consumers' from abroad (1802, p. 180)?

Garnier disputes the contention of Book II, chapter iii, of the *Wealth of Nations* that profits earned in the 'capitalist' productive sphere are virtually the sole source of accumulable savings. Smith himself, as we saw, attributes much of economic growth in history to the parsimony of the self-employed farmer and tradesman. His French translator finds domestic servants equally important sources of saving out of 'revenue'; in fact, no class of consumers has such a high propensity to save as do domestics, on account of the dependency and insecurity of their station (Garnier, 1802, p. 181). The upshot is that *anyone*, even immaterial-service producers, *can save*, and even service producers can generate net inflows from abroad.

The economic rehabilitation of the paid domestic is much advanced by Garnier. Though he does not work out a competent theory of value, the economic survival of menial servants and other purveyors of paid services is explained without recourse to unmotivated transfer, by extending the frontiers of 'production'.

A contribution of a different order is Garnier's notion of alternative cost. The decision to hire a servant is couched in terms of the effort the employer is *spared* in not having to perform the work himself. The germ of the logic of 'opportunity cost' is planted, decades before the Austrians' explicit cultivation of the concept of 'imputation' and von Wieser's introduction of the two terms (Schumpeter, 1954, pp. 917, 1044; Green, 1894; Kauder, 1965, pp. 172 ff.). In Garnier, the idea is confined to an example. From J. R. McCulloch to G. S. Becker the notion of comparative advantage will be invoked to explain decisions over household production and the hiring of personal labor services.

Garnier observes how much more the master can earn in the time spared him by the domestic servant than the domestic has cost, an idea usually credited to English writers a quarter of a century later (e.g. Cannan, 1930, pp. 36–7).

> All these workers, the domestic included, save the person who pays them the labor of maintaining his things himself; it is for this and usually for this alone that [they are hired].
> (Garnier, 1802, p. 172)

Analogous reasoning explains the payment of interest. Garnier's early *Abrégé élémentaire des principes de l'économie politique* (1796) contains an abstinence theory, an idea made central by Senior. In Garnier, interest must be paid to 'indemnify' the lender for his 'privation' in giving others the use of money he might have spent himself. The 'indemnity' will depend on the 'extent of this privation and the [accompanying] risks' (Garnier, 1796, p. 35; Hasbach, 1905, cited in Allix, 1912, p. 331).

4.2.2 Say discovers immaterial inputs

Jean-Baptiste Say (1767–1832), anti-Physiocrat liberal and co-articulator with Smith and James Mill of 'Say's Law' (Sowell, 1972, p. 17), plays an important rôle in extending full economic rights to immaterial goods. It is Say who articulates Garnier's implicit view that the material/immaterial distinction is a red herring for economic science. 'Production', he explains in the first edition of his famous *Treatise* (1803), 'is the creation, not of matter, but of utility' (Say, 1819, p. 63). Worse, 'Objects . . . cannot be created by human means; nor is the mass of matter, of which this globe consists, capable of increase or diminution' (p. 62). In a jibe at Quesnay, it is remarked that

> No human being has the faculty of originally creating matter, which is more than nature itself can do.
> (Say, 1819, p. 65)

The relationship between utility, value (*valeur*) and wealth (*richesses*) remains a puzzle. Price is said to be 'the measure of the value of things, and . . . value . . . the measure of their utility' (p. 62). The primacy accorded 'utility' does not lead Say to reflect more deeply on the choices facing individual consumers, or to give anything like primacy to the 'demand side'. His *Treatise* in fact establishes the 'Classical' order of presentation of the subject matter of political economy (Cannan, 1917, pp. 26–8). Production is addressed first, then distribution, and consumption third and last.

If 'production' is the creation of utility, then 'consumption' must be its destruction. (As noted, in between comes distribution, conceived, in the Ricardian manner, as which factors get what.) Book III traces with admirable consistency the various ways exchangeable values may be destroyed or consumed: slowly or rapidly, now or later, in households by individuals ('unproductive consumption') or by industry in the guise of intermediate raw materials and the depreciation of fixed capital goods ('productive consumption') (Say, 1819, pp. 387–8); see Becker, section 8.4.2 below). The current view of production and consumption as positive and negative flows of exchange value per unit of time thus enters microeconomics at the dawn of the 'Classical' era.

'Producer utility', first analyzed by Say, will add a revolutionary twist to the basic premise of neoclassical labor economics. In it, Jevons's more nuanced position is reduced to the postulate that 'work' is pure disutility and pain, so that 'consumption' by definition must be postponed until 'after work'. (Utopian Marxism, in its belief that man is at heart a *homo faber* for whom work should be a liberation, tries to account for labor supply under capitalism without benefit of a pleasure–pain continuum.) Say's account of the phenomenon is based on the modern notion of joint products: one can make something for a firm to sell to others and generate enjoyment for oneself at the same time.

> When a man executes a painting, or makes any articles . . . for his own amusement, he at the same time creates a durable product or value, and an immaterial product, *viz.*, his personal amusement.
> (Say, 1819, p. 123)

Industrial psychologists indeed endeavor to persuade labor and management to view their interrelations in this light, as a positive sum game. It plays havoc with standard microeconomics, as we shall see in section 8.4.

As in the *Wealth of Nations*, in Say's *Treatise* 'commercial industry' falls within the bounds of 'production', alongside agriculture and manufacturing. Commercial industry covers foreign and domestic trade, wholesaling, retailing, transportation, banking, and the activity of brokers and agents (1819, pp. 100–3). The purpose of transportation and commerce is to bring goods within reach of the consumers who will benefit from them. In another dig at the dogmatic materialism of the Physiocrats, Say explains that the long-distance trader 'avails himself of the natural properties of the timber . . . and of the wind that fills his sails . . . with precisely the same view and the same results, and in the same manner too, as the agriculturist avails himself of the earth, the rain and the atmosphere' (p. 66).

Transportation is the industry that approximates goods to their final consumers. But that is no more than mining and fisheries do, and even Physiocrats grant that *they* are productive (p. 68). As in Adam Smith's analysis of public works in Book V of the *Wealth of Nations*, a well-planned system of public roads and canals enables entrepreneurs to produce the 'same product at less expense' (p. 201).

In a first for political economy, Say's *Treatise* devotes an entire chapter to 'Immaterial Products or Values Consumed at the Moment of Production'. Pondering which adjective best captures the qualities differentiating services from goods, Say, after rejecting 'perishable', 'non-transferable', 'transient', and 'momentary', settles for 'immaterial' (p. 119). A run through Smith's infamous list of unproductive laborers shows them all to be productive of something 'real and exchangeable' that others are willing to pay for (p. 120). Condillac's view of commerce (which he interprets as Marx is to do and not as I did in Chapter 2) is criticized for making every merchant a 'rogue' and every buyer a 'fool', when in fact 'value is really given for equal value' (Say, 1832, p. 8).

With his concern for 'results, not inputs' Say touches on points developed by Kuznets, Bacon and Eltis, and other students of the contemporary mixed economy. Garnier is rather unjustly accused of arguing that

> because the labour of physicians, lawyers, and the like is productive, ... a nation gains as much by the multiplication of that class of labour as of any other... The labour productive of immaterial products, like every other labour, is productive so far only as it augments the utility, and thereby the value of a product: beyond this point it is a purely unproductive exertion.
>
> (Say, 1819, p. 121)

There is more than a trace of accumulation-worship à la *Wealth of Nations* Book II, chapter iii, in the allegation that

> [a] people containing a host of musicians, priests, and public functionaries might be abundantly amused, well versed in religious doctrines, and admirably governed; but that is all. Its capital would receive no direct accession [*sic*] from the total labour of these individuals ... because their products would be consumed as fast as produced.
>
> (Say, 1819, p. 120)

This is a somewhat odd argument for Say to make, for a few pages later at least some public services are said to be intermediate to the production of private marketed goods. Public functionaries, advocates, judges, etc. 'satisfy wants of so essential a nature that without those professions no society could exist' (p. 124). Again, there is the implicit notion of a 'most efficacious proportion' past which public services should not be retrenched.

The wants served by the military are not 'essential' in the same sense as those of civil servants. In an 'error of youth' later modified (Molinier, 1958, p. 102), in the first edition of the *Treatise* Say faults Adam Smith for describing the soldier as an 'unproductive labourer': 'destructive labourer' is more like it (1803, II, p. 427).

Capital vested in human beings is part of total capital. The 'lawyer's opinion, the musician's song' are the fruits of an education that has required years of capital advance (1819, p. 121), both of material inputs to sustain the student and of immaterial lessons. The capital is stocked up as the skill of the professional, and the fees he earns not only reward his 'actual labour and talent, (which latter is a natural agent gratuitously given to him)' but cover 'the interest of the capital expended in his education'. Otherwise, 'capital has been thrown away' (p. 122).

Third, as in Smith but less equivocally, it is maintained that

> [academies], libraries, public schools, and museums ... contribute to the creation of wealth by the further discovery of truth ... thus empowering the ... directors of production, to extend the application of human science to the supply of human wants.
> (Say, 1819, p. 201)

In Say, the entrepreneur is more than provider of capital; he actively *combines* factors of production into a producing organism. Saint-Simon is to develop this view. As Allix remarks wryly about Say's own past (1910, p. 344), 'the former manufacturer of Auchy weaves for himself a pretty crown'. The entrepreneur of the *Treatise* chs V and VI contrasts with the mechanical 'Classical' capitalist whose rôle is limited to refraining from consuming profits in order automatically to reinvest them in labor and materials (Schumpeter, 1954, pp. 555, 645). The latter function, it was later realized by, for example, the Austrians and Knight, involves bearing the risk the investment be lost should the enterprise fail. In contrast, Say stresses the engineering and organizational skills, the human capital, required to found and run a business and to '[reduce scientific] knowledge into practice' (1832, ch. 6, p. 22).

A late work, the *Cours complet d'économie politique pratique* (Say, 1828–9), which is the record of his lectures at the Conservatoire des arts et métiers and the Collège de France, enlarges the capital concept of the *Treatise* to allow for intangible 'immaterial' property.

In the *Treatise*, producers of immaterial goods deal principally in final consumer luxuries. The remarks about the economic needfulness of public functionaries, roads, and bridges, and about the great economic value of skills and habits accumulated in the human mind do not quite elevate those types of immaterial capital to the same 'moral' level as material capital goods.

In the *Cours complet*, 'immaterial' capital is promoted to the status of a real private economic *intermediate* good. It can be traded. Like physical capital, it is owned by but not embodied in human beings.

> One must include in capital several goods which have value even though they are not material. The office of a lawyer or notary, the clientèle of a boutique, the reputation of a shop sign, the title of a periodical, are incontestably [economic] goods; one can sell them, acquire them, make them the object of a contract; and they are capital goods, because they are the accumulated fruit of industry.
> (Say, 1828–9, I, pp. 531–2)

The *Cours* moreover has whole chapters on 'literary property' or copyright (part IV, ch. VI) and on inventors' patents (ch. XXI). Only copyright however is treated as immaterial *movable* property; patents are treated in the section on export bounties and other subsidies and restrictions.

In the spirit of Smith's analysis of mercantilism (*Wealth of Nations*, Book IV), Say portrays the legal system as creator and protector of monopoly privilege. Ability to profit from copyrights or patents, to sell them, to leave them to one's children, depends on the wording of the law. In a performance consonant with Rawls's difference principle (Rawls, 1967), Say comes out in favor of patents and copyright for inventors or the descendants of great writers only to the extent that *society as a whole* may be deemed net benefactor.

Say's writings reached a wide audience in France, Britain, and America during his lifetime. Until supplanted by Mill's *Principles*, the *Treatise*, translated into English in 1821, served as a concise introduction to political economy for those who found the *Wealth of Nations* too long and involved (Say, 1819, Introduction; Gide and Rist, 1913, p. 106) and Ricardo too 'dismally' oriented towards the stationary state. Say corresponded with Ricardo and Malthus and other members of the Political Economy Club in England. His *oeuvre* bore interesting fruit. It inspired the collectivist *industrialisme* of Saint-Simon, whose celebrated 'Parable' contrasts productive industrialists and scientists and their employees, on the one hand, with socioeconomic parasites such as Monsieur le frère du roi, on the other (Saint-Simon, 1819–20, pp. 17–26, 151–8). Say's works also set the tone of free-trading liberal theories of interdependence put forward by a near-century of economists writing in French: Dunoyer, Ganilh, Destutt de Tracy, Bastiat, Courcelle-Seneuil; the Lausanne school; and Say's successors in the chair of political economy at the Collège de France: Pellegrino Rossi, Chevalier, and Leroy-Beaulieu.

Schumpeter (1954, p. 492) finds Say's 'really great contribution to analytic economics [to be] his conception of economic equilibrium, hazy and imperfectly formulated though it was'. Say's theory of immaterial production, part of the *Treatise* from the 1803 edition, postulates equivalent exchange of final goods with services in a closed economy with money as medium of exchange. The theory of immaterial production (ch. XIII) sets the stage for and complements the so-called 'Say's Law of Markets' (ch. XV, added to 1814 edition), which is based on the observation that, since production generates income, what is produced can be bought (Say, 1972, p. 138; Sowell, 1972, pp. 12–28).

The clear and consistent view of production as the adding, and of consumption as the subtracting, of utility or value began the diversion of economists' attention away from stocks as such towards flows *from* stocks. If immaterial lessons can be accumulated as lucrative human abilities and if immaterial movable capital can enhance the value of inputs the same way machinery does, much of Smithian surplus and transfer theory falls under Occam's razor.

Ideas pioneered by Garnier and Say find echo in other works of the Classical period. A principal boast of Lord Lauderdale's attack on Smith and the Physiocrats, *Inquiry into the Nature and Origin of Public Wealth*, is that in it the 'extraordinary distinction' between productive and unproductive labor, 'founded on the mere durability of the services performed', is 'exploded' (Maitland, 1819, pp. xx, 151). Lauderdale's claim to victory rests on what is by now a familiar point: the postulate of equivalence in exchange. Consumers are at liberty to spend as their incomes permit; if they choose to purchase immaterial services there must be a reason, *viz.* the 'satisfaction of . . . immediate desires'. Lauderdale asserts, without grounding it in any theory of the public sector, that members of the government render 'most important services to society' (Maitland, 1819, pp. 151, 152, 315).

4.2.3 Gray: 'No line in nature'

Under the alias George Purves, the littérateur Simon Gray devotes an entire book (1817) to confounding Adam Smith's doctrine of productive and unproductive labor. A major section of a second work (1815, part II) has the same object. Bibliographical rarities, Gray's writings attracted little comment and are not mentioned in the histories of thought of McCulloch, Cannan, Schumpeter, O'Brien, or

Hollander; Blaug (1958, pp. 142, 250) is the exception. The title page of Gray's more substantial effort reads:

> *All Classes Productive of National Wealth; or, the theories of M. Quesnai, Dr. Adam Smith, and Mr. Gray, concerning the various classes of men as to the production of wealth to the community, analysed and examined,* by George Purves, L.L.D.
>
> (Gray, 1817)

The object of those somewhat eccentric works is 'candidly to inquire whether nature has really drawn a line like . . . that of M. Quesnai [and Smith] and [their] followers' (1817, p. 23). Adducing pages of colorful examples in the manner of Garnier, Gray reasons that the physical details of goods or services are irrelevant provided they are what he calls 'chargeable', i.e. earn incomes for the sellers. A good or labor service's passing a market test shows that the buyer values whatever characteristics it may have; these may be more or less ephemeral, serve intermediate or final needs, or be generated in public or private institutions.

> What possible difference then can it make, that one is enabled to charge by means of turning up the soil with a plough, a second by means of bringing tones out of an instrument, a third by raising corn or feeding cattle, a fourth by inculcating the principles of religion or morality, a fifth by thrusting a shuttle between the divisions of the warp, a sixth by making letters with a pen on paper, a seventh by throwing water on cotton cloth to whiten it, an eighth by rehearsing speeches from Shakspeare, a ninth by singeing the wooliness of the surface of muslin off, a tenth by tripping it lightly before an audience on a stage, an eleventh by carrying heavy packages slowly along a street, and a twelfth by collecting the debts due to private individuals or the assessments of the nation?
>
> (Gray, 1815, pp. 59–60)

Meanwhile, operations described as paid services differ little from those usually understood to contribute to the production of goods. '[The] bleacher whitens [flax] and the laundress restores the whiteness when sullied, and they charge for it' (1815, p. 59). The conclusion Gray draws is that '[this] line of Dr. Smith, between really productive and really unproductive, has no existence in nature' (1817, p. 52).

Gray employs the term 'transfer' to characterize the Smithian view of the mechanism by which the unproductive classes acquire their often substantial revenues. The money income (in his terminology, 'circuland') of these classes is 'of the transfer sort', 'not diminishing, though not adding to the national wealth' (1815, p. 34).

For all the stated indifference to materiality, Gray holds public and private modes to represent distinct mechanisms when it comes to determining average wages and total employment in each trade. In the private economy, which is competitive, the number of ploughmen, musicians, weavers, teachers, bricklayers, servants employed cannot be multiplied beyond what is required, because, should that occur, 'the effect of a supply which exceeds the demand would take place', resulting in either unemployment or in reduced earnings of all members of the trade. Exit of workers from the various industries would then 'necessarily decrease the number' back to a more appropriate level. In the 'army and navy classes', however,

> the number is not regulated by themselves, but by the positive vote of others. Their incomes are drawn from the other classes ... through the medium of taxes. The income of these classes being fixed by authority, as well as their number, the natural power of the demand over the supply is in their case taken away.
> (Gray, 1817, pp. 74–5)

Though Gray here introduces the notion of 'voted for rather than bought' into economic literature, his brief remarks may be appended to Smith's analysis of the differences in mechanism between the public and private sectors without disturbing its inner logic. (Say's comments on the incompetence of government as industrial manager are a paraphrase of Smith's; Say, 1819, p. 201).

The several editions of the work of Say and his French disciples herald the subtle change in emphasis from *laissez faire* as instrument to *laissez faire* as end which Marx was to find so unworthy of economics as a science. Say's disagreement with Smith over materiality and exchange of equivalents attracted attention, mainly favorable to Say (e.g. Brydges, 1819), even though some writers, in keeping with the liberal anti-interventionist mood, drew the line at productiveness for state services (Ganilh, 1812, p. 91; Destutt de Tracy, 1817; Thos. Jefferson, 1817). Even Say himself 'in a moment of bad humour against the government' let it slip that in the last analysis government was a final luxury that could be dispensed with (noted by Storch, 1824, V, p. xxx, *re* Storch, 1823, I, p. 47 n.).

Of the disciples of J.-B. Say who embraced the new view of immaterial services while wholly avoiding input–output error, the laurel goes to Denis Boileau. *Introduction to the Study of Political Economy* (1811), written in English, is remarkable for its excellent exposition of many points already discussed in connection with Smith, Garnier, and the Say of the *Treatise*.

4.2.4 Say vs. Storch on 'biens'

The controversy over immaterial goods that soured relations between Say and Heinrich Storch (1766–1837) makes a nice footnote to the history of surplus and transfer theory in the Classical period. Storch, a Baltic German, spent his professional life in St Petersburg, where he was member of the Academy of Sciences and tutor to the future tsar Nicholas and his brother Michael. Storch's four-volume *Cours d'économie politique* was published for the imperial siblings in 1815. In 1823, J.-B. Say had it reprinted with pages of critical notes of his own. Storch's second thoughts filled a fifth volume, subtitled *Considérations sur la nature du revenu national* (1824), which aimed to clarify the economic philosophy of immaterial goods.

The quarrel is over Storch's category 'internal goods' (*biens internes ou [sic] civilisation*). Internal goods are, first, 'leisure, security, religion, taste, and morality', and, second, the more readily acquirable 'health, dexterity, and higher learning'. Internal goods differ from *richesses* in that they are neither material nor transferable. Since internal goods do not reproduce themselves with profit (*sic*), they are only *indirectly* productive of the wealth of nations (Storch, 1823, III, pp. 223, 228–30; 1824, p. xli; also Chalmers, 1832, p. 343).

Say argues in a critical note (Storch, 1823, III, p. 226 n.) that security and morality cannot be distinguished from free goods like air and sunshine, friendship and a clear conscience: though favorable cultural or character traits may certainly be of economic benefit (the way Smith sees the urge to self-betterment making prodigality rare in Scotland and England), there is no simple or direct economic way to 'produce' or acquire them (see sections 3.5.3, 8.4.3 below).

Storch accuses Say, in effect, of imperfectly distinguishing evanescent labor service inputs from their frequently long-lasting results (Storch, 1824, pp. xii, xli). The criticism is not altogether well founded, for, as we saw, Say takes a moderate amount of care to do just that. Consumers of economic literature had to await Léon Walras (1874, p. 213) for an adequate conceptualization of the stock–flow input–output problem, and for G. S. Becker (1965), T. P. Hill (1977), and F. T. Juster (1973, 1981) for writings that leap with true agility over market boundaries.

Storch deserves mention for underscoring the difficulty of separating inputs from outputs in the case of services such as education and medicine. For what it's worth, a Storch-like view of the economic importance of 'national character' – standards of commercial honesty, instincts of workmanship, and the like – is at last out of the closet in development economics, if only in the form of 'geographical dummy variables' (e.g. Timmer, 1986).

4.2.5 A problem in filiation

After Garnier and Say's analyses of marketed immaterial goods, why did it take nearly seventy more years for scope (where to draw the boundary of the economy) and netness (which activities generate investible surplus) to be demoted to mere corollaries of value theory? Even then, the victory was won only in terms of a microeconomics of externality-poor private goods produced in firms earning money profits at the going rate. The application of analogous reasoning to other modes of production and allocation took much longer (sections 7.3 and 8.4 below).

Two hypotheses suggest themselves. According to the first – explicit in Schumpeter but not related by him to the goods–services dichotomy – the problem was not one of persuading Classical microeconomists to make utility a condition of exchange value, but to get them to frame their analysis in terms of diminishing marginal utility *and* increasing marginal scarcity or 'real cost'. That was not done with any consistency until after 1870 because marginal analysis was not until then applied even to the economics of goods. Schumpeter apparently thought 'servants, teachers, and so on' could be 'easily introduced' into either model (1954, pp. 566, 600). By implication, Garnier's and Say's attacks on Smithian unproductiveness doctrine, and the interdependent economy of final private goods and services that they offered in its stead, did not hasten the advent of neoclassical value theory because it was the significance of *marginal* utilities and products that was difficult to grasp, not the notion that *total* utility could be derived from final immaterial services.

A second hypothesis – subscribed to by Cannan (1930, pp. 36–7) and which I find attractive – rather blames things on Ricardo and the intellectual hold his crystal-clear model exerted on his fellows. When Say and Garnier first wrote, Ricardo had not yet worked out the pathbreaking analysis of the no-rent margin. The *Essay on the Profits of Stock* (1815) and the first edition of *Principles of Political Economy and Taxation* (1817) had not yet appeared. Ricardo's rent analysis was the germ from which marginal productivity analysis of labor and factors in general eventually emerged. So much on the intellectual supply side. Then, as far as demand goes, Ricardo utilized and lent his considerable authority to the materialist concept of output, scarcely mentioning services, whether luxuries or necessities, private or state. The rigor of his model and the clarity of its distributional and policy implications attracted and held able defenders, most importantly J. S. Mill, despite the failure of Ricardo's 'dismal' predictions about the falling rate of profit leading to a subsistence-level stationary state. Thus was prolonged the life of both the narrow material definition and the classical theory of surplus production and transfer for over half a century after Garnier's *Notes* and the first edition of Say's *Treatise*.

4.3 Ricardo avoids input–output error

Ricardo adheres to a materialist definition of output and has elaborate views both of the sources of government funds (taxation and borrowing), and of the incidence of that taxation on relative factor and product prices. In Ricardo, tax revenues are irremediably squandered by public authorities; there are no roads or bridges, no legal or defense umbrella, no socially beneficial 'dignity of the Sovereign' by which forced transfer might be commuted to *quid pro quo*. The *Principles* (third edition, 1821) treat with rigorous logic of the economics of material private goods and of the machines, materials, and labor that combine to make them. Final services are scarcely mentioned (a minor exception is 1821, p. 393).

However – and some vaunt this as a tasty fruit of divided intellectual labor, of his having had the intelligence to focus on a narrow set of solvable problems – Ricardo appears to see his way around the sort of input–output error that spoils the grand perspectives of Adam Smith. What preserves Ricardian virtue is not however a device of particular merit. The state is simply treated by him as *entirely* unproductive and *unnecessary* to the private economy – a wholly final luxury. Ricardo never opens the can of worms that is the category 'necessary yet unproductive'. The obligation to deal with the 'most efficacious proportion' problem is denied: the ideal proportion is zero.

What is the evidence for Ricardo's view of government activity as non-necessary final consumption? It is admittedly sparse and implicit. Ricardo's silence on the several issues that created an input–output problem for Smith is indicated by the fact that the editors (Dobb and Sraffa) of the volume-long index to the *Works and Correspondence of David Ricardo* (Ricardo, 1951, XI) managed to dispense altogether with entries for 'productive' and 'unproductive labour'. Moreover, little is said about what the state's tax revenues are spent on. The 'taxation' of the *Principles*' full title refers to *incidence on the private sector*, on the assumption that the revenues raised will be wasted.

Elsewhere it is affirmed that it is 'by the profuse expenditure of Government, and of individuals and by loans, that the country is impoverished' (1821, p. 246). In a comparison of taxation to redeem the national debt with taxation to finance current government services, he writes, 'The one, we might be considered as paying to ourselves, the other was forever lost to us' (1951, V, p. 250). Ricardo's disciple James Mill seconds that emotion (e.g. Mill, 1808, p. 118).

4.4 Malthus's cure for gluts

Unlike the elder Mill, Ricardo's friend and *alter ego* Thomas Robert Malthus puts Smithian parasites to original economic use. Malthus's *Principles* open with a passionate defense of Adam Smith's material concept of output. Unproductives in Malthus are a by-now familiar group of sellers of marketed and non-marketed immaterial services, plus rentiers and landlords. The theory of surplus generation and its transfer provides the framework: service incomes are not derived from a *quid pro quo* sale of services or loan of factors; they are *transferred* from 'productive' producers of material goods. So far the issues are those raised by Adam Smith. Malthus however gives his 'unproductive labourers' a new economic rôle to play – that of preserving the overall economy from trade depression or 'general glut'.

The economic literature studied in this chapter so far has been postulating equivalent, or potentially equivalent, exchanges between public and private sectors. This may surprise readers. *Even where private–public transactions were assumed to be grossly skewed to the benefit of profligate state officials, money played the rôle of mere facilitating medium.* Transfers from productive to unproductive spheres could be imagined to proceed *as if* in kind, in the manner of the barter-like equivalent exchanges of J.-B. Say's private sector.

Malthus's analysis moves away from the barter-economy presuppositions of those models. The rôle he creates for his unproductive laborers is consistent with a wider range of functions for the monetary medium. A basic tenet of textbook macroeconomics has it that *if money is a store of value as well as a medium of exchange, it can lie idle, interrupting the circular flow of sales and purchases* in a closed economy. The fact that production generates money income for workers, and money profits for sellers of intermediate goods, no longer guarantees that all final goods produced will be bought.

Keynes was keen to acknowledge (1933 and 1936) that Malthus's analysis of gluts contains the germ of his own critique of Say's Law and *a fortiori* of Classical–Marxian unproductive-labor doctrine. As noted in Chapter 2 in the discussion of Petty and Mandeville, a major implication of Keynes's *General Theory* is that public spending that maintains demand, employment, and business confidence that would otherwise be deficient ill deserves Adam Smith's 'humiliating appellation of barren or unproductive' if the criterion for judgment is economic welfare of the population (Smith, 1776, p. 628). Keynes lamented that 'the almost total obliteration of Malthus' line of approach and the complete domination of Ricardo's for a period of a hundred years has been a disaster to the progress of economics. . .' (1933, p. 98).

Malthus knew of Garnier, Lauderdale, and Say's objections to the material definition of output that they all associated with Adam Smith. Why did he remain unmoved? Scottish tradition in philosophy and business favored materiality. It is however conceivable that the passion behind Malthus's defense of the materiality criterion was linked to its usefulness for the theory of gluts. Less likely is the inverse, that the glut theory arose out of the attempt to make sense of the non-equivalent exchange implied by the device of a transfer-receiving unproductive class. If organization be evidence of filiation, Malthus commits himself wholeheartedly to materiality in the first chapter of the *Principles* (Malthus, 1820). Objections to Say's Law come near the end. But order of presentation, which would favor the inverse path, cannot be decisive, given what we have seen of the compatibility of surplus generation and transfer models with Say's Law reasoning in Smith and Ricardo, and given that the economic problem of the day, the post-Napoleonic depression, cried out for explanation.

Chapter One, 'Of the Definitions of Wealth and of Productive Labour', gets the *Principles of Political Economy* off on a strict materialist footing. Productive laborers produce material goods that can be transferred and accumulated in stocks. Garnier, Lauderdale, and Say's criticisms of Smith are unfounded. The term 'personal services' is to be preferred over 'unproductive labour' in order 'to remove [the] objection to a classification in other respects sufficiently correct for practical purposes, and beyond comparison more useful in explaining the causes of the wealth of nations, than any other which has hitherto been suggested' (1820, p. 35).

The basis for Keynes's discovery of a kindred spirit in Malthus comes in section IX of the last chapter of the *Principles*, which bears the proto-macroeconomic title 'Of the Distribution Occasioned by personal services and unproductive Consumers, considered as the Means of increasing the exchangeable Value of the whole Produce'. The problem addressed is that of a 'premature failure' or 'want' of 'effective demand' for material wealth, as compared with the supply, such as might occur 'under a rapid accumulation of capital, or . . . a rapid conversion of persons engaged in personal services into productive labourers'.

Premature demand failure would prevent the hoped-for increase in the total value of production, so that 'the motive to further accumulation [would] be checked, before it was checked [as in Ricardo] by the exhaustion of the land' (1820, pp. 398, 407).

> It follows that, without supposing the productive classes to consume much more than they are found to do by experience, particularly when they are rapidly saving from revenue to add to their capitals, it is necessary that a country with great powers of production should possess a body of consumers who are not themselves engaged in production.
>
> (Malthus, 1820, p. 398)

> There must . . . be a considerable class of persons who have both the will and the power to consume more material wealth than they produce, or the mercantile classes would not continue profitably to produce so much more than they consume.
>
> (Malthus, 1820, p. 400)

Malthus's solution to, as distinct from his recognition of, the problem of insufficient effective demand is not really worthy of the *General Theory*. As Sowell points out (1972, p. 96), Malthus's analysis is 'as nonmonetary as that of the supporters of Say's Law'. The economic rôle accorded rentiers, 'statesmen, soldiers, and those who live upon the interest of the national debt' (Malthus, 1820, p. 409) is effective because production of wealth is narrowly defined. Savings, automatically and instantaneously reinvested in the hiring of additional labor by accumulation-minded capitalists, add an increment to output that, it is alleged, will be more readily saleable on account of rentier demand than if the economy consisted exclusively of workers and entrepreneurs.

As national accountants now see matters, luring paid menials away from the domestic and into the industrial labor force by offering the same wages paid out of savings as had been formerly paid out of Smithian 'revenue' does not by itself increase the economy's aggregate output of goods and services. Ex-servants merely increase, together with the providers of machinery and materials, material industrial production at the expense of immaterial service production; the composition of output and the labor force changes in favor of 'industry'.

Malthus's macroeconomics of necessary expenditure by landlords and Smithian unproductives involves some *legerdemain* (Eagly, 1974, pp. 90–102). Rather in the manner of Stalin-era growth accounting (section 6.5 below), in Malthus there is said to be net increase in aggregate supply when domestic servants become surplus-generating workers. Unlike Stalin, though, Malthus is worried about whether the increment will be bought. Insistence on materiality narrows the boundary of 'production' in relation to 'expenditure'; gluts appear by a stroke of the pen. But if that is it, should not the gluts be 'permanent' rather than 'temporary', rather than 'general' as distinct from 'confined to particular trades'?

Say, Ricardo, and McCulloch accuse Malthus of falling for such weak arguments. Malthus bolsters them by assuming backward-bending supply curves of effort for workers and capitalists (Sowell, 1972, p. 63). Having to work for a living at the sacrifice of desirable leisure puts a limit on asset-poor citizens' desire and ability to consume; rentiers do not suffer the same disability since their spending power is acquired *without real cost* (*sic*) (Sowell, 1972, p. 103 and n. 126).

In order to extricate Malthus from the spurious difficulty caused by the narrow definition of produce, R. V. Eagly, in a brilliant stroke of revisionism, adds a second sector, the 'service sector', to 'the one-sector classical model'. In Eagly–Malthus, services differ from commodities in that 'by definition' they require no capital, so that 'there is no profit return and no possibility that the production of services could be regulated by the same sort of mechanism that was specified to keep the one-sector classical system moving smoothly over time ... [The] profit rate does not operate to establish an optimum composition of output' (Eagly, 1974, p. 99).

In Eagly–Malthus, unless aggregate demand is fortuitously 'balanced' between investment and consumption, 'total output [will] not be cleared in the market in the way indicated by Say's Law'. Investment expenditure is 'not regarded [by Malthus] as a policy parameter', since it is mostly determined exogenously rather than, as in later writers, being seen as regulated by the interest rate, which equilibrates supply and demand for 'loanable funds'. The policy implications of Eagly–Malthus are those of Malthus himself, that 'policy measures ... be taken to increase consumption' (Eagly, 1974, pp. 92, 99).

4.5 Goods and services, McCulloch to Mill

4.5.1 *'French' microeconomics in Britain: McCulloch and Senior*

So far, two non-Ricardian and anti-materialist currents have colored my account of the fate of unproductive-labor doctrine in the first half of the nineteenth century. Malthus's confused objections to Say's-Law logic in an expanding material-goods economy led him to call for increases in the spending power of landlords and Smithian unproductives. The reactionary political and regressive distributional implications of Malthus's analysis were met with consternation by liberals as well as radicals (e.g. McCulloch to Ricardo in Ricardo, 1951, VIII, p. 312; Marx, 1867, pp. 160, 495). They need not have worried about the analysis: Malthus's glut-theoretic defense of landlords was too muddled to be a serious threat to the free-traders' anti-Corn Law campaign.

The more serious pretender to the throne of Ricardian political economy was the 'French' tradition grounded, as we have seen, in an appreciation of consumer sovereignty that saw no need to make distinctions of principle between paid services and goods, whether final or intermediate. Among post-Ricardian British writers, Senior, Whately, and Travers Twiss agree with the a-materialist agnosticism of the French. Nothing much that is new is added; the point about equivalent exchange in a Say's-Law world is not taken to its logical, Walrasian conclusion. Nassau Senior does however underline the point that

> the distinctions that have been attempted to be drawn between productive and unproductive labourers, or between the producers of material and immaterial products, or between commodities and services, rest on differences existing not in the things themselves ... but in the modes in which they attract our attention...
> (Senior, 1836a, p. 51)

The productive–unproductive distinction is put down to fuzzy thinking caused by ingrained habits of speech. '[A] shoemaker is said to *make* or *produce* shoes... [A shoeblack] is not said to make or produce the commodity, clean shoes, but to *perform the service* of cleaning them... A servant who carries coals from the cellar to the drawing room performs precisely the same operation as the miner who raises them from the bottom of the pit to its mouth' (Senior, 1836a, p. 52; emphasis added).

Even Ricardo's ally on the inverse wage–profit front, J. Ramsay McCulloch (1789–1864), undergoes a conversion in successive editions of his *Principles* (1825, 1830, 1843, 1849, 1864) to nearly the 'French' view of final immaterial output. By 1843 McCulloch writes that 'wealth' is 'anything involving human industry in its production' and 'possessed of exchangeable value' (O'Brien, 1970, pp. 271–2). Following the reasoning and example of Garnier, recourse to services of domestics is analyzed as a matter of opportunity cost or income forgone. Division of labor that substitutes menials for their masters in low-skill household tasks enables the masters to earn much more from their superior talents than the servants actually cost them. Conversely, if inventors of new technologies (Watt, Arkwright) or businessmen (merchants, bankers) had to cook and clean for themselves, those with incomes of £10,000 would be 'most probably unable to make even £100' (McCulloch, 1864, p. 505).

Nassau Senior's *Outline of the Science of Political Economy* does not altogether dispense with the productive–unproductive vocabulary, but so circumscribes it as to neutralize fully the 'humiliating' and materialist–fallacist connotations of the terms. Pre-empting an important implicit argument of Karl Marx, Senior observes that the typical distinction between productive and unproductive *consumers* is 'less clearly marked than that between productive and unproductive *consumption*. To divide citizens into two economic classes, productive and unproductive, would in fact be a false division, there being few who do not in some respects belong to both classes'. A sizeable fraction of incomes earned in 'productive' material-goods production goes to purchase above-subsistence goods and services, further spoiling any neat duality (Senior, 1836a, p. 55).

In Senior, the only true unproductives are the infants, beggars, and dotards who in Smith 'do not labour at all' and to whom transfers are more or less freely given; to these he adds criminals whose transfers are extorted by deception or force. However, 'though a child or an invalid make no immediate return, their support is the necessary condition of their future services' (p. 56).

Materiality is not an end in itself. Specialization means that productivity increases require correct, 'most efficacious proportions', not minimization of 'unproductive labour'. In a city that replaces a thousand locksmiths by a hundred guards, such 'conversion of productive into unproductive laborers would certainly not diminish [its] wealth'.

> The wealth of the nation [depends] on the *proportion* between [the two sorts of labor] which is best suited to making *most efficacious* the labor of each.
>
> (Senior, 1836b, p. 204)

Modern public choice theory thus owes a fundamental proposition to Senior. 'Division of labour', he explains, 'is the principle upon which all government is founded' (1836a, p. 76). Senior's concept of the 'most efficacious proportion' between public and private sectors is a fruit of that same vine.

4.5.2 The convoluted compromise of John Stuart Mill

John Stuart Mill mans the outpost of unproductive-labor theory so far as 'classical' nineteenth-century political economy is concerned. In his celebrated *Principles of Political Economy* (1848), the work to which most readers in the second half of the nineteenth century owed their education in economics, Mill offers a new lease of life to the moribund Smithian dichotomy. The decision to restrict 'productive labour' to labor engaged in the production of transferable material products is explained with a fatalistic shrug as a consequence of the scholar's obligation to respect 'common usage'. It is a puzzle why at the late date of 1848 Mill declines to follow his compatriots Senior and McCulloch along the road leading away from materiality towards 'characteristics'.

Instead, he makes a contorted defense of Ricardo's and his father's material conception of output. Mill's compromise is the odder for his having, at the age of 23, written an eloquent essay advancing a different and more generous view, closer to that of Say.

The essay, 'On the words productive and unproductive' (written 1829–30, published 1844), argues in favor of inclusion amongst the economy's productive laborers those who contribute to building up the stock of lucrative human abilities. The mystery of Mill's reversion to a cruder Ricardian materialism is compounded by the fact that the *Principles*, chapter iii, Book I ('Of unproductive labour' (1848, II, p. 45), expresses enthusiastic agreement with Say's observation that '[labour] is not creative of objects, but of utility'.

In the essay, the young author protests having to bow to his readers' 'pedantic objection to new technical terms'.

> Every classification according to which a basket of cherries, gathered and eaten the next minute, are called wealth, while that title is denied to the acquired skill of those who are acknowledged to be productive labourers, is a purely arbitrary division, and does not conduce to the ends for which classification and nomenclature are designed.
>
> (J. S. Mill, 1844, II, pp. 279, 281–2)

In an echo of Garnier, it is objected that mere forms of ownership ought not to affect the characterization as productive or unproductive of activities that yield identical use-values. Hedges and ditches dug by the government have the same characteristics in use, including the ability to serve as intermediate inputs, as those dug by private landowners.

J. S. Mill ties himself in an extraordinary knot trying to link the 'productiveness' of a final good or service to that of its intermediate prerequisites. 'Productive' in the essay 'On the words productive and unproductive' is defined to mean capable of adding to the 'permanent sources of enjoyment, whether material or immaterial' (1844, II, p. 284). That proposition is then illustrated by an extraordinary syllogism. The opera-singer Madame Pasta 'labours and consumes unproductively'. *Ergo*,

> the buildings and decorations [of her theatre] are consumed unproductively [even if gradually] . . . But notwithstanding this, the architect who built the theatre was a productive labourer . . . [as were] those who instructed the musicians . . . [and] Madame Pasta [herself, because] all these persons contributed . . . by the production of a *permanent source of enjoyment*.
>
> (Mill, 1844, II, pp. 285–6; emphasis in original)

When final goods are divided into two classes, externality-rich intermediate goods provided by public authorities have to be apportioned *pro rata*. In a foreshadowing of Soviet practice *re* passenger transport (Nove, 1977, p. 266), judges and soldiers have to be considered 'partly productive and partly unproductive'. Public servants who protect (productive) singing teachers, violin-makers or theatre builders are productive by intermediatization, while those who protect unproductive singers and violinists are not.

Nassau Senior noted that the *Principles*' definition of productive and unproductive 'excludes what [the 1844 essay] admitted[:] labour employed in conferring permanent benefit unconnected with the increase of material objects – such as the labour of a teacher or physician' (Senior, 1848, p. 309). Perhaps to avoid 'input–output error in reverse' of the sort objected to by Garnier, Mill in the *Principles* compromises as follows on stocks of abilities:

> [We will] not refuse the appellation productive, to labour which yields no material product as its direct result, provided that an increase of material products is its *ultimate* consequence.
> (Mill, 1848, II, pp. 48–9; emphasis added)

Given a new lease of economic life by that concession are: instructors of engineers and artisans but not instructors of physicians and solicitors, except instructors of solicitors whose clients are engineering firms!

All the while doing what he perceives to be his duty to uphold a materiality criterion for final goods, J. S. Mill bends his argument stoically to the imperatives of producer sovereignty. Productive laborers are whomever the organizers of production find it necessary to employ, directly or indirectly, in order to produce the final material goods that count in annual produce; that part of their consumption which 'goes to maintain and increase the productive powers of the community' is productive consumption (Blaug, 1988). Input–output error is thereby avoided. It is a rare instance in the history of economics of 'materiality without fallacy' (see section 9.2 below).

Mill's economic universe is richer than Ricardo's in that, like Say's, it can accommodate immaterial *intermediate* services. Again one wonders why Mill bothered with materiality at all. His materiality criterion is upheld on the final goods' front only to be lost among the intermediates. Moreover, materiality is merely a proxy for the ability to yield flows of use-values over time, something cherries do not do but the stock of acquired knowledge does (Hollander, 1985, pp. 257 ff.).

In a review of the *Principles*, Nassau Senior argues that the distinction between productive and unproductive remains for Mill 'practically barren' (Senior, 1848, p. 309). To the extent that is true it is a blessing, limiting damage done by absurd and *ad hoc* categories like 'productive producers of immaterial services which are intermediate to the production of final material goods'. Technically, they are the only service producers in the *Principles* who qualify as productive laborers. The implied fractioning of government and education would mainly burden national accountants, but what a burden!

Against the trend of interdependence theories that culminate in general-equilibrium and input–output analysis, J. S. Mill takes 'necessity' back only one period. Government is productive to the extent that it is 'indispensable to the productivity of industry' (1848, II, pp. 49–50). Whether or not Mill's mathematical education extended to matrix algebra, it would have been simple enough for a logician of his rank to admit the cogency of 'infinite regress'. Never mind that the constant-returns-to-scale assumptions of the original Leontief input–output analysis are better suited to a more neoclassical and less Ricardian *Weltanschauung*. Greater appreciation of the importance of coefficients of coefficients would likely have led Mill only to a more sensitive acknowledgement of the difficulty of measuring annual produce.

Mill's deep utilitarianism and his experience of moral crisis left him open-minded on the issue of mode. Government activities are potentially fully rehabilitated by intermediatization; Madame Pasta's frivolous if profitable theatre stays beyond the pale. In a possible anticipation of the mixed economy he would have welcomed, Mill does not make the private/public, market/non-market dichotomies of Smith (and Marx) in any way decisive for welfare (Hollander, 1985, vol. II, p. 256; ch. 5 and section 7.2 below).

4.6 Classicism, marginalism and materiality

In the Advertisement to the second edition of the *Inquiry*, Lord Lauderdale crowed in 1819 that the 'distinction betwixt productive and unproductive labour, as founded on the produce of labour being immediately consumed or reserved for future use, – is exploded' (Maitland, 1819, p. xx).

The history of the economics of immaterial services from Malthus and Ricardo to mid-century shows Lauderdale to have indulged in wishful thinking. There was no bang but rather a slow erosion of the disfavor in which services of domestics, profitable service enterprises, and the state were originally held. The final whimper has not yet been heard.

The microeconomic view of domestics evolved from Smithian hand-wringing at the short duration of the improvements wrought by them, and disapproval of the profligacy of masters who squander 'revenue' on them, to a grudging appreciation of the essential similarity between material goods and immaterial services not destined for resale. Smith's great principle of the division of labor yielded plenty of reasons why unskilled labor might be left to the unskilled.

Profitable service enterprises, to the extent they attracted attention at all, elicited mixed reactions. Theirs was the least troublesome case. The 'French' view of Garnier and Say, accepted by McCulloch and Senior, boiled down to the notion that what consumers were willing to pay money for must be 'product'. Open discrimination against profitable services therefore made little sense, and few economists were so foolhardy as to engage in it (but see Turgeon, 1889).

Nevertheless, it was widely assumed that society would benefit could tastes be turned towards parsimony and away from consumption of luxuries, ephemeral services figuring prominently among them. John Stuart Mill's treatment of Madame Pasta's profitable theatre as 'unproductive' hints at the strength of anti-luxury sentiment that had been characteristic of the Classical outlook since Adam Smith turned around the conceit underlying Mandeville's naughty *Fable of the Bees*.

The diversity of the service category was now better understood. First a class of tradable, immaterial, but long-lasting capital goods such as goodwill and authors' rights was identified by Say. There was also some not very explicit recognition that ephemeral services of single-person professional firms could help enterprises as well as private individuals. That had the potential to place solicitors and architects on a par with producers of raw materials for industry.

Observers disagreed over the state's *de facto* economic rôle. The basic model remained that of surplus generation and transfer; analyses differed in allowing for feedback from state to private sectors. Ricardo envisaged the state as a purely final consumer; his surplus and transfer theory was never in danger of being disqualified on account of input–output error. J. S. Mill, with his complicated final basket, allowed a plethora of public and private services to be intermediate to it. Malthus's unproductive class of final consumers was peopled in the main by landlord rentiers, but also included a generous sprinkling of servants of the public both civilian and military.

The history of surplus and transfer theory in so-called Classical economics draws to a close with Jevons, Walras, the Austrians, and Marshall. In the writings of those pre-public-choice neoclassicals, the unproductive-labor issue disappeared from the intellectual map, a victim of, first, their new analyses of utility maximization by consumers and, second, of roundaboutness in production.

Utility theory firmly and explicitly linked scope with valuation, as the boundary and mix of marketed, final, externality-poor goods' production (supply) was made fully interdependent with what consumers were prepared to pay for (demand).

The general-equilibrium analysis that grew out of the hints contained in Say's Law of markets was based on the postulate of exchange of equivalents in market and barter transactions involving externality-poor private goods and services. Transactions involving transfers without due *quid pro quo* would simply not be agreed to by rational economic men. The emphasis on sovereign consumer choice greatly reduced the probability that low productivity of service occupations would be blamed on their 'immateriality'; such occupations existed because their products were in demand at their current prices.

Austrian capital theory, in studying relations between inputs and outputs, succeeded in inoculating first-rate thinkers against input–output error. Intermediatization of 'necessary' Smithian unproductive labor was taken care of by the assumption of producers' sovereignty over inputs. Marshall's sharp scissors of supply and demand were just as good at trimming fat from producers' expenditure on factor inputs as from consumers' expenditure on final outputs of goods and services!

With the marginal revolution, the distinction of principle between material goods and immaterial services was dropped from economics. Materiality vs. immateriality became as unimportant as any other purely physical quality of goods entering market transactions, such as their color, weight, or chemical composition. It was now realized explicitly (though, as we saw, many Classical writers were on the verge of understanding the implications) that what was consumed in factories and by final consumers after work was not 'matter' *per se* but the useful *services* of capital and durable final goods. Walras, Menger, Fisher, Marshall, and Böhm-Bawerk are crystal clear on this critical point (for example, Walras, 1874, pp. 40, 213 ff., lesson 37; Menger, 1871, pp. 288–94; Marshall, 1890, pp. 44–59; Böhm-Bawerk, 1884, II, pp. 326–7; Fisher, 1896). Even Classical defenders of materiality criteria like J. S. Mill understood the advantage of durable goods à la Petty in terms of their ability to yield flows of final and intermediate capital services over many periods of time.

A consequence of the new marginalist–utilitarian and general-equilibrium analyses was that their focus on valuation was taken to mean that the boundary of the economic was the boundary of the price-making market economy. Only markets were alleged to generate unique prices for private goods and factors. Public servants, despite the subtleties of their rôles in Smith, Malthus, Mill, and Senior, made a premature disappearance from the world of the economist. Menial servants, doctors and lawyers, opera-singers and opera-dancers, though, henceforth fitted into it most comfortably, alongside the captains and workers of industry.

CHAPTER 5

Mode and Matter in Marx: The Factory Paradigm and the Scope of the Base

---

The fox knows many things, but the hedgehog knows one big thing.
(Archilochus, in Isaiah Berlin, 1953, p. 22)

5.1 The productive-labor theory of value and its corollaries

Karl Marx was a Classical economist. In his economic writings is elaborated an 'industrial–materialist' version of the Smitho-Ricardian theory of surplus generation and transfer. He does not manage, nor does he much try, to avoid input–output error within his own original surplus and transfer framework. His main achievement is to clothe the Classical surplus and transfer theory in a rich and exotic overlay of economic, sociological, political, historical, even philosophical implications. The present chapter analyzes Marx's productive-labor theory of value and its corollaries.

Marx is a hedgehog and the one big thing that he knows is that the capitalist mode of production is irremediably irrational and unjust. The moral slant is part of the analysis. The positive economics of how capitalism works *hic & nunc* is interleaved with calls to get rid of it. Capitalism is twice doomed – morally because its true producers, members of the working class, are systematically and progressively cheated of its fruits, and historically because they will someday cease cooperating with non-workers on such unfavorable terms.

The celebrated labor theory of value of *Das Kapital*, it is natural for me to emphasize, is a 'productive-labor theory of value'. Those of Smith and Ricardo are, too, of course (Maitland, 1819, p. 37). But Marx, starting from a narrower base, gets more mileage out of his central hypothesis. Major areas of the Marxian, as distinct from the Smitho-Ricardian, economic and political canon – from the production–circulation dichotomy to self-exploitation of the petty producer to the final expropriation of the expropriators – stand and fall with the central axiom that 'productive labor' is the only basic. It carries on its shoulders the rest of the Marxian economic universe.

The 'productive-labor theory of value' endows *Das Kapital* with a 'proletarian', industrial focus. It yields an apocalyptic harvest of political implication. However, it has difficulty with some of the most commonplace economic phenomena. Of course a primary analytic problem with Marxian economics as a scientific research program is the difficulty of maintaining a strict living-labor theory of value in the first place (Samuelson, 1971; Roemer, 1988). But the extra restrictions Marx imposes on his productive-labor theory create new problems that extend beyond those encountered, for instance, by Ricardo.

The 'productive-labor theory of value' affects nearly every aspect of Marx's grandiose project of social analysis. Key ratios of his economics, movements of which are supposed to seal capitalism's fate, take on different numerical values depending on which citizens count as productive laborers and where the line around capitalist or 'commodity' production is drawn. The basic analytical relationships – the rate of surplus-value or exploitation s/v, the organic composition of capital c/v, the value rate of profit $(s/v) / (c/v + v/v)$ – get low or high coefficients depending on whether industry foremen, bank tellers, high-school teachers, defense plant workers are rated as productive or unproductive. Non-producers are by definition incapable of producing surplus-value. They exploit those who do.

My fundamental contrast between theories of surplus and transfer and theories of interdependence is well designed to shed light on the economics of *Das Kapital*. The size of the national 'mass' of surplus, whether expressed in crystals of 'value' or in money, depends for example on whether immaterial service activities on the outskirts of the factory paradigm are said to be self-supporting, competitive branches of the capitalist economy (as is the case under exchange of equivalents), or whether they are said to be paid out of surplus generated elsewhere and by others. By the same token, applying the narrow definitions of Marx's original surplus and transfer scheme, as is sometimes done (Sharpe, 1982; Kidron, 1970, 1974; Wolff, 1987), to the empirical study of mixed capitalist economies with generous social welfare systems or important military establishments will reveal colossal 'rates of exploitation' of workers in private industry or agriculture.

5.1.1 What Marx knew

To judge from the notes reproduced as *Theories of Surplus-Value*, Marx had read almost everything yet written in English, French, and German political economy. In 1862–3, *en route* to preparing the final version of *Das Kapital*, vol. I, notebook upon notebook was filled with comments on prominent and obscure writers of Classical–liberal and Ricardian-socialist persuasion. It is something of a puzzle then that Marx seems not to have grasped several fundamental premisses of Classical economics. When individuals behave in what to Smith would be ordinary self-interest, the reaction is often surprise and outrage. Occasionally Marx appears not to understand (which is not the same thing as not accepting) the Invisible Hand theorem.

Readers with the stamina to get through the six volumes of *Das Kapital* and *Theories of Surplus-Value* (Marx, 1867, 1885, 1894, 1905–10) learn that later Classical political economy is primarily an exercise in Panglossian apologetics, a 'vulgar' harmony theory. Adam Smith, though his unproductive-labor doctrine is 'essentially correct' (Marx, 1857–8, p. 273), is naïve and misguided in thinking markets regulate economic activity with any success. Competition is impotent to eliminate waste and to undercut monopoly despite rapid introduction of new techniques. Instead of ruling out unemployment altogether, the capitalist system maintains a reserve army of unemployed to keep wages down. *Laissez faire* does not mainly coordinate, it mainly upsets, leaving in its wake miscalculation, anarchy, and crisis. With dialectical skill, Marx has both the coordinating and the chaotic features of competition reduce the system's ultimate chances of survival.

Classical political economy glosses over the division of society into unequal classes based on ownership of the means of production. That is inexcusable, says Marx, because class analysis is the key to both economic and political history. Say, Senior, and Rossi are mere apologists for the activities of bourgeois class parasites. It is absurd to argue that owner-managers or professionals provide value for money, *quid pro quo*, in return for services rendered. The object of Parson Malthus's inquiry into general gluts is to find a means to justify the high incomes of landlords who, like all bourgeois (so unlike workers!), love to reap where they never sowed.

More generally, under capitalism economic liberty is an empty phrase. Consumers, especially workers, do not have genuine freedom to spend their money as they choose; wages are too low to allow meaningful substitution in consumption (*sic*); sick people are *forced* to pay doctors whatever the course of the illness; state services 'are forced on' helpless citizens. Capitalists, too, are scarcely freer; they *must* invest in the latest capital-intensive machinery or be swept into the underclass.

5.1.2 The philosophical background

To understand the frame of reference of *Das Kapital*, it is helpful to situate Marx's economics in its philosophical context, that of 'historical materialism'. Marx places great emphasis on the notion that socioeconomic categories, including those peculiar to the doomed 'capitalist mode', have only temporary, historical validity. What is presented as universal and 'supra-modal' however is the principle that 'the mode of production of material life conditions the social, political and intellectual life-process in general' (Marx, 1859, p. 3). The primacy of base over superstructure is supposed to hold good across modes and historical situations, like the laws of nature.

A consequence for Marx's economics is that the 'capitalist' definitions of 'production', 'commodity', etc. remain in a constant state of tension with the 'philosophical' commitment to keeping a *material base* (whatever that means) upon which to rest the 'superstructure'. As will be shown, Marx is never able to decide whether capitalism or materiality is dominant.

The repeated references to 'material' rather than 'capitalist' production create problems for the interpreter. What weight should we give to rhetoric that violates Marx's own definitions, particularly when it comes in works not readied for publication by Marx himself? *Grundrisse* for example opens with the phrase 'The object before us, to begin with, [is] *material production*' (Marx, 1857–8, p. 83; emphasis in original). The problem is by no means confined to posthumous works. On page one of vol. I of *Das Kapital*, 'commodities' – which he probably meant to define as any saleable goods or services produced for profit under capitalist conditions – are said to be 'things' with 'physical properties' (Marx, 1867, p. 44). People who in principle qualify as 'productive labourers' are in class and 'welfare' terms written off as economic parasites.

5.2 Capitalism or materiality

5.2.1 What is a commodity, who is a worker?

In the definitions of 'productive labour', 'capitalist mode', 'commodity production' given in Marx's mature economic writings, he takes some care to distance himself from Smith's second, materialist, 'storage' definition of output. Marx says he throws in his lot with Smith's first, profit- or surplus-value-earning, 'capitalist' definition. Quotations and examples abound in which the Marxian productive sphere appears to be coterminous with the externality-poor, profit-earning, 'capitalist' or 'private' sector made up of 'multi-person firms'. Materiality of final output is not supposed to be an issue.

> That labourer alone is productive who produces surplus-value for the capitalist and thus works for the self-expansion of capital. *If* we may take an example from *outside the sphere of production of material objects* [n.b.], a school-master is a productive labourer when, in addition to belabouring the heads of his scholars, he works like a horse to enrich the school proprietor. That the latter has laid out his capital in a teaching factory, instead of in a sausage factory, does not alter the relation.
> (Marx, 1867, p. 477; emphasis added)

Adam Smith is praised for having gone 'to the very heart of the matter, [for hitting] the nail on the head' with his profit-earning criterion. That is 'more profound' than the 'second and more superficial' material definition (1905–10, Pt 1, pp. 157, 295). In the trial run for *Das Kapital*, *Grundrisse*, Marx had accused 'A. Smith [of missing] the mark only by somewhat too crudely conceiving the objectification of labour as labour which fixates itself in a tangible object. But this is a secondary thing with him, a clumsiness of expression...' (Marx, 1857–8, p. 846). Via the Spinozan dialectic, *determinatio est negatio*,

> [this] also establishes absolutely what *unproductive labour* is. It is labour which is not exchanged with capital, but directly with revenue, that is, with wages or profit (including of course the various categories of those who share as co-partners in the capitalists' profit, such as interest and rent).... These definitions are ... not derived from the material characteristics [*aus der stofflichen Bestimmung*] of labour... but from the definite social form... An actor ... or even a clown, according to this definition, is a productive labourer if he works in the service of a capitalist (an entrepreneur) to whom he returns more labour than he receives from him in the form of wages; while a jobbing tailor who comes to the capitalist's house and patches his trousers for him, producing a mere use-value [*blossen Gebrauchswert*] for him, is an unproductive labourer. (Marx, 1905–10, p. 157; 1956, 26.1, pp. 126–7; emphasis in original)

Paradoxical situations may arise, but only if the mistake is made of analyzing economic processes in absolute terms, without due regard for historical modes of production, which are 'decisive [*sic*] for material [*sic*] wealth itself'.

> The same kind of labour may be *productive* or *unproductive*. For example, Milton, who wrote *Paradise Lost* for five pounds, was an unproductive labourer. On the other hand, the writer who turns out the stuff for his publisher in factory style is a *productive labourer* ... A singer, who sells her song for her own account is an *unproductive*

labourer. But the same singer commissioned by an entrepreneur to sing in order to make money for him is a *productive labourer*; for she produces capital.

(Marx, 1905–10, p. 401, emphasis in original)

Here the implication is that wage-laborers employed in profitable multi-person enterprises qualify as productive even if their output is not 'material'. Single-person firms are another matter, as we shall see in sections 5.4–5.6.

The reference population of Marxian welfare economics is also a corollary of the productive-labor theory of value. Marxism differs from Christianity just here, in its concern with the salvation of *workers*, as distinct, for example, from the poor or the faithful. Political rights in a just society will be linked with the status of worker rather than, for instance, citizen. It begs the question, *le prolétariat, c'est qui?* Though to be a productive laborer is 'not a piece of luck, but a misfortune' (1867, p. 477), we know that the worst-off members of society are not so lucky; the old, the infirm, the insane, those permanently or temporarily in the reserve army, do not qualify as 'productive labourers' (1867, pp. 602–3). And the class status of individuals who perform 'mere services for the satisfaction of immediate needs' is inferior to that of proletarian. As he delicately puts it,

> From whore to pope, there is a mass of such rabble. But the honest and 'working' *lumpenproletariat* belongs here as well; e.g. the great mob of porters, etc. . . .
>
> (Marx, 1857–8, p. 272)

5.2.2 Mode of production, materiality of product

Officially, then, workers engaged in the 'capitalist' production of immaterial final services are 'productive labourers'. But when that is set against Marx's use of the terms 'commodity production' and 'commodity', the status of capitalist services appears in doubt. *Das Kapital* vol. I opens with the statement that wealth in the 'capitalist mode of production' presents itself as an 'accumulation of commodities', and that '[a] commodity is, in the first place, an object outside us, a thing [*sic*] that by its properties satisfies human wants [whether they spring] from the stomach or from fancy' (1867, p. 43).

Services provided by multi-person enterprises are thus demoted to the status of exceptions of minor importance, so that for all intents and purposes 'commodities' may be taken to be *material*. Anyway Marx opts, no doubt consciously, to build his analysis around 'commodity' (*Ware*) rather than the more neutral term 'good' (*Gut*). *Ware*'s semantic associations are with materiality, transferability, reproducibility – in a word, with the characteristics of products of large-scale industry.

These are, incidentally, the qualities least inappropriately treated in a labor-theory, constant-returns-to-scale framework. Even Ricardo did not try to apply the labor theory to Old Masters. Moreover it can be no coincidence (as Marxists are fond of saying!) that the *physical, material capital goods with which reproducible 'commodities' are produced, in conjunction with unskilled factory labor, turn out to be just those most amenable to 'social ownership'* when the expropriators are expropriated. 'Human' capital cannot be nationalized except under state slavery, and even then it may still have a mind of its own.

Capitalistically-produced services – teaching factories, etc. – are discussed by Marx in disparaging terms. 'A commodity, such as iron, corn, or a diamond, is, . . . so far as it is a material thing [*sic*], a use-value, something useful' (1867, p. 44). Commodities, which may be useful, and which workers buy, are apparently one thing; immaterial services, another: 'These services themselves, like the commodities I buy, may be necessary or *may only seem necessary* – for example, the service of a soldier or physician or lawyer' (1905–10, p. 405).

The tension between capitalist and materiality criteria contributes several layers of ambiguity to the following:

> [Workers] in e.g. luxury shops are productive, . . . as far as they increase the capital of their master; unproductive as to the material result of their labour . . . [and] although the characters who consume such objects are expressly castigated as unproductive wastrels.
> (Marx 1857–8, p. 273

On the one hand the passage conveys the unfairness of the distribution of income by means of productive–unproductive terminology. That terminology was supposed to be value-neutral, a mere description of the capitalist world. In theory, according to the 'value versions' of Smith and Marx (Myint, 1948), 'productive' and 'unproductive' are intended only to communicate whether or not the going rate of profit is being earned under market or, in Marx's case, capitalist-market conditions. Income inequality is, however, by nature a continuous relation, a matter of degree; inevitably it will be poorly captured by a binary distinction.

Marx was, however, not one to lose sleep over value judgments. Productive laborers are not *just* the sole true producers 'in fact'; they are also the chosen, the bearers of revolutionary virtue, who will remake the world for all. What that does to the positive part of the analysis is to link the utility of current final goods unconsciously but somewhat directly to whether or not they are consumed by *workers*.

The distinction between 'necessities' and 'luxuries' carries a normative load not borne by the necessity–luxury distinction in neoclassical consumer theory. There, whether a good is a 'necessity' or a 'luxury' for an individual is an artefact of the interaction of his preferences with given prices and his income (e.g. Marshall, 1890, pp. 89–92).

The ultimate status of service producers in *Das Kapital* is further put in doubt by the astonishing prediction that the development of capitalism will eventually ensure the total disappearance of immaterial services from the capitalist scene. In a section of *Theories of Surplus-Value* that the Moscow editor subtitles 'Manifestations of Capitalism in the Sphere of Immaterial Production', Marx dismisses teaching factories and hack encyclopedia writing in half a page on the ground that they are atypical, 'a *transitional form*' (1905–10, p. 410; emphasis in original). Again there is confusion of matter and mode: that transition looks to be nearly complete, but it is a *transition to capitalism, not to materiality*.

Though the services of individual domestics and singing teachers are luxuries (of high income elasticity), *multi*-person enterprises that provide services that are similar, if inferior in quality, are fated to disappear even though accumulation of capital means greater national total wealth. The upshot of this pessimistic vision is that if *materiality* is not a foolproof way to separate capitalistically-productive sheep from goats today, it will become one in due course. The forecast is that 'apart from minor exceptions, [productive labourers] will exclusively produce . . . immediate material wealth consisting of *commodities* [sic] . . . while [unproductive labourers], with minor exceptions, will perform only personal services' (1905–10, pp. 160–1). That Engel's-Law-denying result is at least consistent with the immiseration postulate, which predicts that, despite frenzied capital accumulation, workers will be no better off.

5.3 The factory paradigm and the production–circulation dichotomy

Marx uses the factory, in which productive wage laborers fabricate material reproducible goods, as the paradigm for analyzing economic life under capitalism. In this he joins the not-too-exclusive club (wisecrack of another Marx springs to mind!) of Economics 101 lecturers who think of factories and of externality-poor, material, artefactual output whenever they draw isoquants on blackboards.

The productive laborers of *Das Kapital* would be those of Smith's value version but for two crucial points of difference. Both have the effect of narrowing the Marxian productive domain down to something less than goods and services produced for market sale. The first point is the distinction much insisted upon between 'production' and 'circulation'. The second, discussed in section 5.4 below, is the difference between 'capitalist' and 'petty capitalist' 'modes of production'. A fruit of Marx's laudable if failed attempt at reconciling history and microeconomics, 'petty' vs. 'capitalist' postulates differences between single- and multi-person firms of a scale comparable to the differences assumed between private firms and state agencies in the *Wealth of Nations*.

The placing of so many theoretical eggs in the basket of factory production, where both inputs and outputs are reproducible 'material goods', multiplies the number of epicycles needed to account for phenomena that some of Marx's more 'vulgar' predecessors managed to treat within a unified framework. For instance, even using 'capitalist' or 'value' definitions of productive and unproductive, transportation and warehousing are protean categories for would-be materialists. Though the inputs are material to the tune of hundreds and thousands of tons, transportation as such cannot be stored (Hill, 1977).

Bookkeeping and wholesale and retail trade, at one more remove from the factory paradigm, utilize material inputs (buildings, paper, ink) but on the product side are less surely adding value in the Marxian sense of the term. Private banking and insurance, not to speak of public works and state services, fit into the factory model even less comfortably, and single-person or family enterprises are said not to fit it at all.

Before running up against the production–circulation dichotomy, the Marxian system differed from the bare-bones Ricardian one mainly in the view of the industrial capitalist as parasite, extracting unpaid labor from workers. Even there it is occasionally implied by Marx that the industrial capitalist 'works', at least in the early stages of industrialization. There is for instance the priceless remark that 'direct exploitation of labour costs labour, as every slave-driver knows' (Marx, 1867, p. 557).

5.3.1 *Circulation proper*

A distinctive feature of the economics of *Das Kapital* is that not all complex activities resulting in goods that can be profitably sold are allowed to come within the boundary of 'production'. 'Circulation' is held to be fundamentally different from 'production'. Circulation is understood as buying and selling in an arbitrage sense, that is, stripped of transportation- or storage-related activities, which may add or preserve exchangeable labor-values. It is here that Marx lambastes Condillac's analysis of pure exchange (Marx, 1867, p. 157; section 2.6 above).

Workers engaged in circulation are not 'productive labourers' even though a capitalist in the circulation sphere hires and exploits labor like the industrial capitalist, and earns the going rate of profit on the investment. The cordoning off of circulation in *Das Kapital* has a scholastic as well as a naïve–materialist flavor; the end-result of the special treatment of circulation is to deny the distributive trades full economic *droits de cité* (Beer, 1938, p. 141).

Sly businessmen that they are, wholesale and retail traders succeed in getting industrial capitalists to *transfer* to them a portion of the mass of surplus-value generated by industrial workers. This is not because arranging for a good to be in the right place or keeping it in its pristine state has a real cost in resources, or alternatively because being in the right place or fresh is a characteristic that buyers are willing to pay for. The explanation offered would not impress a Popperian.

> The process of circulation is a phase of the total process of reproduction. But no value is produced in the process of circulation, and, therefore, no surplus-value. Only changes of form of the same mass of value take place ... If a surplus-value is realized in the sale of produced commodities, then this is only because it already existed in them.
>
> (Marx, 1894, p. 279)

Costs of circulation, it is argued, may be both 'unproductive' and 'necessary'. A none-too-legitimate analogy from the chemistry of catalysis is offered in place of sixty years of economic analysis on 'intermediate yet unproductive'. Catalysts fail to 'participate' in chemical reactions just as 'circulation' fails to add crystals of labor-value to material products. But, since the absence of a catalyst means no reaction, an industrialist would be ill-advised to cross the right amount of catalyst off his constant-capital shopping-list. The logic is simply fallacious in production-function terms. Conjunction of 'unproductive and necessary', it will be recalled, involves a *faux raisonnement*, input–output error. Despite evident study of what Smith, Garnier, Say, Rossi, McCulloch, and Senior had to say on almost those very topics, Marx affirms without a blush that 'the buying and selling agent ... performs a necessary function, ... unproductive in itself although a necessary element of reproduction, ... because [*sic!*] the process of reproduction itself includes unproductive functions' (1885, p. 134).

Why Marx insists on fitting his system at so late a date into that procrustean bed is not immediately obvious. His scientific ambitions were not those of the Schoolmen. There would be an easy gain in explanatory power within the confines of the productive-labor theory of value were the merchant capitalist simply treated as a capitalist, and his employees as laborers like any others, the more so in that the realization function is stated not only to be 'necessary' but to grow proportionately more important as capitalism develops.

CIRCULATION AND THE LABOR THEORY

The issue of giving special treatment to 'circulation' can be separated from that of the validity of the productive-labor theory itself. Marx may have thought that, so long as the labor theory already necessitates invisible 'transfers' of value between branches that differ in capital-intensity, not much is lost at the margin if *additional* transfers of value are postulated, from industrial to other kinds of capitalists. Besides, the production–circulation dichotomy has the political plus of casting aspersions on merchant allies of the industrial bourgeoisie. As with any category of unproductive or superstructural activity, circulation's claim to a fraction of total capitalist product jacks the 'rate of exploitation' s/v of workers in the productive sphere up another notch.

The idea that the production–circulation dichotomy was employed because its acknowledged flaws were thought minor compared to those of the transformation problem, does not seem plausible. It is more likely that Marx simply did not see anything wrong with 'unproductive yet necessary'. The way the labor theory itself is introduced in the first pages of *Das Kapital*, vol. I, lends strength to the second interpretation. The productive-labor theory of value is introduced as a simple and obvious truth, requiring no defense. As Francis Seton elegantly put it,

> the denial of productive factor contributions other than those of labour, on which the whole doctrine of surplus rests, is an act of *fiat* rather than of genuine cognition.
> (Seton, 1957, p. 159)

From time to time economists in the Marxian tradition have attempted to jettison the production–circulation dichotomy. One of the first was the Russian V. A. Bazarov in 1899 (section 6.2.3 below). Insistence that circulation is not production has none the less remained a key tenet of economists who consider themselves true to Marx on basic postulates, as distinct from 'method' (e.g. Gillman, 1957; Baran, 1957; Kidron, 1970; J. Becker, 1977; Gill, 1979, 1986; Fine, 1983; Wolff, 1987; section 7.1 below).

TRANSFERS BETWEEN CAPITALISTS

Activities of enterprises in the sphere of circulation are one of the *faux frais* (incidental expenses) of production, whether the principals work on their own account or have amassed enough capital to employ others. Employees of entrepreneurs rich enough to run a multi-person establishment perform hours of surplus-labor, but their surplus hours do not 'produce value any more than [do their] hours of necessary labour' (Marx, 1885, p. 135). In a large-diameter epicycle on the productive-labor theory, surplus-value is said to be 'transferred' between productive and circulation spheres. Writes Marx, 'by means of [the necessary labor of workers in circulation enterprises] a part of the social product is transferred to them' (p. 135). The logic is one of production time sacrificed to the needs of transportation and retailing (p. 133).

> As far as the entire capitalist class is concerned, [the *faux frais* of circulation constitute] a deduction from the surplus-value or surplus-product, just as the time a labourer needs for the purchase of his means of subsistence is lost time.
> (Marx, 1885, p. 152)

It is momentarily forgotten that capitalists' surplus-value or profit is *never* equal to gross sales except under trivial circumstances, such as monopoly with zero costs of production. That is the case, however ardently Mr Moneybags might wish his realized surplus-value to require no expenses, *faux* or otherwise. The example given of independent direct producers having to waste valuable production time taking their wares to market is perfectly valid. But the conclusions drawn therefrom are not sensible, even in the context of defending a labor theory of value. A solution could have been to submit to production-function logic and to treat as intermediately productive *any* expenses known to be technically and 'socially' necessary for normal 'realization'. Depending on how vertical integration slices things, then, the activities of transportation, wholesale and retail trade, etc., figure either as separate 'branches' of Departments I or II or as workshops of industries that produce 'goods-in-the-right-place' (section 5.6 below).

INTERCAPITALIST EXCHANGE IN THE REPRODUCTION SCHEMES

The determination to keep circulation 'unproductive' precludes mutuality in accords made between industrial and merchant capitalists. Lack of *quid pro quo* is not however uniformly assumed for exchanges between capitalists in Marxian economics, notwithstanding the impression recorded in section 5.1.1. Despite fundamental distrust of the market as a fair divider of gains between buyer and seller and as an effective co-ordinating mechanism, and despite general outrage at the terms of the contract that the worker is forced to sign with the capitalist, Marx does upon occasion employ something like a general-equilibrium framework. In the reproduction schemes of *Das Kapital*, vol. II, exchange between Departments takes place on an equivalent basis. Capitalists producing 'means of production' sell items of constant capital (machines, raw materials) to capitalists who use them to produce final 'articles of consumption'. Abstracting from the invisible value transfers of the transformation problem, interdepartmental trade is a *quid pro quo*, value for value (1885, pp. 402 ff.).

HISTORY AGAINST MICROECONOMICS

Circulation counts as a *faux frais*, even though it may be efficient to divide labor into manufacturing and circulatory functions. When Marx's peasants lay down their hoes to take a hen to market, his opportunity-cost reasoning is perfectly sound, but he misses the point of it. Instead there is focus on the unpleasant Hegelian essences concealed by industrial change.

> It would be a miracle if . . . a transformation [of an unproductive function into a productive one] could be accomplished by the mere transfer of a function . . . from an incidental occupation of many [petty producers] into the exclusive occupation of a few [capitalists in the sphere of circulation].
> (Marx, 1885, pp. 134–5)

Keeping one eye peeled for the historical framework of problems distracts from the analytical task of fixing the holes in the factory paradigm. It is a weakness of historicism generally that analyses are not easily invalidated by anomalies since they can be written off to flux in the framework.

As in the works of his Classical predecessors in surplus generation and transfer, in Marx gains from specialization are treated on an *ad hoc* basis. To be sure, throughout the Marxian *oeuvre* but never more eloquently than in the *Manifesto*, there is wonder at the 'massive' and 'colossal productive forces, [the subjection] of Nature's forces to man, machinery, . . . railways, electric telegraphs' unleashed by the bourgeoisie 'during its rule of scarce one hundred years' (Marx and Engels, 1848, p. 23). The explanation of these gains from specialization is very Smithian: capitalism makes economic the wholesale application of science to production. Division of labor within the firm in industry is the root cause of the worker's alienation – what socialism, with its exciting job variety, promises to overcome.

Division of labor into productive and circulatory is another matter. It is admitted that speedier pairing of final consumer and seller reduces the period of turnover, which raises the rate of surplus-value earned by industrial capitalists. Improvements that reduce costs of circulation for a given volume of final output – like *any* favorable development that lowers costs, he might have concluded! – liberate funds for goods production (1894, p. 280).

Then, as noted, intra-class bargaining (*not* conflict!) brings about the famous 'transfer' of some of the increased surplus-value from the industrial capitalist to the merchant, usurer, financier, and so on (1885, p. 425; 1894, pp. 291–3).

5.3.2 *'Continuation' of production in the circulation sphere*

In practice, of course, enterprises specialize in ways that make circulation proper difficult to disentangle from more laudable activities whose 'productive character [is] merely concealed [*sic*] by the circulation form' (1885, p. 139). Examples of such 'productive' activities taking place under the same roof as pure trade include warehousing, storing and packaging, which retard or prevent the destruction of commodities' use-value.

Of the other borderline cases discussed in volume II, bookkeeping is given out to be a necessary evil, a deduction of labor and resources that could otherwise be devoted to material production. It does possess some transcendent usefulness, as witnessed by the prediction that it will be 'more necessary in collective production than in capitalist production' (1885, p. 138). However, since money will disappear under socialism with the disappearance of the commodity form, resources tied up in the production of goods used as money, as circulating medium, or in holding precious metals are 'unproductively' consumed. They maintain a 'mere circulation machine' (p. 139).

Warehouses have inherent usefulness, similar to that of record-keeping. The holding of inventories prevents costly 'interruptions' in productive processes and is therefore productive (p. 144).

Transportation by rail and water is too 'industrial' and capital-intensive to bear easy relegation to the limbo of circulation proper. Including transportation in the sphere of production puts an unfortunate dent in the pristine materiality of the latter.

> *Quantities* of [material] products are not increased by transportation... it is rather an unavoidable evil. But the use-value of things is materialised [i.e. realized] only in their consumption [by actual consumers], and their consumption *may necessitate a change in location* of these things, hence *may require* an additional process of production in the transport industry.
> (Marx, 1885, p. 153; emphasis added)

By focusing on the physical characteristics of commodities, Marx misses an opportunity to put transport unequivocally on the same footing as industry. That competitive equalization of money-profit rates must have extended to sectors requiring such massive capital investments as railroads should have made it a relatively easy step.

The transport industry forms on the one hand an independent branch of production and thus a separate sphere of investment of productive capital. On the other hand, its distinguishing feature is that it appears as a continuation of a process of production *within* the process of circulation (*sic*) (1885, p. 155). Marx's vol. II notation can be adapted without difficulty to account for transportation even if it is to be denied the status of a separate branch of 'material production' (Weldon, 1977).

$$M - C \begin{cases} P_M \\ L \end{cases} \ldots P \ldots M', \text{ (omitting the industrial } C' - M').$$

In Weldon's formulation, one goes directly from P, now defined as the production of commodities in the factory *plus* their delivery to the point of final sale, to M', their final realization value in money. The innovation involves skipping Marx's usual intermediate stage C', the finished commodity as physical item. Weldon offers this as a way of handling services within the $M - C - P - C' - M'$ framework that 'Marx might well have used consistently throughout to put intangible goods always on the same footing as his obviously preferred tangibles' (Weldon, 1977, pp. 5–6). Alternatively, transport could be elevated to the status of a branch of production in its own right, with its own requirements in labor and means of production. Its C' would then be an (unstockable) immaterial service 'transportation', which would sell for M' (see section 6.5.2 below).

What would Marxian economics lose were it to drop the production–circulation dichotomy? Possibly the hardest pill to swallow would be the implied inclusion, within the productive domain, of financial services capitalistically organized, which he regarded as a straightforward drain on the economy of real producers of things. Despite the obvious differences (e.g. intertemporal ones), there are parallels between financial institutions and transportation and communications firms. In so far as the growing importance of the financial sector was one of Marx's major predictions about the evolution of the capitalist mode, and had an important rôle in realization crises, it is difficult to justify relegating banking and finance to the analytic sidelines, apart from Occam's razor considerations.

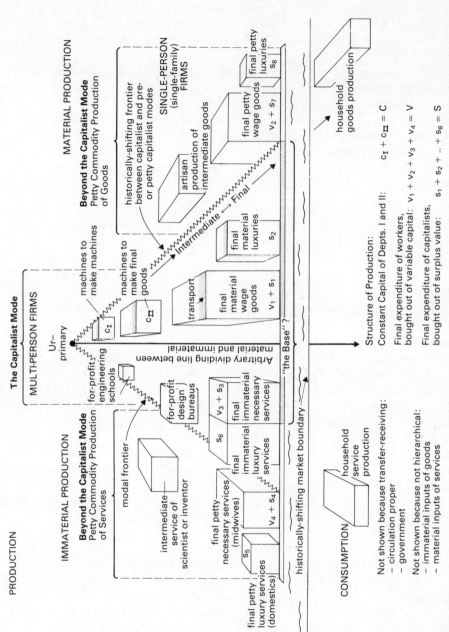

Figure 5.1 Marx's economy: an architectural view showing the *capitalist mode* within the economy; *intermediate* vs. *final*; *necessity* vs. *luxury*; *goods transport* and the arbitrary line between *material goods* and *immaterial services*.

5.4 Beyond the capitalist mode: the petty producer

5.4.1 Self-exploitation of the self-employed

The separate treatment of 'petty commodity production' is the second point of doctrine whose effect is to reduce the Marxian 'capitalist economy' to a subset of the Classics' private sector. The self-employed are consigned to analytical limbo 'outside the capitalist mode' (Figure 5.1). Scattered beyond the pale are a motley crew of individual producers: bourgeois professionals, ignorant peasants, servile domestics. Their 'labor' – for they are not rentiers – may be mental or manual; their 'outputs', while not perfectly reproducible like outputs of large-scale industry, are nevertheless frequently 'material', e.g. those of independent artisans and agriculturalists. But they may also be immaterial, like those of doctors and lawyers. Nothing except the presumption that they are luxuries restricts the output of the petty mode to final goods and services rather than intermediate ones. The stated principle of classification is simply the presence or absence of hired wage workers, since, according to the labor theory (abstracting again from both circulation and differences of capital–labor ratios), the surplus that drives the capitalist system is exploited from hired labor alone.

Individual petty producers are relegated to their own separate mode in *Theories of Surplus–Value*. Petty producers 'belong *neither* to the category of productive nor of unproductive labourers, *although they are producers of commodities*. [Their] production does not fall under the capitalist mode of production' (1905–10, p. 407; emphasis added). The petty-proprietor category is an obvious epicycle and it is unclear why Marx the economist bothered with it at all, or how seriously he intended it to be taken (but see Lenin, 1899). By his own lights, petty producers differ from more successful industrial capitalists in fairly trivial respects. Petty producers behave after all as though they belong to the capitalist mode: they are maximizers and the goods they produce are 'commodities', not primarily for use but for market sale. The only problem is that they do not produce 'surplus-value' (1867, p. 477).

The difficulty of fitting the single-person firm into the framework of the productive-labor theory of value helps to explain their relegation to limbo in a semi-independent petty 'mode'. The petty producer is said to be 'split in two, [exploiting] himself as wage-labourer' (Marx, 1905–10, Pt 1, p. 408). All the examples cited in *Theories of Surplus-Value* involve goods producers – 'handicraftsmen', 'peasants'.

The class allegiance of both producers and consumers of personal services, and the high luxury content of the services themselves, are evidently important analytical considerations. Petty-mode *service* producers flog final luxuries mainly to the bourgeoisie, even though '[the] labourer himself can buy labour . . . the service of a physician or a priest', just as he can buy gin instead of bread (1905–10, p. 404).

> These services themselves, like the commodities which I buy, may be necessary or *may only seem necessary* – for example, the service of a soldier or physician or lawyer.
> (Marx, 1905–10, p. 405; emphasis added)

A further consideration is that petty producers of professional services are members of the '"ideological" classes, . . . government officials, priests, lawyers, soldiers, &c.' and are therefore the class allies of industrial and merchant capitalists and of rentiers who 'have no occupation but to consume the labour of others in the form of rent, interest, &c.' (1867, p. 420).

The old-fashioned argument is revived that, because labor services of domestics and lawyers, etc., are bought with consumers' 'revenue' rather than with capitalists' capital, people who sell them 'cannot [*sic*] fall under the category of productive labour'. In other words, final petty service producers are not productive (Marx, 1857–8, p. 273; see section 3.3.1 above). Analytically the problem is again asymmetric treatment of the different modes, for, as we saw in section 5.2.1, officially, workers who produce profitable final services in capitalist teaching factories and profitable final goods in capitalist sausage faactories are 'productive labourers'.

The 'revenue'–'capital' distinction, it will be recalled, was widely made by Smith and the Classics, being their rendering of the distinction between expenditure on final consumer goods and on intermediate investment goods. But that did not mean to Smith, though he occasionally implied otherwise, that individual *recipients* of 'revenue' could not, by saving out of above-subsistence income, become capitalists themselves. It meant that less and less to his followers, as ground was gained by the abstinence theory of interest and lost by the theory of the subsistence wage.

There may have been an additional reason for breathing new life into that article of Classical dogma. Upward mobility across the boundary between petty- and full capitalist modes runs counter to Marx's analyses both of income inequality and of the direction of technical progress and of industrial structural change. In *Das Kapital*, inequality is not the natural result of differences in parsimony, ability, or luck. The great fortunes of the bourgeoisie originated in 'the so-called primitive accumulation of capital', in plunder and violence. By exploitation did they grow. Personal wealth in capitalism has therefore nothing to do with the innocent incremental frugalities of individuals. Besides, petty production is a mode that is historically doomed to be swallowed up by large-scale 'real' capitalism. The mobility of independent producers may be rapid, but it is always downward!

To have given individual producers of final immaterial services rights to the 'capitalist mode' might have opened the door to that *passe-partout* of vulgar political economy, exchange of equivalents, which was known to come with a heavy baggage of anti-revolutionary corollary. That possibility is sealed off with a bit of class analysis. Marx inveighs against the 'rubbish', 'utter nonsense', 'belletristic trash', 'insipid literary flourishes' of Nassau Senior and Pellegrino Rossi, who would defend the economic productiveness of physicians and lawyers on the basis of consumers' willingness to pay them (1905–10, pp. 288, 294).

'Menials' are not grouped with peasants as petty producers because services are not really commodities, especially when performed by individuals outside the capitalist mode. In criticizing Rossi's view of the servant as someone who enables the master to realize his comparative advantage, Marx reveals familiarity with what he calls 'the *labour-saving idea* of Garnier, Lauderdale, and Ganilh'. Input–output reasoning is invoked to impugn its practical significance. The 'labour-saving idea' would salvage only a small fraction of the domestic labor force.

> [Menial] servants (in so far as they provide only luxury articles [*sic*] and all unproductive labourers who produce merely enjoyment [would still be unproductive] ... [Really] labour-saving personal services would only be productive *in so far as their consumer is a producer*. If he is an idle capitalist, they only save him the labour of doing anything at all.
> (Marx, 1905–10, p. 297; emphasis added)

5.4.2 *Is the capitalist mode the base?*

Allowing that workers' necessities may be produced in the petty mode has implications for the base–superstructure scheme and for surplus and transfer logic generally. It breaks down the neat correspondences between 'productive' laborers working in the sphere of 'material production' and the wage goods consumed by them, on the one hand, and between 'unproductives' engaged in circulation and immaterial petty-commodity production and in luxury goods and services, on the other. Capitalistically-productive laborers consume a non-negligible volume of goods and services from *outside* the capitalist mode – mainly peasants' agricultural produce but also services of petty teachers and physicians.

REPRODUCTION OF LABORERS: MARX'S HOUSEHOLD

A neglected chamber of the Marxian edifice is the household in its rôle of labor supplier and goods demander. Interdependence of production and consumption are on occasion provided for, even though the connection is made not via supply and demand for goods but by treating subsistence wages as the *sine qua non* of the reproduction of the working man himself. Except for the fact of a buffer in the reserve army of the unemployed, the mechanism is in fact quite Malthusian (see Hollander, 1984).

The von Neumann growth model (von Neumann, 1937; section 10.5 below) also treats the worker as 'produced'. Von Neumann's model employs a Malthusian food–population feedback loop like that used with varying degrees of determinism by Ricardo and other Classical writers. The premisses of neoclassical consumer theory are turned around. Methodological individualism falls by the wayside. Consumption is no longer (as Smith proposed) the 'sole end and purpose of all production'. Laborers are just another kind of capital, 'produced by' known techniques, by feeding them consumer-good inputs, like the fodder fed to Adam Smith's 'labouring cattle'. The rate of increase of the number of workers is endogenous; in good materialist fashion you are what you eat.

The reciprocal influence of consumption upon production is not described in a spirit of circular flow and general interdependence, since that is frowned upon in Marxian surplus generation and transfer, but is presented somewhat in the manner of a von Neumann system.

> Consumption . . . falls properly outside the sphere of the economy, *except in so far as it in turn exerts a reciprocal action* on the point of departure thus once again initiating the whole process.
> (Marx, 1859, p. 194)

That 'extent' is likely to be greatest when people are driven to the margin of subsistence, as implied by the immiseration postulate. A functional consumption–working population link would also allow for the possibility of time spent in the reserve army of the unemployed.

That labor power must be reproduced causes another difficulty for unidirectional base–superstructure logic. Reproduction depends not only on wage goods from the capitalist mode, but also on services of professionals (midwives!) from the petty mode.

> Consumption would be productive [*sic*] if it employed labour that produced labour power itself (which . . . the school-master's or the physician's labour *might do*. . .)
> (Marx, 1905–10, p. 292; emphasis added)

Most likely it was the lifelong feud with the ghost of Malthus that kept Marx from taking those lines of reasoning further (see Blaug, 1988).

BASE–SUPERSTRUCTURE LOGIC AND LABOR-VALUE PRICES

Both Marx's surplus and transfer mechanism and his base–superstructure materialism require a capitalist mode that is perfectly 'basic' and self-contained; it must generate all its own inputs and ensure the reproduction of its own labor. In addition it must provide the surplus upon which unproductive modes and actors subsist without taking inputs from them in return. *Das Kapital* and *Theories of Surplus-Value* are riddled with minor instances of interdependence. Both workers' households and capitalist enterprises depend in some measure upon intermediate service inputs from single-person firms and from the state (section 5.6 below).

For the capitalist mode to have succeeded in being the 'base' is in principle 'easier' than to get labor-value prices to work. The latter requires perfect technical hierarchy in production, from Ur-primary inputs to final outputs. There can be no feedback loops or interdependencies of the sort that occur when mining provides iron for machinery production but requires machinery itself (Blaug, 1980b, p. 15). If the capitalist mode cannot survive on its own without intermediate inputs from non-capitalist modes, there is input–output error, but one that is in principle easy to correct by making some larger 'economy' the unit of analysis.

5.5 Mental labor and the 'living production machine'

Class considerations prohibit the placing of 'mental' labor on the same footing as 'manual' labor until such time, not expected before the advent of 'communist society', as the dictatorship of the proletariat eliminates differences between the two that it has been a 'characteristic feature of the capitalist mode' to create (Marx, 1875, p. 347; 1905–10, p. 411). One employment of the mental–manual distinction, as just seen, is to split off members of the liberal professions from petty producers of material commodities.

So far we have looked at luxury services produced in petty and capitalist modes. What of immaterial services as constant-capital *intermediate inputs*? They present interesting problems for economic Marxism. According to the productive-labor theory of value, 'variable capital' is spent on the services of 'productive laborers'. In the majority of cases (abstracting from 'teaching factories'), the commodities produced are 'material'; 'productive laborers' touch and manipulate raw materials directly, and are therefore at the same time 'manual laborers'. But, with complex industrial organization, that simple concordance between productive and manual labor breaks down.

The economic universe of *Das Kapital* is full of 'mental' laborers engaged in the production of 'material' industrial goods. Complex division of labor in large-scale enterprises involves a multiplicity of occupation and grades of hierarchy. Capitalists come to employ 'engineers' and 'overseers' in addition to unskilled 'manual' labor. Are engineers 'productive laborers'? The answer to that scholastic question is: it depends on the mode. Whether or not engineers are in the capitalist mode depends on vertical integration of firms. If capitalists hire them, they are paid wages; by definition wages come out of 'variable capital'; therefore staff engineers produce surplus-value. For freelance engineers and draftsmen in *independent* design bureaux to qualify as 'productive', allowance must be made for immaterial services to serve as intermediate producers' goods in a way analogous to the materials and use of equipment paid out of 'constant capital'. The first case, that of staff professionals, is considered here and the second in section 5.6.

Where there is complex and hierarchical division of labor within the factory,

> all [laborers, unskilled, manual, mental] together as in a workshop, ... are the *living production machine* ... [The] material product [is] the *common product* of these persons [who] are ... *directly* engaged in the production of material wealth ...
> (Marx, 1905–10, pp. 411–12; first emphasis added)

In vol. I of *Das Kapital* the living production machine is called 'collective labour' (*Gesamtarbeit*). 'In order to labour productively, it is no longer necessary for you to do manual work yourself [*sic*]; enough, if you are an organ of the collective labourer' (1867, p. 476).

The quite satisfactory and general treatment of 'intellectual' labor from the viewpoint of overall production requirements (producer sovereignty) rehabilitates to productive status various categories of employees who work in plant offices of industrial enterprises: shipping clerks, secretaries, cleaners, nightwatchmen (Braverman, 1974). It incidentally gives many 'lower-grade' white-collar workers a clearly stamped entry pass into the proletariat. In theory, the device of the living production machine still permits 'production' to be kept distinct from capitalists' exploitative entrepreneurial and ownership functions on the one hand, and from pure buying and selling ('circulation', advertising), on the other. The only question becomes where the lines should be drawn.

5.6 Can immaterial services be constant-capital inputs?

The friendliness to white-collar professionals implied by the living production machine is not of course extended to the class of capitalists themselves. That is fundamental. Less obvious is the reluctance to open the door to contributions by scientists and inventors employed in *separate* establishments: research institutes, consulting firms, and so on. The upshot, in keeping with the shrill commitment to distinctions of mode, is that 'productiveness' of labor depends in the last analysis on purely institutional arrangements such as the vertical and horizontal boundaries between firms (see Figure 5.1).

Circumstantial evidence supports that view. Intermediate services, whether of individuals or multi-person organizations, are treated only in passing, again on the presumption they are a dying breed. The line drawn between capitalist and petty has the surprising effect of absolving Marx of the duty of making a careful distinction between private and public, something that the Classics (except Mill) thought absolutely fundamental. *Das Kapital* turns a strangely deaf ear to differences of ownership and mechanism (non-profit, for-profit) the moment institutions are said to lie 'outside the capitalist mode'.

A practised defender of the distinction between dead and living labor, Marx rejects with horror the idea that *indirect* means of production be put in the same economic basket as direct. The discussion of *indirect* contributions to material production fairly drips with input–output error! Marx is outraged by Pellegrino Rossi's argument that 'the whole labour of government is an indirect means of production' since 'production is almost impossible without it':

> [The] educated bourgeois . . . *grant recognition* even to functions and activities that have *nothing to do with* the production of wealth; and indeed they grant them recognition because they too '*indirectly*' increase, etc., their wealth, in a word, fulfill a 'useful' function for wealth.
> (Marx, 1905–10, p. 288; first emphasis in original)

> It is *precisely this labour which participates indirectly in production (and it forms only a part of unproductive labour) that we call unproductive labour.* Otherwise we would have to say that since the magistrate is absolutely unable to live without the peasant, therefore the peasant is an indirect producer of justice. . . Utter nonsense!
> (1905–10, pp. 293–4)

Marx's more 'Promethean' economic writings such as the *Manifesto* display enthusiastic, even exaggerated, appreciation of the power of reason and 'positive science' to revolutionize 'material production'. None the less, the main passage in *Theories of Surplus-Value* dealing with scientific activity as an intermediate service brands as 'sycophantic underlings of political economy' writers who

> [feel] it their duty to glorify and justify every sphere of activity by demonstrating that it [is] 'linked' with the production of material wealth, that it [is] a means toward it; and they [honour] everyone by making him a 'productive labourer' in the 'primary' sense...
>
> In this matter even such people as Malthus are to be preferred, who directly defend the necessity and usefulness of *'unproductive labourers'* and pure parasites.
>
> (Marx, 1905–10, p. 176; emphasis in original)

The Marxian production-function logic of 'social necessity' runs up against *ad hoc* prohibitions against the crossing of enterprise lines in the case of intermediate producer services. Otherwise it would be producer demand that should establish the productiveness of immaterial, 'mental' inputs acquired from separate legal entities. That would raise the disturbing possibility of immaterial capital-poor labor services being paid for out of 'constant capital', which would spoil things somewhat for the single-factor labor theory and would alter the branch composition of Department I (means of production). The way Marx leaves it, scientists, engineers, or lawyers whose contributions to material production are *'indirect' because subcontracted from a separate establishment* fall in a completely different economic category from that inhabited by their brothers and sisters whose contributions to the living production machine are 'direct'. It is not difficult to imagine what a challenge the modern concept of 'transactions costs' (Coase, 1937) throws down to the 'mode' wing of the Marxian intellectual community.

5.7 The 'most efficacious proportion', a positive fraction

In a revealing comment on Nassau Senior's *Principes fondamentaux* (Senior, 1836b, p. 204), noted in the 'Freutsch' language, Marx cites with approval Adam Smith's determination to 'reduce the "necessary unproductive labourers" like state officials, lawyers, priests, etc., to the *extent* in which their services are indispensable. [For] this is in any case the *"proportion" in which they make the labour of productive labourers most efficacious [die "Proportion", worin sie machen le plus efficace le travail des travailleurs productifs]*' (Marx, 1905–10, p. 289; 1956, 26.1, p. 261, first emphasis in original). I take the liberty of treating the two ideological enemies as co-authors of the phrase that so well summarizes the Classical–Marxian view of the government's economic rôle. Logically, the effect of postulating a 'most efficacious proportion' is to split the unproductive sector into two parts, one intermediate and indispensable and the other dispensable, wasteful, and to be retrenched.

Input–output error helps us understand that Marx's 'most efficacious proportion' is not zero but a *positive fraction*. The 'extent' to which above-mentioned activities are 'indispensable' is, though he does not know this, the same as the 'extent' to which they are 'necessary but intermediate'. If state and petty private professional activity may be 'to some extent indispensable', it means that 'some' activities of state officials, lawyers, etc. are necessary prerequisites, *sine qua non*, to capitalist production as a whole and not just to capitalists' profit.

The Manichaean view that the state under capitalism acts *only* in the interests of the capitalist class and never in the interest of workers or other citizens has been a staple of Marxian political analysis since the *Communist Manifesto*'s famous 'committee' (Marx and Engels, 1848, p. 18). The 'most efficacious proportion' contains the germ of a more balanced, technocratic view in which government is supplier to all rather than protector of the few. The 'most efficacious proportion' is the nineteenth-century equivalent of Kuznets's idea that government, in providing the externality-rich 'regrettable necessities' of the mixed economy's intermediate 'social framework', is a producer of intermediate capital goods of use to business as well as a producer of final goods for consumers and for itself (Kuznets, 1948; section 8.4.1 below).

Marx takes the typical Classical dim view of the little state officials do in return for the taxes they make us pay. In *Theories of Surplus-Value* it is noted that '[*services*] may also be forced on me – *the services of officials*, etc. . . . [One] has the most to pay for the *compulsory* services (State, taxes)' (1905–10, pp. 405–6; emphasis in original).

The simplest models in contemporary public-choice theory reveal systemic bias towards *underprovision* of externality-rich public goods on account of the incentive individuals have to be free-riders, to conceal their true preferences for tax-financed public goods (Samuelson, 1954). That contrasts with Marx's deeply-held conviction – which he shares with Classical liberals excoriated as vulgar apologists – that the bias goes very much in the other direction, towards *overprovision*. There is bitter complaint about

> [the] great mass of so-called 'higher grade' workers – such as State officials, military people, artists, doctors, priests, judges, lawyers, etc. – *some of whom are not only not productive but in essence destructive*, but who know how to appropriate to themselves a very great part of the 'material' wealth partly through the sale of their 'immaterial' commodities and partly by *forcibly imposing*

> the latter on other people... [They are] *parasites* on the actual producers.
>
> (Marx 1905–10, pp. 174–5; emphasis added)

Surplus generation and transfer without *quid pro quo*, which is what this statement says about economic action by state officials, has implications for class analysis and the Marxian revolutionary political program. Moves towards universal suffrage should temper the *Manifesto*'s pessimistic and Manichaean view of the state as 'nothing but' a 'committee for managing the *common* affairs of the whole bourgeoisie' (1848, p. 18). In vol. I of *Das Kapital* there is the implication that even under direct democracy the capitalist bourgeoisie will succeed in maintaining control over the distribution of income and property by allying with the 'ideological classes' (Marx, 1867, p. 420). Pessimism about political reform squares poorly with the prediction that industrial concentration and centralization will increase. If they do, the proletariat will soon constitute the overwhelming majority of the population, with political consequences.

Political science has outgrown the crude Marxian two-class polity. When representatives, bureaucrats, journalists, lobbyists, etc. interpose themselves between citizen and head of state, and for example enter into coalitions to block redistribution, Marx's dictatorship of the bourgeoisie appears as an extreme if interesting case. It does not do justice to the complexities of a world in which many overlapping constituencies and interest groups defend overlapping positions with dollars, 'votes', and 'their feet' (Lindblom, 1977; Hirschman, 1970; Thurow, 1980).

5.8 Marx as welfare economist

As propaganda, the narrowly defined productive-labor theory, with its industrial factory paradigm, was a stroke of genius. But for Marx the scholar, ambitious to work out a system able to account for the grand and commonplace phenomena of economic history, the factory paradigm is more of a liability than an asset. Its epicycles are of such diameter as to stretch credulity and weaken faith in the basic productive-labor axiom on which the call to revolution is based.

The production–circulation dichotomy and the distinction between single- and multi-person firms could – on the assumption that Marx cared more about coherence than politics – be dropped at relatively low cost to the system as a whole. Those two epicycles do not in principle affect the commitment to the single-factor value theory. They do not impugn the rightness of expropriating the expropriators. To jettison them would, it is true, require enlargement of the productive domain to dimensions needed to avoid input–output error.

Had Marx the scientist realized the seriousness of the economic-theoretical and political trade-offs, he might have taken the step of shortening the list of economic parasites and lengthening the list of productive laborers. Technically the message could still have been exploitation. A casualty of the revisions might have been the *ad hoc* class analysis that relegates wage earners in circulatory and immaterial-service professions to membership in unproductive 'ideological' classes. The aim was undoubtedly to keep the revolutionary proletariat industrially pure and untainted by white-collar petty-bourgeois influence. However, that does not square with the axiom that class membership be determined by 'objective' facts of ownership of physical means of production rather than 'subjective' degrees of identification with society's overlords.

Promoting petty and circulatory enterprises to productive status would inevitably dampen some of the fiery dramatics of technical and institutional change that so charge the atmosphere of *Das Kapital*. What to Marx was that qualitatively new creature Modern Industry, sweeping old organizational and technological forms into the rubbish-bin of history, would be transmuted into a humdrum accretion of flows and seepages across the product and occupational boundaries of a behaviorally-unified, lightly-mixed market economy.

How Marx might have received my editorial suggestions may be divined from the apoplectic comments on 'vulgar political economy' of Say, Senior, Rossi, and Bastiat. It was the self-serving defect of those bourgeois writers to think of the capitalist mode as perpetual and eternal, to treat it as a socioeconomic system of general relevance instead of as the nightmare from which the working class would soon awake. To eliminate the fundamental distinction between petty and capitalist modes would open Marx's *oeuvre* to some of the criticisms he levels against the French. It would also diminish the appeal of his system to those economic historians who find the vivid picture of mid-nineteenth-century Britain, with its prodigious, 'revolutionary' tensions between old and new technological and institutional forms, to be the most interesting economics in Marx.

The factory paradigm is defensible, up to a point. Analysis is scarcely possible without simplifying assumptions. After all, *pace* Hollander, the industrial factory model represents a gain in verisimilitude compared with the 'Ricardian corn model'. By 1861, less than one-fifth of the British labor force was still working in agriculture. In the last analysis, both considerations of empirical realism and Occam's razor ought to have driven Marx the scientist back to the drawing boards. The factory paradigm, even as a portrait of mid-century England, simply leaves too much out of account. By the estimates of Deane and Cole (1967, p. 142), manufacture, mining, and industry did indeed employ over two-fifths (43.6 per cent) of the British occupied population, not including housewives, in 1861. But that leaves three-fifths unaccounted for. It takes the epicycles of Marxian surplus and transfer theory to explain how the remaining millions manage to earn a livelihood. Considering the late date of composition and the simplicity and generality of available alternatives, the Marxian productive-labor theory of value fails to satisfy.

The macroeconomics of *Das Kapital* are in a different league. Marx's writings on the trade cycle have elicited reams of careful scholarship, and I shall not summarize it (Robinson, 1942; Sowell, 1972; Bleaney, 1976; Blaug, 1968; Hollander, 1987). The problem is that the analysis of capitalist crises remains poorly integrated with the theory of surplus-value. A number of reasons are advanced as to why Say's Law (i.e. Identity) might fail to hold, among them the inability of the working class to purchase all the goods they produce. Here the circulation category gets a substantive rôle to play, as a source of additional purchasing power with which to 'realize' the labor-values 'crystallized' in material goods. Again, Marx's economic analysis, as distinct from his political conclusions, is closer to that of Malthus than he would care to admit. His crises too should be permanent, not periodic, as in fact he sometimes says they are.

In welfare terms, the capitalist mode is judged on two criteria: first, the efficacy with which it fulfills its historical mission of creative destruction and ultimate replacement; and second, its fairness *hic & nunc* in providing for the members of society whose economic welfare ought to count. On the first score it gets high marks; it is a veritable dynamo despite some errors and miscalculations. But the subsistence wage postulate (not to speak of immiseration) of the labor theory guarantees a low score on the second. Improvements in efficiency made by exploiting opportunities for cost reduction or price increase are proof of *more efficient exploitation of workers*, not of scarce means in general. Competition is lauded for ensuring prompt introduction of technologies, which, *ceteris paribus*, will concentrate the industrial structure, lower the rate of profit, and worsen instability, hastening the final collapse.

Despite competitive capitalism's positive output dynamics, the idea that the market acts with a coordinating and harmonizing Invisible Hand is rejected as quintessential vulgar economy. The market as institution is the agent not of general equilibrium and smooth growth but of cycles, crisis, and waste, with Hobbesian effect on human character. Both the choice-destroying power of competition and the near-parasitic idleness of the factory owner mean there is little need to pay attention to decision-making or management problems inside the enterprise black box. The other side of the coin of the market as irrational is the belief that '[centralizing] all instruments of production in the hands of the State . . . in accordance with a common plan' will overcome its defects (Marx and Engels, 1848, pp. 54–5).

Marx's view of the market as allocation mechanism is thus in spirit antithetical to Smith's despite the many similarities of view on the power of competition and in spite of large overlap in membership of their unproductive classes. With some help from the dialectic, Marx has both the harmonizing and the chaotic aspects of competition work to worsen the system's long-term prognosis.

Capitalism is reprehended for maintaining workers in material poverty despite capital accumulation and technical change. Perhaps equally seriously, it condemns them to a life of political and spiritual poverty, of powerlessness and 'alienation'. The second count means that changes (reforms, policies) that leave the system intact, however much they may lessen productive laborers' material poverty through either homothetic growth or redistributions of original endowments, can *never* provide reason enough to drop the call for revolution. Not just inequality but the ability of privately-owned tangible capital to generate 'unearned' income robs the capitalist mode of universality, disqualifying it on welfare-economic grounds.

Marx's public-choice theory is Classical except for the fact of two classes of citizenry. Ordinary people have state services 'forced on them' by a bourgeois state that acts in the manner of an Arrovian dictator. The true producers – proletarian productive laborers – are disenfranchised and do not influence the quantity or mix of public goods provided by the state, which acts only in the interest of the bourgeoisie. The socioeconomic universe described by Marx would fail to meet the weak Arrow conditions for citizens' sovereignty (Arrow, 1963, pp. 28–30).

Capitalism's distribution of original endowments of tangible socializable capital is far from that which would maximize the value of a Marxian social welfare function *hic & nunc*. Marx gives the (high) total utilities of the economic parasites zero weight and the (miserable) satisfactions of the workers unit weight. Since the disutility of their work is great and the total utility they can buy with their wages is small, the amount of social welfare generated by capitalism's productive potential is way below what a socialized system promises to deliver for the same resources.

Producer disutility (fatigue, alienation) plus class analysis (including the categoric condemnation of private ownership of transferable producer goods) complicate the calculation of total social welfare enjoyed (suffered) by productive laborers under capitalism beyond what is involved in a Benthamite calculus of pleasure and pain. The Marxian welfare economics of *hic & nunc* is not just a matter of applying 'poverty weights' (à la Chenery *et al.*, 1974) to the output of the capitalist economy, or of, say, using a Rawlsian 'difference principle' to distribute it (Rawls, 1967, p. 329; section 9.1 below).

5.9 Inputs, outputs and epochs

To sum up, Marx restricts the analysis to the 'capitalist mode' when, according to his own statements, economic relationships are in force throughout an 'economy' of which the capitalist mode of production is merely the dynamic core. Even during the heyday of Classical liberalism, the 'capitalist economy' was a 'mixed' one. Numerous passages indicate Marx is aware of mixedness if not of its implications. The writings on pre- and non-capitalist modes suggest that the mixed economy is perceived as inherently unstable, perhaps a 'contradiction' in the dialectical sense. That may have been reason enough to keep the basic 'factory paradigm' free of feedback influence from other sectors. The upshot is that Marx's model provides an incomplete account of even the economic life of mid-nineteenth-century Britain.

The underlying difficulty is Marx the philosopher's inability to decide whether 'materiality' or capitalism is dominant. The resulting ambiguities with respect to the scope of production are left unresolved. Confusion about mode vs. matter prevents a clear understanding of the rôle of inputs *intermediate to* outputs that count in production on the supply side. Attempts of Senior and Rossi to allow for interdependence are dismissed by Marx as 'utter nonsense' (1905–10, p. 294), while in adjacent passages he implicitly accepts the principle of opportunity cost (the 'labour-saving idea'), a positive 'most efficacious proportion' of state to private sectors, and the von Neumannesque possibility that immaterial services (primary schooling) may be *wage goods, requisite for the reproduction of labor-power itself*. The professor of historical materialism wasted little time dismissing such trifling anomalies. They imply however that, on Marx's own input–output logic, the economic domain is too narrow. Too much that is 'base' is displaced into the 'superstructure'.

Part Two

IN A NEW MODE

CHAPTER 6

Materiality and Non-productivity under Mixed Socialism in the USSR

> A market economy can operate without anyone knowing how, and indeed, did so for a long time ... However, by definition, a centrally-planned economy operates according to the conscious designs of men.
>
> (P. C. Roberts, 1971, p. 73)

Karl Marx declined to describe in advance the economic institutions of the socialist future. However, the implication of his verdict on the old 'capitalist' economic order was that it be replaced at first opportunity with a 'socialist' alternative. Against expectations, Russia was the first country to forge a new economic system under the banner of Marxism. The Bolshevik revolution could not remake the world overnight; Marx's views of the 'productiveness' of different occupations under real and petty capitalism remained distressingly relevant. Servants of the Soviet state turned naturally if selectively to the Marxian classics. They sought an economic theory, and an institutional and accounting framework, suitable for producing in backward Russia the conditions History had so far failed to deliver.

This chapter, a Part in itself, looks at mode, materiality, and non-productivity in Russian and Soviet economics from Bazarov (1899) and Lenin (1899) to the first years of the Gorbachev era. I examine how workers in non-industrial occupations are said to 'contribute' to economic development under capitalism, socialism, and the inevitable transitional mixtures of the two. How the USSR came to have a 'material product' system of national economic accounts is described. Note is taken of possible paths of influence of Marxist–Leninist surplus and transfer theory on the share of resources devoted to services in the postwar USSR economy. Finally, the current status of the 'non-productive sphere' is examined in light of other pressing economic issues facing Soviet authorities.

6.1 Labor theorists and Austrians

With the so-called marginalist revolution in economic theory of the 1870s, the banner of unproductive-labor theory passed from Classical to Marxian economists. Austrian, French, and British neoclassicists placed private marketed services on the same footing as goods, and indeed were quick to point out that what we consume when we consume durable (including capital) goods are in fact their 'services' per unit of time. The position taken by neoclassicists *vis-à-vis* the German historical school in the *Methodenstreit* of the 1880s implied that non-market modes could be safely neglected as subjects for special treatment. What is now called the theory of public choice did not yet exist.

Marx's analysis of capitalism had by World War I become part of the intellectual baggage of all economists. Böhm-Bawerk's objections to the labor theory, based on its failure to explain why or how labor-values were transformed into prices actually paid, reached a wide audience (Böhm-Bawerk, 1884, I, pp. 281 ff.; 1896; Dostaler, 1978).

6.1.1 Marxian and other socialisms

The connection between 'really existing socialism' and the socialism that can be distilled from the Marxian classics has caused much ink to flow, and much blood. Kolakowski (1977, 1978) and Nove (1964, 1983) are the eloquent authorities. I follow Wiles and Lavigne in defining an economy as 'socialist' if there is significant commitment to 'socialized', 'collective', 'public' ownership of the (tangible, reproducible) means of production and to elimination of 'unearned' property income from same. The notion that socialism is 'about ownership', while a notoriously poor guide to welfare, has the advantage that the rule governing rights to dispose of tangible capital goods (and patents) is an objective legal datum (Tawney, 1929; Kolakowski and Hampshire, 1974; Montias, 1975). Compared to the idea that socialism is 'about equality', the ownership definition also more closely approximates the views of Lenin and the Bolsheviks on the nature of the revolution to be made.

Marxian or Soviet-type socialist economies are commonly distinguished from the mixed capitalist economies of West European democracies run by 'socialist' parties. The latter have not abolished private property in the means of production; such nationalizations as have occurred have been justified by the neoclassical *theory of externalities*, not by the view of property income explicit in the Marxian productive-labor theory of value. When Western economists like Keynes advocated a 'somewhat comprehensive socialisation of investment' (1936, p. 378) the intention was not for 'plan' to eradicate 'market' but rather for state expenditure to restore the private sector to material and mental health (section 7.1 below).

The pure theory of socialism is strangely unimportant in my story. For participants in the famous 'socialist controversy' of the interwar period – von Mises, Brutzkus, and Hayek and also Lange, Lerner, and Taylor – the category unproductive labor under socialized ownership seems to have been an empty set. Both parties to the discussion over 'perfect computation' and 'perfect central adjustment' (Wiles, 1962, p. 189) accept implicitly but without difficulty the neoclassical view of private, externality-poor goods and services as fundamentally *similar*.

The debate over how a fully socialized economy might work took place on a high level of abstraction, however. Concerns of some importance to Soviet theorists and practitioners, such as whether to include retail trade, watch repair, or public transportation within the compass of the plan and its enterprises, do not get near the center of the Lange–Lerner theoretical stage.

6.1.2   Plan of the chapter

Section 6.2 reports the views of Western and Russian Marxists, over the quarter-century of Lenin's pre-revolutionary formation, on the nature of immaterial services, and on the relevance, under capitalist and transitional modes, of such items as the production–circulation dichotomy. The meager attention paid to surplus and transfer theory's unproductive laborers during the Golden Age of European Marxism proves a negative point – namely, that Marx's prejudices against services and his narrow productive-labor variant of the Classical theory were taken for granted as correct. Once the intellectual bridges between Germany and Russia, Marx and Lenin have been sketched in, my focus shifts to Russian and Soviet theories of economic parasitism. The post-Keynesian history of surplus and transfer theory in the West forms the subject of Chapter 7.

The building of a socialist economy out of a backward, imperfectly capitalist one, it was soon realized, could not be done in a day. Section 6.3 looks at the *ex post* economics of revolution as presented by the Bolshevik party's newly-rehabilitated 'biggest theorist', Nikolai Bukharin. Also recorded are Lenin's extraordinary statements about the work of housewives and central planners.

Sections 6.4 and 6.5 look at theoretical and practical origins of the 'material product system' in Soviet political economy, first as it emerged during the New Economic Policy (NEP) and then as it was finalized under the much more socialized and centralized but still 'mixed' conditions of the Stalin plans. A distinction is drawn for Soviet Marxism between 'socialist utilitarians' and 'socialist materialists'.

Section 6.6 examines resource allocation in light of the notion of 'nonproductive sphere'. Section 6.7 outlines the growing criticisms that contemporary Soviet economists, from Vainshtein to Agabab'ian, Shatalin, Rutgaizer, and Oldak, have leveled against the official doctrine that socialist output consists *only* of the 'material' product of the 'productive sphere'. Overall an effort is made to disentangle bias against services from both distrust of private enterprise and determination to maintain a high rate of investment at the expense of present consumption.

6.2 Golden-Age Marxism from Kautsky to Lenin

6.2.1 Overview and problématique

The period from the founding of the Second International in 1889 to the outbreak of World War I has been described as Marxism's Golden Age (Kolakowski, 1978, II). With the exception of V. A. Bazarov, during that period self-proclaimed Marxists appear to have kept rather easily within the 'productive-labor theory' paradigm and to have accepted the Classical–Marxian division of economic activity into productive and unproductive spheres. Non-Marxist critics seized upon the transformation problem, which is basic but in fact a separate issue from that of the epicycles needed to account for transfers between capitalist and other modes in *Das Kapital*. For Russian Marxists, assumptions about the class loyalties of unproductive laborers conspired with pressing decisions about revolutionary vs. parliamentary politics to ensure that such fascinating abstract topics as mode, materiality, circulation, and the superiority of plan over market did not arouse strong passions whether critical or enthusiastic.

The economics that interested the revolutionary intelligentsia was, for instance, whether an active socialist workers' movement was necessary if capitalism was doomed to collapse anyway under the weight of its internal contradictions. In Marx, one-way dominance of 'base' over 'superstructure' challenged Kautsky and Plekhanov to explain how Napoleons and Caesars could affect events (Kautsky, 1887, 1927; Plekhanov, 1908). The 'materialist conception of history' referred to 'immaterial production' only in that the 'base' was identified with 'material production' and the superstructure with 'ideas'.

It is revealing that Kautsky, long-time leader of orthodox German social democracy, author of numerous works on the 'materialist conception of history' and on Marxian economics, barely mentions the productive–unproductive dichotomy in the numerous editions of *The Economic Doctrines of Karl Marx* (Kautsky, 1887). That is despite the fact that it was he who edited and brought out the three volumes of Marx's posthumous history of economic thought, *Theories of Surplus-Value* (1905–10), in which unproductive laborers play a prominent part. Apparently neither proponents nor opponents realized the depth of the revisions to which the factory paradigm or the philosophy of history might be subject were there to be a major re-examination of Classical–Marxian unproductive-labor doctrine.

6.2.2 *Capitalism's resilience*

On the eve of World War I, nearly fifty years after the publication of volume I of *Das Kapital*, the capitalist economic system had still not broken down. Marxist attention had shifted to matters such as the continued vitality of petty-capitalist agriculture, shopkeeping, and trades. Kautsky's revisionist *bête noir*, Eduard Bernstein, notes the persistence of large numbers of small enterprises in which 'productive and service-performing labour are mixed [*sic*] ... as in bakeries, smithies, etc.' (Bernstein, 1889, pp. 59–61). The failure of the industrial and class structure to polarize as *per* Marx's forecast and Kautsky's 1891 *Erfurt Programme* made the standard Marxian two-class sociology look irrelevant and dampened the hope that a dictatorship of the proletariat would be a kind of majority rule. Those developments might have reopened the mode question but did not.

How to account for the delay of *Zusammenbruch* (breakdown) is the problem addressed by Rosa Luxemburg in *The Accumulation of Capital* (1913). The concern is to find an explanation different from that presented as a dynamic equilibrium model by the Russian legal-Marxist economist M. I. Tugan-Baranovsky in his study of commercial crises in England (Tugan-Baranovsky, 1894, pp. 25–6). The Tugan version of Marx's general-equilibrium reproduction schemata accommodates the failure both of the immiseration postulate and of *Zusammenbruch* by showing that growth by accumulation can continue indefinitely so long as there is sufficient investment.

Rosa Luxemburg understood that Tugan's solution – 'production for production's sake' – 'flies in the face of the actual crisis-ridden course of capitalist development' (Luxemburg, 1913, pp. 335, 342). In her view, an economy can continue to have growing output per man-hour while workers remain at the same or an immiserized consumption level only if 'third persons' step into the national market with sufficient demand to prevent overproduction crisis. 'Third persons' are to be found among the goods-hungry masses of the underdeveloped pre-capitalist (colonized) nations of Asia and Africa.

In Rosa Luxemburg, Malthus's unproductive laborers are in effect adapted to a new situation: the 'third persons' are not an idle rentier class within the metropole capitalist economy, but a classless cluster of consumers on the periphery. Malthus's landlords and clergymen are 'unproductive' in the Smitho-Marxian sense; Luxemburg's hewers of wood and drawers of water in the hinterland are not. In retrospect, her sequence seems altogether fanciful considering the constellation of favorable circumstances required for ex-colonial economies to achieve the self-sustaining export-oriented industrialization she predicts. A more serious objection will be familiar to readers: non-equivalence in exchange is asserted, not proven. What, for example, will colonials offer imperial traders in exchange for the flood of manufactures they obligingly snap up from the center? As an anti-revisionist, she rejects out of hand the notion that the necessary 'third market' may come from center workers themselves as their wages rise above subsistence. Luxemburg's scheme was seen to alter 'the whole basis upon which Marx built his analysis of the capitalist system . . . [Wage] labourers of the advanced capitalist countries are no longer exploited but are joint exploiters with the capitalist classes!' (in Tarbuck, 1972, pp. 31–2).

6.2.3 Enter Russia

The intellectual and political conflicts that exercised Russian Marxists during the nearly two decades separating the founding of the Russian Social-Democratic Labor Party and the overthrow of the Kerensky government by the party's Bolshevik faction in October 1917 need not detain us. In Russia, the intellectual lights of the underground revolutionary movement lost little sleep over the rough spots of Marxian economics. It was the so-called legal Marxists (Tugan-Baranovsky, Frank, Struve, Bulgakov, Prokopovich, Kuskova) who looked carefully enough to revise their views under the double impact of Böhm-Bawerk's objections to the labor theory of value and the promising gains made by reformist trade unions in Germany and England (Kindersley, 1962, pp. 154 ff.).

RUSSIAN ECONOMICS AT THE TURN OF THE CENTURY

Marginalist post-Classical economics had only about a decade to make headway before political revolution in the name of Marxism swept through Russian universities and libraries (Karataev, 1956; Shukhov, 1966; Boss, 1984b). But there were many attempts to reconcile multi-factor and marginalist value theory with Russia's peculiar agricultural and industrial institutions. The liberal populist (Ischboldin, 1971, p. 172) professor, A. A. Isaev, while advocating a socialism based on voluntary cooperatives, cites Alfred Marshall as his authority on the production boundary. All occupations are included that contribute 'directly or indirectly' to 'material production'. That means practically everybody – Isaev explicitly mentions doctors, theoretical chemists, street cleaners, firemen, and the police; only those whose efforts are wasted or not in demand are unproductive (Isaev, 1894, pp. 50–2). Such an approach was rejected outright by Marxists as 'bourgeois'.

Lexis, Davydov, and the liberal populist A. I. Chuprov had taken note of Marx's imperfectly transparent views on transportation, bookkeeping, and the mental labor of staff engineers and overseers. Professor Chuprov, following the standard nineteenth-century interpretation of Smith, included trade but otherwise endorsed the idea that production be 'material'. All three refused economic status to paid personal services and allowed the Ricardian–Marxian view of state revenues as transferred without *quid pro quo* (Davydov, 1900, pp. 163–5; Chuprov, 1902, pp. 125–9; Lexis, 1899). The main bone of contention was how to locate the needed boundary between production and circulation.

BAZAROV FINDS FETISHISM IN MARX

Apart from an article that makes similar points (Davydov, 1900), the fifty-page pamphlet published in 1899 by V. A. Bazarov is the only full-scale work I have found in either the Russian or Western Golden Age literature that is given over exclusively and critically to an analysis of Marx's unproductive-labor theory.

Vladimir Alexandrovich Bazarov (real name Rudnev, 1874–1931?) had a distinguished career as a revolutionary (many arrests and exiles), as a philosopher, as co-translator with Skvortsov-Stepanov of *Das Kapital* (the base for the Russian translation still in use), and as a leading economist in Gosplan in the 1920s. Around 1904 Bazarov abandoned dialectical materialism for the Mach–Avenarius positivism that Lenin was to excoriate in *Materialism and Empiriocriticism* (1909). Bazarov was arrested and disappeared at the time of the Menshevik trial of 1931 (Jasny, 1972, pp. 124–8, 55, 83, 137).

Marx's alleged view that warehousing and transportation are 'unproductive' is the subject of Bazarov's critical booklet *Trud proizvoditel'nyi i trud, obrazuiushchii tsennost'* (*Productive Labor and Labor Which Creates Value*). Like Lenin's *Development of Capitalism in Russia*, it was published legally in St Petersburg in 1899.

Bazarov's approach fits the orthodox Marxian mold in being doggedly mode-minded. Answers to analytical problems depend on the stage of capitalist development. Robinson Crusoe has nothing to teach us. There are no economic universals.

Marx is accused of 'commodity fetishism' on account of his less than crystalline views on activities that 'add value' while being carried out mainly in the 'sphere of circulation', which categorically does not. While upholding the orthodox treatment of pure circulation, Bazarov cites with disapproval Marx's remarks in volume II about transportation not augmenting quantities of material products, and finds a conflict between *Das Kapital*, vol. II, chapter VI, and vol. III, chapter XVII (Bazarov, 1899, pp. 23, 39–40). As we saw in Chapter 5 above, the notion of 'processes of production continuing in the circulation sphere' rehabilitates many functions carried out by firms usually described as wholly engaged in wholesale and retail trade. The idea of dispensing with the circulation category altogether does not occur to Bazarov (or to Davydov or Rubin – Rubin, 1928, pp. 271–2) because, occupied as they were with looking over their shoulders at the historicist progress of mode categories, they do not realize that the drawing of the production boundary is a matter of economist's sovereignty and not an objective fact.

In a foreshadowing of 1920s' discussions, Bazarov notices that a peasantry somewhere between 'natural, for-subsistence production' and fully monetized production for the market 'complicates' the analysis (1899, p. 7). Still, he advocates treating a peasant's production of an axe for own use as 'productive labor', since, in the given social formation, axes are 'socially necessary'. Mode dominance does not prevent non-marketed subsistence production from being 'social' under Russian conditions. 'Social necessity' is determined by what everyone else is doing (1899, p. 8). Only theft, for example, which enriches the individual at the expense of society at large, is 'unproductive' within the 'productive sphere'.

The primacy of mode over matter is instead used to argue that materiality criteria are themselves ahistorical and irrelevant. Comparing published works of literature to oral lectures, Bazarov finds that under capitalism both are 'commodities'. The difference between them is quantitative rather than qualitative, reducing to the 'greater or lesser durability of the material which serves as the condition of their appearing as commodities'. Like John Stuart Mill (who had been widely read owing to the 1860 translation made and annotated by the celebrated radical Chernyshevsky), Bazarov observes that 'many food products, objects whose use-values are of an ultra-material character, . . . are distinguished by their exceptionally short durabilities' (1899, p. 18).

Bazarov's little book is not particularly ambitious, being essentially a gloss on Marx's treatment of bookkeeping and transportation within circulation. Published nearly twenty years before the revolution, it deals exclusively with capitalism. The doctrinal and policy dilemmas of those whose task it would be to apply Marxism to a revolutionary situation are altogether absent. Bazarov does not even broach the question of the productiveness or unproductiveness of servants of the capitalist state. The main interest of *Productive Labor and Labor which Creates Value* is in showing that at least one epicycle of the Marxian productive-labor theory of value, the production–circulation dichotomy, came to the critical attention of *Marxkenner* during the Golden Age. Writers such as Lenin, while not subjecting the themes of this book to any systematic treatment, have many more interesting things to say about productive and unproductive laborers under capitalist, socialist, and transitional modes.

BOGDANOV AS PEDAGOGUE

Alexander Alexandrovich Bogdanov (real name Malinovsky) (1873–1928) is best known as the Social Democrat philosopher whose *Empiriomonism* (1904–6) stimulated Lenin's own 'excursion into philosophy', *Materialism and Empiriocriticism* (1909; Kolakowski, 1978, II, p. 447). Lenin and the Russian Marxists first knew Bogdanov from his economic writings, however. Before becoming interested in Mach and Avenarius, Bogdanov, who was trained as a physician and died of the consequences of a blood-transfusion experiment on himself, legally published an economics textbook entitled *A Short Course of Economic Science* which was warmly reviewed by Lenin in one of his earliest published writings (Bogdanov, 1897; Lenin, 1898). Bogdanov's views on materiality and productiveness are interesting because, as Kolakowski put it, 'for many years the entire Bolshevik party learned economics from his books' (Kolakowski, 1978, II, p. 434).

What did they learn? Mainly, historical–materialist stage theory. The *Short Course* spends the first 200 of its 475 pages tracing a long but predictable path from 'primitive communism' to the 'merchant capitalism' of Reformation Europe. Compared to the first volume of *Das Kapital*, relatively less attention is paid to the productive-labor theory and more recourse is had to sweeping historical overview; individual countries and specific events rarely enter in. Expanded reproduction is described, but there is no attempt to present technical problems like the relative growth rates of Departments I and II. It is acknowledged that in 'backward capitalist countries [*viz*. Russia] ..., intermediate classes like the [petty-bourgeois] petty artisans, peasants, and independent small producers ... particularly the peasants, represent the overwhelming majority of the population', and that the onward march of economic history may be punctuated by bouts of decline or stagnation (1897, pp. 356, 378).

The single paragraph on the post-revolutionary socialist future may have struck an odd note when it was reprinted during the Russian civil war. It contains no hint of stormy transitions between modes or of resistance from groups that might prefer not to join the cooperative socialist brotherhood. As in Marx (Carr, 1952, pp. 7–8), the *Short Course*'s socialist economy is a spontaneous affair. Economic decisions are to be made by 'society as a whole ... [distributing] labour and ... the product of that labour' (Bogdanov, 1897, p. 467).

From the *Short Course* the 'entire Bolshevik party' would have learned next to nothing about non-market allocation of the resources taken over by 'society as a whole'. Production functions, whether explicit or implicit, investment–consumption trade-offs, scarce information, distributional consequences of imperfectly equal talent and effort, shine by their absence. This is the 'theory without which' the Bolsheviks intended to plan the economy (see Smolinski, 1967).

The *Introduction to Political Economy, in Questions and Answers* (1917) outlines Bogdanov's views on capitalism vs. materiality. The catechism goes as follows:

> Does every kind of human labor belong to the domain of production?
> – No, not every kind. In science it is the custom to distinguish productive labor, that is, labor belonging to the domain of production, from unproductive labor.
> What is the distinction between the two?
> – Economists have until now understood this distinction in different ways. Some designate as 'productive' only that labor which creates material, tangible products, and consider all other labor 'unproductive'. From this point of view only the physical labor of peasants, artisans, and workers, and even then not all workers' labor is productive: the labor of workers in the carrying trade does not create a new material product, and for this reason should be considered 'unproductive'. – And, even more so, intellectual labor, e.g., the work of managers, teachers, and so forth. Other economists admit as productive all labor that is needed by society, not only physical, but also mental labor: [under this category] comes the labor of the locksmith, the work of the railway engineer or tram conductor, and the activity of the enterprise director and the teacher. Of course here is not included: (1) destructive activity, for example, that of a murderer or a plunderer; (2) work which simply does not concern society, for example, the activity of personal consumption, which is carried out by every individual entirely in his own interest; or with things like chess games, etc. We choose for ourselves precisely this second conception of productive labor, as the simpler and more convenient one: productive labor for us will mean the same thing as socially useful labor: political economy is the basic science dealing with society, and for political economy *the essence of the matter lies not in the materiality or non-materiality of the result of labor but in its social or non-social character.*
>
> (Bogdanov, 1917, pp. 7–8)

Two views of socialist welfare economics are present: the second, which he favors, I christen 'socialist–utilitarian'; the first, 'socialist-materialist'. On the socialist–utilitarian view, socialism is 'about raising economic welfare'. Goods that increase economic welfare the most are those that are most 'socially necessary'. Socialist utilitarianism is related to Tawney's notion that 'socialism is about equality' in the sense that, if people have similar tastes, social welfare will be highest if incomes are equal and production is concentrated on 'necessities'.

According to the socialist–materialist view, what is universal and supramodal in Marxism is its 'materialism'. A socialist economy's aim must be to increase production of material goods irrespective of their finality. Capital is material and material final goods are necessities.

Bogdanov does not ask the turn-of-the-century equivalent of the question of how and by whom 'social necessity' is to be determined under the dictatorship of the proletariat. Bolsheviks were known for pre-Arrovian nonchalance in weighing social costs and benefits. As the proletarian vanguard, they gave themselves *carte blanche* to speak on behalf of 'society as a whole', a right taken for granted in revolutionary Marxian political thought (Lichtheim, 1969, pp. 87–89, 268–9).

LENIN AS ECONOMIST: FROM DEPARTMENT I TO THE HOUSEHOLD DEPARTMENT

Examined selectively but at face value along dimensions of interest to us, the theoretical writings of Vladimir Il'ich Lenin (Ul'ianov) (1870–1924) contain important affirmations of productive-labor-theory Marxism plus several new points of emphasis. Lenin's principal contribution is to have championed a more dogmatic and indiscriminate use of the term 'materialist' than can be found in Marx, Engels, or Kautsky. Interpretation of Lenin's economic and philosophical pronouncements is complicated by their having been written for the struggle, not the dictionary. Still they cannot be ignored. By virtue of his position, Lenin bequeathed vocabulary, emphasis, and tone to Soviet intellectual discourse that lasted long past his premature departure from the revolutionary stage.

Lenin's post-civil war views on moneylessness, peasants, and markets under War Communism and the NEP (Nove, 1967) are currently in vogue as the leadership seeks to legitimize its efforts to modernize the Stalin system of ministerial control. I overlook them in favor of a selective examination of Lenin's views on materiality, the sources of surplus for investment, the nature of household production, and the economic organization of a socialist state. These were more influential until 1986 and serve to temper enthusiasm for a return to the Bolshevik classics in search of a socialist utilitarianism for our times.

Neither Lenin's 'excursion into philosophy' (Kolakowski, 1978, II, p. 447), *Materialism and Empiriocriticism* (1909), nor *State and Revolution* (written August–September 1917; Lenin, 1917a) can be taken as disinterested scholarship. *Materialism and Empiriocriticism* was designed to inoculate Bolsheviks against idealist tendencies discerned in works of Bogdanov and Lunacharsky, fallen under the debilitating influence of the German 'empiriocritics' Mach and Avenarius. In that battle for revolutionary hearts and minds, Lenin propounds a brutal materialism according to which 'sensations, abstract ideas, and all other aspects of human cognition are ... ["nothing but"] copies, photographs, images, mirror-reflections ... in our minds of actual qualities of the material world' (Kolakowski, 1978, II, pp. 453–4). The aim is to corner the market on 'hard', 'objective' materialism, the better to accuse opponents like the ex-legal-Marxist Petr Struve, author of the 'idiographic' treatise *Economy and Price* (Struve, 1913), of such deviations as 'metaphysical materialism', and *'[being] afraid to say the production of material products'* (sic!) (Lenin, 1914b, p. 198, emphasis added). *Materialism and Empiriocriticism* 'enhanced Lenin's reputation among the Bolshevik rank and file as a materialist and a Marxist' (Olgin, 1969, p. 110).

In *The Development of Capitalism in Russia: the process of the formation of a home market for large-scale industry* (1899), Lenin shows he has no bone to pick with the basic axioms and corollaries of Marxian productive-labor value and breakdown theory. On the contrary, the point is to prove Russia is already well advanced along the path Marx correctly foretold for all. Capital accumulation means increasing the stock of material capital. The (industrial) proletarian is the economy's archetypal, if not its only, productive laborer. Later Lenin goes further than even Marx in presenting the self-sufficient smallholding peasantry as reactionary and unable 'by its very nature [to develop the] social productive forces of labor ... social concentration of capital, large-scale cattle-raising, and the progressive application of science' (Lenin, 1914a, p. 70). It is important to prove and capitalize politically on the fact that the poorer peasants are being proletarianized into the natural allies of the working class (Carr, 1952, pp. 10–24; Olgin, 1969, p. 110; Shanin, 1985).

The Development of Capitalism in Russia contains the 'all too well-known assertion concerning the priority of the rate of growth of Department I [means of production] over that of Department II [articles of consumption]' (Nove, 1967, p. 193).

> [The] main conclusion from Marx's theory of realization is the following: capitalist production, and, consequently, the home market, grow not so much on account of articles of consumption as on

account of means of production ... The department of social production which produces means of production has, consequently, to grow faster than the one which produces articles of consumption.
(Lenin, 1889, p. 30)

Besides identifying economic development with industrialization, Lenin makes the statement, which will come in handy in 1928/9, that 'productive consumption [of materials and capital goods] ... can and must increase faster than [ordinary consumption of the population]' (1899, p. 54).

'Reproduction on a progressively increasing scale', i.e. accumulation, can mean either a 'positive' or an 'increasing' rate of growth. Under accelerating growth with a constant capital–output ratio, 'each year a larger proportion of the product would have to be laid aside for future use, and so the share of consumption would fall ... [until] all output would consist of producers' goods and the consumers would all starve to death' (Nove, 1967, p. 196). Soviet economic writing rarely made the distinction explicit before the late 1950s but has done so since (Gerschenkron, 1968b on Pashkov, 1958; Shatalin, 1987c, p. 4).

The distinction between 'production of commodities' in non-capitalist or revolutionary modes of production and 'production of use-values' by individuals in rural or urban households is maintained by Lenin in several connections. Non-commodity-producing domestic household labor is the object of Vladimir Il'ich's undisguised scorn, both on account of low capital intensity and correspondingly low labor productivity, and because of the pre-capitalist organizational form or mode. The essay 'Karl Marx' (written July–November 1914; Lenin, 1914a) presents the Marxist positivist view of *industry* as the mortal enemy of patriarchal attitudes and obscurantism. Cited with approval is Marx's forecast of *Das Kapital*, vol. I, that

> modern industry, by assigning ... an important part in the process of production, outside the domestic sphere, to women, to young persons, and to children of both sexes, creates a new economic foundation for a higher form of the family and of the relations between the sexes.
> (Marx, 1867, p. 460, miscited by Lenin in 1914a, p. 191)

The analysis of housework in Lenin's post-revolutionary speeches is forty, though not sixty, years ahead of its time (section 8.4 below). In an address to non-Party working women in September 1919, it is noted that legislating equality between the sexes in the paid labor force is only a first step towards *de facto* equality. Few feminists today, however, would make Lenin's leap from diagnosis to cure.

> For the full liberation of women and for real equality with men it is necessary for the economy to be socialized [*sic*] and for women to participate in general productive labor.
>
> (Lenin, 1919b, p. 43)

He observes, 'You all know that even when women have full equality under the law there remains actual oppression of women because all the housework is left to them'. Lenin's opinion of work performed in the home is a chauvinistically low one:

> Housework in the majority of cases is the most unproductive, most barbaric, and most arduous labor a woman can do. This work is *exceptionally petty*, containing *nothing* which might in some degree promote woman's development.
>
> (Lenin, 1919b, p. 43; emphasis added)

Rising expectations are cautioned against: 'the building of socialism will begin only when we, having achieved the full equality of women, undertake new tasks together with women who have been emancipated from this *petty, stultifying, unproductive* labor. This is a job which will take many, many years' (Lenin, 1919b, p. 43; 1950, vol. 30, p. 25, my translation, emphasis added).

A pamphlet published in July 1919 ('A Great Beginning') uses exceedingly violent imagery to make the point that

> Women continue to remain *domestic slaves*, despite all the liberating legislation, because *petty domestic labor* **crushes, strangles, stultifies, stupefies and degrades them, chaining** them to the kitchen and the nursery, **wasting** their labor [potential] on work that is **unproductive, petty, insignificant, nerve-wracking, stultifying and forgettable to the point of barbarism.**
>
> (Lenin, 1919a, p. 429; 1950, vol. 29, pp. 428–9, my translation, double emphasis added)

Obviously views such as these did not leave much room for the principle that the welfare-economic *raison d'être* of a socialist organizational form is that it is more successful at increasing use-values that are *truly final*. Faith in collective social institutions joins with mode-mindedness to defend the Classical view that no production worthy of the name occurs in the household.

With high hopes for communal kitchens and day-nurseries and contempt for housework, it was easier for Lenin's successors to interpret the enormous increases in female labor-force participation rates during the prewar five-year plans as yielding *pure net gains* to society as a whole. Those who formerly eked out an existence as unproductive domestic slaves had been mobilized to build the material and technical basis for communism.

A *catalogue raisonné* of Lenin's pronouncements over the course of three decades on the economic rôle of 'the state' is an exercise of mental labor I propose to divide with someone else. Because the success of the overthrow of tsarism demanded that tactics be changed as the situation required and that the pen be an instrument in the struggle, it is difficult for the analytically minded economist to evaluate the degree of *bona fide* naïveté in such semi-anarchist pamphlets as *State and Revolution*, written in hiding in August–September 1917, with its extraordinary promises about 'the economic base of the withering away of the State' (Lenin, 1917a, ch. V, pp. 473–5; also 1917b, pp. 102–6; 1917c, p. 324). An institution whose disappearance is looked to as proof of the victory of the armed workers' democracy over 'exploiters', capitalists, and 'the intellectual gentry' (1917a, p. 474) cannot have been regarded as economically 'productive' in any absolute sense, whatever its historical importance in forcing the transition from capitalism to the 'first phase of Communist society'. Again, the reader interested in Lenin's economic theory of socialism runs up against a strange brew of historical and logical categories. It is Rodbertus's old problem (Pipes, 1980, p. 128) and indeed the basic problem with the application of dialectical reasoning to economic time series. In Chapter 5, I called it 'history vs. microeconomics'.

The link between radical materialist–fallacist unproductive labor theory as the foundation of one's economic *Weltanschauung* and the conception of 'planning' of political or industrial revolution in 'voluntarist' rather than 'determinist' terms is a fascinating subject but not one we can pursue here. It is discussed with some brilliance by Berdyaev (1937, ch. VI.v), Kolakowski (1978, II), Ulam (1979), Nove (1969, chs 3–5), Cohen (1971, ch. IV), and Popper (1947, chs 13–15).

While the Marxian productive-labor theory was not much of an issue in the pre-revolutionary theoretical and factional struggles of the Second International, we have yet to see whether its view of the parasitism of certain classes and occupations is better described as a pawn or a general in the ideological and resource-allocational battles that will shape the institutions of history's first socialist economy.

6.3 Bukharin's economics of revolution

With the Bolshevik consolidation of power, elaboration of laws and operational rules of socialist transformation of the devastated economy became an immediate if difficult task. The problem of the relationship of Bolshevik thought to the letter or the spirit of Marx's economic writings became immeasurably more acute. Anyone who agreed with Marx's mode-minded analysis of 'vulgar economy' would think twice before applying categories worked out for capitalism, such as 'value', 'surplus-value', and 'socially necessary labor-time', to an economic system in which exploitation, *defined as a unique function of private ownership of the (tangible) means of production*, had ceased to exist in major sectors.

The fundamental tenet of revolutionary Marxism - that social ownership of the means of production would *change everything* - encouraged the aim of ultimate victory over the market, over capitalist, 'commodity' production. Government control of crafts production, allocation of labor by decree as in the army, substitution of collective commodity exchange and wages in kind for their monetized equivalents, were among the measures tried during the Bolsheviks' first attempt to transform the economy, the desperate period of civil war and industrial collapse known as War Communism (mid-1918–mid-1921) (Kolakowski, 1978, II, p. 482; Nove, 1969, ch. 3; Malle, 1985; Remington, 1987).

Marx was intentionally vague about the structure and functioning of the socialist economy and polity. What he seems to have expected above all on the economic side was a tremendous spontaneous unleashing of productivity, which would move the economy from the 'realm of necessity' to the 'realm of freedom' (Marx, 1867, p. 715). Now the future had, so to speak, arrived. As foretold, it came into the world bearing the bloody stigmata of the capitalist past.

If the transition to socialism had been truly instantaneous and complete, fidelity to the relativistic, orthodox, 'modist', anti-utopian Marx would have confronted Bolshevik theorists with an ideological and economic–theoretical *tabula rasa*. Two sets of factors conspired against throwing Marx's writings to the winds: the need to legitimize the régime and its policies, and the obvious fact of capitalist remnants. Nikolai Bukharin made an interesting attempt to work out an economics of revolutionary transformation that took account of those factors.

Lenin's earliest and most strictly 'economic' works predate by nearly two decades those of the writer he will describe as 'the party's biggest theorist' (Cohen, 1971, p. 83). After Lenin's anarchistic pamphlet *State and Revolution* (1917a) and 'Can the Bolsheviks Retain State Power?' (Lenin, 1917b), Bukharin presents the most interesting original economic interpretation of the revolutionary process itself and of the nature of the transition to socialism, as seen from the viewpoint of events in the immediate post-revolutionary period.

Bukharin, rehabilitated in 1988 from the charge of treason and remembered now as a defender of NEP against the Left, began his politico-literary career in Bolshevism with a fierce attack on neoclassical distribution theory. Of the 'old' Bolsheviks who lived in exile in Western Europe before 1917, Bukharin was said to be among those best acquainted with theoretical developments occurring in Western Europe in the decades since Marx's death. He knew Western languages, and is said to have been familiar with the post-Marxian sociology of Max Weber, Max Adler, and Werner Sombart, and with the 'new', neoclassical economics of Böhm-Bawerk and J. B. Clark. Bukharin's notions of Austrian economics were acquired at the feet of Böhm-Bawerk himself at the University of Vienna in 1911–12 (Cohen, [1971] 1973, p. 19). But like Marx's readings of the Classics in *Theories of Surplus-Value*, not all of the arguments sank in.

His first theoretical work, *Politicheskaia ekonomiia rant'e: teoriia tsennosti i pribyli avstriiskoi shkoly* (translated as *The Economic Theory of the Leisure Class*; Bukharin, 1919), which was completed in the autumn of 1914, aimed to provide a systematic critique of both the logical and the class foundations of the Austrian school. A second volume was planned, on the Anglo-American neoclassicals, to star the arch-Panglossian J. B. Clark, but it was abandoned during the war to leave room for a more important subject: *Mirovoe khoziaistvo i imperializm (Imperialism and the World Economy*; Bukharin, 1918, translated 1929; Cohen, 1971, p. 22, n. 78).

The Economic Theory of the Leisure Class is Marxian surplus and transfer theory at its crudest, livened with a 'sauce' of the 'hard' materialism that had become a Bolshevik trademark with Lenin's *Materialism and Empiriocriticism*. The emergence of a rentier class, whose assets finance the activities of both the banks and the state, is *the* characteristic feature of 'monopoly capitalism'.

> This [rentier] stratum of the bourgeoisie is distinctly parasitical; it develops the same psychological traits as may be found in the decayed nobility at the end of the ancien régime . . . It participates directly neither in the activities of production nor in trade; its representatives often do not even cut their own coupons. The 'sphere of activities' of these rentiers may perhaps be most generally termed the *sphere of consumption*. Consumption is the basis of the entire life of the rentiers and the 'psychology of pure consumption' imparts to this life its specific 'style' . . . A rentier, if he speaks of work at all, means the 'work' of picking flowers or calling for a ticket at the box office of the opera. *Production, the work necessary for acquiring material commodities*, lies beyond his horizon and is therefore an accident in his life . . . [On the other hand, the] proletariat *lives in the sphere of production, comes in direct contact with 'matter', from which it is transformed into 'material'*, into an object of labor.
>
> (Bukharin, 1919, p. 26; emphasis added)

Bukharin does not hesitate to identify Marx's revolutionary class with 'industrial' workers who produce 'material' goods. Presumably he allows, following Marx, the transportation and warehousing of such goods as proletarian occupations. But otherwise there is not much middle ground. The view of producers and parasites is more Manichaean than even that of the 'political' Marx of the *Manifesto*, not to speak of *Das Kapital*, vols I and III. There at least the capitalist is 'actively' engaged in running his factory (Marx, 1867, p. 557; 1894, pp. 383–7).

As editor of *Pravda* (December 1917 – April 1929) and author with Evgeny Preobrazhensky of the *Azbuka kommunizma (The ABC of Communism,* 1919), and as sole author of *Ekonomika perekhodnogo perioda (The Economics of the Transition Period;* Bukharin, 1920) and *Istoricheskii materializm (Historical Materialism,* 1921), Bukharin established himself as 'Bolshevism's leading, and eventually official, theorist'. Lenin called him the party's 'biggest theoretician' (Cohen, 1971, p. 17, n. 56, p. 22, n. 78). Given Bukharin's 1988 rehabilitation as a moderate, it is instructive to reread his analysis of War Communism.

The *ABC of Communism*, which by the early 1930s had been translated and reprinted in eighteen Russian editions and twenty foreign translations (Cohen, 1971, p. 83), and the more specific *Economics of the Transition Period* (Bukharin, 1920), have been said to reflect War Communism's 'militant optimism, invigorated by the belief that "what Marx prophesied is being fulfilled under our very eyes"' (Cohen, 1971, p. 84, citing Bukharin, 1919, p. 25). A Bukharin scholar observed that

> while a great body of commentaries on the evils of capitalism ... had built up over the years, conspicuous gaps in Marxian revolutionary theory remained – most notably the virtual lack of any detailed treatment of the revolutionary process itself and the nature of the future Communist society which it was to bring about ... Consequently, the *ABC of Communism* became not merely a commentary on the [Party Program, adopted at the 8th Congress in March 1919,] but rather the most complete and systematic compendium of Marxist–Leninist theory produced until that time ...
> (Heitman, intro. to Bukharin and Preobrazhensky, 1919)

The *ABC* opens with an account of the stages of capitalist development standard since the time of Karl Kautsky's *Economic Doctrines of Karl Marx* (1887) and *The Erfurt Programme* (1891) and Bogdanov's *Short Course of Economic Science* (1897). Those works are recommended for 'those who wish to carry their studies further' (1919, pp. 16, 48, 68).

Communism, Marx's second, higher stage of socialism, is the future mode of plenty and social harmony visible 'two or three generations' down the road (Bukharin and Preobrazhensky, 1919, p. 75). Lenin's October 1917 description of socialist organization and planning as essentially bookkeeping is endorsed (Bukharin and Preobrazhensky, 1919, p. 74; see Lenin, 1917a, pp. 473–4, Lenin, 1917b, p. 106). Though the benefits of social division of labor will be retained, under communism citizens will be more or less interchangeable in the workplace. Variety will vanquish alienation.

> The main direction will be entrusted to various kinds of bookkeeping offices or statistical bureaux ... Moreover, in these statistical bureaux one person will work today, another tomorrow. The bureaucracy, the permanent officialdom, will disappear. The State will die out.
> (Lenin, 1917a, p. 474; Bukharin and Preobrazhensky, 1919, p. 74)

The 'Advantages of Communism' (Bukharin and Preobrazhensky, 1919, ch. 3, sec. 22) are not confined to job variety. Communism holds the additional advantage of ensuring *'more* rapid development of the forces of production' than was possible under the capitalist system, which Marx in volume I of *Das Kapital* described as a 'fetter' *on production itself* and not just on its more egalitarian distribution.

> In the first place, there will have ensued the liberation of the vast quantity of human energy which is now absorbed in the class struggle ... Secondly, the energy and the material means which now are destroyed or wasted in competition, crises, and wars, will be saved.
> (Bukharin and Preobrazhensky, 1919, p. 75)

'Thirdly, the organization of industry on a purposive plan' will enable the scale of production to rise and extend the use of machinery even to labor-intensive sectors like agriculture. '[In] so far as large-scale production is *always* more economical [*sic*] ... the communist method of production will signify an enormous development of productive forces', in contrast with the situation under capitalism, where 'there are definite limits to the introduction of new machinery' (p. 76; emphasis added). Fourth, 'parasitism will ... disappear ... The capitalists, their lackeys, and their hangers-on (priests, prostitutes, and the rest), will disappear, and *all the members of society will be occupied in productive labor*' (pp. 76–7; emphasis added).

As we know by now, for Bukharin's fourth proposition to hold, those accused of economic parasitism must not be engaged in activities intermediate or 'necessary' to the production of the now more limited basket of social products. In particular, 'parasites' must not produce anything that 'non-parasites' or 'society as a whole' require as a 'necessity' or 'wage good'. Otherwise it is a case of political economy's common childhood illness 'input–output error'. If the reallocation of 'parasites' to 'productive activities' can be effected without net loss of welfare due to curtailment of formerly 'superfluous' activities, 'society as a whole' can only gain, on the assumption that its goal is to maximize the number of new consumption baskets per period - or, as in the Fel'dman model, the rate of growth of baskets (Fel'dman, 1928a, b).

However smooth distributionally-progressive reaffectations may look in the abstract, Bukharin stands out as the Party theorist who most forcefully *opposes* the naïve prewar social democratic belief of Kautsky and Hilferding that the 'transition to socialism would be relatively painless' (Cohen, 1971, p. 89; Hilferding, 1910, in Fieldhouse, 1967, p. 75; Bukharin, 1920, p. 55).

> The theoreticians of castrated Marxism, like Kautsky, have a truly childish conception of revolutionary upheavals. For them, theoretical and practical problems which pose the greatest difficulty simply do not exist . . .
> (Bukharin, 1920, p. 179, n. 41)

In later chapters of the *ABC* and in the more comprehensive *Economics of the Transition Period*, Bukharin asserts that all great revolutions are accompanied by destructive internal conflict (civil war).

> A temporary decline of productive powers which, objectively considered, in the last analysis extended their strength, occurred also in the bourgeois revolutions.
> (Bukharin, 1920 p. 179, n. 41)

The list of 'real costs of revolution' is a long one. It includes partial or complete destruction of physical and human elements of production, decay of the interconnections between those elements and between sectors of the economy, and an increased budget for 'unproductive expenditures' that are required to wage war in the revolution's defense. Taken together, the result is *'curtailment of the process of reproduction'* and even *'negative expanded reproduction' (sic!)* - a phenomenon that is elevated to an 'historically inevitable stage . . . [of] production anarchy . . . which no amount of lamentation will prevent' (Bukharin, 1920, pp. 42, 97–8; also pp. 105–10). The destruction of the economic apparatus bequeathed by capitalism is subtly related to Russia's troublesome unreadiness for socialism by the lights of orthodox Marxian stage theory. '[By] arguing that this apparatus was invariably destroyed in the process of revolution . . . Bukharin subtly dismissed the nagging question of Russia's relative backwardness (unripeness). He emphasized the "human" rather than the "material" apparatus as the essential criterion of maturity . . .' (Cohen, 1971, p. 90).

In 'The Advantages of Communism', the radiant future is sketched using a *ceteris paribus* comparison between past and future modes. But what is the path like between them? *The Economics of the Transition Period* makes the case for actual Bolshevik policies during War Communism: abolition of money (after inflation had rendered it worthless), attempts to 'plan' industrial and even handicraft production and to distribute in kind, and virtual confiscation of peasant grain supplies for the Red Army and the cities. By 1921, war, food shortages, and industrial collapse had reduced the working class, in whose name the revolution had been made, to half its 1913 size (Nove, 1969, pp. 55–7; Grossman, 1973, pp. 492–3).

Elevating the 'costs of revolution' to the level of basic stage is an embarrassing qualification to the socialist–utilitarian claim that the main advantage of communism is its superior productiveness, the plenty it brings to the people. Between capitalism and communism (Marx, 1875; Lenin, 1917a, p. 469) costly intermediate stages are now inevitable. Depending on how large and over how long a period, these costs may exceed the discounted benefits for cohorts of individuals who must live out most of their lifetimes during the bad years. Under non-lexicographic comparisons between modes, the upshot could be that the economic *status quo* is preferred to very distant improvements. Lenin did not fail to note that possibility, but in *State and Revolution* wisely avoided going too deeply into the matter of the time to elapse before society as a whole could be expected to break even. My rough calculation using a discount rate of zero - which implies absolute indifference between good and bad years (marginal utility of consumption absolutely constant) - reveals that *lifetime average per capita consumption* catches up with the *1913 per capita consumption level* only after 58 years (in 1971) and only for those who survive the entire period (Boss, 1986d).

Despite his book-length attack on Böhm-Bawerk, Bukharin's economics of revolution skirts the question of the low, even negative, rates of time preference implied in projected Bolshevik industrialization plans, even though 'communism' is described as lying 'two or three generations down the road'. In mid-NEP a new, mature Bukharin emerged as an apostle of gradualism and accommodation with the peasantry, resigning himself to moving towards socialism 'at a snail's pace' (Erlich, 1960, p. 78; Cohen, 1971, p. 135). That gave Stalin cause against him, and led to his ousting and eventual execution.

6.4 Output under incomplete socialism from Prokopovich to the Stalin textbook: the theoretical options

6.4.1 Uses of Marxian doctrine

Keynes's *bon mot* about the power of ideas was perhaps never truer than during the plan era. Its ideologues advocated schemes for transforming industry and collectivizing agriculture that looked to be 'ruled by little else' (Keynes, 1936, p. 383).

Some have minimized the importance of ideological factors in fashioning the institutions and practices of the Soviet experiment (Gerschenkron, 1969, pp. 14–17; Berliner, 1964, p. 2). They cite the many violations of orthodox Marxian economic and social doctrine made in the name of consolidation of Soviet power and forced industrialization.

The Bolsheviks' *self-imposed* choices of scope, aims, and institutions cannot in my view be understood without reference to Marx; as Erlich said, 'they did not come from Buddhism'. The speed with which Marx-appointed goals were pursued is another matter.

Marxian mode-mindedness is at the root of the belief that a mixture of modes was ultimately an intolerable threat, a 'contradiction' threatening a dialectical 'catastrophe' that would lead either 'back' to capitalism or in the 'other' direction. The intense concern with whether or not goods were produced and sold under capitalist conditions accounts for the prominence, in the journals and statistical publications of the NEP and the first five-year plans, given to correctly identifying the different ownership types and to recording the mode structure of each industry - concerns placed on a par, or nearly so, with the recovery of output itself (Vaisberg, 1927a; Boss, 1986c). It takes Marx's normative analysis of capitalism to make sense of the virulence of the Bolsheviks' mistrust of the market as institution and of the belief that its alleged antithesis, 'conscious' planning, was a necessity to be extended to the most minor enterprise decision under any socialism worthy of the name.

That is not to say that key elements of the orthodox Marxian stage theory were not set aside by voluntarist Bolsheviks when it came to seizing power and using it to build socialism in a backward country. But once the advanced capitalist stage was seen to have been skipped, bygones were bygones and 'anarchy of social production' was to be replaced at the first opportunity by 'conscious organization on a planned basis'. The economic agenda was modified to one of creating conditions history had not yet managed to deliver.

Here Marxism was used not as a method for deriving objective economic laws of capitalist development, as Berliner argues was its original mandate (1964, p. 2), but rather as the body of doctrine that insisted on the need for, and provided key elements of, a specifically socialist value theory with its own product concept and allocation mechanism. Disagreement over the scope of output under mixed Soviet socialism, revealed in the tension between 'socialist materialists' and 'socialist utilitarians' (sections 6.4.3–6.4.5), can be laid directly to the many ambiguities in the Master's legacy. For example, confusion over 'historical' vs. 'microeconomic' categories produced the dilemma of whether 'materiality' (or money sale) of products would still affect the location of the production boundary once the capitalist 'mode' was declared beaten.

The next sections look at how notions of materiality and non-productivity figured in the Soviet industrialization debates of the 1920s (section 6.4) and at the rôle they played in the formation of the Soviet statistical and data-gathering system that took shape during the NEP and the prewar Stalin period (section 6.5). I also present some data bearing on the question of whether theory affected resource allocation (section 6.6).

Marx said little about the post-revolutionary economy except that it would be the *antithesis* (*sic*) of the capitalist one. Anarchy of production would be replaced by a 'vast common plan'. Wages would not equal per capita GNP because of deductions for investment, administration, basic education, invalid and old-age pensions, etc., and workers would continue to be paid according to their contribution to total social product for the duration of the scarcity phase (Marx, 1875).

But what was socialist social product? Material private goods, food and clothing, 'necessities'? What about literacy? Would resources devoted to planning be treated as intermediate expenses alongside, or 'prior to', inputs used in producing coal and steel? What about the continued relevance of the celebrated distinction, which Marxists insisted on for capitalism, between 'production' and 'circulation'? How to handle the 'immaterial' services of transport and communications, in particular, the fraction of them consumed by individuals? What would be the effect of varying the allocation mechanism? Would the fact that the expenses of the Ministry of Education, say, were paid out of the state budget and distributed directly to the citizenry 'according to plan' rather than sold to them for rubles be enough to render education 'unproductive'?

On a more philosophical plane, would the economic base under socialism still be 'material'? Or would the fact of proletarian control of commanding heights be reason enough to get planned final 'immaterial' services reclassified from the 'superstructure' to the 'base'?

Evidently the theoreticians of the NEP economy had their work cut out for them. In particular, questions *easy for Marxists to answer with respect to full socialism* became decidedly more problematic when applied to the NEP economy, with its 25 million peasant households. As Stalin put it (following Lenin's description of the kulak), these '[breed] capitalism ... constantly, every day, every hour, spontaneously, massively' (Stalin, 1954, vol. 12, p. 43).

6.4.2 *Materialist outlook of some non-Bolsheviks*

In trying to work out the influence of the different currents of self-proclaimed Marxian materialism on the Soviets' choice of plan target, it is important to recall that a materialist outlook on economic life was not a Bolshevik monopoly. Western theorists since Say and Marshall had ceased to treat services sold on markets as fundamentally different from material goods (ch. 4 above). Circumstances virtually guaranteed the non-participation in Soviet economic life of writers holding such 'reactionary' views. But other groups often quite critical of Bolshevik policy participated in economic data-gathering and analysis until the late 1920s.

Mensheviks and ex-Mensheviks for example were prominent in Gosplan and the Central Statistical Administration (TsSU) until the launching of the first plan. Their quarrel with the Bolsheviks concerned the speed and financing of an industrialization and socialization drive that they both ardently desired, rather than, for instance, whether or not immaterial products should be included in the transition economy's productive base.

The most 'Right-wing' current still active before 1929 was the neo-Narodnik school of Kondrat'ev (Kondratieff) and Chaianov. Before the revolution, neo-Narodniks accepted enough of the Marxian view of the evils of private ownership to recommend socialization of the land, with industry to follow (Boss, 1984b; Radkey, 1955).

It is significant that S. N. Prokopovich, a former Social Democrat and legal Marxist, Minister of Food in the Provisional Government and by the civil war an open enemy of the régime, seems to have felt no obligation to revise his view of immaterial services as unproductive. Though he broke decisively with Lenin and revolutionary Marxism at the turn of the century, in the course of a half-century of economic scholarship in Russia and in emigration Prokopovich treated the national economy as made up of only six productive branches: agriculture, fisheries and forestry, industry, transport, construction, and trade (Prokopovich, 1917, p. 83; 1918; 1930, p. 7; 1931–2; 1952, pp. 380–3).

Given NEP politics, this left in positions of potential influence only the few ex-members of other parties still active as economists. What was their attitude to 'immaterial' services likely to be? A reading of Karataev (1956, p. 211) and a quick run through the scores of pre-revolutionary manuals and treatises of political economy leave the impression that Russian economics was only just beginning its marginal revolution, only beginning to think in terms of m goods and n factors, when another revolution swept through its schools and libraries (Boss, 1984b; Shukhov, 1966; Normano, 1945; Seraphim, 1925; Ischboldin, 1971).

Thus not only self-styled Marxists but those whose education had included large doses of John Stuart Mill or Smith (or their Russian exponents such as Chuprov) may indeed not have given much thought to the logic of putting 'immaterial' services on the same footing as goods.

6.4.3 *A Bolshevik socialist utilitarian: S. G. Strumilin*

Among Bolsheviks too there was room for disagreement about what deserved to be included as output in the hybrid socialist economy of the NEP. A 'socialist–utilitarian' scheme for combining the various activities into a product aggregate was advanced in an August 1926 paper (Strumilin, 1926) published in the Gosplan organ *Planovoe khoziaistvo (Planned Economy)* by the prolific economist and future academician Stanislav Gustavovich Strumilin (1877–1974). Strumilin is hard to accuse of being soft on 'geneticism' (Nove, 1969, p. 132): though an ex-Menshevik, by the late 1920s he had become a leading *planovik* who repeated Stalin's arch-voluntarist 'fortress' slogan that was the first five-year plan's unofficial motto. Strumilin's national accounting proposal prefigures that of F. Thomas Juster (section 8.4.3 below) as well as harking back to Marx; the latter's contribution is mainly to provide a short list of social parasites. Output in Strumilin boasts both material goods and immaterial services, including externality-rich public ones. The sole requirement is 'social necessity'. For example,

> the services of a doctor or a teacher are without productive effect only in those cases where they are applied to the healing or the instruction of rentiers, priests, fortune-tellers, thieves, prostitutes and similar parasitical elements of society. In all other cases, when they serve the reproduction of socially-useful labor power, their productive effect is indisputable. In this event they by no means disappear from society without a trace, but have, first in the person of healthy and educated workers, and then in the tangible projects of their labor, definitely a long-lasting existence.
> (Strumilin, 1926, p. 156)

If the term human capital is substituted for labor power, Strumilin appears as a pioneer of the modern concept despite the fact that the present value of his contribution is tarnished by characteristic Marxian reluctance to discount (Blaug, 1970, p. 230). Since labor-power must be reproduced, everyday 'immaterial' services like water supply, electricity, sewage (*sic!*), cafeterias, day-care centers, and so on, deserve to be included in the Soviet total picture on the basis of their wage bills plus profit (if any). It would have been simpler to argue that under socialism all legally remunerated labor should count, even labor employed making consumption goods with no obvious reproductive rôle. But that was alien to the Classical–Marxian tradition of unproductive occupations and supply-oriented value theories. Strumilin smooths the way for inclusion of personal services by endowing them with an investment-like and therefore positive character.

The degree to which a little nationalization could change the picture for those who care about ownership modes and commodity-hood is illustrated by Strumilin's original interpretation of production in the peasant economy. Marx, it will be recalled, had described peasant production as 'outside the capitalist mode' and beyond the pale of economic analysis (1905–10, p. 407). Writes Strumilin,

> [If] in such a country as the USSR there is, on a par with commodity production, an enormous share of the national income produced in *natural* form [without passing through the market], then we have of course to include separately in that sphere, on a par with the natural agricultural production of the peasant farmer, also the unpaid services of his wife or other members of his family in his household. All these: commodities, non-marketed subsistence goods and services [are the product of] socially necessary labor. Any increase in their production in and of itself denotes a rise in the general level of productive forces of the country.
> (Strumilin, 1926, p. 147)

More daringly, considering what Lenin had had to say on the emancipation of women, Strumilin argues that what goes for peasant agriculture holds equally for housework, whether performed by paid domestics or family members. Even the 1968 United Nations revised System of National Accounts, in distinguishing between 'primary' and 'non-primary' production, effectively limits user countries' responsibility in the matter of imputation to subsistence agriculture; unpaid housework is regarded as leisure (section 8.2 below). For housework Strumilin's argument is that:

> we include [in the national income] remuneration of the labor of the servant and all housewives according to the norms for unskilled

urban and rural labor. . . . [The] services of a housewife, paid or unpaid, are in no way inferior in their social usefulness to the services of a hired servant . . . In exactly the same way, bread produced for sale materializes in itself no less socially necessary labor than does bread produced for consumption in the household. And once we no longer impugn the necessity of including in national income all bread, *irrespective of its commodity-hood*, then we ought to include *all services, irrespective of their marketedness.*
(Strumilin, 1926, p. 160)

Finally, for Strumilin, in a workers' state, even the army and the entire state administration are not only 'socially necessary' but wholly productive. Withering-away is not mentioned.

Despite Strumilin's stature as a top figure in Gosplan, his socialist–utilitarian view of the interdependencies linking the components of the socialist economic aggregate did not influence either the prewar yearbooks' product measures or the methodology underlying various other published statistical series - for example, the series on the occupational distribution of the non-farm labor force. Strumilin maintained his outlook on the socialist economy as essentially interdependent through to the end of his long life, daring to portray the economy as a single giant enterprise in the 1930s (Strumilin, 1936a) and attacking the non-productive status of passenger transport in the 1950s. However, the original 1926 socialist–utilitarian blot on his voluntarist record was, unlike his virulent attacks on Mensheviks and neo-Narodniks, omitted from the many reprints of his works published in the late 1950s and 1960s (Strumilin, 1958a and b; 1960–5, 6 vols).

6.4.4 *Two socialist materialists: Petrov and Vaisberg - Marx 'po-shotlandski'*

Strumilin's vision of the Bolsheviks as masters in their own house, powerful enough to determine the optimal mix of material and immaterial final goods and to apply constant and variable capital to those ends, appears, for reasons unknown, to have gone unheeded. A likely explanation is that his proposal appeared too optimistic mode-wise, given the uneven but unacceptably large fraction of the economy still in capitalist hands: 20 per cent of industrial production, a quarter of retail trade, all but an infinitesimal fraction of agriculture (Zaleski, 1971, p. 71, citing KPSS, 1953, II, p. 451).

Neither was Strumilin's 'liberal' and consumption-oriented view of society's economic maximand well suited to underscoring the *industrial* achievements of the Soviet economy in this and the immediately subsequent period.

A quite different view of the proper maximand for mixed socialism was advanced by writers classified here as 'socialist materialists'. A. I. Petrov and R. E. Vaisberg differed with Strumilin in a series of articles appearing in *Planovoe khoziaistvo* in 1927. The most *outré* 'socialist materialist' was undoubtedly the member of the presidium of Gosplan and like Strumilin editor of *Planovoe khoziaistvo*, Roman Efimovich Vaisberg (?–1935). After the first five-year plan ran into trouble, Vaisberg obliged as leader of the official purge of Mensheviks and other 'geneticists' in Gosplan, a campaign that culminated in the trial and disappearance of Bazarov and other prominent economists in 1931 (Jasny, 1972, pp. 33–4, 74–5, 111–13).

Faced with the Marxian dilemma of a mixture of modes, in drawing his version of the boundaries of the productive domain, Vaisberg comes out in favor of a narrow materiality criterion as being valid whatever the mixture of ownership forms. His declared objective is to overcome orthodox Marxian analytical helplessness with respect to peasant agriculture. The materialist compromise made extends to services both 'sold to the public' and provided 'free' out of the state budget. The argument turns on the claim that social product is identical with that of 'material' branches *because* (*sic*) Marx, in the 1859 'Preface' to *A Contribution to the Critique of Political Economy*, had written that '[the] mode of production of material life conditions the social, political and intellectual life-process in general' (Marx, 1859, p. 3).

Unmindful that Marx viewed the output of the transportation industry as non-storable but as production none the less, Vaisberg states flatly that the 'material product of our country is produced in industry, agriculture, and transport. Nowhere else' (Vaisberg, 1927b, p. 136). Moreover, no 'material products or [*sic*] values of any kind are produced in either state or cooperative trade or in credit institutions' (p. 142). This sort of bowdlerized Marxism might have led to trouble later on: Stalin in January 1933 announced a new emphasis on distribution in the second plan by reminding comrades that Soviet trade was after all now 'trade without capitalists' (Stalin, 1933, p. 47; KPSS, 1953, II, p. 722).

By the late 1920s peasant and world-capitalist opposition was dispelling any remaining illusions about the withering-away of the workers' state. In this context Vaisberg advocates retaining non-productive status for public administrators, all the while holding out the prospect that 'the labor of this part of the apparat is becoming productive' (Vaisberg, 1927b, p. 147).

On the distinction between manual and mental labor, Vaisberg confesses to a temptation to declare mental laborers, such as teachers working to reproduce labor-power, productive under socialism. But the temptation is to be resisted, because it would mean drawing a line between labor that reproduces labor-power that ends up employed in the productive sphere and labor that reproduces labor-power that ends up doing other things. 'We would find ourselves', he says ominously, 'in a labyrinth of completely sterile scholastic quarrels and discriminations' (Vaisberg, 1927b, p. 149). Since teachers have to be something, Vaisberg recommends unproductive status, citing Marx's repudiation of Rossi in *Theories of Surplus-Value*, Part 1. Under Soviet conditions, labor in immaterial services 'does not become productive, but remains merely socially useful' (*sic*) (1927b, p. 150).

Connection must be preserved between the revolution's target welfare beneficiaries, the (industrial) proletariat, and their status as the society's sole true producers. There is also a manifest political danger in declaring all types of planned work productive under incomplete socialism:

> The first step is to declare the labor of the intelligentsia equal in value to the labor of a worker; the next step is to declare it more valuable.
> (Vaisberg, 1927b, p. 152)

In similar vein, the future professor and Stalinist survivor A. I. Petrov informs readers of the February 1927 issue of *Planovoe khoziaistvo* that 'commodities' are always material, transferable, and tangible. Only 'material branches' create 'value', the implication being that Marx's teaching factories do not. Both forget that Marx chided Adam Smith for something he often did himself: confusing the material and economic characteristics of productive labor. *Theories of Surplus-Value*, despite its unfriendly attitude to self-employed peasants, scientists, and doctors, boasts the following memorable passage:

> materialization, etc., of labour power is . . . not to be taken in such Scottish sense as Adam Smith conceives it [*ne sleduet ponimat' tak po-shotlandski*].
> (Marx, 1905–10, p. 171; *PSS*, t. 26.1, p. 154)

In Petrov is propounded what becomes the official Soviet pneumatics: 'outside the productive sphere', agents receive incomes that are a *redistribution* of basic incomes, siphoned over from the productive branches (Petrov, 1927, pp. 118–19).

The next point at issue concerns the mixture of ownership types in the NEP economy. For an 'economy of transitional type' the author puts forward a materiality criterion such as is rarely seen in economics since Malthus or the Adam Smith of Book II, chapter iii.

> In so far as under [full-fledged] capitalism and also in an economy of transitional type material production exists not just in commodity form but also in natural and in socialist forms, the question can be

> posed as to the inclusion of all material production. In the latter case, we provisionally evaluate also non-commodity production and natural 'incomes' in value form . . . [Labor] in the form of direct activity not creating any material goods takes the form of derivative income. This division of incomes, in addition to its theoretical premises, shows us how material production of the country is divided between all the members of society and, consequently, what share of material production is spent by the productive members of society for the maintenance [*sic*] of all the rest.
> (Petrov, 1927, p. 121)

Thus commodity-hood (*tovarnost'*) is rejected as delineator of the boundary of the productive domain in favor of materiality alone, irrespective of institutional mode. 'Materiality', as a purely technical criterion, has the advantage of generality; it is therefore well suited to systems with complex mixtures of ownership forms.

A. I. Petrov enunciates the celebrated distinctions between freight and passenger transport (and enterprise vs. household use of telephone and postal services) that are still (1988) a distinguishing feature of Soviet official economics (1927, p. 125 n.). It is evident that what Petrov holds against the 'non-productive sphere' is its alleged inability to generate a surplus for expanded reproduction (growth) (p. 131). But this is assumed, not demonstrated.

6.4.5 Abolin and Rubin on incomplete socialism

Vaisberg's article was roundly attacked by Artem Abolin in two articles also published in *Planned Economy* (Abolin, 1928a, b). They were prefaced by the telltale footnote, 'for discussion only', indicating that editorial opinion was already inclining heavily towards the materialist camp. With a view to discrediting the materialist point of view, Abolin invokes some of the passages I cited in Chapter 5 as proof that Marx allowed that capitalistically-organized services have use-value and exchange-value. Services are not always commodities, but they can be.

> *In the USSR that labor is productive which bears a direct relationship to the creation of social use-value, without distinction as to whether this use-value takes form in a liquid, a gas, a solid, or in a service.*
> (Abolin, 1928a, p. 162; emphasis in original)

Soviet economics should not discriminate against outputs that under capitalism were produced by individual producers (peasants, artisans, artists), or against those of postmen and teachers, because all of them work to fulfill social needs. 'If the labor of a teacher can be productive under capitalism, why is it unproductive under socialism?' (1928a, p. 164).

In the battle of citations of *Theories of Surplus-Value*, Abolin makes short work of Vaisberg's neanderthal materialism. Though not as thoroughgoing a socialist utilitarian as Strumilin (Abolin would still exclude administration and circulation proper as 'not social'), his position rejoins that of Isaak Il'ich Rubin, noted Menshevik professor and Marx scholar also arrested and condemned at the Menshevik trial of 1931.

In the late 1920s Rubin published two major works of Marx scholarship supporting the orthodox 'modist' interpretation of commodity production and circulation and mocking the 'Scottish' materialist point of view (Rubin, 1928, 1929). His strict rendering of Marx's views on what kinds of labor are productive under capitalist conditions does not require restatement. I merely note with Jasny that, by 1931, 'those in power were particularly angry with Rubin because many Bolsheviks accepted his teachings as true Marxism' (Jasny, 1972, pp. 188–9).

Between them, the socialist utilitarian Strumilin and the socialist materialists Petrov and Vaisberg trace out the upper and lower limits for value and output theories considered relevant to a mixed socialist system. Concepts actually used in Soviet statistical agencies during the NEP and the prewar plans drew more of their theoretical inspiration from Petrov and Vaisberg than from Strumilin, and built on the work of the ex-Marxist materialist S. N. Prokopovich.

6.5 The materiality of Soviet 'material production'

How did the Soviet Union come to have a 'material product system' (MPS) of national economic accounts, and just how 'material' is it? The Bolsheviks took power before other countries had much experience in evaluating total, as opposed to partial, economic performance (Boss, 1986c). Owing to institutional momentum and the absence of fundamental reform, accounting conventions in use from the early 1920s have remained in force, with only minor changes, through the Stalin plan era to the late 1980s.

What is 'material' about the MPS is that it aims to exclude from measures of total output 'immaterial services' that Western theory treats symmetrically with goods. This is important because the treatment of 'immaterial' service branches is one of three main reasons why aggregate and per capita economic statistics of Soviet-type economies cannot be readily compared with those of other countries. (The second, much studied reason is that aggregates in centrally planned economies are derived from quantities multiplied by arbitrary rather than scarcity prices; the third has to do with the valuation of foreign trade under inconvertible currencies.) Cumbersome manipulations must therefore be performed to render MPS economic data comparable to those of the market-type economies of the first and third worlds.

Pre-1941 statistical yearbooks and plan documents show what the scope of national income, and of 'planning', were taken to be. The basic convention that 'material production' comprises industry, agriculture, construction, transport, and trade was in place by 1923 (Boss, 1986c, n. 31).

How did this come about? The narrow scope of Soviet economic statistics could have been inherited from pre-revolutionary convention. It could have been a function of attempts to employ 'material balance' techniques elaborated by the imperial German High Command during World War I (Smolinski, 1967). There was also the precedent set by S. N. Prokopovich. In 1917 and 1918 the eminent Constitutional Democrat and former legal Marxist published estimates of national income for 1900 and 1913 employing a narrow, 'materialist' concept.

Though the former Minister of Food in Kerensky's Provisional Government was by the 1920s a sworn enemy of the régime, and was nearly executed during the civil war, Prokopovich's 1913 figure has served ever since as the official benchmark estimate for the last normal year of the imperial Russian economy (Prokopovich, 1917, 1918). Despite new evidence that Prokopovich seriously underestimated tsarist output (Gregory, 1982, p. 10), the matter has not been reopened, doubtless because his was a conveniently low base against which the achievements of the Stalin plans could be set. But we do not know whether this 'index-number card' was a serious factor affecting the choice of conventions for Soviet national product.

On the very day of the October Revolution, Lenin presented Iu. Larin with the job of reorganizing the Soviet economy on principles worked out by the German High Command during the war. By the 1920s, fifty-odd *glavki* (departments) under the VSNKh, the Supreme Council of the National Economy, oversaw the workings of industry, trade, and transport (Carr, 1952, p. 179). Production of consumer services, though not of consumer goods, was not on the agenda of the Supreme Council (Gershgorn, 1921, p. 48).

At the beginning of the NEP, after the hunger and devastation of the civil war, the aim was to derive quantity indicators for a limited number of items (grain, fuel). Current-price value aggregates were all but useless owing to the huge price movements intervening since 1913 (Nove, 1972, p. 91). But practices born of war and hyperinflation were not then abandoned once financial stability returned. Interest in selective indicators, particularly for intermediate industrial goods, was a legacy of the civil war that hardened into a permanent feature of Soviet economic life (Clark, 1940; *Pravda*, 24 January 1988).

6.5.1 The degree of aggregation

WESTERN PRACTICE BEFORE KEYNES

Doubts about the usefulness of global aggregates were shared by a number of Western economists of the period, mainly in Germany (Boss, 1986c, n. 37). Amonn, for example, carried methodological individualism so far as to argue that, since 'the nation' was not an economic agent, its income, being a statistical fiction, could be of interest to no one (Amonn, 1911; discussed in Moskvin, 1929, p. 98). The Americans in the 1920s also favored a high level of disaggregation: apples and oranges were to be kept as separate as possible. For example, under Arthur Burns and W. C. Mitchell, the American National Bureau of Economic Research's 'central concept of economic activity [had become] a somewhat fuzzy cocktail' of (by 1942) 811 monthly series – from which no 'meaningful summary measure' could be derived (Maddison, 1982, pp. 65–6, 211).

However, neoclassical value theory – as illustrated for example in Pigou's view that economics is the study of activities that can be brought '*directly or indirectly* into relation with the measuring rod of money' (Pigou, 1932, pp. 11, 31; emphasis added) – implied that, aggregated or not into some national total, both government and private services fall squarely within the economic domain. In the case of private services, both, and, in the case of the public sector, inputs if not outputs, are traded on price-making markets. In terms of Kuznets's triad, outside Soviet Russia in the pre-World War II period, it was valuation and netness rather than scope *per se* that were at issue.

The Soviets as Marxian socialists had ambitions that guaranteed they would be pioneers in the collection of socioeconomic facts. The magnitude of the data-gathering and planning task was brought home by economists such as Professor Litoshenko, co-author with P. I. Popov of the 1923/4 *Balans* and compiler of the first post-World War I estimate of Soviet national income, *Natsional'nyi dokhod* (Litoshenko, 1925).

> Only countries which are very rich in statistical materials can permit themselves the luxury of calculating their national income and only after eight years of intensive development of state and bureau statistics is there at last the possibility of a more or less well-founded determination of the size of the national income of the USSR.
>
> (Litoshenko, 1926a, p. 113)

But what *was* to be included in income, and how was it to be calculated?

6.5.2 Scope and materiality in practice

'REAL' PRODUCTS VS. 'PERSONAL' INCOMES

National accountants committed to a surplus and transfer theory had the problem of reconciling totals of income got using 'real' and 'personal' (*lichnyi* or *personal'nyi*) methods. Whenever a non-productive sector was postulated – which was always in Bolshevik and Menshevik circles – the 'personal' method's total of incomes exceeded the 'real' method's total of products by the incomes of unproductives. According to the 'real' method, certain branches of the national economy were designated as 'productive'. Funds generated by taxation, or that otherwise fell into the hands of the state and were used to pay the expenses of non-marketed activities, looked like redistributions or transfers.

Following Marshall, J. B. Clark, and Irving Fisher, the 'personal' method treated income as income, from whatever branch or mode. It was therefore open to the criticism of failing to take account of the fundamental *qualitative* differences (*sic*) between incomes earned in the socialized (state and cooperative) and non-socialized (private) sectors, and between bourgeois and proletarian occupations (Vaisberg, 1925a,b, 1927a; Freimundt, 1960, pp. 181–8).

An early inauguration date for the material product concept is indicated by the fact that the statisticians who compiled the first 'balances of the national economy' as a preliminary to more ambitious planning make no effort to defend their narrow scope. The first attempt to construct an actual macro balance sheet occurred during NEP under the auspices of P. I. Popov, ex-Menshevik and director until 1926 of the Central Statistical Administration. Popov's mandate for the balance was confined to figures for agriculture, industry, construction, and publishing (Popov, 1926, p. 80; Wheatcroft and Davies, 1985).

Professor Litoshenko explained in the same document that 'our conception of a national economic account ... does not pretend to provide anything more than a conscientious picture of the process of production and distribution of *physical* commodities' (Litoshenko, 1926b, p. 21, emphasis added).

Economists expressing the intention to extend the planning domain beyond the confines of materiality were actively discredited, even if the 'mistake' consisted of working in monetary rather than in physical units. N. A. Kovalevsky's suggestion for a plan based on Fel'dman's now-famous growth model – which had streamlined Marx's Department I to include only activities contributing net increases to the capital stock – was attacked for using value aggregates rather than physical targets. Another rejected idea was S. Rozentul''s 'synthetic' (monetary) scheme joined to social indicators. It aimed not only to account for enterprises' efficiency '"as measured by their increase in profitability" but also [to record] other secondary effects, such as benefits obtained by the labor force, [social] income from non-productive expenditures (services), etc.' (Spulber, 1964, pp. 89–91).

Lack of equivalence between real and personal estimates of national income was a sore point. F. Dubovikov, a collaborator of the Menshevik Ginzburg in the industrial superministry, the Supreme Council of the National Economy, and A. Nikitsky, a Ministry of Finance budget expert, granted formal equivalence between product and income as two sides of the same coin (Dubovikov, 1923, pp. 66 ff.; Nikitsky, 1926, pp. 92 ff.). Output consists of both newly produced goods *and* 'services'. However, the only 'services' recognized are trade and transport, two branches that all but the earliest official handbooks *already* included as part of final output anyway (see Pervushin, 1923).

Even Professor Litoshenko, who was 'definitely a Kadet' (Constitutional Democrat) and not even a 'Left-wing one', who is described together with Kondrat'ev, Vainshtein, and Iurovsky of the Commissariat of Finance as 'thoroughly versed in contemporary western economics' (Carr and Davies, 1969, p. 740), accepts this same view of output as the output of agriculture, industry, transport, and trade. The nuance again is that transport and trade are said to be 'services' for the legitimate reason that their outputs *cannot be stored* (Kronrod, 1958, pp. 42–43; Hill, 1977; Boss, 1986c, n. 42). Using the label 'services' for transport and trade was the extent of the compromise made between socialist–materialist and socialist–utilitarian views; it left plenty of room for the Classical–Marxian surplus and transfer model to be applied to free services to the population, administration and planning, and defense.

INPUTS AND OUTPUTS OF BORDERLINE CASES

Branches providing non-marketed 'collective' administrative and personal services (education, health, science, and culture), housing, and what by the 1930s went under the name 'communal economy' (municipal water and sewers, public baths and laundries, trams and buses (*sic*), roads and bridges, street lighting, fire-fighting, sanitation, manure removal; Boss, 1986c, n. 43), plus government administration and defense, seem to have been generally regarded as unregenerately final consumers of resources transferred from 'economic' sectors. Strumilin is again the exception.

This produced the irony, unremarked in print as far as I am aware, that the ('immaterial') planning activity of Gosplan itself is treated in Soviet accounts as a final luxury, on a par with opera and ballets at the Bolshoi, instead of as a necessary intermediate activity that is 'Ur-primary' to everything else, from the design of mineral exploration equipment on down!

Such asymmetries meant the personal method gave estimates that exceeded those of the real method by the amount of final 'non-productive' services. This was fully recognized by such advocates of the narrow material definition as the émigré Prokopovich, who correctly argued that for the methods to provide checks on each other's accuracy only incomes earned in 'material' branches should figure on the personal side (Prokopovich, 1930, pp. 6–7). By the 1944 *Dictionary–Handbook of Socioeconomic Statistics*, proper one-to-one correspondence had been established between *excluded incomes of persons* and the labor force of the non-productive sphere (Petrov, Moskvin and Morozova, 1944, pp. 40–3).

However, that was for the future. Menshevik concepts of inputs and outputs appear from the structure of the statistical yearbooks published from 1923/4 on. In them, output and labor-force statistics are set out in adjoining chapters, obscuring the fact that the relationship is of factor-using product to income-earning factor. Estimates of aggregate personal marketed services come not next to industry, agriculture, construction, transport, and trade in the product sections, but at the end, despite data for long lists of entrepreneurial and service-producing occupations in the sections on employment and wages.

Reliance on quantity indicators may have abetted that blurring of the income and product sides, though an important contributing factor must have been unwillingness to accept the positive implications for the productiveness of various 'bourgeois' and superstructural professions (Moskvin, 1929, p. 115).

The hard line against passenger transport and communications was not finalized until after World War II, with the then separate Central Statistical Administration (TsSU) excluding them and Gosplan including them into the 1950s, when the TsSU's narrow version, advocated by Petrov, established undivided sway (Strumilin, 1958b, p. 148). The problem may have originated in the fact that city tranportation was analyzed not together with passenger service by rail and water in the 1920s yearbooks, but separately in 'communal services'. However, the editor of an Academy of Sciences-sponsored volume on *National Income, its Formation and Accounting* was complaining already in 1939 that omitting passenger transport alone amounted to understating Soviet national product by a full percentage point and devalorizing the efforts of over half a million skilled industrial workers (Chernomordik, 1939, pp. 192, 198, 203–4). Strumilin, despite a retreat from his 1926 socialist–utilitarian position, never accepted the exclusion of passenger transport from Soviet material product and ridiculed the pre-Einsteinian physics of 'ultramaterialists' who worried about the propriety of including electric utilities in the sphere of material production (Strumilin, 1958, pp. 148–9).

In an amusing bit of *ad-hoc*ery, around the ousting of the Mensheviks in 1930, Bolshevik socialist materialists found a material stamp of approval for several more kinds of activity that could be cobbled only with difficulty to the Marxian factory paradigm. 'Public catering' (cafeterias and restaurants but not hotels) was relabeled material and *included* next to (all of) trade (*sic*) in the 'material' productive sphere (Boss, 1986c, n. 55)! (UN convention treats all three as 'services'.)

On the other hand, in a notorious case cited by Krasnolobov, it was discovered that ('productive') communications serving the enterprises of material production had been omitted from the national income before 1936 'by mistake' (Krasnolobov, 1940, p. 58).

Non-marketed 'public' services financed out of the state budget were not treated as output or values in the same fashion as goods sold on markets or even as trade and transport. This was despite the fact that their considerable material and labor inputs had to be provided for (e.g. Popov, 1926, p. 81; Boss, 1986c, n. 48). The parallels that could have been drawn between *planned-but-not-marketed public services* and *planned-but-centrally-allocated capital goods* were not drawn, perhaps because of residual commitment to the notion of the withering-away of the state (Daniels, 1953). It is hard, though, to imagine a communism without fire stations.

ACCOUNTING FOR INTERDEPENDENCE

Input–output relations between productive and non-productive activities needed a theoretical and accounting framework. What to do about productive inputs of non-productive branches and non-productive inputs of productive branches was discussed in the theoretical journals of the late 1920s. It was recognized that putting a government agency like Gosplan in Department I (intermediate production) would have violated the fundamental principle that 'living' labor be treated differently from 'dead' (see section 5.6 above). The same A. I. Petrov, for example, declines to include state services in USSR national income on the ground that (assuming tax finance), if public services were treated as elements of the c (non-direct labor, i.e. 'constant-capital' costs) of an industrial good that was subject to tax, instead of being financed out of that good's surplus-value, m, such services would have to be accorded production branches of their own on a par with Department I capital goods (Petrov, 1927, p. 111). This possibility is mentioned in order that it be rejected. Except by Strumilin, the correctness of the surplus redistribution notion seems to have been taken for granted when it came to non-priced ('public') services.

Writing from Germany in 1925, the young Wassily W. Leontief held the omission of non-material production to be unfortunate but not necessarily unsound.

The income side of the economic turnover is considered only insofar as it consists of 'objectivized' material goods. From this point of view it is fully consistent that public administration, whose budget reached almost 1.5 billion rubles, should be represented in the balance by only 475.7 million rubles. *The state does not create any material goods; its income is derived and as such does not have any counterpart in the income of the economic balance.* But neither do its expenditures ... Although this methodological peculiarity limits the attempt to make the balance represent a *complete* picture of the turnover of the economy, it nevertheless leaves the internal organic structure of the balance scheme unaltered.

(Leontief, 1925, p. 94; emphasis added)

Leontief's claim is based on surplus and transfer logic and is free of input–output error to the extent that the state produces no 'necessary but intermediate' goods or services. Should that however not be true, the 'methodological peculiarity' is harmless only if the state intermediates act in a uniform or parametric fashion on material sectors. That would not be the case if, as is the rule in a world of impure public goods, some industries benefit more from goods or services, or are taxed more for them, than are others.

In his invaluable RAND Memo, A. S. Becker explains how material-branch purchases of (intermediate but) non-productive services show up in input–output tables set up according to the conventions of the Soviet material product system (Becker, 1971, pp. 28–9). Unless expenditures on intermediate service inputs are excluded from aggregate gross expenditure, outputs are less than inputs and the table will not balance. Alternatively, the expenditures can be subtracted from the value of gross output so that inputs and outputs balance at a lower aggregate figure.

Citing A. I. Petrov's textbook, *Course of Economic Statistics* (1954), Becker notes that productive-branch expenditures on non-productive services are indeed included in the value of productive-branch output. For example, business travel allowances and interest on bank credit are listed with other components of net product in industrial-sector value added, even though, by themselves, passenger transport and banking and credit activity are non-productive. The same arrangement applies to scientific research carried out in specialized (i.e. non-productive-sphere) institutions and bought by productive enterprises.

Translated into Marxian terminology, such intermediate services are implicitly treated as elements of constant capital, whose value is *transferred* to products in the same manner as the value of thread and the depreciation of looms.

FROM 'UNPRODUCTIVE' TO 'NON-PRODUCTIVE'

By the late 1920s it was conventional to reserve the terms 'productive' and 'unproductive' (*proizvoditel'nyi* and *neproizvoditel'nyi*) for capitalism and history of thought and to employ the polarity 'productive' vs. 'non-productive' (*proizvodstvennyi/neproizvodstvennyi*) for the mixture of Soviet reality (Rubin, 1929; Moskvin, 1929; Zeilinger and Gukhman, 1928; but see Volkov *et al.*, 1979, p. 314, who apply the 'capitalist' adjective to socialist phenomena).

At least one commentator has argued that the Soviet 'material' concept of output is primarily a cold war development designed to facilitate the bringing of Stalinist economics to Eastern Europe (Tsur, 1984b). Tsur's main evidence is Jan Drewnowski's vivid account of the imposition of the material product system on the Polish statistical office in 1948 (Drewnowski, 1979).

Although the final word on passenger transport appears not to have been laid down until the Stalin textbook (Ostrovit'ianov *et al.*, 1954), against Tsur's view we note that the Classical–Marxian 'productive'/'non-productive' terminology, modified from *proizvoditel'nyi/neproizvoditel'nyi* to *proizvodstvennyi/neproizvodstvennyi* to render the mix of capitalist and socialist conditions, was applied from the late 1920s to (i) investment in equipment and structures, as well as to (ii) education and training (cadre formation), just as in current practice (e.g. Zeilinger and Gukhman, 1928; USSR Gosplan, 1930; Barun, 1930). As against Tsur's view of timing, that basic feature of Soviet political economy and national income accounting was present from the earliest discussions of the NEP. It pervades the documents of the first five-year plan (Boss, 1986c, n. 54).

6.5.3 Mind over matter?

It is plausible that planned immaterial services were originally excluded from output under socialism because no one (except Strumilin and, much later, Agabab'ian, Pevzner, Shatalin, and Oldak) saw any need actively to defend them as *intermediate (capital) goods*, capable of contributing in the same manner as machines to make machines to the growth of priority sectors.

What better compromise, then, than something in the Smitho-Marxian tradition already familiar to the statisticians, for example from the work of Prokopovich? The materialist compromise looked Marxist: outputs of *apparatchiki*, rentiers, bourgeois professionals, priests, were 'out'. What was said to be 'matter' was 'in'. Never mind that transportation was more material in its inputs than its outputs, or that even Soviet trade was not all preservation of material values in state warehouses and refrigerators. Serially-produced industrial goods are, of course, easier to count than are comparison-resistant services.

Given the approval accorded by ex- but anti-Marxists like Prokopovich to the narrow material concept, it seems fair to blame the ideology if at the same time we remember that the relevant prejudice in favor of a material output concept was not a Marxist monopoly. It also found favor along a broad front of textbook-Classical, historicist and otherwise non-Walrasian writers who (barring rare exceptions - Slutsky, Shaposhnikov) constituted *non*-Marxian economics in Russia before 1917.

Without access to discussions in Gosplan and the Central Statistical Administration during which the exact boundaries were decided, it is hard to weigh the relative importance of ideological and practical considerations that led Soviet statisticians to relegate not only non-priced 'public' but also priced 'private, personal' services to a separate, 'non-productive' sphere. An imperfect but recognizable post-capitalist version of the Smitho-Marxian doctrine of the inferior productiveness of services private and public was nevertheless built into the Soviet information-processing network in the earliest years of the régime.

Is Marx (or Smith) to blame for conventions that placed Soviet 'trade without capitalists' and the net output of restaurants in a 'sphere of material production'? The heavier pro-material stance as compared with sophisticated readings of *Das Kapital* or the *Wealth of Nations* can no doubt be laid down to the common, not to say 'vulgar', error of identifying 'necessity' with 'materiality', and 'luxury' with its 'opposite'.

The private, marketed services that Smith and Marx can *both* be interpreted as putting on the same footing as capitalistically-produced goods were often those likely to be produced and/or consumed in pre-revolutionary days by non-proletarians: opera-singers, those able to pay private physicians and tutors.

In the case of public services, the familiar Classical prejudice according to which non-market institutions are racked by X-inefficiency got reinforced by a Marxist one that easily survived the overthrow of the bourgeois state and the dawn of the dictatorship of the proletariat. This is the idea that state services are paid out of an extorted surplus and 'forced on' unwilling citizens. Bolshevik political theory would not have had much sympathy for the public-choice notion that education, health, defense, planning should be 'voted for' if they are not 'bought'.

Mensheviks and non-party economists like Litoshenko, being *stricter modists and therefore more inclined to post-revolutionary socialist utilitarianism*, regarded trade, transport, and communications as 'services' but no less output for all that. However the winners in the political struggle of the 1920s swore allegiance to the party of that same Lenin, author of *Materialism and Empiriocriticism* and accusations like '[Petr Struve is] afraid to say "production of *material* products"'. In the atmosphere of Stalin's final defeat of the other party factions and the launching of the first five-year plan, it was good political insurance (witness Vaisberg) to stake out a 'hard' ultramaterialist position.

Strumilin's creative use of Marx's *Critique of the Gotha Programme* must convince us, however, that for the seriously mode-minded anything was possible, in the NEP situation and *a fortiori* for the still 'mixed' but much more 'socialist' economy of the plan era. Stalin declared capitalism destroyed in 1934, but this did not move him to instruct his statisticians at TsUNKhU to transfer planned baths and laundries or the activities of the Commissariat of the Enlightenment to the productive sphere (Stalin, 1934, pp. 245–6). As Wiles and Nove have pointed out, materiality tells only part of the story: agriculture's, or, for that matter, industrial consumer goods' (group 'B''s) materiality was never in doubt (Wiles, 1962, p. 281; Nove, 1963, pp. 294 ff.).

6.5.4 Stalin and after

At the end of his life Stalin himself dabbled in political economy. Throughout the 1930s and 1940s, lack of an official consensus on the basic ownership and inter-enterprise features of the new mode caused much anxiety amongst commentators. What was to be the official status under socialism of, for example, kolkhoz and private-plot production? Were centrally allocated producer goods 'commodities' subject to the 'law of value'? Was the Soviet economy itself subject to 'laws' such as Marx had discovered for capitalism? A high-level working group was set up. After receiving their report, which he discussed in *Economic Problems of Socialism in the USSR*, Stalin declared ominously that it is '*absolutely* necessary to add a chapter on national income to the draft textbook' (1952, p. 479).

The textbook *Politicheskaia ekonomiia: uchebnik* (Ostrovit'ianov *et al.*, 1954) finally appeared a year after Stalin's death and two years before Khrushchev's secret speech denouncing the 'cult of personality'. The Stalin textbook confirms the narrow, 'material' scope of Soviet national income and repeats the doctrine that 'material production' is the economy's base (*osnova*; sometimes *bazis*). Passenger transport is non-productive. So is Gosplan. Wholesale and retail trade and agricultural procurement are confirmed as material (the practice anyway). The plan must aim for priority growth of material over service branches. In all it is the mid-twentieth century's most grandiose monument to input–output error.

[The] greatest economic significance is attached to raising the share of workers engaged in the material production sphere at the expense of the share of laborers engaged in the ranks of the non-productive branches . . . [in order to encourage] the creation of [material plenty] essential to the building of communism.

(Ostrovit'ianov *et al.*, 1954, p. 519)

Like Adam Smith's opera-singers and opera-dancers, servants and kings, employees of the Soviet non-productive sphere, get something for nothing. No matter how socially useful, technically such workers are parasites living off the largesse of the socialist economy's real producers of things.

Note that the term 'material product system' itself is a derivation from Soviet nomenclature, chosen by the United Nations Economic Commission for Europe to distinguish Soviet practice from the UN standard System of National Accounts (SNA) (United Nations, 1959; conversation with M. Kaser, November 1985; Stone, 1985). It derives from the Soviet term 'system of material and financial balances' (SMFB) (conversation with A. Terushkin, Moscow, June 1988). The rendering of *natsional'nyi dokhod* ('national income') as 'net material product' is likewise a Western convention (A. S. Becker, 1971, p. 8, n. 17).

If, as Tsur thinks, the definitive commitment to a material standard was made at the close of the Stalin era rather in mid-NEP, how the deep-seated theoretical and statistical commitment to materiality not only survived but flourished with the rebirth of economics during the first anti-Stalin thaw in the 1950s becomes more of a puzzle (Leontief, 1960; Campbell, 1961). Soviet production boundaries remained essentially unchanged from the 1920s to 1988. True, shoe repair was moved to (productive) retail trade in 1951. Until the so-called Kosygin reforms of the mid-1960s, dry cleaning and dyeing establishments were in the non-productive sphere. Baths and laundries still are. Perhaps on account of the chemicals (!), the 1967 classification reform of industrial and other branches moved dry cleaning to the sphere of material production, alongside made-to-order tailor ateliers, shoe-repair shops, and other repair establishments. That, plus several reallocations within branches of industry, sums up classification changes through to the first years of the Gorbachev era (Gur'ev, 1968, USSR Gosplan, 1969; A. S. Becker, 1971, fn. 92; Vanous, 1986, 1987; *Pravda*, 24 January 1988).

Despite criticism of the entire notion of non-productivity, and hints that the term 'non-productive sphere' should be quietly replaced by its more neutral synonym 'service sphere' (*sfera obsluzhivaniia* or *sfera uslug*), the decade of the 1970s ended with strong affirmation of the doctrine of productiveness of material production and non-productivity of immaterial (Solodkov, 1978; Gatovsky and Kapustin, 1977, ch. 14.3; Volkov *et al.*, 1979; Rumiantsev *et al.*, 1978, II, pp. 176 ff.; on 'service sphere', see Boss, 1982, ch. VI.5.b. and ns 294–7).

During Brezhnev's last years, Soviet authorities were apparently so committed to having a different, non-bourgeois, Marxian system that they went to the trouble of lobbying the UN, which had adopted the Keynesian system of GNP accounts in 1947 (United Nations, 1947; Stone, 1985, p. xix), to commit itself in turn to the principle of 'separate but equal' on the national accounting front. Elaborate methodologies were brought out for reconciling the SNA and the MPS (UN, 1969a, b, 1971, 1977, 1981a; Ivanov, 1987). The unsightly banks of blanks for the Soviet Union and its Comecon allies in the UN's GNP league tables were to be partly filled by a *Dienstrein* compromise statistic, 'gross domestic product excluding services'. Since 1981 the UN *Statistical Yearbook* has published this universal if indefensible measure of economic performance for all the countries of the world, East, West and South (UN, 1981b, p. 89; see Marer, 1985 and sections 8.2 and 8.3 below).

Finally, to celebrate the marriage of *glasnost'* and *perestroika*, the renamed State Committee on Statistics gave a figure for the growth rate of Soviet GNP (*Pravda*, 24 January 1988). In April 1988 it advised economic agencies to prepare to 'change the system of methods of calculation of socioeconomic indicators' in the interest of international comparability (interview with D. S. L'vov, Moscow, June 1988; Medvedev, 1988a). The new attitude to the legitimacy of comprehensive comparisons of economies with different modes is evidenced by the State Committee on Statistics' reported intention to join the UN's International Comparison Project at the 1990 round (information supplied by L. Dreschler of the United Nations Statistical Office, New York, December 1988 – see ch. 8.2 below).

6.6 Effects on the service share?

Did officially sanctioned prejudice against services retard their development? An uncowed socialist utilitarian dared complain as late as 1940 that the material system employed in the statistical agency TsUNKhU understated the output of social labor by that fifth contributed by the 'non-productive sphere' (Kursky, 1940, p. 105). Since then, Abram Bergson and Simon Kuznets and a generation of their disciples have provided re-estimates of Soviet GDP and its growth and structure over time using SNA concepts, making it possible to compare Soviet growth and structure with those of other countries (Bergson, 1949, 1953, 1961, 1963; Bornstein *et al.* 1961; Kuznets, 1963; A. S. Becker, 1969; Block, 1979; Pitzer, 1982; Kurtzweg, 1987).

A study by S. H. Cohn found Soviet growth rates in the period 1928–66 to be pretty much the same whatever the definition of output or 'coverage' (Cohn, 1972, pp. 125–7). The implication is, however, that Soviet growth was 'growth without tertiarization' at a time when advanced (and some not-so-advanced) economies saw declines in the share of 'industry' including construction, in product and labor totals, and substantial increases in the share of 'services' in income (Kuznets, 1963, 1966, 1971; Chenery and Syrquin, 1975).

The share of services (narrowly defined, excluding transport and communications, i.e. Kuznets's S-) in recalculated USSR net national product actually declined from 1928 to 1958 (1937 factor prices; Kuznets, 1963, using Bergson, 1961). Instead of growing faster than the rest of the economy, S- services held quite steady at around 30 per cent of reworked GNP from 1960 to 1980 according to a number of Western estimates. Using 1970 prices, Block (1979, tables A-1 and A-6), the CIA (1981, table 39) and Pitzer (1982, table A-4) get shares ranging between 31.6 and 29.9 per cent of GNP for that period. A 1980 share of 30 per cent for S- is barely half the US share and 15 or so percentage points below those of Italy and Japan (Boss, 1982, table VI.2; United Nations, 1981a, table 29). G. Schroeder's 1985 figure for S- is 27.2 per cent of GNP, lower than Pitzer's and CIA's for 1980 but slightly above the share she reports for 1980. Schroeder's series has the share of S- in GNP changing less than a percentage point in the quarter-century since 1960 (1987, p. 249).

Is Soviet economic structure significantly different from that of Western countries at comparable levels of per capita GNP? Gur Ofer, in an interesting cross-section econometric comparison of the Soviet Union with some seventy developed and underdeveloped countries for 1958–60, found the share of service labor in the Soviet labor force to be significantly smaller than predicted by per capita GNP converted from rubles to dollars and by several other indices of development and structural transformation. The lower-than-predicted service share in 1958–60 is explained as a combination of a much lower retail-trade share, which was expected for a 'socialist country', and also, somewhat oddly, by a low share of labor force in 'general administration'. Ofer indicts not only Soviet Marxist economic doctrine (according to which, as we saw, even planners are non-productive laborers), but also especially the industrialization strategy adopted by Stalin, which restrained both consumption and urbanization and therefore held down outlays on passenger transport, housing construction, repair, and retail-trade services to city-dwellers (Ofer, 1973, pp. 148–61).

Ofer's cross-section study using 1958–60 data led him to conclude that, despite the Stalin past, the Soviet Union might eventually converge to a more typical developed-country pattern. However, more current data, published in his and Schroeder's 1987 surveys, demonstrate persistent lags in service shares behind what the Chenery and

Syrquin research on 'patterns of development' predict for a country with levels of dollar GNP per capita similar to those estimated for the Soviet Union.

The Chenery and Syrquin 'norm' for countries having the per capita incomes estimated for the USSR in 1950 (600US$ 1965) and in 1980 (1,500US$ 1965) is for residually defined service shares (Kuznets's S) in GNP to reach, respectively, 50 per cent and 54 per cent (Chenery and Syrquin, 1975). Instead of growth to 54 per cent from the high base of a 50 per cent share of product, Soviet output of services broadly-defined started much lower and showed little proportional gain. On Ofer's measures, the service sector accounts for nearly the same fraction of GNP in current prices in 1980 (40 per cent of GNP) as in 1950 (38 per cent) or even 1940 (37 per cent of GNP), despite over 4 per cent annual GNP growth from 1950 to 1985 (Ofer, 1987, pp. 1792, 1778). The actual 1980 service share in total output is thus 14 percentage points or about 30 per cent (geometric mean) lower than predicted by Chenery and Syrquin. Schroeder finds slightly lower shares of services including transport and communications in GNP: 37.7 per cent for 1980 and 38.1 per cent for 1985 (Schroeder, 1987, p. 249).

Ofer points out that shares estimated for 1980 are probably too high: differences of definition (of manufacturing, agriculture, and labor force) between Chenery-Syrquin and the CIA Handbook, which is the source for the 40 per cent share for 1980, 'make the Soviet Union seem closer to "normal" than it really is' (Ofer, 1987, p. 1793 and n. 32).

Over the period 1950–80, during which the Soviet consumer-service economy might have made proportional gains, Schroeder and Denton note an overall flat share of resources devoted to services to the population within the service sphere, despite movement up for personal services and for transport and communications and down for housing, education, and health (Schroeder and Denton, 1982, pp. 325–7, 333, 343–52).

With respect to employment, Chenery and Syrquin predict that, for countries having the Soviet Union's income level, the share of the labor force employed in service industries in 1950 and 1980 should be 37 and 50 per cent respectively. Actual Soviet shares of service employment in total employment in those years are 22 per cent and 37 per cent; in other words, the USSR attains in 1980 the employment share it 'ought' to have had (given its per capita ruble GNP converted to dollars) in 1950. The 1980 share figure is 13 percentage points behind or 25–30 per cent lower than predicted by Chenery and Syrquin for countries having the per capita GNP of '1,500$ 1965' which the USSR had in 1980 (Ofer, 1987, p. 1792). Schroeder reports a USSR service labor-force share for 1985 of 38.7 per cent, as against for example 54.3 per cent for Japan and 48.0 per cent for Italy. On the narrow definition of services favored by Fuchs (1968) and Kuznets (1963), which omits transport and communications, 1985 service employment is only 29.6 per cent of total employment (Schroeder, 1987, p. 243).

Those low shares give a somewhat false impression owing to the incomplete specialization of Soviet enterprises classed as 'industrial'. Horizontal integration means that branches that are nominally 'industrial' in reality fulfill many 'service' functions: on top of running kindergartens, clinics and apartment buildings for workers, factories sometimes even grow and process their own food (Rumer, 1981). Expenses of such auxiliary activities are included in enterprise output.

Kravis *et al.* have drawn our attention to the valuation and index-number problems that distort international comparisons, including studies of the original Chenery–Syrquin and Ofer type. Services have relatively low prices in traditional, poor societies: they are labor-intensive and and wages are low. Low price *weights* yield low apparent service *shares* in GNP even when the actual 'number' of services enjoyed per capita may not really be so far inferior to the 'number' consumed in richer countries, or in the same countries when they get richer. Conversely, the apparent 'tertiarization' of final consumption in rich countries is partly an illusion due to high wages (Kravis *et al.*, 1982, p. 193, n. 13; Baumol *et al.*, 1985, p. 8).

The derivation of internationally comparable purchasing-power prices, which is a first step to comparing an economy's real output level and mix with those of other countries, is made more difficult in the case of socialist countries by the fact that socialist prices are arbitrarily set and only imperfectly reflect relative scarcities. *A priori* that could bias the service share in GNP either way. Kravis *et al.* hypothesize, though, that in socialist countries the fact of *public* provision of 'comparison-resistant' services like health may have dampened average money wages overall. Assuming services to be relatively labor-intensive, the measured share of services in socialist GNP would be decreased by an additional factor (Kravis *et al.*, 1982, p. 193, n. 13; Kravis *et al.*, 1983; section 8.2 below).

Subsidies for housing and other services also make the volume of services produced in countries such as the USSR look lower than it is when valued at cost. Low established rents on state housing bias downward the ruble value of the important housing and utilities component of the consumer-service index. Revalued to reflect resource costs rather than consumer outlays, the share of services in total 1982 consumption of Soviet families goes from 21 to 34 per cent (Schroeder, 1987, p. 254, n. 27). Schroeder and Denton remark that if volume indices of consumer expenditure are not adjusted for undervaluation of housing, etc., 'the ratio of all goods to all services resembles that of India' (Schroeder and Denton, 1982, p. 333; Prell, 1986).

Even when adjusted to reflect factor costs, Soviet service shares defined on the SNA and ISIC definitions of output and employment are low by OECD standards in real terms (Schroeder, 1987, pp. 254 ff.). Moreover, as we saw, the overlap between Western statisticians' notion of services as the residual category 'non-industry, non-agriculture' and the Soviet non-productive sphere is not exact. Non-stockables such as freight transportation, retail trade-without-capitalists, and repair of material durables are, as noted, *already* in the sphere of material production.

To decide whether the 'humiliating appellation' of non-productive influenced planners' decisions about allocation of resources, the relevant share is that of non-productive services. An idea of the *non-productive* sphere's share of resources emerges from an interesting study by R. W. Campbell. After adjustment of 'industry' for services bought from independent research laboratories, from insurance agencies, doctors, etc., Campbell's reworked Soviet GNP in 1980 exceeds official 'net material product' by only 28.6 per cent. Of that, 8.5 percentage points are for the difference between gross and net investment (depreciation) and only 12 points are wages and estimated profits on capital in 'non-material', non-productive' branches. Imputed rents on private housing and military personnel costs make up the balance (Campbell, 1985, p. 8 and table 7).

Campbell's wildly varying US dollar figures for Soviet ruble GNP (e.g. from $6,824 to $2,751 per capita for 1980) serve as a rude reminder of the logic behind the original Chenery–Syrquin-type deviations from cross-section patterns. (A more recent Chenery, Robinson and Syrquin study, 1986, makes many more adjustments for exchange-rate distortion.) Campbell tries out the obvious hypotheses and obtains a disturbing range of ruble/dollar exchange rates (Campbell, 1985, table 9). Dollar GNPs for the USSR and other countries thus calculated form the shaky foundation of the international league tables and the econometric work that makes use of them (section 8.2 below). Predicted pattern values and structural gaps are meaningful to the extent that faith can be put in the conversion factors (one exchange rate per country) needed to reduce world output to a common denominator. Such exercises, while fascinating and suggestive when prices are right, resist interpretation when prices are set by bureaucrats and currencies are non-convertible.

6.7 Perestroika and Soviet economics

6.7.1 *Revising the notion of economic good: from matter to 'characteristics'*

At the time of writing, *perestroika* has not yet led to a restructuring of the basic definitions of productive and non-productive activity despite loud hints that there are plans to do so, and despite personnel and name changes at the Central Statistical Administration (Vanous, 1986, p. 4; discussions at the Central Mathematical–Economics Institute, June 1988). Continued improvements in the quality of the literature devoted to the non-productive and service spheres raise the hope that a normalization of the treatment of services in Soviet economics and statistics may at long last be in the offing.

In addition to works on general economics, optimal planning, and national income accounting (Boss, 1982, ch. VI, ns 293 and 294), since the 1960s scores of articles and monographs have been devoted to the non-productive sphere (Boss, 1982, ch. VI, n. 295), the service sphere (1982, ch. VI, n. 296), and to specific topics such as the economics of education, health, housing, R&D, and management science (Bogomazov, 1981; Boss, 1982, ch. VI, n. 297).

The Stalin textbook's definitive exclusion of passenger transportation rankled, especially since several East European countries declined to follow the Soviet lead (Kudrova, 1969; Campbell, 1985, p. 3).

In the late 1950s the prominent and quite orthodox (Katsenelinboigen, 1980) political economist Ia. A. Kronrod suggested that passenger transportation, while not productive of material 'products', is 'of material character' and 'helps secure the material existence of people'. It therefore deserves its own category, 'material services', which would also include passenger transport and consumer energy supply, 'etc'. Kronrod's scheme fell short of dispensing with non-productivity altogether: doctors and sculptors still belonged in the non-productive sphere even though they too 'materially affect nature' (Kronrod, 1958, pp. 62–9).

Kronrod's material services were perceived as the thin edge of a wedge. Were passenger transport allowed in, other communal and personal services could press their claim for productive status (Sobol' in Riabushkin, 1958). A worker unable to get to work cannot produce much industrial output. Therefore passenger transport may be a necessary intermediate à la Kuznets to industrial production. If that is admitted, transportation to vacation spots could be productive too, because 'rest [is] necessary for the restoration of the person's work capacity' (Savin, 1969, cited in A. S. Becker, 1971, p. 55).

Savin's logic leads in either a G. S. Beckerian or a von Neumannesque direction, depending on the maximand (sections 8.4.2 and 10.5). Dutiful hardliners like Riabushkin and Sobol' (Riabushkin, 1958; Sobol', 1960, p. 141) prevented the Beckerian can of worms from being opened at all far. It is not known how explicitly the link was made between allowing the productivity of services and admitting that Marshall and Pigou had been right all along. It is reasonable to assume that the ideological high authorities understood that tampering with the doctrine of non-productive activity called into question, however technocratically, the productive-labor theory of value upon which the call to anti-capitalist, communist revolution and ultimately the legitimacy of the régime were founded. Tinkering with the official surplus and transfer theory risked invalidating Soviet claims to a distinctive economic 'mechanism', complete with its matching value theory and economic 'laws' (see Karataev, 1966; Khavina *et al.*, 1975, 1976).

The first wave of deStalinization came with a winding down of opportunities for extensive growth. There was concern about the persistent backwardness of agriculture and consumer services. Criticism of the doctrine of non-productiveness first arose in the main philosophy journal in 1958 in connection with education, health, planning, and public administration. Not only laborers in material branches were productive, but also those whose labor is intellectual or spiritual. Spiritual labor involves 'science, art, care of children, teaching, management, organization of the national economy, state administration and so forth'. As in Strumilin and Kursky, lexicographic modism saves the situation. State service workers under socialism are entirely different in character from those described so unflatteringly by Adam Smith and Karl Marx. Students and soldiers are not rehabilitated by the scheme; soldiers' labor is neither material nor spiritual, though 'socially necessary and highly respected' (Rachkov, 1958, p. 187).

Rachkov's proposal was attacked by the old-time materialist–fallacist M. V. Solodkov, later dean of Moscow University (1959, p. 48). It made no imprint on the classification reform of 1967. Still the Khrushchev period witnessed the opening of new fields for economic analysis: education, health, scientific research, and public administration (Krylatykh, 1985). But it was not until 1974 that the Moscow University Economics Department acquired a *kafedra* and degree program for the study of the non-productive sphere, under Solodkov's direction.

A survey of the Soviet economics of education is beyond the scope of this history (G. G. Bogomazov, 1981, has kindly provided a useful bibliography). The Soviet capital concept remained closely identified with machinery and buildings: 'basic funds' originate in such branches as machine-building and construction, not in labs or educational establishments.

Mathematical economics began to be more widely disseminated when it was realized(!) that it could improve the feasibility of plans. Mathematical followers of Nemchinov, Novozhilov, and Fedorenko, like Raiatskas, had no difficulty with production-function type relationships between inputs and outputs. Output was related to welfare by the postulate that planners choose investment priorities and consumption mixes benevolently, in consumers' near-term if not immediate interest, and assign resources to them efficiently. The study of such choices they called SOFE, for optimal functioning of the economy. Advocates of SOFE were accused by the political economists of being closet marginalists, insufficiently respectful of the labor theory of value, and, later, of such mode offenses as favoring 'market socialism' (interview with N.Ia. Petrakov, Moscow, June 1988; Katsenelinboigen, 1980). For example, optimality is presented in *Social Usefulness of Production and its Cost in Labor* (Val'tukh, 1965) in a way that leaves no room for Classical–Marxian service-bashing.

> [The] essence of an economic optimum lies in obtaining with the aid of [society's material and labor resources] the maximum of utilities from the viewpoint of the development of society ... [In so far as] labor in non-material production [raises] the well-being and [leads to] the all-round free development of the members of society, it is productive labor. In other words, all socially useful labor is productive labor.
>
> (Val'tukh, 1965, pp. 62, 66)

Val'tukh's socialist utilitarianism has a neoclassical precision not found in Bazarov, Bogdanov, or the Strumilin of 1926. Service-sphere workers produce value since they and material production workers buy services, and

> *payment for services is a form of equivalent exchange.* There exists distribution and redistribution of the results not only of material production, but also of the results of non-material production ... This is in full accordance with the principles of social division of labor (which apply of course not only to material production) and with those of socialist cooperation between workers.
>
> (Val'tukh, 1965, p. 67; emphasis added)

Val'tukh moreover explains that workers in the non-material sphere are 'productive' of surplus since the products are worth more than they cost in labor and materials. As did Kursky, he complains that exclusion of services 'lowers the mass of [measured] real wealth obtained by members of socialist society'; the more important the size of the non-productive sphere, the more serious this distortion becomes. It is misleading to include only material expenses of the non-productive sphere in net material product because not material inputs but service outputs are what constitute bona fide goods or utilities to consumers. On the supply side, the production processes of non-material outputs lend themselves to and indeed require economic analysis, further undermining the case for asymmetric treatment (Val'tukh, 1965, p. 68).

Calls to rehabilitate the non-productive sphere on socialist–utilitarian grounds reached a chorus in the late 1960s. Articles with titles like 'Value of Services: reality or fiction?' and 'No Such Thing as Double-Counting of Services' appeared in widely read journals such as that of the Institute of World Economy (Kovyzhenko, 1967; Pevzner, 1969; Boss, 1982, ch. VI, n. 296).

A Russian translation of the émigré Paul Studenski's monumental study *The Income of Nations* (first edition, 1958) was brought out in 1968. It began with an important introduction by the eminent non-Party scholar A'lb. L. Vainshtein. Studenski's book traces from earliest times the progress of the 'comprehensive' concept of output (by which he means the Keynesian $C + I + G + (X - M)$), given statistical flesh by Keynes's disciples Meade and Stone (Meade and Stone, 1941; section 8.2 below). Studenski documents the spread of standard SNA methodology to all countries except those of the Soviet bloc. Vainshtein (1892–1970) had been among the neo-Narodniks associated with Kondrat'ev (Kondratieff) at the famous Conjuncture Institute in the 1920s. Kondrat'ev was purged; Vainshtein survived a quarter-century in the gulag (Jasny, 1972, p. 208).

Vainshtein's monograph displays easy familiarity with the work of Marshall, Pigou, Meade and Stone, Kuznets, Bergson, and of course Studenski. It refers to education as investment in human capital, a view that was to gain wide currency in specialist circles (Vainshtein, 1969, p. 16, n. 2; Kapeliushnikov, 1977). Vainshtein himself supports a Kuznets-type variant of the Western concept that demotes government administration to the status of intermediate input, part of the regrettably necessary but only indirectly welfare-enhancing 'social framework' (section 8.4.1 below).

Pre-*glasnost'* Soviet publication practices were such that, in an introduction otherwise highly favorable to Studenski, Vainshtein justifies *excising* from the Soviet edition Studenski's detailed accounts of pre-revolutionary Russian and Soviet estimates of national income, and his views of the controversies over unproductive labor and the boundary of the economy. Readers of the Russian Studenski are told that their edition 'has been slightly shortened [by about 20 per cent] in comparison with the English original'. The Aesopian message is plain: Studenski's devastating judgment of the baneful influence of Adam Smith and his view of the Marxian as 'nearly a copy' of the Smithian conception are rendered almost in full and in the same unequivocal language (Studenski, 1968, pp. 51–2, 57–62, 278–85). It was a compromise of the type, 'cut the numbers but keep the concepts'.

In 1969, statistical material cut from the Studenski translation was restored in Vainshtein's own historical and critical study, *The National Income of Russia and the USSR*. The index-number problem ('1926–7 and all that') and the proper price deflator for 1913–28 are discussed in this important work with some frankness (Gregory, 1982, p. 104). The 1967 classification reform is criticized for not having enlarged the sphere of material production to include at least 'material services' like public baths and laundries and for not allowing into net material product scientific research organizations 'connected with production' such as geological prospecting and engineering consultancy bureaux. But readers are once again reminded that, under capitalism, inclusion of all service incomes grossly inflates the total and is moreover socially reactionary since rent and interest are included on a par with wages. Imputation of rent for owner-occupied dwellings paints a false picture of the housing situation. Under socialism, productiveness should be based on the distinction between 'necessary' and 'surplus' labor and product; on his view, health, education, and even original works of art belong in socialist national income.

> In socialist society necessary labor and product should encompass all goods and services going into *direct* consumption of all workers participating in socialist production: strictly speaking, in a socialist country only the services of the army, militia, courts and prisons, and the purely administrative [i.e. non-planning] apparatus should be excluded . . .
>
> (Vainshtein, 1969, p. 18)

A 1970 article by P. G. Oldak explains the favoring of goods over services as a misunderstanding of the distinction between stocks and flows. Oldak's is essentially the argument presented with penetrating clarity by Léon Walras in 1874 (section 4.6 above). Utilities enjoyed are flows of services consumed per unit of time. Adam Smith did not see that it is all relative.

> If we take a century-long time period, stocks will be seen to consist only of mined precious metals, precious stones, and goods made of them, as well as certain engineering installations - roads, dams, canals, some buildings. On a ten-year scale, the stock [of produced wealth] will now appear to include many types of means of production as well as a large group of instruments of consumption (durable consumer goods). In a one-year framework the stock will encompass now almost all instruments of labor and equipment (except for tools which wear out rapidly), a definite fraction of raw materials, fuel, and [other] materials (the increase of annual reserves), and instruments with long and medium-term service lives. If we take a period of a single day, the stock concept appears to include almost all material products of production (with the exception of certain

types of prepared food), as well as specific kinds of services (for example, furnishing of heat to consumers' dwellings). And finally, if we take a very short interval of time, the difference between a flow and a stock disappears ... Theoretically, this means that in comparison with the stock concept, the flow concept has the wider and more comprehensive meaning.

(Oldak, 1970, p. 115)

By 1977 V. N. Bogachev could write that ability to tell stocks from flows 'has become what distinguishes the economist from the dilettante' (1977, p. 2).

The terminology used to describe the service sector yields a convenient rule of thumb for dividing old-style Stalinists from reform-minded modernists. The old-style writers maintain the value-laden official term *neproizvodstvennaia sfera* (non-productive sphere) while the mathematically literate, both optimal planners and decentralizers – among whom we may cite Kvasha, Shatalin, Val'tukh, Agabab'ian, Medvedev, Vainshtein, Pevzner, Petrakov, and Oldak - reliably employ the more neutral term *sfera uslug* or *obsluzhivaniia* (service sphere). Use of the term 'service sphere' is associated with a more matter-of-fact focus on the best use of economic resources in order to raise consumers' welfare and with reduced concern for the scholastic Classical–Marxian issues of materiality and 'inherent' capacity for producing a surplus.

As we saw in the case of Strumilin (not to speak of Marx and Lenin if we give them generous benefits of the doubt), socialist utilitarianism is quite compatible with a belief in the efficacy of strict central ownership and control. That is the tacit theme of the monograph *Production and Consumption of Services in the Tenth Five-Year Plan* by E. Agabab'ian (1977). Immaterial services are treated as comparable in every respect to material goods, and as such may even make up part of the nation's medium-term accumulated wealth. Forms of wealth that provide use-values over multiple time periods include not only the physical capital stock but also the 'level of skill, professional experience and physical capacity of the total labor force, the achievements of science, the accumulated products of art and culture and the [personal] property of the population' (Agabab'ian, 1977, p. 122). Moreover, exhaustion of factor reserves means that future growth will depend on improved quality of factor inputs, particularly management, and on technology developed by the (non-productive mental laborers of the) scientific and technical intelligentsia (Agabab'ian, 1977, pp. 122–3).

Management science saw promotion to the status of independent academic discipline during the Kosygin reform debates of the mid-1960s; institutes to disseminate managerial know-how were set up. Traditional Marxism's faith in the powers of 'science' and in conscious man's victory over unconscious but not-too-niggardly nature was extended to the 'science of running the economy' (Beissinger, 1982, ch. 2). In that spirit, Agabab'ian looks to the 'convergence, the growing together of administration and science' into a more effective if still centralized system of information-gathering and resource allocation.

The promotion of administration to scientific status involved a small step in the 'Austrian' direction of formulating the planners' problem as one of coordination between specialized units under the scarce or low-quality *information*. Increasing enterprise specialization increases the number of transactions between enterprises (Arrow, 1979). Imperfections of 'central adjustment' are not only due to the fact of 25–34 million different goods in the Soviet economy and to geometric increases in the complexity of their interrelationships. There is also – as a generation of Western and a growing number of Soviet scholars have noted – a built-in tendency under Soviet planning for the information provided from enterprise to Gosplan to be *false*. Risk-averse enterprises overstate requirements and understate capabilities in order to get easy plans (Bergson, 1948; Liberman, 1955; Berliner, 1976; Kornai, 1980). Agabab'ian's analysis is a step on the road to a more modern appreciation of the nature of economic goods as multi-faceted 'bundles' of 'characteristics' (Lancaster, 1966).

While it scarcely bespoke a revolution in Soviet microeconomics, especially in the teaching of undergraduates, a number of important Western textbooks became available in Russian in limited editions starting in the 1960s. Samuelson's *Economics* came out in 1964, Baumol's *Economic Theory and Operations Analysis* in 1968, and Seligman's detailed *Main Currents in Modern Economics* in the same year. Lancaster's *Mathematical Economics* was published in Russian in 1972 and Malinvaud's *Leçons de théorie microéconomique* in 1985. Böhm-Bawerk and Schumpeter are promised for 1990.

Analyses that placed productive and non-productive spheres on an equal footing remained open to criticism from the ideologists however. Until 1988, political economy taught to students was essentially the contents of the Stalin textbook, reworked in scores of dictionaries, courses, outlines, and essays. The collective efforts of, for example, Gatovsky *et al.* (1977), Rumiantsev *et al.* (1979), Volkov *et al.* (1979, 1985), Kolesov (1979), Tsagolov (1982), Buzuev and Buzuev (1986), and Chukhno (1988) only marginally temper traditional Leninist materialist-fallacist rhetoric – to the extent of paying the non-productive sphere many more compliments than previously on its social usefulness. When all is said and done, though, the kind words and phrases merely compound the input–output error. In the textbooks as in the national income accounts, citizens employed in the *neproizvodstvennaia sfera* are still technically and theoretically portrayed as *transfer recipients* living off the backs of the productive members of society, the real producers of 'things'.

Official materialist fallacy has been an albatross for Soviet economics. It went hand in hand with the branch average cost approach to price formation and the gross value of output approach to plan fulfillment. Before Gorbachev's revolution from above, no one had the authority to deal with the political and philosophical implications.

There are several ways to shoo the bird away: one, Kuznetsian in spirit, takes the route of valorizing 'socioeconomic infrastructure' as a worthy if intermediate form of socialist economic activity, and notes that services too may be 'intermediate'. The other delves back into Marxism's socialist–utilitarian and utopian past for the notion that the revolution was made not in order to maximize the output of heavy industry but to increase the number of 'final economic results' enjoyed by the target beneficiaries, workers and peasants. Services to the population are such final economic results (see Abalkin, 1978).

Quarrels over ends and means continued throughout the well-named 'period of stagnation'. 'Final results of production activity' (note the qualifier) was one of the few new entries in the 1981 *Dictionary of Political Economy* (Volkov *et al.*, 1985). The items 'final social product', 'production', 'productive and non-productive labor under socialism', 'service sphere', 'ownership', 'essential distinction between mental and physical labour', 'vulgar bourgeois political economy', and so on, remained defined as before. But 'final results of production activity' and perhaps also the entry 'personal subsidiary small holding of a collective farmer' hinted at possible movement away from the traditional focus on material intermediate goods to emphasis on what consumers might prefer. There is a downplaying of mode, as if the 'net material product' concept were already under fire and 'final results of production activity', which is very similar to the SNA's 'Keynesian' $C + I + G + (X - M)$, were being groomed to succeed it.

> Final results of production activity [are] a form for implementing the objectives immanently *inherent in any mode of production* ... Socialist production is aimed at meeting the needs of society and achieving the all-round development of each individual objectively highlights *social use value* ... All these demands are most fully met by the physical volume of the national income [*sic*] ... In the socialist economy, the final economic results reflect the movement of the product along all the phases of social reproduction up to its *ultimate* consumption by the people [$C + G_c$], for the purposes of accumulation [I], export [X] or strengthening the country's defences [G_d]. Thus, in agricultural production it is important

not only to grow products, but *equally* important to transport, store and process them, as well as to sell them to the consumer ...

(Volkov *et al.*, 1985, pp. 137–8; emphases added)

6.7.2 Mode and matter under perestroika

The doctrine of the non-productiveness of immaterial services under Soviet socialism has remained a heavily-defended bastion of the official economic scene since the defeat of the Strumilin proposal in the mid-1920s. But like the planning system introduced under Stalin which it complements, non-productivity is portrayed by the more sophisticated economists and economic journalists of the Gorbachev era as an increasingly misleading guide to Soviet reality and aspirations.

The redistributive and pro-growth ideals of Marx and Lenin have sought expression under Gorbachev in terms more socialist–utilitarian than socialist–materialist. Even the 'socialist' today sounds partly for show, a legitimizing link with the mode of the founding fathers. The fanatical appeal to eliminate market links, to root out private ownership and destroy rentier incomes - outstanding features of revolutionary Marxism since Lenin, as we saw in sections 6.2–6.4 - is now something of an embarrassment. Under Gorbachev, Lenin is being made (not without protest from historians - e.g. Seliunin, 1988; Tsypko, 1989) into a passionate defender of cooperatives as fully socialist and into a lifelong advocate of an NEP mixed economy in which not the plan but 'commodity–money relations' govern relations between units.

A World Bank report (on China but not irrelevant) couches the connection between expansion of a socialist economy's 'non-productive sphere' and reform of its economic mechanism as follows:

> Rapid service sector expansion and reform of the system of economic management are closely related options. Expansion of commerce would go hand in hand with expansion of market regulation and increased specialization of production units and localities. Expansion of enterprise support services, including finance, accounting, and law, would likewise be a corollary of increased enterprise autonomy and specialization. And expansion of personal services would reflect a change in the relative weights attached to planners' priorities and people's preferences. Moreover, rapid growth of services probably could not be accomplished through administrative directives and centralized resource allocation, but would have to be pulled by demand. Individual and collective enterprises may also be better suited than state enterprises to providing many types of services.
>
> (World Bank, 1985, p. 2)

Service-bashing is increasingly seen to be symbolic and symptomatic of the low priority accorded to the wants of consumers. The need to move from an extensive growth strategy built on the mobilization of surplus rural labor to an intensive one based on raising total factor productivity has been an insistent theme since Brezhnev and Kosygin. Providing a more attractive array of consumer goods *and* services is perceived by the Gorbachev leadership as a key to the problem of raising labor productivity, of motivating workers to work while at work (Rutgaizer, 1985, p. 2; Rutgaizer and Sheviakhov, 1987). A widening of wage differentials is being justified by a view of unearned income that harks back to the neoclassical notion of monopoly rent. In the writings of the influential sociologist T. Zaslavskaia, 'unearned income' is earned not just by black marketeers and profiteering middlemen, but by shirkers and drunkards on the shop floor who take home pay without doing their share for social product. Also profiting unfairly from unearned income are citizens able to take advantage of heavily subsidized prices for housing, bread, and meat and of undifferentiated rents for fertile private plots (Zaslavskaia, 1986). The similarities between Zaslavskaia's and Rutgaizer's views on economic just desserts and those of Bukharin's neoclassical nemesis J. B. Clark have, understandably, not been overstressed.

How a de-ideologized, restructured, and 'feasible' Soviet economy might make its peace with a multiplicity of ownership types was discussed before *perestroika* got under way by the eminent economist Alec Nove (Nove, 1983, Part 5). Different goods and services have different production and consumption characteristics. Scale of establishments, ownership rules, and invasiveness of central control should in theory vary with techniques of production and of delivery of goods to their final destinations. For Nove, a 'feasible' scheme might keep 'natural' monopolies such as rail, mail, and telephone services under central control. (The naturalness of such monopolies depends on the cheapness with which technical advance adds flexibility: when satellites rather than wires are the capital equipment in telecommunications, a plurality of suppliers becomes feasible, such as occurred in the US telephone industry in the 1980s.) In their case, technical economies of scale are likely to be so huge that a region or nation does best by regulating a single monopoly producer.

In restaurants, tourism, commerce, and the legal and 'helping' professions, however, it is unlikely that regulated monopoly is the institution of choice. The analysis relies on not only the Smithian view of the benefits of competition but the 'characteristics' of the goods themselves. In these industries, producers deal with clients face to face. Under capitalism, ownership and incentive structures induce sellers to *conceal* the fact that they are in the business of earning a living, making money. The illusion of voluntary service has welfare rationality because politesse, promptness, friendliness, care - in a word, 'service' - are part of the bundle of 'characteristics' of service outputs that consumers look for.

In individualized undertakings such as restaurants, the 'amount' or quality of service rendered is frequently negatively related to the size of the plant if not the whole enterprise. Non-homogeneity (differentiation) is the rule; a mass cafeteria serves needs (and meals) quite different from those of a fancy restaurant. Economies of scale in production and organization are typically less important in paid service enterprises than in industry. Indeed, alienatingly excessive scale is blamed for tax-revolt and the world-wide shift to the Right in Western countries, as consumer-voters underestimate the true volume of services received from the faceless bureaucracies of the welfare state (Dahrendorf, 1981).

In public catering, raw ingredients come from agriculture, itself a domain in which products are easily but sharply differentiated by quality and freshness. Perfectly homogeneous bushels of corn exist in treatises on perfect competition, not in Soviet vegetable warehouses. Failure to capture differences in quality in prices generates non-price allocation modes (such as queueing, pilfering, tipping, outright bribery) that distort labor incentives and increase policing costs for the economy as a whole.

Before *perestroika*, untold gains in value added and consumer satisfaction went untapped because small-scale enterprises were not allowed to provide services legally at prices that reflected quality differentials. The activities did not disappear; they were driven into the second economy, where information was naturally scarce and prices exhorbitant on account of low volume and high risk.

Taking a cue from the Soviet law on cooperatives of 1986, J. S. Berliner develops a model of how *perestroika* might progressively overcome the Stalin system's problems of high cost and low quality. The idea is gradually to marketize the command economy by keeping plan targets stable and letting new cooperatives, private farmers, and the old state enterprises freely buy and sell above-plan production. With growth, the state sector would experience a relative decline. The cooperative sector would run on inputs sold to it out of above-plan production of state enterprises and the output of private plots. The catch is that, in order for state enterprises to *want* to increase above-plan output, plan targets (now called state orders) have to be stable, pre-empting the annual upward ratchet of tasks that made it rational for firms to underperform in the past.

Assuming productive capacities do increase with investment (i.e. that the capital–output ratio does not shoot to infinity), enterprises in a three-sector Berliner system should generate a growing surplus and ever-more-competitive prices. If the ratchet is broken and enterprises are allowed to dispose freely of their proceeds, the surplus should be as large and as appropriately mixed as sovereign consumer-workers wish. The liberty of earning income by selling over-plan production to the highest bidder harks back to Lenin's 'tax in kind', a further selling point.

> Among the goods and services to be produced by the cooperative sector would be a variety of consumer services (repairs, taxis, catering), specialized consumer goods, special order production for enterprises that require quick turnaround-time and high reliability, small-scale construction work, high-tech consulting services, and of course foodstuffs. The three-sector model would have a number of advantages: 1/ It would divert much of the entrepreneurial effort presently confined to the illegal portions of the second economy into legal and productive activity under state regulation ... 2/ It could reduce the degree of supply uncertainty ... 3/ It would significantly increase the supply of consumer goods and services, of higher quality ... 4/ [The size of it] can be controlled by the licensing of coops and by varying the degree of plan tautness ... 5/ The prices that emerge ... may increase the pressure on the state sector to [make prices closer to market-clearing ones] ... 6/ It is defensible on ideological grounds ... [and] is a distinctly Soviet model ...
> (Berliner, 1986, pp. 25–6)

The law on state enterprises that went into effect on 1 January 1988 threatens to present firms with a more difficult challenge than Berliner's tri-mode scheme, though how strictly failure will be punished is unknown. The aim of the law is to put a sizeable fraction of state firms onto 'full *khozraschet*' (economic accountability). Were this principle to be fully implemented (which shows little sign of happening) firms would have to survive as in capitalism by their wits and the desirability of their products in the marketplace. The first stage, though, retains a large share of the old system of guaranteed supplies and orders from the state network, at prices not to change until the 1990s.

The November 1986 decree permitting 'individual labor activity' - as family-scale, state-regulated, non-agricultural private enterprise is disingenuously called - has not to date legalized much more than was already technically legal according to the Constitutions of 1936 and 1977. (Auxiliary private farming and marketing of agricultural produce had even been encouraged in the late 1970s, as the state and kolkhoz food situation worsened (Rumer, 1981).) Confirmed in the 1986 law on self-employment is the existing right to produce and sell food on a family basis, as well as to perform repair, tailoring, tutoring, counseling and similar services, upon receipt of the requisite permit, and provided one pays income tax and does not quit the paid labor force if already in it. Permission to rent rooms and to operate cars as taxis are the novelties (Schroeder, 1987, p. 259).

Individual labor activity was introduced with ominous warnings about 'unearned incomes', corruption, and speculation (*Pravda*, 28 May 1986). Since these have not been clearly defined, the individual-labor initiative looks as much like an attempt to tax and police the existing 'second economy' as like a low-outlay way to increase consumer satisfaction (Blough *et al.*, 1987). The 'Marxist' ban on exploiting the labor of others (*sic*) and the provisions designed to prevent mere substitution of private for state activity threaten to reduce the effect of the provision on total private activity.

Similar regulations governing the formation of cooperatives to provide consumer services, food, and consumer goods (e.g. *Izvestiia*, 20 October 1986, 12 February 1987) went into effect in May 1987. They have attracted a modest number of initial takers on account of fears of policy reversal, official limits on eligibility, and overly strict interpretations of the law by local authorities. The State Committee on Statistics reported that 200,000 people had registered for individual labor activities and 80,000 were working in cooperatives producing consumer goods and services in October 1987; by the end of 1988 the total in the two new forms of activity had increased sevenfold to just under 2 million (*Sotsialisticheskaia Industriia*, 22 January 1989, p. 2). Prognoses of the scale envisaged in the medium term range from 5–7 per cent for self-employment, mentioned by Gorbachev himself, to 4 per cent cited by Abalkin. It is thought, for example by Abalkin, that cooperative production could reach 10–12 per cent of Soviet national income by 1996, with regional differences (Blough *et al.*, 1987, pp. 266–70).

In July 1988 yet another initiative was introduced to try to address the stagnating food situation. It was announced by Gorbachev that peasants should be given the option of taking out a 25-30- and even 50-year lease on *kolkhoz* and *sovkhoz* land, on the theory that peasants would raise production if they could keep the proceeds over and above the lease payment and any personal taxes. Reportedly there have been very few takers - proletarianized rural dwellers still show the demographic and emotional effects of dekulakization and are either afraid to incur neighbors' envy or simply lack the energy and ambition for above-*kolkhoz*-minimum work effort (Abalkin, 1988).

Along with the newly sanctioned private- and cooperative-sector initiatives in industry, agriculture and services, state services have also been set more ambitious growth targets. At the 27th Congress, Gorbachev stated the Party's intention to assure the 'development of a modern service sector as quickly as possible' (*Pravda*, 26 February 1986). If growth of services keeps pace with or exceeds growth of material goods, there would no longer be a case for exclusion on the ground that inclusion of services in global success indicators would diminish their measured growth rates.

The well-disposed observer of the *perestroika–glasnost'* new thinking scene does not know whether the play is a comedy or a tragedy. The wheel is being reinvented; introducing it demands great energy and political courage, since drivers still put their faith in sledges and profit from their monopoly of them. Traditional Marxism's favoritism of centralized, large-scale, state-owned units, its identification of material production with production of necessities and of services with luxury production appear on the point of being totally discredited, after causing seventy years of untold losses in potential utility. Serious commentators eschew the old rhetoric about the inherent across-the-board superiority of large-scale state-run units, the 'logical' primacy of material production, the perfectibility of directive central planning, and the inability of the non-productive sphere to produce intermediate goods, or even to add value. As we saw in Chapters 4 and 5, the entire detour was unnecessary: the counterarguments were there in the writings of nineteenth-century economists.

Perestroika as an economic program has not yet proven it can deliver the goods. Unpopular measures such as price increases for food and housing are on the agenda. The post-Stalin social contract is further undermined by the law on state enterprise, which is capitalism without private ownership and should for that reason strike fear into the hearts of Soviet managers and workers. No one knows who is a speculator or what constitutes unearned income. People have been told since 1917, and many believe, that production on its own account is antisocial if not criminal, that capitalist profits are extorted, that attaining an evened-out income distribution by expropriating the bourgeoisie was a primary aim and achievement of the revolution. Such people are understandably of two minds about the new opportunities.

The economic theory that might incline them to think otherwise is still officially limited to specialists, not taught, and apparently not entirely grasped even by prominent and mathematically-trained economists and sociologists amongst Gorbachev's advisers. Mathematical economists have, it ought not to be forgotten, numbered among the USSR's most confident central planners.

Adam Smith pointed out two centuries ago that producers vastly prefer monopoly to competition. The latter's low-price benefits are appreciated by citizens only in their rôles as consumers. Marx, as we saw, associated market competition with chaos, exploitation, and crisis rather than with a servo-mechanism for breaking down privilege.

Increasing computer literacy and awareness of the export achievements of certain third world countries has prepared the Soviet managerial and technical intelligentsia to understand the information-theoretic arguments, now that they can be voiced.

Beyond sheer ignorance of the Invisible Hand theorem and the conditions under which it holds, there is the touchy question of its relationship to basic values of Soviet society. The current enthusiasm for competition between enterprises and the flip-flop on non-planned, non-state-owned money-making must inevitably lead to a re-examination of the legitimacy of the revolution and the non-capitalist economic system it sought and succeeded in imposing. While the cruder Bolshevik ton-materialism seems *en route* to being discreetly weeded out of Soviet philosophy and economics, anti-market, centralizing modism has deeper and hardier roots in Soviet Russia. It remains to be seen how well the fragile small-scale enterprise plants will survive.

6.7.3 Beyond the pale

How have Soviet economists dealt with activities in the non-market household sphere, a mode beyond the pale? We saw how in the 1920s S. G. Strumilin advocated a full, 'socialist–utilitarian' accounting of household production. Home-produced care of the sick and the young as well as home-baked bread and self-built houses were to be included in the national income of the people's state. Though the purpose was to capture the full range of peasant production, behind that lay the idea that such a scheme did justice to the class compromise that underlay the New Economic Policy.

One of the first postwar economic analyses of non-marketed household production was made in Academician Strumilin's 85th birthday *Festschrift* (Sonin, 1962). 'On the characteristics of labor and employment in the domestic and private auxiliary [private-plot] economy' acknowledges that domestic labor devoted to household services ('care of children, shopping, food preparation, washing and mending of clothes, etc.) enables families to reduce money outlays. This is helpful even though no actual money is earned, as is usually the case in private-plot agriculture. Home-produced services are none the less susceptible of valuation via the measuring rod of money. Market values can be imputed to them just as the material product system imputes for home-produced food and housing.

Writing after Khrushchev's crackdown on private plots, the author bemoans their 'low productivity' and reminds us that they 'bear the stamp of individualism' and deprive their workers, mainly women, 'of the many joys inherent in collective forms of work' (Sonin, 1962, p. 278).

Although the boundary of the official NMP domain falls between household service and private-plot goods production, neither produces a 'social' surplus-value since there is no wage labor. Continued growth of productive forces promises to reduce shares of both sorts of individual activity, though only labor producing privately consumed material goods will disappear altogether. Performance of 'services for oneself' will always remain a 'necessary element of family, as indeed of individual existence' (Sonin, 1962, p. 275; sections 8.4.2 and 8.4.3 below).

The extra burden of 'work after work' imposed on Soviet citizens by the underdevelopment of consumer services is a major point made in an excellent 1972 study, *Man after Work*, by the sociologists Gordon and Klopov. The authors go beyond traditional productive-labor-theory Marxism in using 'time . . . as a means of describing everyday behavior' of people in their capacity as consumers as well as producers. Not all time after working hours is really free, leisure time. For example, in the late 1960s women in European Russia spent an average of six hours a week on queueing and shopping alone (Gordon and Klopov, 1972, ch. 2 and p. 84). Gordon and Klopov provide a fascinating statistical glimpse into the uses of workers' time during the sample survey week (see Table 6.1).

The old utopian communalist and Leninist view that the state should eventually supply the full range of Beckerian X-goods is rejected in favor of recognizing the moral and economic autonomy of what the young Marx called 'civil society'. Gordon and Klopov's argument can be related to the notion of diseconomies of scale in the production of goods and services of given qualities (characteristics). The use-value of a meal or of time spent entertaining friends, caring for infants, or tutoring children depends on the small, intimate scale of the household unit. Services rendered to citizens who frequent state theatres, crèches,

Types of activity	Women	Men
Labor in social production	39.40	40.10
Activity directly connected with production	9.50	13.00
Housework	27.20	11.40
Activities with children	5.50	6.00
Extrafamilial social intercourse	3.50	6.30
Daily cultural activity	11.50	19.50
Sleeping, eating, caring for oneself, idle time	60.30	66.30
Other	9.10	4.20

Table 6.1 Basic time expenditures of workers surveyed (hours and minutes per week)
Source: Gordon and Klopov, 1972, p. 263.

or schools (to which a dystopian might add other sorts of establishments) have 'characteristics' altogether different from the analogous ones 'produced' à la G. S. Becker in the privacy of one's home or communal apartment. Gordon and Klopov conclude that 'complete replacement of the household economy by socially produced services' is neither possible nor desirable.

> [It] is not just technical difficulties that [explain why] . . . the sphere of social services will not, over the next few decades, fully replace family production of services . . . It is a matter of the very nature of housework, which is, in effect, the last stage in the movement of many of the products and services produced by society to the consumer, and in this respect housework cannot but be individualized. Every family is *sui generis*, and its household is adjusted to the habits, tastes and temperaments of its members. In the final analysis, the household serves to consolidate the family, and so, many or some aspects of housework cannot be wholly absorbed by the service sector even when the latter is able to take on itself the production of corresponding services . . . Understanding that a complete replacement of the household economy by socially produced services is a utopian expectation helps to develop a broad and . . . realistic program for easing and reducing housework.
> (Gordon and Klopov, 1972, p. 78)

The authors employ the notion of substitution between bought goods and services (detergents, washing-machines, dry-cleaning services) and the work performed in the home without them. The 'most important reason why families [do] not use cafeterias [is] the expense of eating out in comparison with the domestic preparation of food' of a given quality (p. 80, n. 1).

Although the mix of personal services rendered in the household is presented as at least partly the outcome of an economic calculus, and although household 'production' is distinguished from household 'consumption', *Man after Work* does not mount a frontal challenge to the then-official boundary of the Soviet economic domain, as indeed its title indicates.

Agabab'ian, Oldak, or Rimashevskaia, economists by profession, would seem better placed to have housework (what little of it there can be, given participation rates of around 90 per cent of the adult labor force) reclassified as 'work'. Oldak, it will be remembered, found fault with the logical untidiness of Pigou's paradox (as did, by implication, Strumilin) and saw no reason why the output of housewives should be treated differently from that of cooks (Oldak, 1970, p. 119). In the USSR in 1970 'more than half of all yard goods consumed were used by private people for the sewing of clothes, sheets, etc. under household conditions' (p. 119, n. 16). He cites Studenski's summary of Western prewar studies, which estimated household production at 20–30 per cent of GNP.

Three years into *glasnost'*, *perestroika*, and new thinking, would-be Soviet socialist-utilitarians have their hands full advocating full economic citizenship for paid and unpaid state services. The non-productive sphere is still held to be such by university departments and official statisticians. Full conversion to world-conventional Pigovian–Keynesian national income accounts is a bright but unrealized prospect. Rimashevskaia's Institute for the Socioeconomics of the Population was founded only in 1988 to study participation, income distribution, and so on. A futile attempt to raise 'work after work' to full output status might merely play into the hands of the hard-line defenders of non-productivity and 'otherness' - followers of Tsagolov, Solodkov, Pravdin, Korchagin and Sbytova, Sonin, Kapustin, G. P. Ivanov, Kozak and authors of the Brezhnev-era textbooks on political economy and histories of thought.

Should the material product system and corresponding value theory be quietly dropped as part of a *glasnost'–perestroika* package, as looks probable now that GNP growth rates for the USSR have been published and major overhauls promised for economics and sociology after the 19th Party Conference, that would be a blow struck for both welfare-relatedness and international comparability. Ultimately, though, it would reopen another lost chapter of Soviet economic history. If the current studies of queueing time, e.g. those of Sheviakhov, Rimashevskaia, and Latsis, are extended backward to earlier decades and added into an equation that allows for reduced home production and enjoyment of housing, the much-vaunted reductions in the length of workers' working day might shine in a colder light. The production feats of the Stalin period, during which participation rates in target sectors rose dramatically, would get a second revaluation downward, past that required to incorporate the results like Seliunin and Khanin's (1987) on inflation.

It should come as a surprise, especially to Marxists, if an economics profession that has built careers around maintaining at least the semblance of fundamental theoretical disagreement with Western economics, should of a sudden abandon that commitment. The paradigm of the factory in which productive and revolutionary workers turn out material goods is part of the Soviet mythos. In circumstances in which productive status is still denied to public transportation, and ruble prices are inaccurate scarcity weights, it is hard to imagine the State Committee on Statistics stealing a march on Western national accountants and adopting as principal economic success indicator some new, more truly 'final' measure of goods and services 'produced', with the assistance of Beckerian X-goods, 'in the home'.

It was still *de rigueur* well into the 1980s for political economists to dismiss as 'subjective' the 'neoclassical' theory of production and distribution of marketed goods and services (see the Volkov *et al.*, entry 'Political Economy, Vulgar Bourgeois'). Though Hayek and Friedman as marketeers have received important attention from scholars (for example, Makasheva, 1987, 1988), Buchanan has not. The study of public goods and public choices in the USSR is in its infancy.

Karl Marx may be said to have popularized Say's notion of producer utility by underscoring how little of it workers got in capitalism's satanic mills. He also kept alive the not-unrealistic hope that, given the right arrangement, work could give pleasure, not just pain. Soviet economics has yet to take up those ideas in their modern Beckerian guise.

Nor has *glasnost'* yet sent lexicographic modism to the rubbish-bin of history. The notion that Marx's productive-labor theory of value may have been needlessly hard on barbers, hawkers, inventors, and postmen was a theme of a June 1988 paper I presented to the *kafedra* of the Non-Productive Sphere of the Department of Economics of Moscow University (Boss, 1988). The ensuing debate was closed by the host's reminding the assembly that their interlocutor was, after all, a 'bourgeois economist'.

Under full communism, concern to maximise the flow of truly final, Beckerian use-values actually enjoyed by citizens might be a logical first objective of benevolent custodians of state property. Measuring that progress might be considered the principal task of socialist metricians. But, to invoke a *bon mot* of Karl Marx, 'it is not the consciousness of men that determines their being, but . . . their social being that determines their consciousness' (Marx, 1859). If the determinists are right, it may be a long wait.

Part Three

REVISIONS AND EXTENSIONS

CHAPTER 7

Old Left and New Right on Government as Parasite

> A plague o' both your houses!
> (*Romeo and Juliet*, Act III, scene i)

From the marginal revolution to the Great Depression, the economics of public- and private-service sectors and of households were relatively neglected subjects. Gaps and anomalies in the Classical and Marxian approaches to the boundary problem were acknowledged, but caused little loss of sleep. There *was* indeed Wicksell's article inaugurating the economics of public choice as the study of goods rich in externalities (Wicksell, 1896). Marshall (1890) noticed the problem of jointness in supply and demand, and analyzed external economies. Attention was, however, principally focused on money pricing of private goods and factors exchanged on markets large and small. The Great Depression and the new research program of macroeconomics changed all that.

First, Keynes produced an antidote to the disease he identified – the failure of labor markets to clear in a slump. In the absence of state intervention, unemployment could be expected to last seriously and for a long time. The good news was that governments might cure the disease by intelligent use of monetary and fiscal policy. A search for successful policy recipes was launched. Second, Keynes's analysis of propensities to consume implied that good macroeconomic effects might be had from redistributions away from rich but timorous savers toward reliable big spenders such as government bureaux. A fatter government slice of the cake benefited not only defense contractors and the poor but all who stood to gain from a strong economy. Third, large volumes of national income and product data were required to support the enlarged policy effort; on Keynes's advice it was agreed to place government expenditures on non-marketed goods and services in the national income and product accounts on the same, 'final' footing as consumption and investment (Meade and Stone, 1941; Stone, 1985). Conventional measurements of economic success henceforth gave government the benefit of the doubt utility-wise. Fourth, the Keynesian treatment of government as just another sector made a permanent breach in the traditional mode boundary of economic science, drawing economists ever deeper into non-market territory.

A revolution so successful in changing the agenda of economics and economies created new problems as it treated old. Vocabulary expanded to take in political business cycles, cost-push, entitlement creep, stagflation, crowding-out, egoism of bureaucrats, rationality of expectations, slowness of productivity growth, inelasticities of supply in general. With the dashing of the initial hope of combining high growth, rising entitlements, and low inflation, a new class of explanations looked to differences between public and private goods, to the disrepute of the former, and also to symmetries of information in the hands of policy-makers and businessmen. For if private citizens know just as much about the economic mechanism as do government policy-makers, how might the latter fool the former into favorable macroeconomic behavior (Sargent and Wallace, 1976; Rymes, 1979)?

Politics still relies on the device of a 'Left'–'Right' linear spectrum. Economic theory and policy debate *post* Keynes seemed to range itself along such a line. If space is curved, however, opposites may touch. A prime suspect for ideational warp in economic science is the Classical–Marxian theory of surplus-generation and transfer. Economists at polar ends of the politico-economic spectrum may end up with similar analyses of a range of basic issues. The monetarism of Marxian analyses of inflation is a notable example (M. Lavoie, 1987).

Radical modism, for instance, rises at the antipodes. Both 'old' Left and 'new' Right make their models rely, with a fervor foreign to Keynesians who occupy the political middle, on the postulate of unique productiveness for the market mode of production within mixed capitalism. Government in general and defense in particular are parasitic excrescences upon the real economy of private producers of things. In the name of the Keynesian delusion that governments *can* fine-tune the economy, resources have been shunted to an unproductive state sector, starving the engine of postwar growth.

Though late twentieth-century revival of unproductive-labor doctrine comes in 'Left' and 'Right', Marxian and conservative variants, it would be absurd to try to downplay obvious differences between self-proclaimed opposites. There is fundamental disagreement on the ultimate welfare value of market outcomes, particularly as they touch on to the distribution of income and wealth. But the two sides share some intellectual ground avoided by the Keynesians who take positions between them in politics. On the common territory flourish a number of common themes:

(i) that tertiarization is a menace and that industry deserves encouragement as more 'productive' than ephemeral services;

(ii) that, since effective demand may be taken for granted as more or less adequate, attention should shift to supply, to saving, and to provision for future as opposed to present generations. Individuals have myopic telescopic faculties and cannot be trusted to provide for capital accumulation to benefit their children and grandchildren or even to see to their own sustenance in old age;
(iii) that it makes a great deal of difference in which mode supply occurs.

Post-Keynesian Classical–Marxians of both Left and Right pay close attention to commodity-hood and *de jure* marketability. Market and non-market modes are non-comparable as to both process and result; in particular, the latter is not an *as if* analogue of the former. The services of state officials are not supplied via some roundabout public-choice mechanism in response to revealed demand for them, but are rather, as Marx put it, 'forced on us'.

Left and Right evaluate results differently, as Marx differs from Smith. The Left, as we shall see, finds little fault with the familiar Marxian portrait of capitalist development except for scale and timing of the final crash. Business and government may now be 'big', but the capitalist system is neither stable enough nor fair enough to deserve any positive long-term prognosis. In contrast, conservative academic economists have taken up questions left unanswered by Classical–Marxian unproductive labor theory and tried to rework them into a more respectable intellectual product. Costly and possibly asymmetric information is integrated into a competitive market model, amended to allow as best it can for externality-rich public and other state goods.

The political life of Western democracies in the late 1970s and 1980s was dominated by voter-consumer feeling that state agencies were not providing reasonable *quid pro quo* for taxes paid (Dahrendorf, 1981; Stockman, 1986). Representatives who promised to lower the cost of complying with government regulations and to reduce the share of resources passing through state hands found themselves in power. Since the end of the postwar boom *circa* 1973, the problem of the 'most efficacious proportion' of public to private action has been *the* issue in economics as well as politics (e.g. Thurow, 1986).

7.1 Post-Keynesian Marxism: capitalism spared by an unproductive war sector

Fewer than two decades separate the end of European Marxism's Golden Age, in World War I and the October Revolution, from the

Great Crash of 1929. The long depression that followed shook the remaining countries of the industrial capitalist world to their foundations. J. M. Keynes's *General Theory*, published in 1936, combined novel analysis of protracted slump with the practical recommendation that deficit-financed public works be instituted to put purchasing power into the pockets of the unemployed. With World War II, the situation turned around and faith in both capitalist institutions and in non-Marxian economics was largely restored. Orthodox Marxian value, class, and breakdown theory received a serious intellectual challenge. Among non-aligned Marxists writing in English, the challenge was most energetically taken up by Paul Sweezy, Paul Baran, Joseph Gillman, Paul Mattick, and Harry Braverman. The American journal and press *Monthly Review* provided a widening forum for their ideas in the 1960s. Since then, Michael Kidron, James F. Becker, A. Sharpe, and Edward N. Wolff have passed more recent macroeconomic numbers through the sieve of the old Marxian anti-capitalist parasite theory.

Paul M. Sweezy's *Theory of Capitalist Development* (Sweezy, 1942) introduces Marxian political economy to an American readership. The book is something on a classic because of its early post-Keynesian timing, non-polemical tone, and fair-minded if enthusiastic exposition of the work of Marx and his European successors. Sweezy is faithful to the great radical of scope, valuation, and netness. Only 'labor' in production creates 'value' and 'surplus-value'. Circulation, for instance, is 'unproductive commercial activity ... unproductive because it does not create surplus-value but rather absorbs it from the other sectors of the economy' (1942, p. 227 and n.). He pooh-poohs Adam Smith's difficulties with the designation of some laborers as unproductive, though Smith has committed a 'logical error'. The materialist cast that Smith's heirs so clearly perceived in the *Wealth of Nations* comes from a too literal misreading of Smith's intent. What Smith aimed to render with the productive/unproductive distinction is the historically- shifting mode boundary that is Marx's contribution to the scientific study of capitalist development. As for the Menshevik Rubin (section 6.4.5 above), for Sweezy material definitions of output are ahistorical and irrelevant to social science.

Material definitions of output and productive labor carry a high risk of 'unproductiveness fallacy'. Sweezy is not immune. Despite the post-Keynesian flavor of the work, Sweezy singles out a special category of consumers – rentiers, civil servants, and commercial workers – as ultimately 'unproductive', all the while describing in detail how 'necessary' and important they are in keeping the capitalist system afloat. For example, merchants are able to extract some of the surplus-value generated in 'production' because 'under capitalism commerce cannot be dispensed with; in an unplanned economy [sic] the bringing together of buyers and sellers is an absolutely necessary function' (1942, p. 279). Advertising executives and military personnel fill the shoes of Malthus's landlords and parsons. 'Production' covers only 'industry', agriculture, and transport' (p. 228). Without examining how a non-Stalinist centralized socialism might function, Sweezy asserts it would overcome the present system's tendency to deficient aggregate demand without reliance on expenditures of unproductive consumers. The 'applied Tuganism' of a Stalin-style investment strategy, logically a candidate, is presumably not what he has in mind.

Despite the Keynesian echoes, Sweezy is ultimately an underconsumptionist (Bleaney, 1976, ch. 12). Crises and recessions are caused by the limited 'consumer power of the population, primarily of the working class but also of the rentiers who receive a certain share of the profits'. This means that '[investment and government expenditure] have to be brought in to fill the gap' (Bleaney, 1976, p. 230).

Given that avoiding crises and depressions is an unambiguous desideratum (a point not obvious to revolutionary modists), successful macroeconomic policy should yield a Pareto-improvement, benefiting not only would-be unemployed and owners of underutilized tangible and intangible capital, but everyone, including those still employed but in a slack economy. The superior state of affairs would be in part due to expenditures that Sweezy characterizes as 'unproductive': they are responsible *ceteris paribus* for the *difference* between the low and high levels of aggregate activity. Treating state expenditures as exclusively final consumer goods when employment of resources is less than full involves, as I have said, the input–output error of 'unproductiveness fallacy'. Even if it is maintained that some categories of state expenditure lack final utility in themselves, they – like sulfuric acid, dynamite, and miners' lights – may still be necessary if only intermediate means to the worthier, more 'final' ends.

Sweezy is not sure that 'Keynesian' avoidance of crisis is desirable, however, since it is doubtful whether piecemeal demand management that aims to preserve such an inherently cruel, wasteful, and philistine system as monopoly capitalism can really be justified.

Sweezy's longtime friend and collaborator Paul Baran, who lived in Poland, the Ukraine, Germany, Moscow, Latvia, and England before coming to the United States, brought out *The Political Economy of Growth* in 1957. It is an exciting work in which sparks fly from every page. Baran excoriates the injustice, irrationality, waste, militarism of the American economic system, the dehumanizing manipulation of the consumer, the contemptible hypocrisy of the monopoly capitalist and his advertising minions; the unredeemable vulgarity of American culture, which 'systematically and relentlessly destroys all intelligent thought among young and old, . . . ignorant and educated, in the advanced countries no less than the backward' (Baran, 1957, p. 298). Analytically his work turns on the 'concept of economic surplus'.

Baran's concept of surplus epitomizes the defects both of logic and of intolerance in aesthetic matters that dog attempts to dictate who should count as an economic producer and who should not. Baran's avowed subject is 'economic development'. What is development? In a passage requiring no comment he suggests that

> economic growth (or development) be defined as increase over time in *per capita* output of *material* goods. . . . *Especially* troublesome [in measuring it] is the services sector, the expansion of which would cause an increase in Gross National Product (as conventionally defined) suggesting thus 'economic growth' - although in most countries [*sic*] it would be considered to be a *retrograde* step rather than one in the direction of economic progress. Pigou's famous gentleman marrying his cook and thus reducing national income comes readily to mind. Equally easily one can imagine a tremendous expansion of national income caused by the introduction of compulsory payment to wives for services rendered.
> (Baran, 1957, pp. 18–19; emphasis added)

Colin Clark's definition of economic progress 'simply as an improvement in economic welfare' (Clark, 1940, p. 1) is rejected because it would leave out of account increases in leisure but include increases in material output that 'bear no relation to welfare', such as 'currently-produced investment goods, armaments', and (*sic*) 'patent medicines, beauty parlors, narcotics, and items of conspicuous display, etc.' (Baran, 1957, p. 18, n. 6).

As in Book II, chapter iii, of the *Wealth of Nations*, in Baran the size and disposition of the economic surplus determines the rate of economic development. Baran admits that 'the concept . . .is undoubtedly somewhat tricky' (p. 22), but proceeds to set out three varieties of it.

[1] *Actual* economic surplus [is] the difference between society's *actual* current output and its *actual* current consumption [that of consumers, the capitalist class, and government's spending on administration, military establishment and the like]

[2] *Potential* economic surplus [is] the difference between the output that *could* be produced in a given natural and technological environment . . . and what might be regarded as essential consumption . . . [It] *excludes* such elements of surplus-value as what [above] is called *essential* outlays on government administration . . .[but] it comprises what is not covered by the concept of surplus-value - the output lost in view of underemployment or misemployment

of productive resources . . . Its realization presupposes a more or less drastic reorganization of the production and distribution of social output. . . (Baran, 1957, pp. 22–4)

[3] *Planned economic surplus* [is a concept] relevant *only* to comprehensive economic planning under socialism. It is the difference between society's 'optimum' output attainable . . . and some chosen 'optimal' volume of consumption [representing] a considered judgment of a socialist community guided by reason and science.

(Baran, 1957, pp. 41–2)

'Potential' consumption exceeds 'essential' by four categories of superfluous expenditure: (1) the 'excess consumption' of middle-and upper-income groups; (2) the volume of output not produced because of the existence of 'unproductive workers'; (3) the output 'lost because of the irrational and wasteful organization of the existing productive apparatus'; and (4) the output forgone 'owing to the existence of unemployment caused primarily by the anarchy of capitalist production and [*sic*] the deficiency of effective demand (1957, p. 24).

Baran does not flinch from deciding what it is people actually want. 'Essential consumption', whether in underdeveloped or in advanced economies, 'is far from being a mystery'. In poor countries

> essential consumption can be circumscribed in terms of calories, other nutrients, quantities of clothing, fuel, dwelling space, and the like. Even where the level of consumption is relatively high . . . a judgment on the amount and composition of real income necessary for what is socially considered to be a 'decent livelihood' can be made . . . [This] is precisely what has been done in all countries in emergency situations such as war, postwar distress, and the like. What an agnostic apologist of the *status quo* and the worshipper of the 'consumer's society' treat as an unsurmountable obstacle, or as a manifestation of reprehensible arbitrariness, is wholly accessible to scientific inquiry and to rational judgment.
>
> (Baran, 1957, pp. 30–1)

On his view,

> a not insignificant part of the output of goods and services marketed and therefore accounted in the national income statistics of capitalist countries represents unproductive labor . . . [All] of it is altogether productive or useful *within the framework of the capitalist order*, indeed may be indispensable for its existence . . . most generally speaking, it consists of all labor resulting in the output of goods and services the demand for which is attributable to the specific conditions and

relationships of the capitalist system and which would be absent in a rationally ordered society.

(Baran, 1957, p. 32)

Into that category fall most of the usual Smitho-Marxian professions except for 'scientists, physicians, artists, teachers, and similarly occupied people'. Baran has his own twist to add to Smitho–Marxian unproductive labor doctrine. Since his goal, like Smith's, is to isolate the maximum of resources available for consumption and accumulation ('rational utilization'), but since 'labor [such as that of teachers] may be necessary without being productive' (*sic*, citing Marx, *Grundrisse*, 1857–8, p. 432), the resources spent on these unproductive activities are not 'surplus' in the sense of 'free for the tapping'. As Marx promised, in a 'rationally ordered society' total demand for doctors and teachers 'would become multiplied and intensified to an unprecedented degree'. Still there is no real economic *quid pro quo*: a surplus and transfer mechanism is what drives the system; professionals are 'supported by the economic surplus' (Baran, 1957, p. 33).

Baran's deep dissatisfaction with the *status quo* has as its vehicle a rather flagrant materialist input–output error. As with Marx and the Stalinists, in Baran modernization is to all intents and purposes synonymous with industrialization and the formation of an industrial working class.

His experiences in the Soviet Union caused no fundamental revision of faith in socialized ownership and centrally planned use of the physical means of production. Not only 'Stalin and Beria' but 'the "entire system" are responsible for . . . the crimes and errors committed in the Soviet Union before the Second World War'. The Soviet experiment, however, shows that rapid transformation of a backward economic system can be achieved by any country, however small and autarchic. What is required is to reduce actual consumption to essential consumption by taxing and expropriating middle and upper incomes, by forcing resources out of luxury industry and unproductive services like banking and advertising, etc. into basic industry, and by reducing managerial slack and waste. How this structural and efficiency shift might be engineered without resort to a Soviet-style command economy is not gone into.

Harry Braverman gives his *Labor and Monopoly Capital* (Braverman, 1974) the subtitle 'The degradation of work in the twentieth century'. The book's novelty as a contribution to Marxian economics is that it gives 'unproductive' white-collar service workers a clearly-stamped entry pass into the proletariat. Whereas, for Marx, 'to be a productive worker was not a piece of luck, but a misfortune' (Marx, 1867, p. 477), in the 1970s monopoly-capitalist mixed economy this misfortune falls upon all 'wage workers' in for-profit sectors (Braverman, 1974, p. 419). Marxism has been losing ground to other doctrines, says Braverman, because it has foolishly targeted itself at a declining population of industrial workers (p. 13).

Although commodity-centered and mode-minded, as Marxists must be, Braverman moves towards a less overtly materialist position. Still, his case for service-worker membership in the working class is made in part by reminding readers how 'material' certain service-industry tasks are. Service-sector jobs are increasingly automated and have been stripped of that variety of task that used to make them less alienating than factory work. Echoing the logic that Gray and Senior applied to Adam Smith (Gray, 1815; Senior 1836a), Braverman observes that

> When the chambermaids in hotels and motels, or the aides in hospitals and other institutions make beds, they do an assembly operation which is no different from many factory assembly operations – a fact recognized by management when it conducts motion and time studies of both on the same principles – *and [sic] the result is a tangible and vendible commodity.* Does the fact that porters, charwomen, janitors, or dishwashers perform their cleaning operations not on new goods that are being readied at the factory or construction sites for their first use, but on constantly reused buildings and utensils render their labor different in principle, and any less tangible in form, from that of manufacturing workers who do the factories' final cleaning, polishing, packaging, and so forth? ... The capitalist ... does not care in the last analysis whether he hires workers to produce automobiles, wash them, repair them, fill them with gasoline and oil, tend them by the day, drive them for hire, park them, or convert them to scrap metal.
> (Braverman, 1974, pp. 361–2; emphasis added)

Like Sweezy, Gillman, and Baran, Braverman finds the share of unproductive and superfluous laborers, as judged against an inner standard of what their share might be in a 'more rational' society, to be 'too high' and rising. It is not high income-elasticity of demand for services but greater output per productive laborer on the supply side in goods that has permitted the unfortunate trend.

Bourgeois economists, with their belief in consumer sovereignty, shrug their shoulders at tertiarization (e.g. Baumol, Blinder and Scarth, 1985, pp. 565–7). Society, they think, is just moving up its hierarchy of wants.

> Instead [of worrying about structural change in favor of unproductives], the measurement of the productivity of labor has come to be

> applied [by bourgeois economists] to labor of all sorts, *even labor which has no productivity*. It refers ... to the economy with which labor can perform any task to which it is set by capital, *even those tasks which add nothing whatever to the wealth of the nation.*
>
> (Braverman, 1974, p. 41; emphasis added)

As in Marx, the entire social surplus is owing to 'production workers', though millions are hired by capital in circulation activities, and despite the fact that, for the concept of surplus-value to be operative, surplus must be 'realized'. The argument makes use of the stagnationist thesis that the monopoly capitalist system will implode unless sustained by the unproductive expenditures of advertisers, the military, and the administrative and other branches of the state sector.

Underconsumption theories may be distinguished from Keynesian 'theories of effective demand' if we look at whether they allow that 'a government pound note, or an investor's pound note, is just as good as a consumer's...' (Bleaney, 1976, p. 230). Does a munition worker's dollar have the same effect as an automobile worker's? What of the spending of advertising executives, employees of teachers' unions, welfare mothers, those living on social security? As we saw in the case of Malthus, how such citizens affect total demand depends on whether they are said to be engaged in supply as well as demand, whether they produce as well as consume.

Left Keynesians like Kalecki and Joan Robinson, as well as Heilbroner and Galbraith and many other commentators, credit favorable macroeconomic performance in the period 1950–73 to a high level of military expense. However, since they think the economy is not close to its capacity limits, effective demand can come from *any* sector and equally stimulate the macroeconomy, except for the possibility that accelerator effects may be influenced by sectoral differences in capital–output ratios. Consumers do not remember in what sector they earned their wages when they come to spend them (see Kalecki, 1967, pp. 146–7, 153–5; Robinson, 1951, pp. 27–8; Robinson, 1966, p. 26).

Post-Keynesian orthodox Marxists put many more eggs in the military basket. Baran and Sweezy (1966) assert that capitalism has survived almost exclusively on account of spending on wars hot and cold. 'If military spending were reduced once again to pre-Second World War proportions, the nation's economy would return to a state of profound depression, characterized by unemployment rates of 15 percent and up, such as prevailed in the 1930s' (Baran and Sweezy, 1966, pp. 151–3).

Michael Kidron, of the International Socialism group in Britain, raises the cold war economy thesis to the status of historical epoch. Outdoing the Lenin of *Imperialism*, he finds a new, more recent 'latest, final stage of capitalism – the permanent arms economy' (Kidron, 1974, ch. 1). Kidron's arguments are strongly 'ideological' and do not cast much in the way of glory on Marxian economics as a progressive scientific research program. They do, however, bring into unmistakable focus the premises of the Marxian scheme of producer and parasite, surplus and transfer, in its post-Keynesian guise.

> The drain provided by arms budgets since World War II has constituted a far more effective mechanism for stabilizing the system than classical imperialism ever could, for it has involved a systematic destruction of values. . . . Capital is taxed to sustain expenditure on arms and so deprived of resources that would otherwise go towards further investment [sic]. The expenditure itself constitutes a net addition to the market for [final] goods, all the more significant for being expenditure on fast-wasting products in constant need of renewal and change. [One] obvious result of such expenditure is high unemployment and, as a direct consequence, rates of growth since the war amongst the highest ever. . .
> (Kidron, 1974, p. 19)

Who is unproductive? Kidron identifies economic parasites using a combination of input–output table *cum* high-handed value judgment to arrive at a measure of the scale of superfluous ('waste') production. Unproductive waste producers then spread their ill-gotten gains throughout the economy, maintaining a false prosperity. There is awareness that designating a particular subgroup of citizens or workers or ISIC industries as the sole and unique source of accumulable transferable surplus is a matter of definition. But the insight is applied by Kidron to conventional definitions and measures, not to his own materialist–fallacist one.

> Classing waste-goods production as unproductive rather than productive activity has far-reaching consequences: if it is productive, there can be no [sic] inner barriers to the growth of the system . . . Depending on the way you're looking at it, the system grows or it doesn't. The choice is arbitrary . . . [Classing] waste-goods production as productive makes nonsense of the concept of necessary labour [and] of the concept of surplus as all output . . . over and above necessary output, and therefore [sic] [it] makes nonsense of the labour theory of value and everything that flows from it (including the locating of the basic conflict in the system at the point of surplus production.) Capitalism now employs hundreds of millions of people who by no stretch of the imagination can be said to contribute to growth. . . . Their consumption is unproductive. The equipment they work with is waste. The surplus goods they create and absorb

are sterile. Together they constitute a huge waste sector within an increasingly maleficent system.

(Kidron, 1974, pp. 40–1)

Kidron's concept of waste industries is modeled on Sraffa's understanding of luxury as non-input (Montani, 1988, pp. 1008–9). Among sectors of the US economy said to be 'non-basic' and 'in principle unassimilable as inputs into further production' are cited: entertainment and gifts, finance, insurance and real estate, business travel, management consulting, and engineering (Kidron, 1974, p. 43). Apart from the usual PR men, lawyers, and judges, waste professions include sales engineers, social and welfare workers, farm managers, managers except self-employed, bridge tenders, and bookkeepers. Perhaps out of utilitarian – quite unMarxian – sympathy for the little guy, an exception is made for self-employed petty proprietors provided they are not in 'trade'.

Waste output is netted from total output within non-waste industry because 'large parts of industrial activity are devoted to financial (as distinct from material) record keeping' (Kidron, 1974, p. 43). This operation is colored by a strong modism. No less an authority than Vladimir Il'ich had described 'book-keeping' and 'country-wide accounting' as providing 'something in the nature of the *skeleton* of socialist society' (Lenin, 1917b, p. 106). A methodologue of some daring, Kidron separates waste from non-waste trade by taking the *Soviet* percentage of trade employment in total employment for the year 1964 'as a rough measure of the necessary minimum proportionate size of a distributive network', permitting the conclusion that 'US trade could be deflated to 22 per cent of its actual size' without affecting real output. In sum, that powerful scientific weapon, definition, permits the conclusion that 'productive final demand' is a mere 39.71 per cent of conventional final demand; the rest is waste (Kidron, 1974, p. 48 and n. 18 and p. 54).

It does not take much economics to see materialist fallacy here. As in primitive Bolshevik economics, the 'Austrian' coordination problem is not addressed. Kidron is silent on the possibility that the smooth functioning of even material production may require costly information about techniques, input availability, and output demand. Nor does he, as a non-believer in the Invisible Hand, have much patience with the notion that a market system will divide and specialize that labor like any other.

In the tradition of Mandeville and Smith, Bukharin and Baran, Kidron appoints himself taste tsar of Western civilization, with amusing if ultimately disturbing consequences. Since taxi-driving and hairdressing are waste occupations, the possibility that ordinary consumers might 'prefer' more taxi rides to more private automobiles, or more visits to the hairdresser to arranging a homemade coiffure, is not considered. Loved ones will have long lives once capitalism falls under the rationalist's knife: 'funeral directors and embalmers' are waste occupations. Nor will there be accidents, fires, or theft after the final crash, 'insurance' being a superfluous luxury.

Passing from the 'horizontal' spread of professions of workers in their prime to the 'vertical' problem of retirement in the life cycle, we find Kidron again silent on a key point, the problem of intergenerational transfer and retirement pensions (e.g. Samuelson, 1958). 'Old age and retirement benefits' – even those disbursed to workers formerly in industries he has as productive - fall under his heading 'waste production generated by unproductive government expenditure other than military'. All in all, Kidron's is not the sort of performance that bolsters the orthodox productive-labor-theory-of-value Marxists' claim to an alternative scientific research program.

There is not space to discuss the many other variations and formalizations of the Baran–Sweezy thesis that monopoly capitalism has survived by virtue of a rising share of unproductive, particularly military, expenditure in conventional GNP. Worthy of mention, but subject to the same litany of objections (taste-dictatorship, input–output error, failure to weigh 'monopoly capitalism' against 'really existing socialism') are works by J. Gillman (1957 and 1965), J. Becker (1977), B. Fine (1983) and E. Wolff (1987).

That is as much attention as can be paid to postwar orthodox Marxism. Other attempts were made to develop hybrids of Classical–Marxian surplus and transfer theory sturdy enough to survive the hostile atmosphere of the postwar academy (e.g. Resnick and Wolff, 1987; Roemer, 1988). Most of the English-language variants have been (sympathetically) reviewed by I. Gough (1972), B. F. Hope (1979), and E. K. Hunt (1979). There is also a large European and Canadian literature in the French language that depends for its conclusions on acceptance of a productive/unproductive dichotomy (Berthoud, 1974; Delaunay, 1971; Nagels, 1974; Gill, 1979, 1981, 1986; Poulantzas, 1975). With the rise of feminism there appeared a rather different source of danger to the orthodox Marxist parasite paradigm: sex.

7.1.1 Marxists and housewives: the 'humiliating appellation' and the domestic mode of production

Some say Marxism has little to do with the productive-labor theory of value or a material base for the superstructure at all. It is, rather, a romantic *cri de douleur* against what was thought to be the avoidable alienation of urban industrial life. Converts fall for a utopian promise of a post-capitalist mode in which Christian selflessness will flower along with a self-actualizing job variety made feasible by technological advance.

Marx on this view belongs to a line of egalitarian moral philosophers going from the early Christians to John Rawls (1967). The capitalist mode is unjust, wasteful, etc. because it fails to maximize social welfare – itself, as in Bergson–Arrow, 'some function of' the utilities of all the citizens who count (Bergson, 1938; Arrow, 1963; section 5.9 above). Inequality of original endowment, a worsening aspect of the capitalist scene since primitive accumulation (Marx, 1867, pp. 667 ff.), engenders inequality in consumption, which is at the root of the system's failure to maximize social happiness despite technical improvement (Boss, 1986b).

Expropriation of the expropriators being the only sure means of eradicating forms of property that generate inequality, another *courant* of Marxian thought, which might be called modist socialist revolutionary, takes pains to identify groups in society underprivileged in terms of political enfranchisement, producer utility, earnings, and self-actualization generally. Both they and the socialist egalitarians intend have-nots to benefit relatively and absolutely from the post-revolutionary once-over redistribution of tangible physical assets (means of production), as well as from a longer-term, dynamic redistribution of acquirable human assets and 'life chances'. Revolutionary politicians also have a need to identify groups who might, whatever their situation, be prepared to support them in political struggle.

Such concerns stimulated Marxist economists to examine the claims of the women's liberation movement to see what, if anything, objection to male chauvinism and to the stagnation of women's life chances had to do with the critique of capitalism.

The attempt to give traditional Marxism a feminist perspective inevitably drew attention to long-standing difficulties over boundary-drawing and input–output error. The bare-bones productive-labor theory of value is innocently gender neutral: wage-working women employed in more-than-single-person industrial and agricultural firms are just as exploited as male workers, but not more exploited. Accounting for wage differentiation is something else again. Extra sociological and cultural factors, or else that Marxian bugbear, demand, must be invoked to explain why, for example, women, but also blacks and hispanics, tend to be employed in low-status, low-paying, low-quality jobs and why white, prime-aged males have the highest wages, the strongest unions, and the lowest rates of unemployment. Still, within the traditional Marxian production boundary with one rate of surplus-value s/v, women workers are no worse off than other proles.

'Socialist utilitarians' play down some of the specifics of the laborer's relationship to the dominant mode of production. Braverman, as we saw, treated highly-alienated, poorly-paid, sporadically unionized wage-laborers in non-productive circulation (bank tellers, clerks, keypunch operators) as members of the working class. An unintended but swift consequence was to force re-examination of the status in Marxian economics of self-employed, low-wage, non-unionized, overwhelmingly female domestic workers and their unpaid *alter egos*, women working in the home.

The domestic servant has been a perennial problem child for Classical and Marxian surplus and transfer theorists. It was thought anomalous that the servant's *de facto* labor contract covered production of a myriad of different and differently durable use-values. Ephemeral material eggs and milk are transformed before they go bad into ephemeral material soufflés. Dishes are restored to very temporary cleanliness; mended trousers get only a slightly longer expected useful life. Materialist fallacy is the mote in the economist's eye that has him see in the master's instruction to the servant to bake this, fix that, an act *not fully analogous to* the same master's decision to buy a keg of wine from, say, a peasant smallholder. The mode-mindedness that seizes on the fact of resale is what makes the domestic, who is not paid separately for each item on the evening menu, look fundamentally different from the country doctor who may be paid separately for specific procedures like a visit or the setting of a limb (see section 3.3).

Whether or not the doctor, the peasant, and the cook are seen as 'part of the economy' depends then on whether employment of wage-labor is the key to everything. Pigou's paradox shows the slipperiness of the measuring rod of money. Should the mistress marry the chef, the peasant press wine as usual, and the doctor leave his wife and hire a nurse, other things equal, in an economy of three households the per-period flow of disutilities and utilities is unchanged, casting doubt on conventional GNP as a proxy for welfare.

Workers and capitalists grow old and die. Maintenance of the system requires that the categories of ownership and authority be carried over from one generation to the next. One link in the 'reproduction' process is the physical reproduction of the labor force: the begetting, gestation, and care of children. Human infants possess no saleable labor-power; *au contraire* they absorb adult labor – they must be looked after, either 'for free' by their parents or well-disposed third persons, or else by paid caregivers who specialize in child-minding and make it their profession.

With no more ado, I take a brief look at the Western Marxism's 'domestic labor debate', drawing heavily on an article in the *New Left*

Review of July–August 1979 by Maxine Molyneux, which surveys the feminist and Western Marxist literature on housework as a separate mode (Molyneux 1979). Featured are two strands of feminist Marxism, Margaret Bentson's notion that domestic labor directly produces the marketable commodity labor-power (Bentson, 1969) and John Harrison's notion of domestic labor as a 'client mode of production' (Harrison, 1973a and b). The questions are: is housework 'work', and how does it fit into the scheme of the productive-labor theory of value?

Molyneux makes short work of Bentson's argument that housewives deserve reclassification as Marxian productive laborers because they are fully engaged in the direct home reproduction of the commodity 'labor-power', a process having an exact socially necessary real cost in women's time (Bentson, 1969, cited in Molyneux, 1979, p. 8). Bentson's idea is in the tradition of Malthus, Ricardo, von Neumann, and Marx himself (Hollander, 1984), but it is a poor rendering of how modern housewives spend their time.

Molyneux goes on to defend orthodoxy against the more plausible if *ad hoc* stratagem of John Harrison, which is to treat domestic labor as a 'client mode of production' appended to the dominant capitalist one.

> There is one important sense [Molyneux writes] in which housework is correctly characterised as 'non-capitalist', namely that it lies outside the sphere of commodity production and is therefore not itself governed by the law of value [sic]. It is Harrison's recognition of this which leads him to conclude that it must therefore constitute a separate mode of production...
> (Molyneux, 1979, p. 16)

Housework is said in many respects to resemble 'petty commodity production: both are marked by the absence [sic] of a division of labour, a low degree of socialization of labour, and the fact that the producers work on an individual basis' (Molyneux, 1979, p. 8). A problem in promoting households to even partial Marxian productive status is that, in contrast to single-person firms and farms, they do not produce goods and services for *resale*.

Harrison stresses that housework 'depresses the value of labour power by providing ("for free") the labour necessary for its day-to-day reproduction' (Molyneux, 1979, p. 9). It stretches the 'family wage' paid to male workers who earn enough to be the sole family members in the paid labor force. For Harrison, it is 'primarily capital, rather than, for instance, men, which benefits from women's subordination' (Molyneux, 1979, p. 22).

Molyneux makes welcome allowance for the evident fact that the amount of housework performed by women who can afford to stay home is not some fixed quantum but varies within wide limits. Eschewing 'monism and economism' as incomplete explanations of women's second-class socioeconomic status in home and workplace, Molyneux grants partial validity to the Bentson household production-function argument with the fudge remark that unpaid domestic labor 'provides use-values for the reproduction of the labourer' (p. 8).

Molyneux seems undecided whether on balance housewives and -husbands are privileged to have spouses who earn a family wage, or whether a slack economy has relegated them to the economic sidelines against their will. The author's uncertainty in fact springs from a profound difficulty in the economic analysis of household production. Between some undefinable minimum and the totality of the homemaker's waking hours, the amount and quality of housework and child care performed allows of enormous variation, from compulsively neat to slob. For this reason, economists in sympathy with the Chicago time-utilitarians (G. S. Becker, 1965; section 8.4.2 below) have trouble regarding the housewife as 'working consistently as hard as' those subjected to the specific duties and/or constant supervision of a Coasian labor contract (Coase, 1937; Leibenstein, 1976).

With the decline of subsistence agriculture, housewives and -husbands can no longer be said to be engaged full time in domestic production of wage goods. It is therefore impossible to pick a reasonable rule of thumb with which to divide the home workers' day between 'work', where net utility is negative, and 'leisure' where it is positive.

When the spouse's wage is inadequate or becomes so because of inflation (or rising expectations), women's labor-force participation rises, reducing *maximum* but not necessarily actual home production. In totting up putative costs and benefits to 'the state', Molyneux draws a useful distinction between possibly sporadic cooking and cleaning and more likely full-time care of young children.

> The cost to the state is undoubtedly one reason why capitalist societies have tended to resist providing nurseries, but it is not the only reason. Under the conditions of advanced capitalism where high unemployment prevails, it would be extremely problematic. . .to create the conditions which would help to free women from the domestic sphere because the labour market provides an insufficient number of jobs to accommodate them. In this sense the 'family wage' and the 'housewife syndrome' help to conceal high unemployment. . .Women [make up] a stratum of the reserve army, called upon in times of war or rapid accumulation. . .
>
> (Molyneux, 1979, p. 26)

While Molyneux notes the large increases in paid labor-force participation of married women during the postwar period, no attempt is made to differentiate cyclical influences from changes in trend.

The all-or-nothing Classical–Marxian view of the unproductiveness of domestic activity is a mode-bound convention that, *faute de mieux*, Western GNP accountants took over from Pigou. The compromise proved highly unpopular, as we shall see in section 8.4. For starters, it violates the rationality postulate at the core of economics. *A fortiori* the sacred neoclassical principle of substitution is said not to apply to the choice between home production and market purchase.

At the instigation of socialist utilitarians and radical feminists, orthodox productive-labor-theory-of-value Marxists were moved to examine the housewife's claim to the status of 'productive laborer'. The claim was rejected. Molyneux's summary of the domestic labor debate needs no exegesis.

> [It] is doubtful whether the creation of use-values for private consumption.. .justifies the use of the concept 'means of production' to designate the implements utilised in such activities. . .[The] absence of a productive base, and the absence of any social [exchanged] production within the [domestic mode of production], renders problematic the very use of the term 'production' in this context.
>
> (Molyneux, 1979, p. 18)

7.2 Post-Keynesian Classicism: capitalism starved by an unproductive state sector

7.2.1 Bacon and Eltis: too few producers

The mid-1970s saw a series of attempts – sociological, monetarist, and otherwise – to explain phenomena like stagflation, disappointing factor- productivity growth, and other manifestations of unforthcoming supply. Growth of the public sector in the postwar period was offered up as scapegoat. Opinion as to whether government should or even could do anything about social and economic problems moved towards the conservative end of the Left–Right political spectrum. David Stockman describes it vividly (1986, pp. 19–48).

A fascinating consequence of the sea-change in socioeconomic opinion was to send new wind into the sails of the archaic, supposedly discredited crypto-Marxist doctrine of productive and unproductive labor. The grand conservative *laissez-faire* mode-mindedness of Classical political economy began to be touted not as a dangerous

Treasury-view recipe for prolonged slump, but as a superior analytical approach to increasing the real supply of things people want.

As we now know, to define productive labor and its product restrictively implies that there are unproductive laborers able to siphon resources over to their side of the economic fence. Adam Smith describes such a côterie of economic parasites in Book II, chapter iii, of the *Wealth of Nations*. Smith's growth model employs a binary dichotomy: whosoever is not a productive laborer is an unproductive one, and savings and investment are correspondingly lower, the more of them there are. Rather than the more subtle analysis of public institutions and works of *Wealth of Nations*, Book V, the productive/unproductive dichotomy of Book II, chapter iii, contained a message easy to sell to a tax-weary public as the true wisdom of the Classics. The anti-government revival gave a new lease of life to the unproductiveness–fallacist, if not the cruder materialist–fallacist, dichotomizations of the Smithian theory of economic growth.

The classical revival of the 1970s also stressed another feature of the so-called 'value version' of Adam Smith's growth model, namely its emphasis on price-making markets. Productive laborers are workers whose products pass through the chastening channels of competition. Economic new-Classical conservatives, as distinguished for instance from other conservatives in sometime political coalition with them – big-spending 'defense conservatives' (the Committee on the Present Danger, the Pentagon), anti-abortion activists, or paternalist interventionist 'taste conservatives' (E. J. Mishan, Prince Philip, PBS, the Canadian Broadcasting Corporation) – defend untrammeled markets as promoters of efficiency and growth. Abstracting from problems of the 'second best', the *laissez-faire* conservatives suggest that the state should endeavor progressively to disengage itself from what they think is 'the economy'. To minimalists, some types of GNP are more equal than others.

The analysis underlying the new Classical remake of Smitho-Marxian parasite theory is rendered in the title of a book first published in the London *Sunday Times* in 1975 by the Oxford economists Robert Bacon and Walter Eltis – *Britain's Economic Problem [is] Too Few Producers* (Bacon and Eltis, 1975a and b; 1976; 1978a). Aha, we ask, who are Bacon and Eltis's producers, and what is it that they produce? The roster of 'producers', of whom there are too few, bears a striking resemblance to the old-fashioned list of 'commodity producers' advanced by Classical–Marxian modists from Smith to Molyneux.

Bacon and Eltis purport to advance a terminology that is value neutral. 'Producers', they say, are merely producers of goods and services that are 'marketed'. Following Adam Smith, Bacon and Eltis allow for-profit services that strict Marxian materialists disallow as belonging to the sphere of circulation (section 5.3 above). The United Kingdom's slow growth, relative to its OECD peers, and balance-of-payments difficulties suffered prior to the development of North Sea oil and adoption of monetarist interest rates are attributed by the authors to a state-sponsored employment shift away from the (productive) market sector and toward the (unproductive) non-market sector, effected in the name of Keynesian demand management.

The analysis starts with consideration of a variety of proposals for bisecting an open mixed economy in which both marketed and non-marketed goods and services are produced. Few citizens except those born wealthy rentiers are able to live their whole lives entirely on the income their human and financial assets earn them as individuals: transfers of wage and property income occur between parent and child and between citizens. In the search for the Smithian grail that is the locus of the economy's accumulable surplus, Bacon and Eltis first reject the materiality criterion and the goods/services dichotomy. The Smithian 'storage version' (Myint, 1948) is rejected on the ground that, while all investment consists of (material) industrial production (*sic*), 'it is not only industry that exports', since one-third of British exports *circa* 1975 are 'invisible' items (Bacon and Eltis, 1976, pp. 16, 25). A materiality criterion would militate against services, whether marketed or not.

Bacon and Eltis attempt to distance themselves from the materialist fallacy by giving out, with some justification, that it is a disease of the Left. Labour MP Tony Benn's 'Left solution' of taxing the rich and subsidizing manufacturing is a mistake because 'a crude pro-industry policy which increased the output of the wrong products at the expense of the services that sold heavily overseas could make the balance of payments still worse, ... curtail investment still further, and leave yet greater shortages of the goods workers actually want' (Bacon and Eltis, 1976, p. 26). So far so good.

Next considered is a distinction between 'tradables' and 'non-tradables'. However, it is rejected because sufficient exports of tradables can earn the economy an accumulable surplus via the balance of payments. Note that the tradability criterion disqualifies on-the-spot activities like construction and instruction except in cases where foreigners pay for them (see Marris, 1984). Equally, the tradability criterion excludes most outputs of government except for Concordes, Exocet missiles, and souvenir stamps.

Bacon and Eltis opt on the third round for what they bill as a generous and reasonable dichotomy between goods and services that are 'marketed' and those that are not.

> [Everyone] who produces anything 'marketed', i.e. *that is sold* at home or overseas, produces a potential surplus. As the whole

nation's exports and investment are sold, and everything that is privately consumed in addition, the economy's 'market' sector has to provide for all of these.

(Bacon and Eltis, 1976, p. x)

The marketedness criterion is nearly identical to Adam Smith's familiar value-adding or private-goods criterion – or to Marx's notion of commodity production stretched to include circulation and petty proprietors. There are a few improvements. One is a downward adjustment of marketed private output when the private sector receives net subsidies from the state, and an upward adjustment when, conversely, state enterprises behave like private enterprises and sell goods and services to the public at cost-covering (*sic*) prices.

Marketed output is therefore the output of goods and services, whether produced in institutions owned by private or collective entities, which are sold for money at cost-covering prices. Non-marketed output comes out of the non-commodity-producing, public-goods-producing, transfer-dispensing agencies of the state sector. Together, these two entities make up 'the economy'. By recognizing that the Post Office may cover some of its costs by selling stamps and that direct state subsidies may inflate measured profits of private firms, Bacon and Eltis are able to assert that 'the distinction between the market and non-market sectors of the economy is not the same as the distinction between public and private sectors' (Bacon and Eltis, 1976, p. 29). *Indirect* subsidies conferred on business by, for example, tariffs and quotas or in the form of tangible and human infrastructure paid for out of public funds are not considered.

As defined, the two sets of adjectives do not modify precisely identical vectors of goods and services. In practice, though, the terms 'public' and 'non-marketed', and 'private' and 'marketed' are used interchangeably.

Why bother to bisect the set of wage and income earners and their products into mode-bounded subsets at all? Isn't demand demand? The market/non-market dichotomy is defended on the ground that modes matter to consumers. Fear of the political consequences of each cyclical recession has the government skew the composition of output and employment in ratchet fashion ever further in the direction of the non-market sphere. This is no innocent change in the product mix. Consumers underestimate the 'social wage' of goods and services that they do not pay for directly. When taxes and benefits rise evenly, they feel worse off, with the result that they seek and get higher money wages to offset tax increases. Misperception of the true size and composition of the consumption basket, failure properly to evaluate the social wage of goods and services 'voted for' rather than bought, is behind wage-push inflation. Not much attention is paid to the monetary authorities; they are assumed accommodating.

Bacon and Eltis's worker-citizens act as though they had no input into decisions that determine the 'proportion' of public to private goods (or employment) in Britain. For instance, workers' wage behavior casts doubt on whether the *de facto* social choice function meets Arrow's condition of non-dictatorship. Bacon and Eltis's worker-citizens behave as though state services are, in Marx's immortal phrase, 'forced on them' – imposed from without by officials insufficiently constrained to give them value for money.

Several interpretations are possible. One, workers are too stupid to appreciate what they do not pay for directly; two, that they are too smart to accept the state's claim that it is returning them full *quid pro quo* for their tax money; or three, that the costs of ascertaining the degree of equivalence between taxes paid and state services received are so high that workers adopt an information-saving rule of thumb, which is to assume that they have been on balance losers from structural and intermodal change.

The argument is on more solid ground when extended to the foreign sector. That Britain is not an autarchy is said to aggravate the consequences of worker-citizen ingratitude over the intangible social wage. Money wages driven up by lack of appreciation are passed on as higher goods prices, which then hurt exports and, with propensities constant, encourage imports. Sooner or later there is either devaluation (pre-1972) or depreciation of the currency, and either can trigger a further round of wage and price increases. Profits and investment are squeezed. (Investment decisions in Bacon and Eltis are made by the private, for-market sector by definition.)

The authors' pro-market argument with respect to international competitiveness hinges on the relative strength of direct and indirect effects. While non-marketed goods cannot be sold to foreigners, and thus do not directly improve the balance of payments, the indirect effects of, say, publicly-funded R&D may yield highly successful technologies that find ready overseas buyers. At least some public agencies produce goods and services that are directly sold abroad. The ill-fated Concorde aircraft was developed primarily for export, as are many kinds of military hardware. The Japanese Ministry of Trade and Industry apparently enjoyed a productive streak identifying and subsidizing export winners.

If secondary effects of the non-market sector on the market sector can be ruled out, and if non-market employees consume tradables but do not produce them (as Bacon and Eltis affirm), the trade deficit will indeed be greater, the greater is the fraction of the workforce employed in the non-market sector. But since indirect feedback effects exist and may be substantial, and since products may be tradable but inappropriate in mix, quality, or timeliness, how important is tradability *per se*? The decline in Britain's share of world manufacturing exports beyond that due to catch-up by other countries (Maddison, 1982; Baumol, 1986) has been blamed on the poor training and complacent attitudes of British management (Peaker, 1974, p. 63). Bad habits and ignorance of scientific and managerial techniques are to some unknown extent the consequence of inappropriate and inadequate schooling, received for the most part from the non-market sector. To change that situation requires mainly public efforts.

The contention that only the market sector invests is a dubious one. As in Smith's analysis of accumulation, a lot depends on what is meant by 'capital stock'. If capital includes the accumulated stock of embodied and disembodied scientific knowledge and technical know-how, then pretty obviously in our society the public sector creates new capital stock, that is, it invests.

By the same token, public authorities also invest in physical assets and in tangible infrastructure, though such investments show up in GNP accounts as (marketed) sales by private firms and as government consumption of goods and services, undifferentiated as to finality of use-values created.

Restricting the term 'investment' to production of marketable intermediates – to the exclusion of improvements in knowledge, in human capital, in tangible infrastructure, or in the quality of the 'social framework' of peace, security, and public order – implies that such evidently economically beneficial 'goods' belong to non-basic, luxury consumption. Resources devoted to them drain resources away from, directly compete with, growth of basics. A different view has it that ports and bridges, schools and colleges, research establishments, military bases, police departments, the mint, the bureau of the census, etc. are desired by voter-consumers not mainly for their own sake, as thrilling final utilities, but rather because they are necessary intermediate inputs into the production processes of goods people want. To call these sorts of intermediate goods 'unproductive', is yet another instance of our familiar bugaboo, input–output error.

It does not take Solow–Denison growth accounting to give credibility to the Marx–Senior notion that there is some 'most efficacious proportion' of public to private activity (see chs. 4 and 5 above; Denison, 1974; Solow, 1957; Davenport, 1976). Still, the more one is convinced by Solow's researches, which yield a huge residual labeled 'technical change', the more one may be prepared to view the public sector's varied activities in providing educated citizens and new processes as contributing positively to the private component of GNP growth rather than as diminishing it. Bacon and Eltis admit as much, without acknowledging that the indirect effects, if they are non-negligible, ruin their case for the market.

> [The] size of the non-market sector can be expected to have two general effects, one favourable and one unfavourable, on the long-term rate of growth of productivity. First, many public-sector activities which do not result in marketed outputs are likely to have favourable effects on the rate of growth of productivity. Of these, education, government-financed research and development, and defence spending can all be expected to have favourable though sometimes lagged effects on technical progress that are not easily quantifiable. On the other hand, the larger the ratio of employment in the non-market sector, the smaller will be the aggregate amount of market-sector output in any given year, and this means that market-sector investment (which is a fraction of market-sector output) will be less. Growth models have been put forward by Arrow and others which make technical progress a function of the amount of investment, and if there is less market investment, there will be less 'learning by doing', and research and development departments may be smaller with the result that they discover less per annum. On this line of argument, productivity will rise faster where the market sector is larger in relation to the non-market sector.
>
> (Bacon and Eltis, 1976, pp. 142–3)

So much for the market sector's alleged unique ability to produce intermediate capital assets and new technology. Bacon and Eltis compound input–output error with a pro-industry argument borrowed in part from Nicholas Kaldor's *Causes of the Slow Rate of Growth of the United Kingdom* (Kaldor, 1966).

> [The] crucial advantage of a large market sector is . . . that this will be associated with high industrial investment which will have favourable effects on research and development and 'learning by doing'.
>
> (Bacon and Eltis, 1976, pp. 142–3)

Only the private sector invests; public expenditures are unable to induce private industrial investment (no asphalt or cement works, no tank factories, no blackboard factories!); the whole of the private for-market service economy mimics manufacturing, sliding down Kaldorian economies of scale and Arrovian learning curves such as are never to be found in government.

The Bacon and Eltis case against the non-market sector rests on the method of comparative steady states – alternative scenarios for the future made by extrapolating assumed values for key parameters. The extrapolations presume knowledge of characteristics of the economy that we would like to have but cannot presume to. Is the UK economy macroeconomically near or far from its steady-state trend line? Is technical progress Harrod-neutral, so that generous additions to capital make generous additions to output, or is incremental capital–output ratio rising? How illuminating can it be to treat investment decisions as autonomous, as Bacon and Eltis do, when entrepreneurs' intentions vary with 'animal spirits', with expected differences of receipts over costs? Direct costs to firms are influenced by the level of services provided 'for free' by state authorities, by new technologies, by government policies concerning energy, public health, pensions, and so on, not to mention monetary and fiscal policies that influence real interest rates. Without a feeling for the importance of such factors, the authors' anti-publicsector prejudice reduces to little more than Korchagin-and-Sbytova-like expostulation against featherbedding and waste. That sort of complaint, while legitimate (especially if the economy is thought to be operating close to the production-possibility frontier), *requires a different sort of analysis* from the speculative comparative static arithmetic used to justify the authors' pro-market stance.

The different sort of analysis required for their real gripe against the non-market sector – its alleged inefficiency in providing those public goods that are wanted, are consistently evaluated by recipients, and are conducive to growth in that they provide not only macroeconomic incentives but also intermediate tangible and intangible capital goods for it – has to make provision for public goods and public choices. For the 'full' input-output analysis that must underlie policies designed to move the economy's structure in the direction of its presumed 'most efficacious proportion', there must be some theory about how civil servants and elected representatives behave, whether their budgetary and political constraints are 'soft', etc. Confident when reading the mind of the wage earner, Bacon and Eltis have only the productive/unproductive dichotomy to offer as proof that state employees automatically, *by virtue of their mode*, fulfill their tasks less effectively than do the workers and rentiers in the private sector.

By what standard is efficiency or inefficiency in public activity to be judged? Outputs that are not sold may have money costs but they do not have ordinary prices. Productivity and profitability are straightforward concepts only under market competition where quantities and prices of inputs and outputs are known, and budget constraints hard. Extension of those notions to the non-market sphere is by analogy, but the analogy works only to the extent that the measure of the output is complete. Public activities tend to look bad because a high proportion of them are services, whose productivity improvement may be slow and is in any case hard to measure, and because favorable external effects on other parts of the economy, and on the level of overall activity generally, get credited to the private sector.

As Oskar Morgenstern scathingly observed, constrained maximization is an appropriate mathematical tool only in situations where 'the individual or firm (or whatever other entity) controls all variables on which the maximum depends' (Morgenstern, 1972, p. 116). Accusing the public sector of inefficiency means it should behave (officials and representatives should be instructed to behave) *as if* it (they) really maximized. However, even if they program all their own robots, even heads of family firms do not fully control every variable. All the more reason to think public officials and representatives may not be interested in maximizing a single, scalar goal, by analogy with the maximization of profit by the private firm. Beset by demands from diverse constituencies, officials may satisfice down a list of imperfectly compatible goals, such as labor peace *cum* introduction of labor-saving machinery, or expanded public works or retraining simultaneous with deficit reduction. The efficiency calculus copied from the linear model of the single-plant, single-product, perfectly competitive firm may be the wrong model. But it is the one Bacon and Eltis adduce to demonstrate that Britain's economic problem is 'too few producers'.

The Marx–Senior 'most efficacious proportion' problem would not *be* a problem if varying the proportions of public to private action produced effects of predictable magnitude and direction. Bacon and Eltis, assuming *quod est demonstrandum*, end up with a less than convincing case even for sign.

7.2.2 Feldstein: too few savers

Bacon and Eltis's *Too Few Producers* originally appeared in a Sunday newspaper. As Adam Smith said, if the rod be bent too much one way, in order to make it straight you must bend it as much the other. The authors no doubt overstated their case with a view to catching the public's attention. Much of the so-called supply-side literature is journalism rather than serious economics. But that accusation cannot be leveled against Martin S. Feldstein, professor of public finance at Harvard and Chairman of the Council of Economic Advisors in the first years of the Reagan administration. What is a serious empiricist like Feldstein doing in a history of unproductiveness fallacy? Feldstein devoted several articles in the 1970s to the effect of pension schemes on aggregate saving. His methods and assumptions are revelatory of the new Classical concern over the adequacy of private saving and accumulation, and the negative effects on measured GNP growth of transfers made by entitlement rather than 'deserts'.

Assuming demand can be taken for granted as adequate, aggregate supply cannot grow without a commitment of resources to capital formation (investment). Where do investment resources come from? In a closed economy, they come mainly from domestic saving. Who saves? In Feldstein, the axiomatic answer is private individuals and private corporations. The case against state-managed pension plans assumes that only the private for-market sector can save. We consume too much and save too little because we assume the state will save for us. But the state schemes are not fully 'funded'; they are paid for out of current tax revenue and are therefore transfers from potential current producers and savers to those elderly unproductives who, as Adam Smith put it, 'do not labour at all'.

In the old days before the New Deal, the institution of retirement scarcely existed. Workers and businessmen died in harness. A few could live as rentiers in old age, but the difficulty of accumulating enough of a nest egg, Great Crash apart, kept full retirement beyond the reach of the majority, whatever their leisure preference or state of health. Feldstein's research in the 1970s inquired whether the institution of state-managed social security had positive or negative effects on private saving.

In a 1977 paper, the impact of social security on private savings is analyzed in light of 'two opposing effects: wealth replacement and induced retirement' (Feldstein, 1977, p. 174). Wealth replacement is the replacement, by a public benefit system, of income from private assets that would otherwise have to be saved up during one's years in the labor force. The presence of a benefit system 'permits working individuals to reduce their [private] saving and still plan to enjoy the same level of consumption during retirement' (Feldstein, 1977, p. 175). Retirees get entitlement to consume a basket imperfectly related to what they have individually contributed.

There is a potential countervailing force. Instituting a public pension scheme induces retirement among those who would otherwise not have retired at all but have planned to work to the last. Those people maybe saved *less* in the days before social security. The practice of retirement may therefore generate additional *private* saving since the publicly funded system does not replace 100 per cent of pre-retirement income. *A priori* the net effect of wealth replacement and retirement on saving is unknown. Feldstein estimates a life-cycle model for a number of OECD countries and finds that the first effect predominates.

> [The] provision of public pensions for the aged substantially depresses the rate of private saving. If this is not offset by other government policies, the result is a decline in the rate of capital accumulation, with important long-run effects for the level and distribution of income.
> (Feldstein, 1977, p. 175)

An earlier Feldstein study on US data stated that 'nearly all the estimates imply that, in the absence of social security, personal savings would be at least 50 per cent higher than they are now and probably closer to 100 per cent higher' (Feldstein, 1974a, p. 916).

The tone of Feldstein's academic writings is scholarly to the point of colorlessness; no playing to the galleries here. Assumptions and operations are carefully expounded and sensitivity analyses performed. But what *are* the assumptions? On the one hand, the argument is couched in terms of long-term comparison of steady states; consumption, saving, and investment are extrapolated for decades. Such a procedure, while suggestive, has its limitations. More to the point is Feldstein's presumption that only the private sector saves and invests. This is simply assumed. The state's use of the proceeds is to consume them in unproductive handouts to the profligate old.

Feldstein voices calm regret that his fellow-citizens do not share his and Adam Smith's enthusiasm for future over present consumption. *De gustibus non est disputandum*. But supposing tastes and ends granted, what about means? Like the Classics and the Bolsheviks, he argues as though only by increasing the stock of real, tangible, alienable private capital assets, which depend exclusively on investment of private surplus, can there follow increases in the economy's annual produce of measured output. But is brute abstinence at a constant ICOR the tastiest recipe for economic advance?

A propos, the researches of Denison suggest, quite the contrary, that business-sector

> capital formation has not been the dominant source of economic growth in the past [in the US, in Canada, or in other OECD countries]. Economies of scale, advances in knowledge, improved resource allocation, and increased employment accounted for over 80 per cent of [e.g.] Canada's growth between 1950 and 1967; increases in business capital formation, though they were very large, contributed to less than 20 per cent.... [The implication of this high ICOR is] that exceptionally large increases in capital formation would be required to significantly influence the rate of economic growth. The contribution of capital formation to economic growth was even less in other countries [over similar periods, for example, 16 per cent in West Germany, 12 per cent in France and Japan, and 9 per cent in the United States]... The differences in overall growth are explained far more cogently by differences in output per unit of input, which reflects the efficiency with which capital and labor are used in the production process.
> (Denison, 1976, cited in Economic Council of Canada, 1979, p. 51; see also Eisner, 1988a, pp. 26–7)

The distinction between funded and not fully funded pension programs is crucial.

> Since the US social security system is not 'funded' but operates on a pay-as-you-go basis, the reduction in private saving is not offset by any increase in public saving ... In providing a 'fiat' asset as a substitute for real capital formation, social security is similar to absorbing saving by a growing money supply ...
> (Feldstein, 1974a, p. 922, n. 26 and 27).

Private accumulation is 'crowded out' by the full amount of transfer consumption in the Feldstein analysis of pay-as-you-go. If pension schemes are partly or fully funded, though, the government may choose between saving or consuming any net revenues. If the government saves them, there are two limiting cases. In the first, if social security taxes are treated by consumers as perfect substitutes for personal saving (perfect wealth replacement), there is no change in total saving, just a shift from private saving to public. In the second case, consumers continue to save as before (no wealth-replacement effect), such that public and private savings are complementary: total savings go up by the net pension fund revenue.

In the first case, private investment is 'crowded out' but public investment is 'crowded in'. For some reason (mode-mindedness? unproductiveness fallacy?), 'crowding out' is seen asymmetrically, from the private-sector viewpoint (Weldon, 1981).

Feldstein finds that the second case, in which private saving is not reduced, can be dismissed because empirically the wealth-replacement effect swamps the retirement effect. Criticisms of his negative findings of the consequences of making old age less financially insecure have centered on the size of retirement, longevity, bequest, occupational pension, and demographic effects which work in the opposite direction (Economic Council of Canada, 1979, pp. 45–7).

In a report on the aging of the Canadian population, pro-market modists express similar fears about too little saving.

> [If social security does indeed replace personal saving,] private investment will be 'crowded out' – ... [either] by increased government consumption [or] by increased government investment. In fact these options describe two of the most common worries about public pension schemes: that the funds generated will either be 'wasted' on government consumption (although that may include investment in human capital through expenditures on health or education) or at least diverted into public investment – and thus perhaps into less productive uses than in the private sector [*sic*].
> (Economic Council, 1979, pp. 47–8)

The Feldstein sensitivity analyses of old-age pension schemes breathe a scientific breath of life into the pro-saving tradition of Smitho-Marxian and Stalinist unproductive-labor doctrine. The link with Smith and the Classics is in the unashamed preference for a reduction in profligacy and an increase in parsimony. Oldster consumers reap where they never sowed. Saving more today to increase future consumption is to be preferred to giving more to them. That is despite the fact that, so long as there is some net investment per head and ICORs are not infinite, future generations may be expected to be richer than we are. If the unborn could vote, Feldstein hints, the pro-saving party would obviously carry the day. Since our great-grandchildren and their children are disenfranchised, the economist volunteers to stand in as benevolent dictator in order to assure a just weighting of present and future utilities, even as he sketches for society a social welfare function after his own heart (Feldstein, 1974b, pp. 16–16a; p. 45).

A propos of social welfare functions, it is interesting that Feldstein finds the present pay-as-you-go system to be distributionally regressive in so far as it raises *infragenerational* interest rates and lowers wage rates (1974a, p. 924). But, somewhat in the manner of Lenin and Bukharin, Feldstein is less concerned about intergenerational regressivity, so long as the bias favors future generations over citizens alive *hic & nunc*.

A less obvious affinity links mode-minded empiricist macroeconomists like Feldstein to otherwise strange bedfellows among orthodox Marxists and Stalinist Bolsheviks. It turns on the implicit denial of uncertainty about returns to investment – uncertainty that forms the essence of Keynes's analysis of the importance of 'animal spirits of the entrepreneur' (Keynes, 1936, chs 5, 11, 12; Shackle; Weldon, 1981, p. 4). Feldstein's arguments rely on steady-state reasoning. The future is known, because it will be like the past, and information about the past is all we have, so we should use it. Feldstein calculates an average interest rate, for example, that is then used to figure how generously, without a social security system, workers currently entering the labor force could provide for their own retirement consumption assuming their current savings earn that rate of return. But who knows what will be the actual realized yield, forty-five or fifty years (or three years) hence, of such placements? How will inflation, recession, technical change, political change, resource exhaustion or discovery, affect the performance of workers' portfolios? The answer is unknowable, uncertain in the profoundest Knightian sense of the term. As P. Jeanjean said in a commentary on Feldstein's 1977 paper, 'an individual preparing for retirement, with a choice between private savings and a subscription to a public retirement plan, would be well advised to select the latter. Public retirement plans have a much higher real rate of return, because they are reassessed according to a cost-of-living index' (cited in Inman, 1977, p. 482).

On these accounts it has been argued by J. C. Weldon that Feldstein's analysis has little to do with social *security per se*. *A priori*, it is not obvious why a Feldsteinian modist would limit himself to the payroll tax (Weldon, 1981, pp. 9 ff.). Public goods that are not sold are not 'funded' either; how well they cover their costs item by item is not easy to work out. If that is the case, why limit one's sights to the payroll tax? Why not abolish the income tax? With a stroke of the legislative pen, there could be a wholesale redistribution away from prodigals and towards Smithian undertakers. What a material free-enterprise paradise on earth that might bring about, 'two or three generations down the road'!

7.3 Public goods, rent-seeking, and the new neoclassical economics of mode

7.3.1 Public goods, public sector, public choice

The neoclassical research program launched by Jevons, Walras, and Marshall handled the transferable, wastable surplus question begged by Smitho-Marxian surplus and transfer theory mainly by clarifying the notion of productive *factor* (sections 4.6 and 6.1). Paid mental labor in the market economy was placed squarely on the same footing as manual labor. J.-B. Clark, for instance, taking a cue from Euler's exhaustion theorem, shows how the entire value of competitively-valued social production may be accounted for by factor contribution. By implication, all incomes received in connection with the production of externality-poor marketed output are *earned*. The private economy *has* no surplus (Clark, 1899, p. 46; Robinson, 1934, pp. 398 ff.)

Walras's grand vision of an economy of innumerable goods and factors in a general equilibrium analogous to the solution of a set of simultaneous equations was dimmed by the mathematical rigorists who supplied formal existence proofs (Arrow and Debreu, 1954; Debreu, 1959; Arrow and Hahn, 1971). Walras's 'unlimited competition' and law of one price turn out to be necessary but not sufficient for equilibrium to be general. Production and consumption sets have to be convex. Agents must be endowed with at least one valuable asset. Then there is uncertainty about future states of the world, which fits the framework only if there are futures markets in conditional contracts for all *l* goods and services (Debreu, 1959, p. 102; Weintraub, 1977, p. 119). Worse, as Blaug put it in a trenchant résumé,

> global stability of such an equilibrium depends in turn on ... some dynamic process that guarantees that every economic agent has knowledge of the level of aggregate demand ... Some

of these assumptions may be relaxed a little to accommodate increasing returns to scale in a minority of industries and even a measure of monopolistic competition in all industries. But the existence of oligopoly, *not to mention the presence of externalities in consumption and production, destroys all [general-equilibrium] solutions as it does all other notions of competitive equilibrium.*
(Blaug, 1980a, pp. 188–9; emphasis added)

External effects in production and consumption thus conspired to spoil things for general-equilibrium theorists but they yielded interesting partial dividends for students of non-market modes. The next item on the neoclassical agenda was to extend the notion of economic good to externality-rich public goods. In an act of intellectual imperialism from which political scientists are still smarting, neoclassical economists invaded non-market territory *en masse*. They were armed with three powerful intellectual weapons: methodological individualism, *homo economicus*, and politics-as-exchange (Hirschleifer, 1985; Buchanan, 1987).

Modern public-choice economics begins with the 'Scandinavian' school, with major contributions by Wicksell (1896) and Lindahl (1919). They argued that taxpaying should be a *quid pro quo*, assumed public servants to be selfish not altruistic, and rediscovered Hume's 'free-rider problem' (Mueller, 1976, pp. 396–8; Phelps, 1985, p. 114). The impossibility of keeping rational consumers from enjoying pure public goods (non-excludability) allows them to *conceal* their true preferences for such goods in hope of avoiding a contribution. Other things equal, too *few* pure public goods are then supplied rather than too many; society's expenditure on them is too low, rather than too high as Classical and Marxian economists had always supposed.

It was further noted that it is rare for externality-rich goods to be completely pure in the sense of being in evenly joint supply for all citizens. Even defense does not spread its protection smoothly over the population: some live nearer the missile silo or the Maginot line. When benefits are localized either in space or by category, average net cost of provision may not decline indefinitely with each additional taxpayer on the rolls. Scale economies may begin to be exhausted; congestion may lower benefits (Mueller, 1976, p. 413).

Economic stabilization practised by governments can be viewed as such a quasi-public good. It is evidently rich in external effects (Wallace, 1983–4). For example, inflationary monetary and fiscal policy confers uneven but hardly excludable joint costs and benefits on creditors and debtors (Greider, 1987a).

Complicating the picture of demand and supply for public goods is the fact that exclusion is often technically possible, if costly. Broadcast signals can be scrambled; membership and user fees can be charged for clubs, pools, bridges. Internal passports may restrict voting-with-the-feet in the direction of city lights, better housing, or more buoyant labor markets (Tiebout, 1956; Hirschman, 1970).

How best then to satisfy a polity's collective wish for public and quasi- public goods? A variety of decision rules (majority rule, dictatorship) have existed in history. Others have been proposed. The Scandinavians advocated hard-to-satisfy unanimity rules (Phelps, 1985, pp. 215 ff.). Arrow (1963) showed it was impossible to derive a social choice function for taxing, redistributing, and spending even if such weak conditions are imposed on it as non-dictatorship, unlimited domain for preferences, not leaving any citizen's welfare out of account, and the sort of consistency that maintains social rankings of options A and B whether or not some C option exists ('independence of irrelevant alternatives'). The solution most often adopted in practice is to relax the paralyzing Pareto principle and plunge into the icy waters of interpersonal comparison. Government cannot act if it is constrained to make everyone either indifferent or a winner all of the time.

Even as the desired scale and mix of public-goods demand is determined as best it might, there remains the problem of efficient mode of supply. While it assumes price-making competitive markets, original neoclassical theory is actually rather silent on mode as such. The socialist controversy of the 1930s established that, at least in theory, other modes besides perfectly-competitive private ownership might get prices right; a central planning board could mimic the Walrasian auctioneer. In both discussions, production is instantaneous; inputs are transformed into outputs as if in a 'black box' (section 6.1.1).

Early neoclassical economists' lack of interest in process and in the internal workings of institutions extended to establishments in the public sector. Pre-public-choice public-goods theory treated state agencies in effect also as black boxes run by people with no interests of their own. The beginnings of a more sophisticated view came from studies of motivation and hierarchy in large firms in the private sector. The distinctions between principal and agent, stockholder and manager, advanced by Berle and Means, Scitovsky, Williamson, and Leibenstein were easily extended to public 'firms' that finance their operations out of tax levies and borrowing rather than out of revenue earned selling products on markets.

Neoclassical public-choice theory thus applies the *homo economicus* self-interest axiom to bureaucrats and representatives. Evaporated is the myth of the altruistic public *servant*, employed in a transparent benevolent state apparatus that costlessly and democratically transmutes incompatible citizen preferences into roads and bridges, high schools, and defense establishments. Machiavellian political science defended itself better on that score. A huge literature now studies the economics of interest groups and multi-level representative government (for example, the references in Boadway, 1979). A sample of the trend towards behavioral consistency across institutional modes is Niskanen's dictum that 'the rational bureaucrat maximizes the size of his bureau' (Niskanen, 1971).

Mode matters to neoclassical students of public-goods' supply because 'hard' budget constraints are different from 'soft' (Kornai, 1980, 1982). Adam Smith's analysis of the reasons for government waste still provides the basic rationale for asymmetry between enterprise and bureau (section 3.5 above). Budget constraints on government bureaux, though they exist and may even be 'zero-based', are alleged to be 'softer' than those faced by, say, the Chrysler Corporation. A bureaucrat's boss must ultimately face the constraint of re-election. Even monarchs may be overthrown. But between campaigns, officials of modern mixed economies have at their disposal not only seignorage and the power to tax but privileged access to credit markets. They are under less urgent pressure, so the story goes, to minimize cost for given services rendered, if that is what it is their intention to minimize.

Complex governments have more on their agendas than to minimize the tax cost of defense protection, the school system, the interstate highway network, or the post office. The most obvious general economic goal is maintenance of favorable animal spirits in the economy as a whole. By extension of Kuznets's 'social framework' notion (Kuznets, 1948; section 8.4.1 below), it can be argued that, next to law and order and property rights, animal spirits are among the most externality-rich and relatively pure of public goods. If governments behave so as to satisfy lexicographic orderings of objectives, improving the state of confidence would be likely be near the top of the list. Reliance on the state to take a politico-economic rôle in turning things around is evident when the climate of confidence turns bad, as after the stock market's Black Monday of October 1987.

Depending on whether or not one thinks that they work, maintaining buoyant consumer and investor animal spirits has been said to require: (i) fine-tunings of monetary and fiscal policy, (ii) conscious featherbedding in public works' projects to create jobs and work records for the hard-to-employ (Danziger and Weinberg, 1986), and (iii) generous allocations for defense. The economic goods 'bought' by military spending include, conceivably, not only a sense of security for the country itself (Juster, 1973; Juster *et al.*, 1981) plus the regular Keynesian multiplier effects and technological spinoffs, but also realignments of the global political situation in ways favorable to trade and specialization.

7.3.2 Rent-seeking and directly unproductive profit-seeking: a neoclassical unproductive-labor theory

The public-goods-augmented neoclassical research program put another generation between itself and its Walrasian ancestors when it joined forces with international economics. Neoclassical political economy, as proponents have baptized the new subject (Colander, 1984), takes a rather jaundiced view of the possible interplays between self-interested actors. Modes matter. Not for the new political economists the Panglossian harmony theories of J. B. Clark and the rational expectationists, according to which all is for the best in the best of all possible worlds and the state is impotent for good or ill.

Neoclassical political economy responds to Panglossian defenders of the *status quo* with arguments that hark back to Adam Smith's celebrated critique of mercantilism (section 3.5.2 above). Governments may be poor fine-tuners, but they are all too good at creating monopoly rents for private citizens to fight over. Pork-barrel politicians hand out rents to win votes and influence people. Constituents equally rationally find it worthwhile to spend resources up to the expected value of the rents in order to get them.

The day it is able credibly to distinguish growth-diminishing rent-seeking from growth-enhancing profit-seeking, the public-goods-augmented neoclassical research program may yield an unproductive-labor theory grounded in the distinction between competition and monopoly and free from input–output error. So far, in the conservative tradition, new political economists have produced analyses of government's problematic economic rôle that conclude that waste is principally caused by parasitic and feckless big government's having too much money and power. Conservative economists have, of course, decades of experience casting doubt on the proposition that allowing big *business* to earn monopoly rents is ultimately bad for consumers (Schumpeter, 1912; Harberger, 1954; Stigler, 1971)!

Terminology in neoclassical political economy has been somewhat confusing. 'Rent-seeking' is the term pioneered by Anne O. Krueger in a classic analysis of trade quotas (Krueger, 1974). It is in wide use in public economics (for example, Buchanan, Tollison and Tullock, 1980; Phelps, 1985, pp. 207–8). It is observed, though, that not all rent-seeking is bad. Cost-cutting allows firms to earn Marshallian quasi-rents but hardly to the detriment of consumers (Olson, cited in Colander, 1984, p. 8). Nor is rent-seeking the exclusive prerogative of those who would constrain markets. The nineteenth-century pro-market legal framework extolled by public-choice minimalists 'did not just happen; people were seeking rents' (Samuels and Mercuro, 1984, p. 58). Moreover, in a second-best world, successful rent-seeking by A may simply offset distortions negotiated by B, with stimulative effect on 'real' output (Bhagwati and Srinivasan, 1982).

A more general nomenclature, 'directly unproductive profit-seeking (DUP)', has been introduced by the international economist Jagdish Bhagwati and his co-authors (Bhagwati, 1982a and 1983b). DUP is a question-begging term with Classical–Marxian overtones and Classical–Marxian problems. 'Directly unproductive profit-seeking' is said to refer not just to the seeking of rents yielded by quantity restrictions in international trade, but to any tariff-seeking, revenue-seeking, regulation-seeking, monopoly-seeking activity that may be said to create incomes without (*sic*) augmenting the 'real' flow of goods and services (Colander, 1984, pp. 5–6).

The rents and gains to be captured arise from poorly designed tax, tariff, welfare, or similar rules and regulations which confer restrictive monopoly advantages on some firms or citizens that they will spend money to get and to keep. Those who are left out or harmed have an interest in bidding away the licenses or overturning the harmful legislation. Alleged examples of DUP are firms' or their lobbyists' efforts to land import licenses, to keep favorable tax treatment of depletion and depreciation, to maintain acreage restrictions and agricultural price supports, and so on. The complaint is that 'real' output is reduced because lobbying to get a monopoly costs money and monopoly restricts output. The bureaucrat who grants the permit or subsidy is not acting in the public interest at the same time as in his own; redistribution occurs from the general public to bureaucrat and lobbyist. If it is plausible that no countervailing second-best considerations are involved, there has been a net loss of public welfare. Worse, lobbying may be succeeded by wasteful cycles of counterlobbying, tariff-yes, tariff-no, because the transactions costs of agreeing to disagree are too great.

It will come as no surprise that the success of the DUP research program is a function of the observer's ability to make convincing distinction between rent-seeking or DUP and its presumed opposite, directly productive profit-seeking (DPP). In designating as 'directly unproductive' activities in which freely contracting individuals are able to earn incomes and even fortunes, there is evident risk of input–output error.

Following a well-trodden path, neoclassical political economy's DUP variant draws an arbitrary line between 'good' and 'bad' activities. The level of 'bad' rent-seeking is 'too high' because incompetent and meddlesome bureaucrats advance their careers handing rents out, thinking up industrial policies, and so on. Competition for elected office is too clumsy a mechanism to ensure that state activity is limited to just the level of roads, police, silos, and bridges that it is in people's interest to have. Though the means are more sophisticated, the end is that government is again proved a wasteful economic parasite because it aids and abets DUP.

There is an obvious asymmetry. From Condillac (1776) (section 2.6 above) to Gilder (1980), capitalist 'profit-seeking' has been viewed in the *laissez-faire* tradition as a positive-sum game: firms are justly rewarded with profits by virtue of the fact that they are providing the food and clothing that people want. Even hostile takeovers are evidence of consumer (shareholder) sovereignty. The private sector is DPP.

Why does not the Gilder logic apply in mixed economies to activities carried out by the state? Under dual private/public-choice systems in which elected officials pay some heed to citizens' 'voice', how can it be maintained as a matter of dichotomous principle that certain activities – free use of the political process by lobbyists, say – are by their very nature carried out at a cost in 'real' (welfare-related) goods and services (Musgrave, 1985, p. 306)? One suspects that 'real' activities are distinguished from DUP by DUP theorists according to the time-honored principle of economist's sovereignty. Under censorless *samizdat*, writers are free to designate as productive the activities they themselves prefer (ch. 1). Tullock, for instance, describes his 'good' non-rent-seekers as producers of 'social assets in the physical sense' (in Samuels and Mercuro, 1985, p. 60).

Since DUP is based on the public-choice extension of the rationality postulate, DUP as a research program avoids the principal defect of Marxian modism. Neoclassical political economy takes *homo economicus* for granted. No promises are made that human nature will be revolutionized by changes in the ownership rules over tangible means of production. DUP writers nevertheless make institutions matter. Public-choice mechanisms transmit citizen preferences to state officials less accurately, and voting, lobbying, and 'voice' discipline them less stringently, than do the myriad individual, private voluntary acts of consumer purchase of marketed goods and services. The state is not some sort of non-market market.

Early Keynesian public-choice theory, such as it was, implied that governments were inexplicably, naïvely benevolent in carrying out the new macroeconomic tasks vouchsafed to them. That economist-observers could study demands for public goods like stabilization policy, without analyzing how conscientiously public functionaries might be moved to supply them, in hindsight looks nearly as naïve as the Marxian promise of government benevolence towards workers in the first stage of communism.

Keynesians avoided input–output error by treating government as final, but in no way luxury, expenditure. As we shall see in section 8.2, the original Keynesian national accountants gave government bureaux the benefit of the doubt utility-wise, downplaying the issue of mode on the demand side. Consumer-voters were thought to be enjoying public goods and high animal spirits which only non-market institutions could efficiently provide – another triumph of rational division of labor. Such gains from specialization between public and private spheres were noted by Senior and Rossi in the 1830s (section 4.5). Richard Nixon let slip in 1971 that 'we are all Keynesians now'. The anti-Keynesian minimalists who have sought to dominate economic discourse since then would convince us of something else: that we are all modists now.

CHAPTER 8

Drawing the Boundary: The Main Variants

> In fact the whole dispute about the nature of 'material' and 'immaterial' labor reduces to the definition of use-value and to the drawing of the production boundary.
>
> (A. Abolin, 1928a, p. 154)

8.1 From producers to products

The present history has been dedicated to exploring the implications of the idea that any restrictive definition of the economy and the economic implies a boundary with a non-economic world. On the economic side of the boundary, activities that are economically productive produce outputs that have utility. Directly or indirectly they serve to augment the welfare of some member of society. More is better than less.

This chapter moves from the history of who says who is a producer to a more modern-sounding but not much more tractable query: 'what is output?' The reciprocal tautology of surplus and transfer theory is that output is what designated producers produce; those involved in producing output are productive laborers. Unproductive non-producers may greedily consume what is transferred to them out of the nation's product, but their contribution to production is nil; they live on our generosity.

Economic theory, if it is more than an intellectual pastime, serves as the handmaiden first of measurement and second of policy, however minimalist. The choice of national accounting system is of interest because the numbers it organizes affect how successful governments appear to their enemies and friends. Second, the system of national accounts affects how readily performance of country A can be compared with that of its neighbors. A scheme once chosen acquires institutional momentum. Policy may be designed to enhance growth rates of standard indicators that the scheme valorizes. The likelihood of indicator-strategic behavior is perhaps worst under central planning in cases where planners insecure about their legitimacy are yet potent enough to set prices in addition to allocating resources to favored sectors at the expense of others lower in priority. In mixed democracies, the pressure felt by incumbent governments to generate good-looking numbers has been said to produce 'political business cycles' (Lindbeck, 1976).

The problem of measuring the annual product of a polity is fruitfully broken down into decisions about 'scope, valuation, and netness' (Kuznets, 1973, pp. 580–3). Sections 8.2 and 8.3 of the present chapter compare scope, valuation, and netness across the two official national accounting schemes, the Keynesian System of National Accounts (SNA) and the Soviet Material Product System (MPS). Choice of scope, of production boundary, has implications for netness if input–output error is to be kept at bay.

What are we trying to measure? Gross national product has many deficiencies as a measure of economic welfare. Section 8.4 examines alternative attempts at making the aggregate output index a better indicator of how much is produced of what people want and value. Section 8.4.1 discusses Kuznets's 'intermediatization' of part of government in a 'social framework'. Section 8.4.2 looks at the Chicago theorist Gary S. Becker's 'intermediatization' of consumer goods that count as 'final' in GNP. Section 8.4.3 outlines the rationale behind Tobin and Nordhaus's 'measure of economic welfare'. It also mentions several other sets of conventions designed to improve the capture of goods in, and the exclusion of bads from, measures of annual net output.

8.2 Intermediate and final output in the System of National Accounts and the International Comparison Project

Comprehensive annual national income and product accounts are creatures of the Keynesian revolution. Before the Great Depression, doubts about the feasibility and utility of *aggregate* measures of product and incomes were strong. As noted in section 6.5.1, the German economist Amonn, for instance, held that, since the nation as a whole was not an economic *agent*, its income was a statistical fiction of no special interest (Amonn, 1911; discussed in Moskvin, 1929, p. 98). Americans in the 1920s also wished to keep apples and oranges separate. The National Bureau of Economic Research's 'central concept of economic activity' was not aggregate output but 'a somewhat fuzzy cocktail' of, by 1942, 811 monthly indicators from which no 'meaningful summary measure' could be derived (Maddison, 1982, pp. 65–6, 261).

Keynes refocused attention from potential supply of saving to actual demand and supply of goods overall. In order to test hypotheses about the consumption function and the multiplier and to work out monetary and fiscal policies that the *General Theory* deemed necessary to maintain demand and employment, reasonable measures of the volume of income and expenditure were needed. Further, 'distinctions among the major sectors in terms of their motivations and behavior patterns suggested the development of interrelated sectoral accounts...' (Kendrick, 1970, p. 305).

Though attempts to measure the income of a whole country were made by Gregory King in 1696 and by a growing handful of writers after him (Studenski, 1961), it was Simon Kuznets who pioneered the modern estimation of national income and product from detailed censuses of individual industries. With meticulous concern to avoid double-counting, Kuznets built up to national income from data on wholesale and retail sales, farm production and consumption in kind, government purchases, wages and employment in personal services (Kuznets, 1934). The methodology for interlocking GNP accounts was worked out in the early 1940s by James Meade and Richard Stone, also future Nobel laureates, 'with encouragement and detailed advice from Keynes' (Kendrick, 1970, p. 308). Both early Kuznets and Meade and Stone opted to include all government expenditures and revenues in *final* national expenditure and income. In terms of scope and netness, therefore, our heritage from them are the textbook identities Gross National Product = Gross National Expenditure = Consumption + Investment + Government + (Exports − Imports) = Income of nationals in the form of Wages + Interest + Profits + Rents + Transfers (e.g. Baumol, Blinder, and Scarth, 1985, pp. 133–7).

In a British White Paper of April 1941, Meade and Stone present income at factor cost and outlays on final goods and additions to stocks as the two sides of a double-entry production account for the entire national economy. 'National expenditure was thus firmly established as a coordinate variable'. According to Kendrick, 'the idea of double-entry national-production accounts led [Meade and Stone] to the related idea of constructing income and outlay accounts for each major sector of the economy... They suggested four sector accounts – for households, business enterprises, governments, and the rest of the world' (Kendrick, 1970, p. 308).

The 1941 paper recognizes the theoretical possibility that government may 'invest', but decides not to account for it as a separate item. Moreover, unlike Simon Kuznets's 1948 reconsideration (section 8.4.1 below), Meade and Stone have all government activity as final (none of it is regarded as intermediate to other sectors), so all of it counts in GNP. Government purchases of reusable capital assets (additions to the state stock of post office equipment, construction of new public housing) show up in the Meade and Stone scheme as 'home investment'. They concede that [there] is ... a certain degree of arbitrariness in deciding what items of Government expenditure should be regarded as investment expenditure, [although] the principles to be adopted for the purpose of balancing the tables are clear. If, for example, expenditure on roads and on battleships is excluded from current expenditure by the Government, then it must be included in home investment, and vice versa.

(Meade and Stone, 1941, p. 337n.)

Meade and Stone's Cambridge predecessor A. C. Pigou suggested in an oft-quoted passage that national income be understood as an annual flow of goods and services that 'can be brought directly or indirectly into relation with the measuring rod of money' (Pigou, 1932, pp. 11 and 31).

Meade and Stone take a more agnostic view of the requirement of monetization and market exchange. How production and income in kind are handled in the accounts depends on convention and ability to estimate. They observe that 'a whole host of transactions occur that either involve the payment of money from one owner to another *or [that] may be imagined to be accompanied* by such a money transaction' (Meade and Stone, 1941, p. 338; emphasis added).

For instance, with respect to the room and board that domestic servants receive from their employers, which counts as part of 'Wages' in the table for Net National Income at Factor Cost, Meade and Stone say,

we may imagine that the employer pays to the domestic servant the whole of this wage in money, and that the domestic servant then purchases from the employer the food and lodging provided in kind. In order to preserve the balance [between Net National Income and Net National Expenditure at factor cost,] if the whole of the wages of domestic servants is included in ['Wages'] the whole of it must be included in ['Personal Consumption Expenditure at Market Prices'].

(Meade and Stone, 1941, p. 340 and n. 1)

'In order to avoid unprofitable complications of the tables', Meade and Stone treat non-profit institutions like clubs, charities, voluntary hospitals, and so on 'merely as a channel through which persons receive and spend income'. In other words, such institutions go in the household sector, a practice later deemed unwarranted. (Meade and Stone, 1941, p. 352; Palmer, 1966, pp. 130–3).

Meade and Stone's 'new departure ... spread rapidly' (Kendrick, 1970, p. 308). The original United Nations System of National Accounts (SNA), for which Stone was principal consultant, dates from 1947 (United Nations, 1947). Since the 1940s all countries of the first and non-communist third world have employed the SNA to estimate levels of aggregate economic activity.

The SNA is the official accounting-manual embodiment of Keynes's and Meade and Stone's idea that it is useful to analyze total aggregate product Y (GNP) as the sum of four classes of expenditure on goods and services: on consumption goods and services C, on net investment goods and services I, on government goods G, and, in open economies, on net exports $(X - M)$. $Y = C + I + G + (X - M)$. GNP is 'gross' only in the sense of being gross rather than net of depreciation. Net national product (NNP) is the Meade-and-Stone final total of $C + I + G + (X - M)$ available after deducting the cost of maintaining business capital intact.

It is a common misperception that the SNA draws the GNP boundary around firms and government and excludes all non-marketed production of households. Except for illegal transactions, all activities resulting in production of goods or provision of services, whether personal or collective, are treated as part of production and are therefore supposed to be counted. The sole exceptions are for activities described as 'own-account non-primary'. What it means is that imputations are not supposed to be made for housewives' services in rich countries but values are to be imputed for, for example, food grown and housing constructed for own use, without passing through the market (United Nations, 1968, pp. 10–11).

The 1964 revision of the SNA made a major effort to overcome the understatement of per capita GNP of poor countries caused by failure to include non-market production. The SNA makes no bones about the conventional nature of the drawing of the production boundary. As the anonymous authors put it, 'Once the production boundary has been established for an exchange economy, certain flows will be found to cross the boundary. Those which flow out of the region could be said to make up the constituents of final product', while those that do not cross the boundary are listed as 'intermediate products' (United Nations, 1964, p. 6). It is 'reasonable to regard' direct personal services (such as those of domestics) that 'one household buys from another' (*sic*) as 'part of production'.

The 1964 SNA recognizes therefore 'a limited amount of production within households'. As in the original Meade and Stone, the domestic servant is a one-person 'household' that not only consumes but produces services that it sells to other households. The servant is not quite a bona fide capitalist firm since the consuming household is said to buy the servant's services 'at cost'. The production account to which is debited the cost of the servant's services, 'like any other production account, lies within the production boundary and what flows out of it is part of final product' (United Nations, 1964, p. 5). Depending on the degree of 'surplus' presumed to be factored into the 'cost' at which the servant sells his or her services, the SNA formula seems to hark back to Marx's portrait of the petty producer as 'exploiting himself', though not, of course, to the Marxist view of the petty producer as 'outside the economic domain' (section 5.4 above).

Again with respect to single-person (single-family) firms and farms, the SNA notes the difficulty of separating members' transactions into those that belong to production and those that are said to be part of consumption. Despite good intentions, the SNA makes a somewhat unsatisfactory compromise on the question of household production. The arbitrariness and inaccuracy of price and quantity estimates of home production of heterogeneous non-agricultural products are evidently thought to be the main obstacle to extending the recommended program of imputation much beyond the primary and secondary activities of traditional agriculture (see Reynolds, 1983, p. 947). The SNA's division into primary vs. non-primary seems designed as a proxy for a host of value-laden distinctions – business vs. family life, good vs. service, necessity vs. luxury; and the authors sound not too confident about making it.

> The ... rules have as their object the inclusion in production of household activities *that are clearly akin to those which are usually undertaken in enterprises* and the exclusion of those for which the analogy with enterprises becomes tenuous [*sic*] and which do not lend themselves to any precise definition. It is convenient in stating these rules to *draw a distinction between primary and other producers...* As a result ..., there is *omitted from production* the net amount of *all non-primary production* performed by producers *outside their own trades* and consumed by themselves. Non-primary production may be defined broadly as the transformation and distribution of tangible commodities as well as the rendering of services...
>
> (United Nations, 1964, p. 5; emphasis added)

Presumably, if you are a clown, clowning for your family is formation of human capital. The distinction between primary and non-primary seems designed to sharpen inter-country comparisons by limiting national accountants' responsibility for imputation to subsistence agriculture in poor countries. Unpaid housework belongs to leisure, not to work.

The primary category is, however, generously conceived and the SNA is commendably determined to make imputations for whatever can be measured within that class. Not only strictly primary agricultural and mineral production but simple transformation into 'such items as butter, cheese, flour, wine, oil, cloth or furniture', whether for market sale or own use, are to be estimated for GNP. Moreover, the SNA encourages user countries to treat *tangible* investment on own account with the same respect accorded to investment carried out by enterprises.

> All production of fixed assets on own account should, in principle, be included in the gross output of commodities... [If] possible, a separate establishment should be delineated where households or governments engage in own-account construction of structures, roads, and similar works. For the same purpose, the value of tools, instruments, containers, and similar items which have an expected life of use of one year or more ... should be recorded in gross output.
> (United Nations, 1968a, p. 96)

Production in the 1968 revised SNA is divided by ostensible mode into two main subcategories, 'commodities' and 'other goods and services'. Commodities are 'goods and services normally sold on the market at a price which is intended to cover the costs of production', i.e. to turn a profit, whereas other goods and services 'are supplied by the producers of government and private non-profit services and [*sic*] by domestic service; and may also be imported' (1968a, p. 94). As in Bacon and Eltis, all investment goods are 'commodities', as are all exports.

On the question of government as intermediate or final, the SNA follows its consultant Sir Richard Stone and not the Kuznets of 1948.

> In the case of government ... when expenditures of use to business are provided by the government ... expenditures appear as final products even though it might be possible to regard them as intermediate products. For instance, seed, fertilizers and other supplies given free of charge to farmers ... might be treated as intermediate products by replacing the government purchases of these products by an imputed subsidy to farmers. It is difficult to think of quantitatively important cases in which a clearcut separation of the business element in government services could be made and in practice such imputations are not attempted in national accounting.
> (United Nations, 1964, p. 6)

The 1968 SNA description of government makes no reference to government activity as demanded by anyone other than government itself, and betrays a Smith-flavored modism.

> The producers of government services furnish, but normally do not sell, to the community those common services which cannot otherwise be conveniently and economically provided, and administer the State and the economic and social policy of the community. Their activities therefore differ substantially in character, cost structure,

and source of finance from the activities of industries. The activities of the government services are largely financed by the government itself [sic]; and they are consequently considered to be the final consumers of most of the services and goods which they produce [sic]. Their cost structure does not contain an element of operating surplus [sic]; and [sic] is made up, to a substantial extent of compensation of employees. A very minor portion of the gross output of the producers of government services may be disposed of in the market on terms which will result in classification as a commodity [sic].

In addition to [for example, bodies which engage in administration, defence and regulation of the public order; health, educational, cultural, recreational and other social services; and promotion of economic growth and welfare and technological development], the producers of government services should include social security arrangements and certain other non-profit bodies . . . which, by virtue of the relations with a government, are clearly instruments of the social or economic policies of the government.

(United Nations, 1968a, pp. 74–5)

Despite two centuries of argument in economics over the nature of capital and its increase, not to speak of contemporary work by Schultz and G. S. Becker, which developed Say's and J. S. Mill's insight that human and intangible capital often outlast physical capital (Schultz, 1961; G. S. Becker, 1964), the 1964 SNA distinguishes consumption from 'capital formation' on a one-year exhaustion criterion. Education is a short-lasting service.

> Capital formation is confined to tangible assets in national accounting. Services, such as education received by individuals, are excluded, even though their benefits are realized at a later date, because [sic] human beings are not regarded as capital assets.
>
> (United Nations, 1964, p. 8)

Long-lasting tangible assets can, however, accept short-lasting bought intermediate inputs in the form of intermediate business services. Repairs or alterations partially reverse depreciation, lengthening useful lives and enhancing physical or value productivity. They partially substitute for capital investments embodying new technology. Paint jobs, overhauls, retoolings, new software, management reorganizations are examples. Services in SNA are not therefore automatically confined to the 'final goods' category as in official Soviet doctrine. But gross capital formation is distinguished from outlays on 'intermediate consumption'. Inputs bought for purposes of R&D are classed as 'intermediate consumption' for the reason that they 'may not yield concrete benefits and are usually not embodied in tangible assets'. The same goes for 'advertising, market research and activities such as public relations which are designed to improve the goodwill [capital] of business units' (United Nations, 1968a, p. 101).

Aside from the difficulty of imputing values for human capital, the SNA's ruling against it is made for the reason that, as with the journey-to-work ruling, *all* consumption is regarded as final, not just consumption over and above some socially-defined subsistence minimum. Since there is no way of calculating the 'minimum' amount of education needed to keep a citizen going in a given society, 'total' education cannot be calculated as some multiple of it to yield a 'stock' of minimally and supra-minimally educated labor-power, which might be viewed as the result of capital-forming activity on the part of teachers and educators.

The revised 1968 SNA supplements the 1964 system with detailed instructions first for setting up highly disaggregated input–output tables. Another addition is of matrices for financial flows, it being observed that financial decisions are 'frequently taken in much larger units' (central governments, head offices of conglomerates) than those in which operating decisions are taken.

The SNAs are impressive if conservative documents. It is difficult to convey the extent of their commitment to maximizing the volume of consistent, disaggregated information that double-entry income–outlay and input–output tables can yield. Carrying out their recommendations requires governments to hire armies of scribes and number-gatherers. The fruits of that effort benefit not only researchers but also the subsistence farmers, artisans, and workers in 'informal' sectors of developing economies whose productions of goods and services are often written off as of marginal welfare significance.

With scope and netness standardized across countries, GNP data collected and aggregated according to SNA methodology in national currency units are amenable to conversion at some conversion factor to a common-denominator currency, making possible inter-country comparisons of total and per capita GNP and of its subcomponents. International league tables thus generated can be used by development assistance and financial agencies and in empirical research into patterns of growth and structural change (Ofer, 1973; Chenery and Syrquin, 1975; Chenery, 1982; Chenery, Robinson, and Syrquin, 1986).

Rank and dispersion of country standings in the league tables naturally reflect the factors by which GNP or GDP in local currency units are converted to the common denominator that permits ranking. *Faute de mieux* the commonest rate used is the average annual official rate of exchange of the local currency *vis-à-vis* the US dollar. The dollar–local currency rate is, however, a specific price generated in a very particular market, the foreign-exchange market. It depends only on the market for tradables, not on the market for all outputs figuring in the SNA's GNP. It reflects, on the one hand, the purchasing power of US dollars over local goods that succeed in penetrating the channels of international trade. To acquire them, foreigners demand the local currency. On the other hand, it reflects the local country's demand for imports from the United States and from third countries such as the oil exporters who quote in US funds. Locals offer their own currency in order to obtain dollars with which to buy those imports.

Relative standing in ordinal rankings and the dollar distances between richest and poorest countries emerging from exchange-rate conversions are quite misleading. Converting, for example, a high volume of local construction, domestic service, and government expenditure on primary education and health by a price ratio that may reflect not much more than the low purchasing power of tea over imported oil and vehicles may give a deceptively unfavorable dollar GNP for the tea-exporting country. Phases I and II of the International Comparison Project (ICP) 'showed that the purchasing power of the currency of low-income countries relative to that of very high-income countries is often two or three times as great as the exchange rate would indicate . . . [leading] to a correspondingly large understatement of the low-income country's relative real income' (Kravis, Heston, and Summers, 1982, p. 3). Moreover, large annual swings in exchange rates between the currencies of rich countries since the move to floating exchange rates in 1971 make the US dollar a less-than-ideal world *numéraire*.

Since poor countries are not miniature replicas of rich but differ from them in sectoral structure, relative prices are naturally skewed so as to favor the goods that poor countries produce relatively cheaply, namely labor-intensive goods and labor-intensive services. Capital-intensive goods tend to be relatively more expensive than they are in rich countries. As Kravis, Heston, and Summers express it, 'the deviation of purchasing power parities from official exchange rates is not uniform for all kinds of goods . . . Exchange-rate conversions thus tend to exaggerate the relative proportion of GDP that is taken in the form of capital goods in poor countries', pumping up the share of industry, for example, and giving a false impression of the real volume of services (Kravis, Heston and Summers, 1982, p. 4).

The distorted picture of production and consumption relativities created by the practice of exchange-rate comparisons led the United Nations and World Bank to fund an ambitious multi-stage International Comparison Project (ICP). By its Phase III (Kravis, Heston, and Summers, 1982), the ICP calculated purchasing power parity (PPP) conversion factors for 151 final-expenditure categories for thirty-four countries. Phase IV (Kravis, Heston, and Summers, 1986) covered sixty countries for 1980; Phase V's results, for 1985, cover twenty-five developed countries, with those for the remaining forty-five countries to be available in late 1988 (World Bank, 1988, p. 220). The Soviets have expressed the intention of joining at Phase VI with data for 1990 (information supplied by L. Dreschler of the UN Statistical Office, December 1988).

Upon reaggregation to GNP or GDP these factors permit cross-section comparisons of income and product that take into account the heightened purchasing power of local currencies over units of local output. The results are striking. For example, in 1975, India's per capita GDP converted at the official dollar/rupee exchange rate was $146 per head, a mere 2.3 per cent of the US's 1975 per capita GDP of US$7,176. But, converted at purchasing power parities for the 151 classes of good, India's GDP comes out at $470 'international dollars', or 6.56 per cent of the US figure. India's 'exchange-rate deviation index' is therefore $470 divided by $146 or 3.23, a useful number if stable or evenly evolving over time. The deviation index, laboriously calculated by researchers who found out quantities of the 151 categories of goods and services that rupees could buy in various regions of India in 1975, can thenceforth be used cheaply to convert annually published and readily available rupee GDPs for other years into dollars at the dollar/rupee exchange rate, and then to adjust the resulting dollar GDPs upward by simple application of India's dollar-exchange-rate deviation factor of 3.23.

An adjustment in the opposite direction must be made for the developed countries of Western Europe. It is needed to capture among other things the lower purchasing power of local currencies over living space. For example, in 1975 West Germany's per capita GDP in dollars converted at the official rate was 94.7 per cent of US GDP. Reworked via PPPs, though, it came to only 83 per cent of the US level; the West German/US exchange-rate deviation index was therefore less than unity, 0.88 (Kravis, Heston, and Summers, 1982, p. 12).

Important empirical research has since examined the extent to which the Phase III and IV exchange-rate deviation indices are representative of deviations from PPP for countries not included in those studies, and the extent to which the indices behave predictably over time (Chenery, Robinson, and Syrquin, 1986).

With 'real' GDP calculated in purchasing power prices, the ICP studies subaggregate it back to its components consumption, investment and government in an original, mode-blind way, one that is arguably more welfare-related than the SNA practice. In SNA, GDP is the sum of resident households' C + enterprises' I + government's G. This is a subaggregation essentially by mode except for additions to private-sector C and I needed to accommodate 'primary' activity done on own account by households.

ICP's object is to 'ensure that [inter-country] comparisons for [the subgroupings consumption, investment, and government are] *independent of the degree to which a country's expenditures for them are made collectively* by the society on the one hand and out of household budgets on the other'. The ICP is interested in consumption from whatever source, and therefore *removes* government and non-profit expenditures for health care, education, welfare, and recreation from the 1968 SNA's tables 5-3 and 5-4 ('government' and 'non-profit bodies serving households') and adds them to 'consumption expenditure of the population', in approximate correspondence, the authors write, with 'the distinction between public and private goods that is made in the theory of public finance'. The ICP's 'public final consumption expenditure' (abbreviated 'government'), consists of 'final [sic] products that most societies, regardless of economic and social system [sic], provide through public organizations and finance by tax revenues. [They] take the form largely of [externality-rich] services that provide citizens with physical, social and national security' (Kravis, Heston and Summers, 1982, pp. 33, 62, 67). The affinity with Kuznets's 'lost' proposal of 1948 will be plain shortly.

8.3 Matter and mode in the Material Product System

As we learned in Chapter 6, what the Soviet Union decided it wanted to measure was 'material product', a concept narrower in scope than GNP (Boss, 1986c). Countries using the 'material product system' (MPS), present and former Soviet allies, are not included in the international league tables of GNP and shares in GNP because of lack of comparable data. The rebel stance of advocates of the Material Product System manifests itself as banks of blanks for the USSR, China, and Eastern Europe in the economic yearbooks and atlases of the World Bank and UN (e.g. World Bank, 1987, tables 1–5). Conversion of MPS numbers to standard GNP methodology is possible, but it is an arduous task that has till the 1980s fallen on individual scholars rather than constituting the routine business of supranational agencies (e.g. Bergson, 1961; Pitzer, 1982).

Interestingly, the UN seems to have acquiesced to the principle of 'separate but equal' as far as the rival systems of national accounts are concerned. Elaborate methodologies have been published to aid reconciliation of the SNA and the MPS (United Nations, 1969a, b, 1971, 1977, 1981a).

In dissenting from the 1968 SNA, the Soviets furnished a document that assisted the UN Economic and Social Council's Statistical Commission in understanding scope, valuation, and netness in the MPS

(United Nations, 1969b). The Commission published the first of several pamphlets outlining procedures for converting from SNA to MPS and vice versa (United Nations, 1969a).

According to the Soviet document (United Nations (1969b), global social product (*valovoi obshchestvennyi produkt*) is 'the entire mass of material goods produced in the branches of material production during a given period'. It is therefore 'gross' in a much more worrisome sense than GNP, for grain is added to flour is added to bread. National income (*natsional' nyi dokhod*) is 'the sum of net outputs . . . generated in the sphere of material production' (1969b, pp. 18–19). The aims of the MPS's 'system of balances of the national economy' are stated as follows.

> The balance of production, consumption, and accumulation of the global product (material balance) . . . reflects the process and results of the production of the global product in its material form. This balance permits us to establish the tangible physical and social structure of the production of the global product and its utilization for intermediate material consumption [*sic*], for final consumption, for net capital formation, for replacement of losses, and for export.
> (1969b, p. 52)

'Material production' comprises production of material goods and 'material services' of transport and trade (*sic*). Ostensibly for practical reasons, passenger transport is given as a material service, alongside freight transport, against Soviet practice (see A. S. Becker, 1971, p. 55). With reference to the International Standard Industrial Classification system (ISIC), the following groups are determined by the 1969 reconciliation to be 'non-material services' in MPS:

6320 Hotels, rooming houses, camps, and other lodging places
8210 Financial institutions
8220 Insurance
 831 Real estate (not ownership of dwellings)
 832 Business services except machinery and equipment rentals and leasing (except 8324, engineering, architectural and technical services, which count as material services when attached directly to construction enterprises [Gur'ev, 1967]
 910 Public administration and defense
 920 Sanitary and similar services
 931 Education services
 932 Research and scientific services
9331 Medical, dental, and other health services
 934 Welfare institutions
 935 Business, professional, and labor associations

939 Other social and related community services
941 Motion picture and other entertainment services (except 9411, motion picture production) [film is material]
942 Libraries, museums, botanical and zoological gardens and other cultural services not elsewhere classified
949 Amusement and recreational services not elsewhere classified
952 Laundries, laundry services (part)
953 Domestic services
959 Miscellaneous personal services
960 International and other extra-territorial bodies

In addition, the UN noted that 'there may be some other activities which are treated as "non-material" activities in MPS, for example:

(i) distribution of gas and water (part of ISIC 4102 and 4200);
(ii) certain services incidental to transport (part of ISIC 7191) such as tourist agencies, tourist development services;
(iii) storage of household goods (part of ISIC 7192);
(iv) certain types of engineering, architectural and technical services, notably those which are not connected with construction (part of ISIC 8324);
(v) part of veterinary services, namely those which are not connected with agriculture (part of ISIC 9332).

(United Nations, 1969a, pp. 11–12)

Other accounting differences attach to: capital consumption in the non-material sphere; business travel; actual as compared to written-off value of scrapped assets; imputation of rents for owner-occupiers of dwellings (not included in MPS, important in SNA); depreciation of public assets and of dwellings; fixed assets and equipment bought by the military, which in MPS are apparently counted in fixed capital formation (Wiles and Efrat, 1985); in-kind consumption by members of the armed forces (food, shelter, dress uniforms vs. everyday); enterprise outlays on amenities for workers – recreation, day-care, food plots (Rumer, 1981); goods and services furnished by government institutions and accruing to households but for which consumers control neither source nor amount (in MPS, the 'social consumption' component of 'total consumption of the population'); unfinished construction as creation of finished fixed asset vs. change in stock; monetary vs. other gold; unforeseen vs. normal capital losses; imports and exports of non-material services; license fees; net incomes of unincorporated enterprises (private plots, tips); social security and employer pension contributions; banking and insurance (United Nations, 1969a, pp. 12–27).

The great merit of this and successor documents is that they identify adjustments and reclassifications needed to convert either set of tables into 'elementary flows' that can then be arranged according to the rule of either system.

The impenetrable bureaucratese of the United Nations pamphlet (1969a) is unable to conceal a striking implication of 'Conceptual relationships between the revised SNA and MPS'. Once the labor of making the adjustments, additions, and subdivision needed to arrive at 'elementary flows' is performed, there remains no substantive reason – aside from thinking that non-material services involve a genuine *quid pro quo* – to favor one methodology over the other. The cold war of the central statistical offices should have been over! Countries on the two sides of the Comecon boundary ran low on excuses for not offering their 'elementary flows' according to either methodology, for not examining the economic universe through stereoscopic glasses.

The new tolerance did not catch on easily. SNA countries stood by their SNA, having little inclination to exclude 'non-material services', their fastest growing sector, on either politico-strategic or economic–theoretical grounds. The subtext of a Gorbachev-era discussion of problems and possibilities of reconciliation of the SNA and the MPS in *Review of Income and Wealth* written by a Soviet staff officer of the Statistical Office of the United Nations Secretariat is that the MPS is just as good as the SNA and is here to stay (Ivanov, 1987).

By the early 1980s, the stalemate that had produced unsightly gaps in the international league tables for such important countries as the Soviet Union and the other members of Comecon was partially broken. The UN *Statistical Yearbook* began a series for East, West, and South prepared according to a *Dienstrein* but otherwise incomprehensible compromise statistic, 'gross domestic product excluding services' for example, United Nations, 1981a, p. 89). Meanwhile Hungary, Poland, Romania, and Yugoslavia began publishing alternative GNP statistics as part of a drive to normalize relations with the international financial community.

Extension of the ICP could have made the SNA–MPS stalemate a minor nuisance. With its slow advance a tone of frustration settled on agencies that *faute de mieux* must rely on exchange-rate comparisons. The World Bank's 1987 *World Development Report* replaced the neutral descriptive term 'East European Non-Market Economies' for its banks of blanks (in use since 1978) with the stonier designation 'Non-reporting Non-Member Economies'. The change reflects on the one hand statistical defection from unilateral MPS by Poland, Hungary, and Yugoslavia (and China); and on the other, addition to the East European MPS hard core of Angola, North Korea, and Mongolia (World Bank, 1987, tables 1–33).

In a series of special reports, GNP conversions for 1980 were derived using a variety of exchange rates for China, the USSR, and six members of Comecon (World Bank, 1983, p. 244; Marer, 1985). Campbell's report for the USSR stresses the extreme sensitivity of dollar measures of Soviet per capita GNP (e.g. ranging from $2,751 to $6,824 in 1980) to the exchange rate chosen, casting doubt on the whole exercise (Campbell, 1985, table 9 and pp. 23–4).

Since the price structures of centrally planned economies are so idiosyncratic and so distort the image of their real incomes in exchange-rate comparisons, the prospect of applying ICP methodology to MPS-using Comecon members was greeted with keenest interest. In 1982, the Kravis, Heston, and Summers UN–World Bank ICP Phase III published 1975 benchmark data for thirty-four countries including four centrally planned economies, Hungary, Poland, Romania, and Yugoslavia, but regrettably not the USSR. ICP 'real incomes' for centrally planned economies are comparable in scope, definitions of consumption, investment, and government, and detailed branch classifications, and in their use of purchasing power price weights, to those made for other, 'capitalist' members of the world community.

Despite criticisms in the Soviet press (Shatalin, 1987a, b), *perestroika* and new thinking have at time of writing (summer 1988) not yet produced outright revision of the doctrine that 'non-material services' are redistributions that deserve to be in a 'non-productive sphere'. The new political economy textbook under the editorship of the Kremlin's new chief ideologist reaffirms that the service sphere does not create independent final products but instead contributes to the creation of a 'production and social infrastructure' (Medvedev *et al.*, 1988a, pp. 18–19). Though Soviet authorities reportedly asked the United Nations for assistance in setting up GDP accounts, for many years GDP figures were not estimated even for internal consumption (Vanous, 1986, p. 4). Things are changing, though. I was informed by a group of economists at the Central Economic–Mathematical Institute that the State Committee on Statistics in April 1988 issued instructions for planning and monitoring agencies to prepare to adopt 'international methods of calculating indicators of socio-economic development'. A growth rate, though no level, for Soviet GNP in 1987 was included in *Pravda*'s January 1988 report on the economy, alongside the usual list of industrial indicators. B. Riabushkin published a how-to introduction to the GNP concept in May of that year (Riabushkin, 1988). The new textbook pays a compliment to the UN's GNP concept for its nearness to the '[Soviet] concept of final product' and announces that as of 1987 'in the interests of international comparability' the USSR will include a GNP figure in its official statistics (Medvedev *et al.*, 1988a, p. 27).

8.4 New measures of final supply: towards an economics of use-values

8.4.1 Intermediatization of a social framework: Kuznets

The great pioneer of national income accounting and Nobel laureate Simon Kuznets posed the problem of measuring output and its growth through time in terms of 'scope, valuation, and netness' (Kuznets, 1948, p. 152). Kuznets's proposal for the evaluation of a society's net product is a critical reaction to the US Department of Commerce's outline of an SNA-type Keynesian scheme, which, as we saw, treats all government as final. Kuznets's aim is for the arbitrary accounting definition of net output to encompass just those goods and services that he thinks pass the test of welfare-relatedness. 'National income is for man, and not man for the increase of the country's capacity' (Kuznets, 1946, p. 114). For goods or services to count in a final product that is welfare-related, more of them must be better than fewer from the standpoint of final consumers.

As we saw, pre-public-choice neoclassical microeconomics regarded scope and netness as functions of valuation (money price formation). Scope of production is delimited by what has market value because it is both useful and rare. Since it allows the generality of the principle of opportunity cost, the neoclassical approach somewhat fudges the problem of actual versus potential value that arises in connection with valuing activities of government, non-profit organizations, and households. While costly to supply in actual and/or opportunity-cost terms, government, household, and charity goods are not resold individually to citizen-consumers free to choose the unit from which they come.

Valuing them for the national accounts requires convention *re* both valuation and netness. The Keynesian SNA values government and non-profit expenditures at cost, assuming zero implied profit, places them entirely with products and expenditures classed as final, and leaves household production out of account entirely except for 'primary' as noted above.

The Keynes – Meade and Stone decision to locate the economy's official accounting boundary around $C + I + G + (X - M)$, while theoretically informed by the *General Theory*'s analysis of monetized effective demand, remains just one convention on scope and netness out of many. GNP is well suited to capturing production and consumption possibilities, but the link to welfare is somewhat paradoxical. More GNP is not always better than less as far as consumers are concerned. In the first place, net investment yields no current utility, only the promise of increased future utility. Foreigners enjoy our net exports, not us. The idea behind GNP as a measure of consumption possibility is that we *could*, by shifting around the output mix, consume what we now invest and export, so that GNP indicates something resembling 'potential consumption, given the actual state of animal spirits'. Since it is sovereign consumers who refrain of their own free will from consumption in order to invest and export, a Panglossian purist can readily make the link to welfare for the private goods $C + I + (X - M)$. Citizen sovereignty expressed via some sort of democratic political process accounts for the welfare-relatedness of G. For all Keynes's dismissal of Marx, the *General Theory* gives a faint nod of analytical respect to the anti-Jevonsian notion of *homo faber*: since mass unemployment is such a social evil, working can be construed as in some degree an end in itself, not exclusively a painful means to consumption (section 7.1 above).

The neoclassical tradition starts with individual or household preferences and effective demands and works backward to what those demands make it profitable for firms to produce, given technology and terms of acquisition of inputs. Only final outputs, by hypothesis, yield utility; inputs, material or immaterial, are forever lost to us. But the efficiency requirement that inputs be minimized for a given output does not by the same token make them 'bads'.

Simon Kuznets (Kuznets, 1941, 1946, 1948, 1951) was the earliest and most articulate advocate of the suggestion that several classes of goods and services that the Keynes – Meade and Stone national accounts treat as final are more properly regarded as *productive yet intermediate*. Taking up the core of the Classical–Marxian unproductive labor doctrine while purging it of input–output error, Kuznets 'intermediatizes' a 'regrettable but necessary social framework' of government services, which he describes as useful to business, not consumers. '[Most] government activities are designed to preserve and maintain the basic social framework and are thus a species of repair and maintenance which cannot in and of itself produce economic returns' (*sic*) (Kuznets, 1951, p. 184). Expenditures preserving the social framework include, according to Kuznets, 'all types of economic legislation, administration, and adjudication' but not expenditures on education and health. The ICP theoreticians' affinity with Kuznets's mode-neutral attitude to the line between 'government' and 'final consumption' is plain. Kravis, Heston, and Summers, however, agree to treat government activity as final and do not attempt to 'intermediatize' it.

Kuznets's social framework is not unproductive just because it is intermediate. Kuznets is no 'fallacist'. The social framework is described as entirely necessary, a *sine qua non* for the production of 'final' marketed consumption goods. In the manner of capital goods, the part of government expenditure that goes to maintain the social framework is a condition of consumer satisfaction, not a source of it (Kuznets, 1948, p. 156). '[The] flow of services to individuals from the economy is a flow of economic goods produced and secured under conditions of internal peace, external safety, and legal protection of specific rights, and cannot include these very conditions as services' (Kuznets, 1951, p. 193). Accounting of such activities should therefore avoid the implication that more of them is better than fewer, if we care that national income be welfare-related.

Kuznets's objection to the Department of Commerce is that their concept (Keynesian in the manner of Meade and Stone) is said to involve unwarranted duplication. The distinction between net and gross in all national accounting 'hinges on how duplication is avoided' (Kuznets, 1946, p. 112). GNP adds government services beneficial to business to the net output of the business sector. 'The implication of adding into net national product both the cigars at full market value and the wages of government workers is that the latter produce goods that have nothing to do with the cigars, i.e., are final products not embodied in them' (Kuznets, 1948, p. 158). It is argued that the legal, protective, and administrative fraction of government services should be netted out analogously to bakeries' purchases of flour before calculating final business product, namely goods and services that provide utility to consumers (*sic*), and net investment. The solution is to 'construct the account for government on lines parallel to the account for the business sector ... [distinguishing] within total sales to government between sales on consumer and government capital account [on the one hand] and sales on business or cost of society account [on the other]' (Kuznets, 1948, p. 153).

Citizens' sovereignty does not imply finality for all the products of government.

> [The] fact that in democratic societies decisions on the volume and character of governmental activity are made by legislatures responsive to the interests of the men and women who comprise the nation ... means merely that the activities are considered necessary; they may, however, be essential costs just as easily as essential final products.
> (Kuznets, 1948, p. 156)

All this is noble and hard to quarrel with. The aim is to translate neo-classical welfare economics into an input–output accounting scheme. However, beyond asserting that property-rights legislation, etc., is of benefit to business alone, Kuznets does not explain on what basis the suggested 'functional analysis of government expenditures' will reveal just which are intermediate and which are of final utility to citizens. Splitting government activity à la J. S. Mill rules out the plausibility that a legal, infrastructural, and administrative framework benefits producers and consumers *at the same time. Jointness in consumption is after all a principal cause and characteristic of government production.* The difficulty of segregating government functions into those beneficial just to business and those giving consumers direct utility is the Department of Commerce's and the Keynesians' principal excuse for refusing to try (see Hicks, 1940, p. 118). The Department of Commerce authors eloquently contest Kuznets's contention that 'economic legislation' is of no utility to end users.

> [Regulation] of security dealings, administration of anti-trust laws, control of child labor, provision of minimum wages, and regulation of public utilities are . . . services to individuals. Economic legislation generally provides rules for the operation of the private enterprise system in order that it may function with great equality of opportunity and income, and with greater protection to the individual against fraud and the hazards of industrial life. These benefits are over and above the output of the business system, which could be quite the same even though the benefits of economic legislation were not obtained.
> (Gilbert *et al.*, 1948, p. 185)

The Department of Commerce economists also indict 'National Income: a new version' for alleged waste of information. 'Vast segments of production and income, recorded in our national accounting system, would be obliterated from [Kuznets's] because they do not constitute capital formation or the flow of what he regards as final goods to consumers' (Gilbert *et al.*, 1948, p. 180). But Kuznets is concerned with product having direct impact on consumers' welfare, describing the Keynesians' willingness to 'measure what one can measure rather than what one wants to measure' as 'fatal to any meaningful statistical estimation' (Kuznets, 1948, p. 156, n. 4). 'National Income is not a measure of activity, of how much effort, toil and trouble economic activity represents, but of its contribution, of its success in attaining its goal' (1946, p. 114). '[The] total we are seeking is that of *product* . . . not of the volume of *activity* itself. Despite a great deal of activity, the product from the viewpoint of a clearly-defined end, in this case services to ultimate consumers, may be quite limited' (1948, p. 157).

Kuznets's insistence that product be recognizably final broaches the subject of 'von Neumannesque' elements in consumption. He objects, for instance, to the Department of Commerce's practice of including 'miners' expenditures on explosives, lamps and smithing' in 'personal consumption expenditure' (Kuznets, 1948, p. 157). Consumers, on the other hand, may regard a basic ration of consumer goods as mere subsistence (inputs) and only above-basic consumption as yielding 'real' utility. But in that case (which is why he is against it), 'the whole category of ultimate consumption disappears' (1946, p. 117).

Kuznets's argument that expenditures on defense, the courts, and so on are 'gross' but not 'net' failed to carry to the day. Western governments flocked to set up Meade-and-Stone GNP accounts after the war (Studenski, 1961). Kuznets went on to publish pioneering comparative studies of long-term modern economic growth: rate, structure, and spread, for which he won the Nobel prize in 1972 (Kuznets, 1963, 1966, 1971). These studies declare a truce with the SNA definition of $Y = C + I + G + (X - M)$, the better to focus on shares in Y of agriculture, industry, and services, including government, across countries and over time (for example, Kuznets, 1966, p. 371 and table 3.1). By the 1970s, Kuznets was however again reminding us that the 'end and purpose of economic activity' is results, not inputs (Kuznets, 1973).

8.4.2 Intermediatization of marketed consumer goods: households as firms in G. S. Becker

In his earliest estimate of the national income (1934), Simon Kuznets explains the decision to exclude from measures of production what he supposes must be a large volume of home-produced services rendered in the US's 30 million households by wives and other family members.

> [The] organization of those services renders them an integral part of family life at large, rather than of the specific business life of the nation. Such services are therefore quite removed from those which gainfully occupied groups undertake to perform in return for wages, salaries or profit.

Moreover, 'no reliable basis is available for estimating their value' (Kuznets, 1934, p. 4).

The decision to exclude household production of services was imbedded in harder institutional concrete in the various SNAs and adjoining documents (United Nations, 1947, 1960, 1964, 1968a). As we saw, the Revised 1968 SNA still in use outlines an ambitious program of imputation for own-account 'primary' production (including a lot of 'secondary'). Values are to be estimated for crops, firewood gathered, homemade wine, cheese, cloth, and furniture made on own account, as well as for own-account 'net capital formation' (home construction of houses, barns, roads, irrigation channels). However, the SNA instructs countries not to bother working out estimates for 'non-primary' own-account services (child-minding, instruction, cooking and cleaning, study).

Application of standard microeconomic tools to the behavior of individuals *qua* producers and consumers casts doubt on the soundness of that particular manifestation of the Classical–Marxian goods–service dichotomy. It has inspired a fascinating series of attempts to evaluate all classes of home production in order to derive more convincing aggregate measures of truly final consumption of use-values, fully net of 'work after work'.

Kuznets questioned the finality of defense, subways, and police. The Chicago time-utilitarian Gary S. Becker contests the finality of store-bought lentils, turkeys, textbooks, floor mops, TV sets. In a series of brilliant forays into non-market territory (1964, 1965, 1981), Becker firmly establishes the locus of 'final' production beyond the market boundary, in the household. Store-bought goods are demoted to the status of intermediate inputs. Lingering materialist resonances of the Classical and neoclassical notion of 'good' are all but silenced. What we consume and what augments our welfare in the last analysis is a flow of services, sometimes but not always the services of goods. These flows of services are enjoyed by individual members of households per unit of time.

Time-utilitarianism extends the neoclassical notions that work is the antithesis of leisure and that time is money. In 'A theory of the allocation of time' (1965), Becker carries the principle of opportunity cost first introduced formally by D. I. Green (1894) to its logical resting place beyond the market boundary. The full cost of goods and services consumed is not their market price, but 'the sum of market price and the forgone value of time' required to prepare store-bought items for actual enjoyment (Becker, 1965, p. 494). In Becker, all 'free' time, even in the middle of the night, has a price tag. The sleeper could be using it to earn money, which is our reward for participating in the production of capitalist and state X-goods.

Becker seconds Cairncross (1958) in accusing the economics profession of schizophrenia in assuming different degrees of rationality during and after labor-force work. The household is not some province of non-rational impulse but a 'small factory', a multi-person unit that 'combines capital goods, raw materials, and labor to clean, feed, procreate and otherwise produce useful commodities'. These final use-values are what 'directly enter utility functions', making individuals well or badly off (Becker, 1965, pp. 495–6). 'Useful commodities' are christened Z_i to set them apart from X_i, the marketed goods sold in malls and supermarkets which count as final production of consumer goods and services in GNP. Becker does not explicitly include state goods in the set of X-goods, but they are easily incorporated. In the case of immaterial services final in SNA (for example, those of subsidized public television stations, private restaurants, or state schools), the X_i and Z_i coincide (assuming the enjoyer does not remember them afterwards!).

Becker avoids the SNA modism that has business as pure producers and households as pure consumers. Households may be 'producing units and utility maximisers' at the same time. Households 'combine time and market goods via "production functions" f_i to produce the basic commodities Z_i and they choose the best combination of these commodities in the conventional way by maximising a utility function $U = U(Z_i \ldots Z_m)$' (Becker, 1965, p. 495).

The full price of a home-produced-and-consumed Z-commodity (meal on the table) is the sum of the prices of the bought inputs and of the time used in preparing it. For instance, the 'full price' of the Z-good 'an evening watching TV' is earnings forgone by the couch potato plus depreciation of the TV set, the couch, the house it is in, the extra lifetime earnings lost by not studying, etc. The income losses are offset to the degree that some relaxation is necessary for maximum earnings (Becker, 1965, p. 495).

Becker's approach revives J.-B. Say's concept of 'productive consumption', said to have had a 'long but bandit-like existence in economic thought' (see Blaug, 1988). The cost of time nets out to be lower for Z-commodities that contribute restoratively to productive effort. 'A considerable amount of sleep, food, and even "play" fall under this heading. The opportunity cost of the time is less because these commodities indirectly contribute to earnings' (1965, p. 503).

Since time can always in Becker's world be converted into goods by using less of it watching TV and more preparing for or participating in paid employment, the traditional distinction between work for pay in the labor market and off-hours leisure goes by the board. The relativity to look for at the margin is that between activities that are 'earnings-intensive', i.e. time-intensive without being X-goods-intensive, and those that are 'not earnings-intensive'. The latter contribute positively, indirectly or directly (though perhaps not netly), to earnings by contributing to the production of X-goods.

The other side of his coin that 'free time' is being used day and night to produce Z_i is that 'work time' may afford some consumption component, i.e. may be enjoyable to a degree. The implication is that

> Not only is it difficult to distinguish leisure from other non-work but also even work from non-work. Is commuting work, non-work, or both? ... The notion of productive consumption was introduced precisely to cover those commodities that contribute to work as well as to consumption. Cannot pure work then be considered simply as a limiting commodity of such joint commodities in which the contribution to consumption was nil? Similarly pure consumption would be a limiting [Z-]commodity in the opposite direction in

which the contribution to work [earnings] was nil, and intermediate commodities would contribute to both consumption and work.

(Becker, 1965, p. 504)

Becker's concept of productive consumption overrides economics' longstanding binary division into a 'sphere of production' and a 'sphere of consumption'. In treating 168 hours per person per week as consumers' only genuine constraint, the traditional Jevonsian production/consumption, labor/leisure dichotomies get hopelessly blurred. The economic domain of production is no longer a set territory with clear mode boundaries, such as the 'private for-profit business sector plus non-profit institutions plus government' of the GNP accounts. *Production appears rather as a protean effort to improve the finality of intermediate inputs, up until the moment of their perfection as Z-outputs.* It may occur 'anywhere', on the freeways and in the restaurants and bedrooms of the nation, completely oblivious to the bought-input bi-mode boundary of $C + I + G$. Utility-wise it stretches in declining balance from pure work and painful sacrifice (whether in the labor force or in the home), through the less alienating 'productive consumption', to purely enjoyable, wholly earnings-intensive, non-restorative, non-productive-of-intermediates 'final consumption', which is reduced to the status of a limiting case. Input–output-wise, production flows of the final Z_i are consumed like immaterial services in the *Wealth of Nations*, in the instant of their performance.

In Becker, the 'imperialism of economists' so upsetting to priests, poets, and psychologists is distilled into a clear, subtle, and seemingly harmless elixir. But one drop, and sleep, fasting and prayer, armed robbery, taking one's infant to the learning enrichment center – all are stripped of independent motivating power by the logic of time-constrained utility maximization. The domain claimed for economic logic expands to the totality of human experience for the reason that time cuts across mode boundaries and is the only real constraint. Life is short and *de gustibus non est disputandum*. In Becker, life's brevity gives us the 'economics of everything' and the 'economics of Dr Pangloss' in a single package.

In Becker, except to the extent that 'work' is fun, final net production of use-values (Z_i) takes place not in businesses, charities, or government bureaux, but in 'the home'. With scope and netness thus reconsidered, the problem of valuing the opportunity cost of people's time and their use of their X-goods returns to center stage. Teacher-training colleges and steel mills recede further up the production chain. Apples and oranges become intermediate inputs; TV sets become capital. Safety procedures, office cactuses, and muzak fall under productive consumption. Comparing the time-utilitarians' premisses to the respectful attitude to mode boundaries shown by Smith, Marx, or even Keynes, it is a brave new world.

8.4.3 Improving on GNP

GNP's $C + I + G + (X - M)$ covers a large number of products that have positive opportunity cost on account of resource scarcity. Innumerable transactions that add estimable values are totted up by standard methods into national aggregates. However, the chief global success indicator of the economic performance of 130-odd countries West and South leaves out many demonstrably economic goods while neglecting to subtract flows of economic bads. Assuming people are not masochists, that makes it an imperfect index of welfare.

GNP's architects thought this was simply unavoidable. Reacting negatively to Kuznets's 1948 proposal, users such as Jaszi and Denison were content to have a measure of activity, forgetting happiness. The ruling out of interpersonal comparisons of utility and the absence of cardinal measures were thought to make that impossible in any case. Denison for one was concerned to prevent complication of the analysis of productivity change that he thought would be a consequence of including non-profit institutions, not to speak of households, in the productive sphere. (Moss, 1973, p. 6).

Probably the most significant exclusion from the SNA's GNP on the goods side is that of 'non-primary production of services on own account', chiefly housework, of which more below. Household services have obvious utility and obvious positive opportunity cost, and imputed values for them can be readily estimated.

GNP excludes production of demanded but illegal 'goods' such as narcotics. It fails to capture underground production and construction, which while not strictly illegal are not recorded because agents attempt to avoid safety regulations, immigration laws, taxes, and so on (Simon and Witte, 1982). In terms of ability to form capital, in SNA government and non-profit institutions are not put on common ground with businesses. The treatment of consumer durables is similarly idiosyncratic and conventional: buying a house is purchasing a capital asset, but buying a washing machine is consumption.

On the bads side, GNP accounts do not endeavor to net out negative outputs caused by declines in quality of natural and man-made environments. The line between maintenance or protection and improvement is notoriously hard to draw even if we are not in a von Neumann system and consumption remains the 'sole end and purpose of all production'. A great deal of GNP is already protection (bicycle locks, winter clothing, storm windows, staple foods?). Putting bads-prevention (defense, police, pollution abatement) on the same footing as goods-production has worried political philosophers and economists since Nassau Senior (section 4.4.1). Beginning with Kuznets's 'National Income: a new version' of 1948, measurers dissatisfied with the GNP's omissions and distortions have attempted to correct for them.

Gary S. Becker's reconstitution of microeconomics both inspired and discouraged efforts to revise estimable product concepts in the direction of final welfare-relatedness. On the one hand, his 'productive consumption' notion implies that utility and X-goods can be joint products: people can be having fun while at work in the labor force. But how much fun? Empiricists despaired. Second, his notion of Z-commodities denies rather than exploits differences between tasks that can and those that cannot be delegated to third persons. Non-market tasks susceptible of delegation can be accurately estimated because the fact that some people *already* delegate them makes it less probable that they consistently afford large amounts of joint utility. 'Economic household services' (Hawrylyshyn, 1977) are therefore more apt to have some usable going price in the market.

'Economic household services' yield Beckerian Z-goods of the sort 'clean house', 'tasty meal', 'well cared-for child'. The distinction, superfluous in Becker, is whether individuals *have a choice* between either producing and consuming the Z-goods themselves at an opportunity cost in earnings forgone, or contracting them out.

Adjusting GNP for what Hawrylyshyn (1976, 1977) calls 'leisure–pleasure activities' (watching TV, enjoying the sunset) is more problematic. Scholars who would attach values to such activities must rely on estimates of the opportunity cost of the enjoyer's time. There are no per-task market reference rates because such services cannot be performed by hired labor. 'Leisure–pleasure activities' are equivalent to the Z_i that Becker has individuals 'buy for own consumption with earnings forgone' but that cannot be done for them by third persons.

If someone else watches a film or a sunset for you, the Z_i you get is not the same as the Z_j you would have got had you done it yourself. That we cannot pay third persons to sleep, jog, or cram for us is fairly clear. T. P. Hill, in a brilliant but flawed article (Hill, 1977), disputes the contention that eating, drinking, learning, and studying are productive in the economic sense at all, even were it possible to derive useful measures in the Beckerian spirit of the value of time spent on them or of the additions to earnings from the human capital created by them.

Hill suggests using the delegation criterion to delimit economic from non-economic. The intent seems to be to stem the tide of conversion to Becker's view of the economic domain as embracing the totality of human uses of time. While appreciative of Classical writings on the permanence of some services affecting persons, Hill maintains that inalienable physical and mental self-improvements are *qualitatively different* from shaving or cooking and 'cannot be treated as productive in an economic sense'. 'Otherwise', he argues, 'the rich of this world would possess not merely large mansions, but encyclopaedic knowledge and batteries of skills' (Hill, 1977, pp. 326, 317). Stressing the differences between human and other capital conceals the fact that rich ignoramuses may have large command over the services of savants and artisans, procuring Z_i if not Z_j.

The earliest estimates for the value of the housework component of non-market production in developed countries came to over 20 per cent of their GNP. The first attempts to estimate the value of housework were made in Denmark and Germany for the 1920s (Studenski, 1961). W. C. Mitchell made an estimate for 1919, and Kuznets in 1944 relented and made one for 1919. Kuznets's approach was to apply the actual wage rate of hired domestics to the number of families having two or more members. Rural families were weighted with lower rates. Kuznets regarded his estimates as merely suggestive and not in the same league as calculations based on market-sector statistics (Kuznets, 1944, II, pp. 431–3, cited in Hawrylyshyn, 1976, p. 104).

In 'Is Growth Obsolete?' (1973), William D. Nordhaus and James Tobin attempted to put statistical flesh on the most tractable objections to GNP as a welfare index. They present an alternative aggregate, labelled MEW (measure of economic welfare), for 1929–65. Getting from GNP to MEW required three categories of adjustment: redefinition of final product and final consumption; imputation of values for consumer durables, for leisure, and for the product of household work; and correction for 'some of the disamenities of urbanization' (Nordhaus and Tobin, 1973, p. 513).

Their category 'instrumental expenditures' closely resembles Kuznets's 'social framework' of regrettable necessities. Under that rubric the authors place commuting costs and a large fraction of government purchases – for police, sanitation, road maintenance, and defense, which, paraphrasing Kuznets, are described as 'among the necessary overhead costs of a complex industrial nation-state'. 'No direct satisfactions' are yielded by them, even though 'given the unfavorable circumstances which prompt these expenditures, consumers will ultimately be better off with them than without them' (Nordhaus and Tobin, 1973, pp. 515–16). They are inputs, not outputs.

In MEW, consumers' expenditures on durables are conceived as investments that yield annual flows of direct services. Government and private expenditures on education and health go in investment, but the yields are assumed to be intermediate rather than final. The fruits of spending on education and health are expected to be realized in 'labor productivity and earnings, [so Nordhaus and Tobin decline] to count them twice. [MEW thus] understates economic welfare and its growth to the extent that education and medical care are direct rather than indirect sources of satisfaction' (1973, pp. 514, 517).

The imputation for leisure dwarfs all the other pluses and minuses. For 1965, personal consumption in US GNP comes to $397.7 billion. Leisure Nordhaus and Tobin calculate at $626.9 b., and non-market activity at $295.4 b. Factoring out disamenities and personal instrumental expenses, MEW consumption amounts to $1,243.6 b. (over three times the official figure), of which more than half is leisure, and between a fifth and a quarter is non-market production. Per capita NNP in 1965 (1958 $) was $2,897; 1965 MEW per capita the authors work out at $6,391, 2.2 times the conventional level. Rates of growth of per capita MEW were positive over 1929–65 but 30 per cent below growth rates of per capita NNP (1.1 per cent per annum vs. 1.7 per cent) (Nordhaus and Tobin, 1973, p. 521).

It was objected that when the two measures diverge, per capita MEW is not always easily defended as an unambiguous improvement over per capita NNP. For the Depression years 1929–35, MEW per head is 'stable or slightly rising', a phenomenon that sheds doubt on the MEW interpretation of leisure time (Moss, 1973, p. 20).

Nordhaus–Tobin and a number of other researchers (Sirageldin, Weinrobe) measure household output using a 'naïve Becker–Lancaster notion', which is labelled WOCT by Hawrylyshyn (wage = opportunity cost of time). WOCT does not take due account of a ubiquitous phenomenon that is the obverse of Beckerian productive consumption in the market sphere. It is that direct pleasure and indirect result-yielding housework may be joint products (Pollak and Wachter, 1975). Estimating money values for housework by WOCT is therefore biased upward, since not all housework hours are as painful in dollars as the dollars one earns (Hawrylyshyn, 1977, p. 90).

A second way to evaluate 'economic household services' is by using the formula MAHC (market alternative = housekeeper cost). The idea is that the hired domestic 'has absolutely no reason to spend extra time' on a task since it gives him or her 'no direct utility'. The nanny does not bond to the child. MAHC can be fine-tuned in that different hourly rates can be introduced for different grades of domestic skill or arduousness: cooking, gardening, babysitting, spring cleaning, snow shovelling, tutoring.

A third variant, MAIFC (market alternative = individual function cost), weights each hour spent by the household member on economic household service i by the market wage for its delegable equivalent. But because of scale economies and transactions costs of Coase type, MAHC is said to be preferred (Hawrylyshyn, 1977, pp. 90–2).

A fourth possibility, theoretically the most elegant and closest in spirit to Juster (1973), is what Hawrylyshyn refers to as the full production approach. The value of gross household output is the value of bought inputs plus the value added by labor services and capital services respectively. Estimation with this approach requires knowing people's opportunity-cost wages and values of stocks and flows of household capital. Valuation of capital services is a more uncertain enterprise in the home than in the factory. 'Hiring housekeepers is likely, renting or leasing all one's durable goods is far less so' (Hawrylyshyn, 1977, p. 94).

Modified WOCT tries to net out the direct utility component, either by reducing hours allegedly spent scrubbing to some minimum or by docking the opportunity-cost wage by some reduction factor. The 'minimum necessary time' might be derived from actual estimated hours spent on 'economic household services' by observing the behavior of either extremely busy or extremely messy people. What minimum should one adopt as standard?

Elsewhere Hawrylyshyn compares thirteen adjusted estimates of housework's share in GNP for several countries and periods. The ratios of the estimated value of household services of all family members to conventional GNP range from 28 per cent (Sirageldin, 1964, MAIFC) to 39 per cent (Weinrobe, 1974; WOCT net of putative tax); Kuznets (MAHC, 1929) arrives at 35 per cent and Nordhaus and Tobin (after-tax WOCT, 1965) are close behind at 34 per cent. When WOCT is adjusted for putative income tax, its average share in GNP across the studies surveyed is the same, 35 per cent, as is average MAHC, lending credibility to the attempt to value the fraction of non-market work that is susceptible of delegation (Hawrylyshyn, 1976, pp. 108, 114).

The 1980s saw a series of ambitious reworkings of conventional GNP in the direction of including sources of present and future utility and of netting out regrettables, intermediates and bads. Probably the most ambitious scheme theoretically is that of F. Thomas Juster, Paul N. Courant and Greg K. Dow (1981). (More recent extensions of the official US national income and product statistics into non-market territory, for instance the work of John W. Kendrick, Robert Eisner, Dale W. Jorgensen *et al.*, and Xenophon Zolotas, came to my attention too late for inclusion in the present study. Eisner (1988b) provides a fascinating summary.) Juster *et al.*'s 'theoretical framework for the measurement of well-being' is founded on the admirably consistent axiom that flows of societal resources are 'limited by two basic factors: the amount of available human time, and the stock of wealth inherited from the past' (Juster *et al.*, 1981, p. 1). Juster's 1981 scheme 'adds Becker (or rather: Pollak and Wachter, 1975) to' the framework of another interesting scheme that Juster had advanced in 1973. The 'basic proposition' of Juster I was that 'income comes from wealth and from no other source'

(1973, p. 42). The 1973 scheme supplemented conventional GNP accounts with accounts for (i) tangible capital assets of households (consumer durables) and of governments, (ii) intangible capital of households and enterprises, (iii) pollution and its abatement, and (iv) household services as well as goods.

In the more grandiose 1981 scheme, the stocks from which all blessings flow need to be combined à la Becker with inputs of human time (divided between 'market work, household production, leisure and biological maintenance') to yield their true utility potential. 'Process benefits' of the 'producer utility' type are allowed for, so that one can prepare food that will later yield gastronomic utility *and* gain enjoyment from the process of cooking at the same time. Juster, Courant, and Dow's stocks come in six kinds:

(1) TK: Conventional stocks of tangible assets, such as machinery and housing.
(2) KK: Stocks of abstract knowledge about the history and properties of the world, not embodied in specific individuals.
(3) HK: Human capital associated with specific individuals, such as health, skills and knowledge.
(4) OK: Organizational capital reflecting networks of relationships among particular people populating society. Types of networks include families, associations of friends and neighbors, public associations such as towns and state and federal governments, and various voluntary organizations.
(5) SK: Social–political capital stocks reflecting the institutional arrangements for the performance of collective or societal activities, and the context of individual behavior provided by legal and habitual rules for social interaction.
(6) EK: Environmental stocks reflecting the physical and biological surroundings of human society. These include the weather and the availability of natural resources.

(Juster, Courant, and Dow, 1981, p. 9)

They observe that, if all intermediate products could be properly netted out, 'all the final products [would] be process benefits' (1981, p. 31). If one day Juster *et al.*'s output and capital account frameworks could be filled with numbers for the world's 150-odd countries, and the totals converted to some common denominator reflecting purchasing power parities, it might gladden the shade of Simon Kuznets, who so consistently and gently reminded us to measure results, not inputs.

As noted, the housework performed in Western countries amounted at participation rates of the 1970s to something like 35 per cent of GNP. One can speculate that the consumption component of GNP might have to be multiplied by a factor of at least four in Western countries to capture Beckerian Z_i. This might be so even if distributional weights from a Bergsonian–Arrovian social welfare function were applied in order to proxy for lower marginal utility of Z_i to the rich, who, while richer in X-goods than the poor, still have the same allotment of 24 hours a day in which to transform them into Z_i (Burenstam Linder, 1970). The amount by which GNP would have to be altered to allow for flows of Justerian well-being might be positive or negative, depending on how much people suffer from socio-political 'contexts' such as fear of nuclear war or AIDS, or from proximity to slum housing or coal-fired power generators or garbage in public parks.

The scope of the output boundary can be enlarged or narrowed at the statistician's or dictator's pleasure without real-world consequences, so long as producers are sovereign. The danger lies in attempting to interpret index changes in welfare terms, rather than in terms of military potential (for example). What a scheme designates as final may be far removed from, and not in one-to-one correspondence with, the welfare-related Beckerian Z-commodities that provide final utility. The consumption component of an indicator's final output measure may even fail to capture the totality of Beckerian X-goods if X-goods are to a large degree entitlements or goods produced for home use. If it can be demonstrated that society's aggregate economic indicators are in only remote correspondence with presumed flows of Beckerian Z_is, both growth rates over time and international comparisons of indicator performance lose a good deal of their very great intrinsic interest.

Public-choice theory suggests that policy efforts of state authorities will be distorted by selfish attempts to generate good-looking numbers. Governors and general secretaries would like to appear to be mere instruments of the people's will, and to be able to report success in fulfilling their desires, but they have their own agendas. Input–output error on the part of central authorities has implications for resource allocation when private-goods producers and consumers are not fully sovereign – as they *cannot be* in mixed and centrally planned economies. Success indicators may, for example, focus on elements *far up the production chain* from Beckerian Z_i.

Even benevolent economist-observers have on occasion fallen victim to index-number illusion. But their political masters can be assumed to espouse index-number illusion rationally and intentionally: their political fortunes may depend on it.

CHAPTER 9

Necessity without Materiality, Materiality without Fallacy

It is hard to forgo two last chances to test surplus and transfer theory's usefulness as a window into economics. In this chapter, the basic contrast between theories of surplus and transfer and theories of interdependence is applied to two subfields: development economics, in both its Lewis 'classical' and 'basic needs' variants (section 9.1), and Polanyi–Pearson economic anthropology (section 9.2). In Polanyi–Pearson, 'the economy has no surplus'.

9.1 Necessity without materiality: 'basic needs' in development economics

Materiality criteria were commonplace until the 1970s in development economics, a field that, scandalous to say, scarcely existed until World War II, the decline of the British Empire, and the emergence of the Union of Soviet Socialist Republics as a superpower. Although non-Comecon poor countries did not adopt Soviet-style national accounts, thereby avoiding institutionalization of materialist fallacy, poverty was nevertheless widely conceived as material poverty, and 'industrialization' was viewed as the principal means of escape.

During the heyday of GNP growthmanship in the 1950s, when 'overtaking and surpassing' was the objective of politicians and economists alike, it did not much matter whether one looked 'Left' or 'Right': 'more' seemed to mean more 'things' to all men. Paul Baran's views on the correspondence between material-goods output growth and 'economic development' were sketched in Chapter 7. Baran's intellectual formation, however, took place under historical conditions in which materialist fallacy was rife (Sweezy, 1965), so determinists may find him an excuse.

Baran was a fiery radical and, while influential as a link between 'old' and 'new' Lefts, was more of a gadfly than a model-builder. The same cannot be said for to-be Nobel laureate W. Arthur Lewis, whose avowedly Classical analysis of causes of and cures for low levels of GNP per head became, with Rostow's (1960), a model for the first generation of students of third world development. Lewis's celebrated article 'Economic Development with Unlimited Supplies of Labour' (1954) takes a Smithian look at the sources of capital accumulation and productivity increase. Lewis has in mind Adam Smith's growth analysis of *Wealth of Nations*, Book II, chapter iii, set in a social framework of political peace, *laissez faire* and security of property, and fuelled by 'unlimited' supplies of raw labor whose marginal productivity in its original, subsistence occupations is alleged to be zero or worse.

The Lewis model contains two sectors, the 'capitalist sector' and the 'subsistence sector'.

> The capitalist sector is that part of the economy which uses reproducible [tangible] capital, and pays capitalists for the use thereof. This coincides with Smith's definition of the productive workers, who are those who work with [physical] capital and whose [tangible] product can therefore be sold at a price above their wages.... The subsistence sector is by difference all that part of the economy which is not using reproducible capital. Output per head is lower in this sector, because it is not fructified by capital (this is why it was called 'unproductive'; the distinction between productive and unproductive [having] nothing to do with whether the work yielded utility, as some ... have scornfully but erroneously asserted). As more capital becomes available more workers can be drawn into the capitalist from the subsistence sector, and their output per head rises as they move from the one sector to another.
>
> (Lewis, 1954, pp. 407–8)

Lewis's reading of the *Wealth of Nations* is that Smithian unproductive labor is 'just' labor of low physical productivity, low output per man-hour. With this I cannot agree. While some of the phenomena Smith describes may be better rendered by Lewis's model than by Smith's, the mechanisms differ as dichotomies differ from continua. Smith's growth model is one of surplus generation by productives and its transfer to unproductives 'and those who do not labour at all'. The distinction has to be a *binary* one for the coordinating Hand of the market to equalize returns to capital and labor across some sectors but not others. Unproductive laborers are maintained by transfers; they do not earn 'returns' (ch. 3 above). It saves confusion if the view that 'unproductive labor' is 'labor of low productivity' is referred to as the Lewis version.

The Lewis model involves no transfer, but ordinary 'neoclassical' *quid pro quo* exchange of goods between the two sectors of a single economy. Returns to factors would be equalized between them were labor not stuck in the capital-poor subsistence sector. In fact, in the Fei–Ranis extension of Lewis, equalization of marginal labor productivities across sectors, once capital accumulation has sufficiently absorbed labor into the modern, capitalist one, is what marks the completion of the process of 'unification' of the dual economy (Fei and Ranis, 1961).

In Lewis, development is mainly if not exclusively (plantation agriculture) a process of *industrialization*. Industrialization reduces the share in output and labor force of low-productivity subsistence agriculture, domestic service, and petty trade. The 'capitalist sector' produces physical tangible exportable goods. There are a few other materialist resonances. *Faute de mieux* (savings out of profits as in the *Wealth of Nations*), Lewis suggests using 'inflation for the purposes of capital formation' because if there is a large enough 'industrial class', who will be 'pretty certain to reinvest its profits productively', the inflation will be 'self-liquidating'. 'Only the industrialist's passion drives towards using profits to create a bigger empire of bricks and steel' (Lewis, 1954, p. 429).

Who exactly counts as capitalist-sector capitalist is left somewhat open. The 'class of industrialists' is contrasted on the one hand with the 'middle class', the 'merchant class', the 'bankers', and the government class, and, on the other, with the peasantry. Redistribution in favor of merchants etc. does not generate output increases that counteract the inflationary push. Elsewhere, though, state capitalists are shown to be in theory just as good as private ones at investing a high fraction of their revenues. Some respect is indeed shown for Stalin as taxer and mobilizer of Lewis-version unproductive laborers and as builder of industry (Lewis, 1954, p. 422; Lewis, 1978, p. 42).

Lewis's subsistence concept is nowhere automatically limited to a particular basket of goods – food and clothing, for example, as distinct from food, bicycles, and weddings. Just which activities go in the subsistence sector is not an issue. The model is, however, built around the terms of trade between it and the (presumably different) outputs of the capitalist sector.

The necessity–luxury distinction is relevant to that part of growth economics that relies on hard sacrificial investment rather than the magic of technical change. It illuminates why Classical–Marxian growthmen – Smith, Lewis, and Stalin among them – have reservations about consumer sovereignty. In libertarian neoclassical utility theory, consumers' own free decisions about how to spend marginal increments in income determine whether or not a good rates as a 'luxury'. Luxuriousness is a revealed statistical result, not a sectoral prejudice of would-be economist-dictators.

Necessities in consumer theory are defined as goods and services that individuals placed in hypothetical choice situations say they would not cut back on proportionally if their incomes should fall and that they would abandon proportionally if their incomes should improve. That is, they are goods whose income elasticity of demand is less than unity (it may be negative). Evidently, goods that work out to be luxuries at low levels of income may show up as necessities at higher levels, with growth and across households.

The logic is that, if a good rates as a luxury, its production is least painfully scaled back and the resources liberated, most easily committed to capital accumulation. Smith finds unproductive laborers unproductive not because they are of low productivity (though they may also be that), but because they produce superfluous luxuries and therefore ought to be reassigned in order for the annual produce of goods that ought to count to increase.

From the perspective of modern welfare and consumer theory, it might be supposed that the lower incomes are, the lower the income elasticity of demand for goods actually bought, and the likelier tastes really are exogenous, truly independent of extraneous influences like advertising and the demonstration effect. The closer the goods are to being 'necessities' with very low income elasticities, the less legitimate for economist-dictators to override citizen-consumer preferences for these goods in favor of others they are assumed to 'need more'. However, development economics is based on the *dirigiste* proposition that consumers in traditional economies do not know what is good for them (Lal, 1983).

'Development' has growth as a necessary if not sufficient condition, but growth of what? A simple answer in the Smitho-Marxian tradition would be baskets of necessities per annum. The operation of ranking what people want must first be run through on the consumer side in order to ensure that growth in the number of baskets produced and distributed is welfare-related.

It is popularly thought that the poorer the country, the more appropriate are materiality criteria for measures, means, and ends (see Marcovitch, 1958; in Mandel, 1962, p. 340). Where millions die yearly of starvation, exposure, deficiency diseases, contaminated water, 'subsistence' may be thought to have a purely physical, biological resonance, one of an absolute and not a social minimum. People on the margin of physical survival may be thought to require in the first instance more physical, tangible, edible, wearable goods for consumption, accumulation, and export. Private and public services that perish in the instant of their performance may appear to be luxuries that such poor economies can ill afford.

Singling out some average basket of necessities for a polity composed of individuals with disparate tastes and unequal incomes presents overwhelming theoretical difficulties in the absence of a social welfare function. The problem of deciding on distributional weights is simplified by going over to a lexicographic ordering, such as might be made by a benevolent Rawlsian dictator who would put consumption of the poorest first. Rawls's theory of justice (Rawls, 1971) is not a crude but a sophisticated argument for egalitarian constitutions and policies. Since 'before birth' we do not know how generously the gods will smile upon us, rationally we should set rules so as to maximize the minimum, improve life chances first for the least fortunate. Divergences from egalitarian outcomes are permitted to the extent that 'differences' are necessary to elicit outcomes that raise the welfare of the worst off (Rawls, 1971, p. 329).

A Rawlsian dictator might interview the least favored group in the society in order to discover what goods and services are in its necessities basket. Growth of this group's per capita income of basket-equivalents (and their means of production) could then with justice merit the name 'development'.

The 'difference principle' means that anything required to up the flow of basket-equivalents to the poorest (training of hydraulic engineers abroad, instruction for barefoot doctors, establishment of central statistical administrations, agricultural research stations, more progressive tax collection, construction of water purification plants, secondary schools) can be justified, since it is intermediate to basket production. This renders the subtle Rawlsian qualification that 'inequalities [like paying engineers more baskets per capita than the target group] are just if and only if they are part of a larger system in which they work out to the advantage of the most unfortunate representative individual' (see Arrow, 1973).

With that in mind, I turn to a fruitful and distributionally non-regressive approach to development theory and policy, the notion of meeting 'basic needs'. 'Basic needs' was in vogue during the tenure of Robert S. MacNamara at the World Bank; it has since fallen out of favor as too much of a wager on the weak. The Reagan sea-change and the performance of the East Asian 'Gang of Four' shifted opinion toward stimulating supply of food and exportables by 'getting prices right' (Timmer, 1986).

Basic needs, however, gives the *coup de grâce* to the Smitho-Marxian materiality criterion as welfare instrument. Once its logic penetrates past the industry-worshipping blinkers of dictators, politicians, and advisors, there is no longer any excuse for identifying services with luxuries or growth of industry with economic development.

The basic needs strategy was elaborated at the World Employment Conference in 1976. It is expounded in a 1977 joint International Labor Office – Overseas Development Council report, *Employment, Growth and Basic Needs* and summarized by one of its architects, Paul Streeten, in an eloquent article (ILO, 1977;

Streeten, 1977). Basic needs are said to include the following:

> First, they include certain minimum requirements of a family for private consumption: adequate food, shelter and clothing are obviously included, as would be certain household equipment and furniture.
>
> Second, they included essential services provided by and for the community at large, such as safe drinking water, sanitation, public transport, and health and educational facilities.
>
> (ILO, 1977, p. 31)

The presentation is notably free of both modism and material bias. In describing the basket of goods and services deemed essential to improving the life chances of the least fortunate, access to education, water, sewage disposal, irrigation, agricultural extension, and other public and municipal services are placed *on an equal footing with access to the (services of) the usual private goods*. The targets are rather vague even so; each country is to retain its sovereign right to determine the needs that are basic to it.

The ILO report ends with a 'Note' outlining the criticisms of the basic needs strategy made by the capital-intensive industrializers, the anti-imperialists, the East Europeans, the Panglossian non-redistributors, and the export-promoters more interested in working out a new international trade and debt order. From that it may have seemed unlikely even at the time that more than a handful of countries would find it politic to treat satisfaction of basic needs as anything but incidental to more traditional industrial and export objectives. Nevertheless, the idea that some collective services are 'basic' managed to gain 'rhetorical momentum' (Paolillo in ILO, 1977, p. 185).

Declining recourse to Classical–Marxian dichotomies like 'material good' vs. 'immaterial service' and related appositions like Lewis's 'traditional subsistence sector' vs. 'modern capitalist for-profit sector' went hand in hand with recognition that the choice of private vs. public-sector provision was principally a question of *scale*. Mainstream development economists' heightened mode-neutrality shows up in World Bank publications at about the same time that Kravis, Heston, and Summers rewrite the SNA's definition of 'consumption' to include publicly-provided education and health (section 8.2 above). The *World Development Report* for 1979 describes health care, safe water, and sanitation services as 'essential' even though they invariably come from outside the 'subsistence sector' for reasons of efficient minimum scale. 'While malnutrition can be largely overcome if the incomes of individuals are raised, adequate access to essential public services cannot. Safe drinking water, sanitation, health and education are supplied by public agencies, and the complete absence or poor quality of these services afflicts the poor even in Middle Income countries' (World Bank, 1979, p. 35).

It was conceded that meeting basic needs by the year 2000 was an ambitious goal. Simulations by Joseph J. Stern suggested that for the poorest 20 per cent of the LDC population to reach certain minimum targets by the year 2000 (FAO caloric recommendations per person per day; UN standards of living space per person; and schooling for 98 per cent of the 7–16 age group) would require roughly a doubling of the rate of GNP growth and a sharp reduction in population growth rates. But with 'substantial' income redistribution, 'most developing countries [could] achieve basic-needs objectives by [GNP] growth at an annual rate of approximately 7 to 8 per cent, . . . higher than those currently experienced in the majority of countries, but not markedly higher' (Stern, 1975, discussed in ILO, 1977, pp. 39–42).

Changing fashions in development economics led naturally to new measures of development (Baster, 1972). One tack was taken by Ahluwalia and Chenery in *Redistribution with Growth* (Chenery *et al.*, 1974). They re-weighted GNP using data and value judgments about income distribution to highlight the degree to which the poorest groups were sharing in measured GNP growth (Chenery *et al.*, 1974, ch. 1). It is stressed that the undoctored GNP growth rate *already is* a weighted sum of growth rates of each fractile (decile, quintile), with the weights being the fractile's share in GNP (Todaro, 1985, p. 163). GNP weighted not by actual shares but by population or priority weights generates measures that may better translate a researcher's or society's value judgments as to the relation between growth of GNP and 'development'.

For example, should increases in GNP be entirely captured by the society's richest quintile and should it be decided to weight improvements going exclusively to them with zero weights, the welfare-related success indicator would show zero improvement no matter how impressive the increases enjoyed by the best off. Similarly (to give a numerical example), if the bottom two quintiles of the income distribution should see their per capita income rise 0.5 and 1 per cent respectively, while 'poverty weights' of 0.6 and 0.4 are applied that give all priority to changes in their situation and zero importance to improvements accruing to richer groups, the 'poverty-weighted' growth rate would be $(.005)(.6) + (.01)(.4)$ or seven-tenths of 1 per cent, which might be a very pale reflection of the rate change of GNP per capita.

9.1.1 The 'physical quality of life' index

Basic-needs-inspired emphasis on reaching target minima rather than raising growth rates of national averages brought forth a daring pretender to the throne of GNP, the so-called 'physical quality of life index' (PQLI) (Morris, 1979). The stated aim of the PQLI is to capture the most basic *sine qua non*s of human civilization.

What Morris D. Morris chooses as basic and describes as 'physical' in the PQLI may come as a surprise. The index's components are hardly 'physical', whether by the standards of English usage or Classical-Marxian materiality criteria. The PQLI is an index formed of equal weightings of three statistics: (1) an index of life expectancy at age 1, (2) an index of infant mortality per 1,000 live births, and (3) the percentage of illiterates in the adult population aged 15 and over. These features of the LDC socioeconomic profile are chosen by Morris on the one hand because they illustrate performance at some very minimal level, and on the other because data on them tend to be widely available and to cover relatively accurately even the least well-off groups in the poorest societies.

> The Physical Quality of Life Index is a limited measure. It makes no attempt to incorporate the many other social and psychological characteristics suggested by the term 'quality of life' . . . Thus it is labelled a physical quality of life index, even though there is some question about calling literacy (and what it represents) a physical feature of existence. . . [But] the literacy indicator provides information about the potential for development and the extent to which poor groups can share the possibilities and advantages of development activity. . . [Among] the poorest of the poor in developing countries, the achievement of even basic literacy is itself a step that increases the potential for participation. . . [Unlike e.g. elite or secondary school enrollment] a basic literacy indicator not only records gains going to the very poor but is able to mark literacy gains made by informal mechanisms as well as those resulting from formal schooling.
> (Morris, 1979, pp. 35, 37–38)

Unlike GNP, the PQLI has the great merit of measuring results, not inputs or potential inputs, with something like a Beckerian understanding of what seems to count for welfare (section 8.4.2 above). A child who makes it to his or her first birthday is arguably more of a 'result' than are retail sales of infant formula or wages of government midwives or water specialists.

PQLIs are presented for 150 rich and poor countries *circa* 1973, for 74 countries by sex for 1947–73, and for the US and 50 individual states by sex and by race for 1900–74. The relativities are fascinating and quite different from league tables made with per capita GNP or using PPPs. The PQLI is not very sensitive to differences at the top, between first and second worlds, clustered with PQLIs of 90 and over out of a possible 100. Canada and Poland are practically indistinguishable. But money isn't everything in the third world. Sri Lanka, with a per capita GNP of only 179 1974–6 US $ at official exchange rates, earned a PQLI of 82, miles ahead of much richer countries (Kuwait, Chile, Portugal), and not just on account of her supposed 81 per cent literacy rate but because of even better performance on infant mortality and life expectancy at age 1 (Morris, 1979, Appendix A).

Morris as sovereign researcher is free to select literacy and the two indicators of child health for his index, and to weight them equally. Infant mortality is a good proxy apparently for water quality and sanitary conditions in urban and rural areas, and of the health and status of women, is harder to reduce, and therefore sets the globe's poorest countries off from those somewhat less miserable. Life expectancy at age 1 is said to reflect the nutritional, medical, housing, and general environment of the rest of the population, child and adult (Liser, 1979, p. 132). In such exercises it is the researcher who as play-dictator writes the recipe against which, say, Iran's or Kuwait's performance is to be judged. The PQLI's components are chosen presumably not because they yield levels and rankings close to those of GNP league tables, as Beckerman and Bacon intended their composite index to do (Beckerman and Bacon, 1966), but because they capture what Morris thinks people want when they have least. Still, it measures both what the economist-dictator finds to be in high correlation with growth in countries that already have outgrown direst poverty and ignorance, and what he thinks poor people think growth should bring, what will reward them for their efforts. The distinction is not trivial. Development experts from Rostow and Lewis onwards have counseled poor countries, telling them they can alter the physical quality of their lives by reassigning surplus currently consumed by unproductive wastrels. But what if the economy *has* no surplus?

9.2 Materiality without fallacy: Polanyi–Pearson economic anthropology

> Two pyramids, two masses for the dead, are twice as good as one.
> (J. M. Keynes, 1936, p. 131)

In provocative works of economic history and anthropology published between 1944 and 1968, the Hungarian economic historian and polymath Karl Polanyi challenged the neoclassical marketocentric view of rational economic man in a way that surplus and transfer theory can readily illuminate. Polanyi's thesis is that the ambitious textbook haggler-after-profits of Adam Smith's imagination *did not exist* before the 'Great Transformation' of the late eighteenth and early nineteenth centuries (Polanyi, 1942, pp. 43 ff.). In Western Europe for the first time in world history the 'economy' became 'disembedded' from a network of traditional reciprocal and redistributive social relations and came to form an independent institution in which division of labor is mediated by money exchange of inputs and outputs on 'free', 'price-making' markets.

For economies and societies of other times and places, Polanyi suggests, 'material production' may *not be analytically separable from* activities that appear to Smitho-Marxian materialists or even pre-public-choice neoclassical economists as falling 'outside the economic domain'. Though there may be institutions called markets (the agora), they may not 'make prices'. They may serve as social cement rather than as the institution through which prices of goods, land, and labor move up and down until they come into some sort of equilibrium balance (Polanyi, 1957b).

> The human economy... is embedded and enmeshed in institutions, economic and non-economic. The inclusion of the non-economic is vital. For religion or government may be as important for the structure and functioning of the economy as monetary institutions or the availability of tools and machines themselves that lighten the toil of labor.
>
> (Polanyi, 1957a, p. 148)

The implication is that if the ceremonial and integrative social activities cannot be disentangled from activities oriented towards 'supplying [people] with the means of material want-satisfaction' (Polanyi, 1957a, p. 139), then, in the phrase of Polanyi's disciple and co-author Harry Pearson, 'the economy has no surplus' (Pearson, 1957). Faithful to deeply-rooted traditional practices, societies may not regard 'non-economic' activities as dispensable, as luxury drains on the production of things. Immaterial ceremonial activities, for instance, may be regarded by people as the most important things that they do, integral to their cultural existence and *raison d'être*. Researchers interested in calories per head must then recategorize such activities as *intermediate* to efforts aimed at assuring material subsistence. While, for example, ceremonial activities may be interpreted by Marx- or Lewis-minded Western observers as potential sources of accumulation, as unproductive labor free for the tapping, such presumptions may lead to serious errors when taken as bases for policy, for the planning of 'economic development'.

If the ministrations of a shaman are 'socially necessary' for the yam crop to be large, and if the shaman is sent by a Baran- or Lewis-trained economist-dictator to redeem his economic parasitism in the salt mines, *ceteris paribus* no yams will be planted. The spells of the shaman are *intermediate to* final material production. At the limit of our imaginary traditional case (of Malinowskian inspiration), yam production may require garden labor, seed, and the shaman's blessings in something like fixed proportions, as in Leontief production functions. Remove the shaman, and output falls to zero!

While the Polanyists conceive of the 'economy' as the locus of activities wherein material output is produced, and while they identify 'production' with 'material production' on almost every page (e.g. Polanyi, Arensberg, and Pearson, 1968, pp. 120–7), theirs is a rare materiality without materialist fallacy. Polanyi, Pearson, and their disciples simply avail themselves of scholars' sovereign freedom to define the final output basket as they find convenient.

In an argument inspired by concerns of Rousseau and Marx, Polanyi maintains it is unhistorical and misleading to conflate two different meanings of the term 'economic'. 'Economic', in what is said to be its primary, 'substantive', supra-modally universal sense, refers to man's 'interchange with his natural and social environment, insofar as this results in supplying him with the means of material want-satisfaction', his subsistence (Polanyi, 1957a, p. 139). All societies derive their subsistence from nature, but nature is not always seen to be niggardly. It depends on what you expect.

The 'substantive' meaning of economic is contrasted with what Polanyi calls the 'formal', logical, choice-theoretic meaning, which has echoes of 'economizing', 'economical', 'rational' choice-making. The 'formal' meaning of economic is said to have relevance not generally but specifically, for market economies after the Great Transformation to capitalism, seen à la Marx as a powerful but world-historical anomaly. The 'formal' meaning covers situations in which acts of exchange are induced by 'insufficiency of means', a situation by no means universal (see Sahlins, 1972).

Polanyi's noble savages are therefore not societies of economizing Crusoes. Nor is his ancient Greece or socialist Russia. 'Outside of a system of price-making markets economic analysis loses most of its relevance as a method of inquiry into the working of the economy. A centrally planned economy, relying on non-market prices, is a well-known instance' (Polanyi, 1957a, p. 145). While the naïve view of the socialist problem brands and dates him, Polanyi may be on more solid analytical ground with 'primitive and archaic'.

Polanyi strenuously contests the neoclassical view of human behavior as economic in all situations, as tautologically rational regardless of institution or mode. He is particularly concerned to wound the witty dragon that is Lionel Robbins. In *An Essay on the Nature and Significance of Economic Science* (1932) Robbins had poured elegant ridicule on the Physiocratic materialist remnants in Smith and other Classics. Scouting out non-market territory later settled by the public-choice and time-utilitarian schools, Robbins in that work staked the modern claim that economists can talk equally coherently about businessmen, peasants, bureaucrats, Trobrianders, and housewives, since all must relate means to ends in conditions of scarcity, and 'Economics is not concerned at all with ends *as such*' (Robbins, 1932, p. 30). Robbins claimed all of those agents for our discipline with the immortal definition of 'economics' as 'the science which studies human behaviour as a relationship between ends and scarce means which have alternative uses' (Robbins, 1932, p. 16).

In his quest for a more nuanced framework able to distinguish the modern world as a transformation of the ancient and primitive, Polanyi argues for decomposition of the Robbinsian scarcity postulate.

> [For] insufficiency [of means, i.e. scarcity] to induce choice there must be given more than one use to the means, as well as graded ends ... ordered in sequence of preference. Both conditions are factual.
> (Polanyi, 1957a, p. 143)

'Facts' in Polanyi are whatever people happen to believe. People may think that means have only one proper use, and interdict their application elsewhere. Castes, medieval guilds, and British trade unions restrict the use of labor. Interdictions and beliefs are 'facts' in the sense that production functions for ends must take them as 'socially necessary', as part of the social technology. The Leibensteinian concept of X-inefficiency (Leibenstein, 1966) is founded on the notion of single world best-practice technology, not a series of them individualized to allow (for instance) for socially necessary tea breaks or interdictions against men and women working together in the same building. '[It] is rational for the suicide to select means that will accomplish his death; and if he be an adept of black magic, to pay a witch doctor to contrive that end' (Polanyi, 1957a, p. 143). Robbins would, of course, not disagree with that, since his argument is that ends are not at issue.

Where Polanyi and Robbins part company is in the relationship between rarity and choice. The scarce means must have alternative uses if a price-making market system is to be the relevant paradigm. Robbins writes as though scarcity of means induces people to play freely around with input combinations until they arrive at the one that gives the best and cheapest, most efficient link between means and results. Polanyi thinks this seriously unrealistic as a portrait of production decision-making in 'primitive' and 'archaic' situations.

In terms of my 'Melanesian' example, if 'in fact' a society happens to believe that witchcraft, seed, and garden labor need to be applied in fixed proportions, it would not be 'rational' for them to allocate the resources in any other way, and 'in fact' they may refuse to do so. Development planners can suggest any number of consistent plans for increasing the output of yams, huts, and canoes; but 'in fact' substitutions, alternative uses of time and resources, may not be allowed. Where there are no alternatives, there can be no calculus (see Morgenstern, 1972). Where there is no calculus, it makes no sense to speak of higher or lower marginal productivity of Lewisian unproductive labor. Until beliefs change, reassigning the shaman or the gardeners will not necessarily cause average product of subsistence-sector yams to rise, but possibly to fall.

In my 200-proof distillate of the Polanyi–Pearson primitive economy, the chief sorcerer is provider of the Ur-primary input prerequisite for the production of all substantial and ephemeral intermediate goods required for the ultimate production of 'material means of want satisfaction'. This economy has no surplus; there is no slack to be taken up, no unproductive labor free for the tapping. Tradition is the economy's production function and five-year plan. In the manner of Kuznets's government, the sorcerer provides not the final luxury of prayer but the economy's intermediate social and engineering framework. Even the most Stalinist economist-dictator might appreciate the madness of abolishing the one occupation that, 'in actual, Polanyist fact', makes all production possible.

CHAPTER 10

Results, Not Inputs

10.1 On Sombart's torment turnpike

Hell hath no more fitting punishment for the sins of the political economist, suggested Werner Sombart in 1897 in a Pooh-Bah mood, than to spend eternity studying the chapters on productive and unproductive labor out of some nineteenth-century textbook. The punishment comes from unproductive-labor doctrine's tantalizing combination of analytical imprecision and insufferable smugness. Confusion over unproductive labor is, however, altogether understandable: unproductive laborers are exceptions to all the rules. The issues that they force us to confront – necessity, materiality, finality, publicness – defy easy resolution. The smugness too is in some degree an occupational hazard. Drawing a boundary around some 'economy', some line between it and what is exogenous to it, was in the eighteenth century and still is the economist's fundamental declaration of faith in his or her subject. Writers confident that they know which laborers are productive and which are not are drawn to offer policy advice. If annual produce is so designed as to constitute a reasonable index of welfare, it may make sense to shift the production structure away from parasites and towards producers.

Thinking to gain salvation by a short ride on Sombart's torment turnpike, I did look at those chapters on productive and unproductive labor in mercantilist, Classical, and modern economics. My pre-emptive, otherworldly motivation was abetted, though, by Popperian curiosity. Classical–Marxian unproductive laborers – unpromising raw material – rewarded it by revealing what looks to be a new core paradigm for economic science: the model of surplus-generation and its transfer.

Tired, perhaps, from a similar mental journey, Joseph Schumpeter haughtily dismissed the 'famous controversy' over productive and unproductive labor, saying that the 'only reason why this dusty museum piece interests us at all is that it affords an excellent example of the manner in which the discussion of meaningful ideas may lose sight of their meanings and slip off into futility' (1954, p. 628). But that is the fascination. The controversy was never fully resolved; the meanings are those of the nature and significance of economic science itself.

10.2 Review of the parts

Theories of Surplus and Transfer aims to be the most comprehensive analysis in economic literature since Schumpeter of the historical debates over the nature of the economy and of the limits of economic behavior. Economists' understanding of the relations between inputs, outputs, and welfare, Petty to the present, West, East, and South, are studied using a conceptual framework that incorporates recent developments in public and comparative economics. That framework, based on the useful distinction between theories of surplus and transfer and theories of interdependence, is designed to treat the widespread but problematic notion that not all incomes involve *quid pro quo*.

Part One of *Theories of Surplus and Transfer* examined the origins of surplus and transfer theory in the unproductive-labor doctrines of the Physiocrats, Smith, and Marx, and speculated on the theory's ability to survive into the second half of the nineteenth century despite strong criticism. Part Two followed the Marxian productive-labor theory of value into action in a new mode, Soviet socialism. Part Three surveyed contemporary reinterpretations of the Classical–Marxian issues: the sources and measures of economic growth and its relation to human welfare. It studied modern attempts to separate sense from nonsense on the question of which laborers or citizens are producers and of what.

The 'archaic' Classical–Marxian productive/unproductive shorthand is found to stand in for a much richer complex of distinctions: necessity vs. luxury, final output vs. intermediate input, externality-rich vs. externality-poor, private good. The modern bifurcated sets overlap quite imperfectly. They correspond but badly to dichotomies employed in pre-public-choice Classical and neoclassical writings: material good vs. immaterial service, enterprise sector vs. state sector, multi-person capitalist vs. single-person petty or pre-capitalist firm. Unravelling the complex and changing relations between those dichotomies has been a major challenge for even the great economists.

Observers' original explanation of incomes received by citizens engaged in government, private-service, and household spheres was that they lived on transfers of surpluses produced in 'the economy'. Service producers looked to be transfer recipients because they did not on first inspection fit into economics' early 'factory paradigm'. The factory of Classical and Marxian microeconomics is a multi-person firm whose owners hire unskilled labor and physical capital to produce reproducible, externality-poor, private, material goods under favorable returns to scale; market sale of these goods returns the going rate of profit.

Surplus and transfer theories were found to highlight long-standing continuities of subject matter in economics at the sectoral level.

Public, private, and household service producers who threatened to spoil the analytical schemes of seventeenth- and eighteenth-century writers remain problem categories for academic specialists in the late twentieth century. That is in spite of the fact that contemporary economists see many more similarities than did their predecessors between market and non-market modes of choice. 'Mode' of supply has been largely discredited as a reliable indicator of the 'publicness' of the goods or services that result.

As for earlier centuries, for the contemporary period it was found useful to divide transcriptions of the productive/unproductive shorthand into surplus generation and transfer theories, on the one hand, and theories of interdependence and equivalent exchange, on the other. The more elaborate 'new Right' version of Classical–Marxian surplus and transfer theory starts with anti-mercantilist, pre-Keynesian, minimalist views of the private sector's alleged superior ability to 'supply'. Into that complex of traditional ideas are being incorporated public-goods- and imperfect-competition-augmented explanations of the public sector's alleged unique ability to insulate itself from demand discipline. Self-styled 'neoclassical political economy' revives the value-laden productive/unproductive vocabulary of Classical surplus-generation and transfer models as a distinction, theoretically promising but very hard to draw in practice, between 'rent-seeking' and 'profit-seeking'. Like the 'sophisticated' Adam Smith of the *Wealth of Nations*, Book V, the new neoclassical explanation of why mode should matter maintains behavioral unity across mode boundaries to a degree not found in brute *laissez-faire* Classicism, in Marx, or, in the 'opposite' direction, among early followers of Keynes.

In preceding chapters, growth and welfare theories of a number of well- and not-so-well-known economists have been passed through Kuznets's filters of scope, valuation, and netness. The concepts that result from that exercise clarify a wide spectrum of opinion about how most fruitfully to define the scope of production, on the one hand, while accounting for the existence of resource-using activities that fall outside the conventional production boundary, on the other. Surplus and transfer theory illuminates the logic behind both narrow and wide definitions of the productive domain.

Kuznets's second problem, valuation (absolute and relative price-formation), has played a subordinate rôle in this history except in so far as writers have insisted that certain kinds of boundaries, for instance the boundaries of the price-making capitalist market, are what set the limit of output production itself.

Kuznets's third element, netness, provides whatever link there can be between 'output' and 'welfare' in a world of free-riders. In Smith as in neoclassical consumer theory, the 'sole end and purpose' of economic action is consumption, not production. According to all but idiosyncratic social welfare functions (sections 10.4 and 10.5 below), it is not costs, not production of intermediate materials or machines, but final, 'net' outputs that matter, for the reason that they alone by hypothesis raise the total utility enjoyed by citizens who count.

The value-laden distinction between necessities and luxuries, which underlay a good part of the Classical and Marxian dismay at the 'excessive' share of resources consumed by 'unproductive laborers', is still in use. This is despite widespread acceptance of the recommendation that positive and normative economics be kept separate. There has been, of course, since Marshall a technical meaning to the terms 'necessity' and 'luxury'. It corresponds to goods' below- and above-unitary income elasticity of demand under consumers' sovereignty. How to tell necessities from luxuries under other kinds of sovereignty was an important question for the first generation of post-World War II writers on economic development and the environment.

Such distinctions inform the not-unrelated contemporary effort, described in Chapter 8, to devise summary output indicators that can be defended as more 'welfare-related' than for instance GNP. The idea is that indicators be chosen for their ability to serve as proxies for socioeconomic happiness of citizens, since, once they are enshrined as official measures, they tend to take on lives of their own. Policies are designed to enhance them. We know from the work on methodology that, whenever boundary-drawers restrict the object of their study by strokes of the pen or truncate data banks by strokes of the key, value judgments are involved.

Economist-observers from Quesnay to Bacon and Eltis, and even so-called neoclassical political economists like Krueger and Bhagwati, retain a division between producers and non-producers amongst citizens who have entitlement to consume. The problem is of course that in some systems income may be transferred without *quid pro quo*, in addition to being earned. The criterion for exclusion from the class of true earners has been failure to pass a test of contributing either (i) necessary intermediate inputs to, or (ii) net outputs included in, the chosen aggregate output index.

10.3 Finality, sovereignty, and the efficacy of policy

Aggregate output indices are built up, using valuations, from per-period vectors of goods and services produced within the boundary of 'the economy'. Where the economy is and where the boundary is drawn are ultimately a matter of research-suppliers' sovereignty; consumers of economic literature may buy or not buy the conventions proposed; boundaries too must pass market tests! Materiality, necessity, publicness, marketability of goods are interesting to the extent that they figure among researchers' criteria for inclusion in summary indices of 'annual produce'. If an index is indeed perfectly welfare-related, in that it registers only truly final goods (such as leisure time) and leaves out intermediates and bads, the maximal index growth rate attainable given technology is also the optimal growth rate.

Scope, valuation, and netness belong to the problem 'what is output?' To choose the economic boundary and name the vector of truly final, welfare-related goods and services, both ancient and modern observers have divided labor and resource uses into (i) those that produce the final goods and services favored by the welfare-related maximand, (ii) those productive of superfluous luxuries, which, while desired by those lucky enough to afford them, are weighted by economist-observers in ways implying that social welfare is lower than it need be on account of too large a share being devoted to them, and (iii) those productive of items *necessary but intermediate* to final production of (i) and (ii).

If producers are truly sovereign, whether they are trying to please sovereign consumers, Langean planners, or Arrovian dictators, intermediate requirements for production will be ordered as technology and tradition demand. Inputs will, so to speak, take care of themselves. Economist-observers have no need to pronounce on their productiveness, and risk input–output error if they do.

Out of curiosity, observers may be anxious to acquire many types of technical and factual knowledge about input–output relationships within the boundary of the economy they study. Promoting growth of welfare-related output by state policy (if it works at all) requires similar, even asymmetrically superior, knowledge on the part of government. In addition to socio-technical information summarized in production functions for private goods, there must also be knowledge of the numerical value and product composition of the Marx–Senior 'most efficacious proportion' of state to private goods.

Surplus and transfer theories, because they are not afraid to make value judgments, yield a rich harvest of policy recommendations. Society, so the the story goes, would enjoy more baskets of welfare-related output and therefore more welfare, if only surplus presently accruing to economic parasites could be returned to true production. If only unproductive laborers could be reassigned to productive tasks, the index number that summarizes the total final net product of the economy would grow faster, and that would be a 'good thing'. In Classical–Marxian theories of surplus-generation and transfer, conversion of unproductives primarily means individuals changing their job description or occupation in order that the overall structure of industrial branches might shift in the right direction.

Applying surplus and transfer theory, making the non-productive productive, invariably requires more than patience and faith in the accuracy and motivating power of price signals. These may be feeble! Why wait for market forces to make profitable a W. A. Lewis-type increase in the capital/labor ratio for unproductive laborers in their old jobs in their old industries (section 9.1)? Short-cuts are available that are superior to do-nothing *laissez faire*.

The surplus and transfer paradigm, for all its Smithian roots, harbors a nagging mistrust of consumers' sovereignty even under free competition (section 3.3.3). Allowing consumers to spend and save exactly as they please may not ensure sufficiently rapid conversion from unproductive to high-productivity jobs and branches. Unproductive-labor theorists tend to live far from the Panglossian *laissez-faire* world where, with tastes, technology, and endowments given, *consumers themselves* may be permitted, by percolation through the system of their sovereign choices, to determine the final composition of demand and employment – not to speak of its rate of change in response to decisions to save and invest.

While disgust with *de facto* economic outcomes may not surprise us in the case of the arch-rebel anti-Panglossian Karl Marx, unhappiness with 'what is' amongst pro-market surplus and transfer conservatives like Eltis, Stockman, and Feldstein (section 7.2) at first inspection looks harder to understand. Mercantilistic imperfections of competition in the over-regulated economy's private sector, and, analogously, the public sector's deafness to 'voice', color their perception that 'all is not for the best' even under something approaching consumer and voter sovereignty.

10.4 Styles of dictatorship

Dissatisfaction with the *status quo*, as we saw, can move surplus and transfer theorists to action. Society, they believe, would be both richer and happier if it reallocated labor and resources so as to produce more of those goods and services that ought to count. Surplus and transfer theorists thus often sound like would-be Arrovian dictators (Arrow, 1963, pp. 28–31).

Whenever a line is drawn between labor or output that is productive and labor or activity that is not, and if product according to the observer's system is defined with pretensions to welfare-relatedness, the observer expresses a preference in favor of industries or branches that, under full consumers' and voters' sovereignty, he hopes would be chosen voluntarily by society as a whole. Wherever, for reasons of asset inequality or of impediments to free market exchange or to political expression, the observer feels that citizens' welfare is lower than socio-technically it needs to be, perhaps something can be done about it. The observer may pronounce as to the policies, productive sectors, and occupations he would favor, and the unproductive ones he would discriminate against, were he not just a powerless economist on the sidelines but an economic pharaoh or tsar. An economic dictator might hope to control, if not technology and the stock of productive assets inherited from niggardly nature and past history, then at least the size and disposition of the economy's investable surplus. Rivers of blood have flowed in our century in the name of welfare-related reallocations for growth.

Before attempting to convert parasites into producers or to maximize growth by accumulation, the efficient observer or dictator is well advised to study the *status quo ante* for clues as to the nature and sources of the economy's accumulable surplus. Maximizing growth by accumulation requires data on the input–output relationships like the overall 'most efficacious proportion' and the ingredients of the 'social framework'. It must be decided, by observation of actual 'factual' behavior of inhabitants, to what extent the economy of the society is 'disembedded' in the Polanyi sense from the web of social and psychic phenomena that influence and perhaps determine how people may react to the proposed conversion of unproductives. In a von Neumann dictatorship (section 10.5 below), knowledge is required about the minimum wage that will permit survival and reproduction of the labor force, and about elasticities of resource supply at other wage and interest rates.

In general, for the comparison of policy alternatives and for justifying the reassignment of unproductives as a 'good thing', there are as many boundaries as there are sovereign boundary-drawers. There can be no 'correct' boundary. Out there, in life, in each interval of time, a finite vector of heterogeneous activities – some pleasurable, some less so, some torturous – are engaged in by members of society. The length of the subvector of activities to be labelled 'economic' is limited by the research-supplier's or dictator's imagination and good or bad judgment. One subvector might be weighted with a set of arbitrary prices in order to yield an index named 'net material product'; another, weighted by market *cum* imputed prices, could be labeled 'gross national product'; another, 'marketed consumer goods plus non-marketed government goods and services thought to provide final utility to consumers' (Beckerian X-goods); a fourth, with some other name, might aim to capture only the harvest of yams.

If by some miracle the exact moment of transition from production to consumption, from the adding to the subtracting of value, could be pinpointed, and output data were available not as the arguments of individuals' utility functions but as the actual 'util' values subjectively accorded in those functions by all the individuals who count in society, then we would be in possession of the individual totals to be weighted by the Bergsonian–Arrovian social welfare function. If that seems too high-flown, the researcher might settle for estimation of the per-period crop of Beckerian Z-goods. Truly final annual produce would then be the goods and services 'produced' not by 'firms' but by 'households'. Their inputs would be store-bought and publicly allocated X-inputs, made fit for enjoyment by after-work 'free time' of varying opportunity cost.

To calculate a summary index from the vector of products chosen as being in the economy, 'weights' are needed. Here is the 'valuation' of 'scope, valuation, and netness'. Shadow prices or opportunity costs are the candidates with the good choice-theoretical pedigrees. They obviate artificial mode restrictions of the production boundary – for example, restriction to products exchanged on price-making markets. As we have seen, observers or policy-makers who lack the faith of Voltaire's Dr Pangloss that 'all is for the best in the best of all possible worlds', who disbelieve that relative prices observed in this vale of tears represent the valuations of the Great Matrix Algebraist in the Sky, have often opted for weights of zero and unity. Black and white, unproductive and productive, seemed like good first approximations. The vocabulary was both medieval and microcircuitous.

It is a sad fact that economic logic and ability to estimate empirical relationships are not on the same level. No national income accountant – not Juster, not Nordhaus and Tobin – expects to derive accurate weights for aggregate national, or world, production of Beckerian Z-goods. Measurability has been continually invoked in the history of economics as an excuse for not making the chosen output index relate very closely to welfare at all. The question 'promote the growth of what?' gets the fudge answer, whatever we can measure with reasonable accuracy. What is deemed reasonable has changed from the seventeenth century to the twentieth, from country to country, from writer to writer.

Since he must, the observer or policy-maker traces a boundary for his economy and relates its output to the (possibly different) output of goods that he thinks are the goods that count for the welfare of the citizens who count. Historically, commentators like Pigou and Studenski note a trend towards ever more generous drawings of the production boundary, though, as we saw in Chapter 2, that widening depends on where the story is said to begin. Early eighteenth-century writers were somewhat more tolerant of non-market modes and immaterial products than were their Physiocratic and Classical successors. Weighted geographically, the twentieth century displays confusing movements in several directions. Pol Pot depopulates real cities in an orgy of Marxoid Physiocracy (Shawcross, 1979, pp. 239 ff.). Safe in the realm of literature, Gary S. Becker expands the domain of rare and economic production to encompass Marx's whole superstructure, Polanyi's whole society, the neoclassicals' whole household. In the same direction, the sociobiologists outdo even the time-utilitarians.

Indeed, as Juster reminds us (Juster *et al.*, 1981; section 8.4.3 above), were economists to draw boundaries far enough down the production chain so as to separate final, net results from intermediate inputs with real success, economic success indicators would take on a quite different countenance. A polity's success in adding final value might be measured not in dollars of GNP but in flows of what used to be thought of as 'non-economic' medical, psychological, social, and cultural well-being: longevity, self-rated happiness including job satisfaction, low incidences of disease, illiteracy, crime, pollution, gridlock, war.

In a dictatorship (which from a public-choice perspective is one of the simpler types of society), a dictator whose preference it is to return parasites to true production may choose product and welfare weights in such a way as to maximize the difference between the index numbers in the original and post-conversion situations (i.e. the measured growth rate). Or he can concentrate on raising the absolute level of a subset of its components in some period two (as in a maximin basic-needs strategy). Primitive, archaic, or modern dictators can, of course, choose to do neither.

Such exercises, in which history and economics abound, have applied zero weights to the outputs of: priests and sorcerers, men of letters of all kinds, generals and soldiers, criminals and madmen, merchants and ad men, opera-singers and opera-dancers, entrepreneurs and rentiers, prodigals, bureaucrats, bus- and tram-conductors, and, not least, the dictators themselves. The zero accounting weights are relatively painless, occurring as they do in the privacy of ivory towers and Central Statistical Administrations. A stroke of the pen, and people who enjoy incomes and suffer producer disutility are converted into transfer recipients. Luckily that does not by the same token mean that the transfers will be zero.

Welfare weighting can have more worrisome consequences. A Rawlsian economist-dictator would give zero welfare weights to all but the least fortunate representative individual. Earthlings have not yet lived in a Rawlsian society. They do, however, have experience of real historical dictators giving zero or negative welfare weights to the entitlements of middle peasants and kulaks, capitalist roaders, Jews and gypsies, city-dwellers.

Somewhat benevolent or insecure economist-dictators may think to derive their legitimacy and their place in history from such growth in aggregate want-satisfaction as occurs during their sway. If a dictator is able to assume that the populace that counts is made up of identical representative individuals whose wants are to be progressively satiated, total utility will grow fastest now if the first wants to be attended to in his regime are the most pressing wants. That is why Benthamites make good egalitarians. Which X- or Z-goods satisfy the most pressing wants? By definition, 'necessities' do.

10.5 Von Neumann systems

> In the von Neumann system, consumption has disappeared; products have no purpose except to serve as inputs into future production; for maximum growth, growth must be growth, just for its own sake!
> (Hicks, 1965, p. 212)

What is at stake in growth-maximizing dictatorship shines through more clearly if we relate it to history and theory's von Neumann systems. Von Neumann systems invert micro theory's holy premise that consumption, in Adam Smith's immortal phrase, 'is the sole end and purpose of all production' (1776, p. 625).

John von Neumann's celebrated growth model (von Neumann, 1937; Hicks, 1965, ch. 28; Koopmans, 1964) proves an existence theorem for a maximal proportional growth path for intermediate producers' goods, otherwise known as capital. To maximize the rate of growth of producers' goods, wages are kept as low as possible and all non-wage output is reinvested in production. Consumption is minimized, non-consumption is maximized and all of it is accumulated. Like the fodder fed to Adam Smith's 'labouring cattle' or the fuel, raw materials, or repairs fed to machines, wage goods in von Neumann's growth model are 'mere inputs'.

Laborers themselves are produced in order to cooperate to produce more capital goods, including more laborers. Labor *is* capital. Growth of the part of the capital stock that is human occurs by ingestion of inputs of necessary subsistence. These, as noted, are minimized like any other cost.

The von Neumann system is therefore Malthuso-Ricardian in its subsistence concept; what is original is the maximand. Human capital in Schultz and G. S. Becker is also invested in as a means to an end, but the end is still traditional: final utility; ordinalist time-utilitarians are still utilitarians! Von Neumann systems sever the product–welfare link that economists from Petty and Smith to Kuznets, Juster, Hill, and Becker worked so hard to establish.

In von Neumann systems, subsistence is whatever is technically and socially necessary to keep the laborer productive of goods and reproductive of laborers. As Polanyi underscores and as was realized by the more careful Classical writers, just what is in the subsistence basket is a question of cultural, behavioral *fact*. If the supply of labor at a given wage is perfectly elastic, we know the wage basket is full enough. The necessary minimum may be high or low, but, once it is determined, so is the 'surplus'. A change in wages shows up as a change in 'technology', altering the rate of return on the old techniques (Hicks, 1965, p. 210).

With the entire surplus accumulated, von Neumann systems grow as fast as techniques allow. All consumption is purposeful Beckerian 'productive consumption'; none is simply for pleasure (section 8.4.2). Capital goods produce capital goods to produce capital goods, in a sort of divine (Tugan-Baranovskian) parody of Adam Smith's growth model. The system is, interestingly, a dynamic relative of the growthless Sraffian one in which 'commodities are used to produce commodities'.

A scheme that treats consumption as something to be minimized might not be thought likely to win friends and influence people who are Jevonsian utilitarians or Bergsonian-Arrovian welfare economists. However, Robert Dorfman, Paul Samuelson, and Robert Solow (1958, ch. 12) in their turnpike theorem salvage the reputation of the von Neumann system by making it 'temporary'. The von Neumann model's objective is modified from one of maximal proportional growth of producers' goods 'forever' to one of attaining a maximal capital stock at a specific terminal date. Then, the sacrifice period over, the maximally-enlarged stock of physical and human capital (putty) can be wholly switched back to production of consumer goods.

Since its maximand is growth of capital rather than utility, von Neumann's model can admit of no genuine agents – entrepreneurial, proletarian, or governmental; since life is short, self-interested humans would never cooperate. There is only one mode; with strictly constant returns to scale for all commodities in the system, there can be no market failure and thus no need for a higher, 'public' authority to remedy it. Robots, however, could be programmed for a von Neumann world.

History's would-be growth-maximizing economist-dictators deal with real citizens. Flesh and blood labor is not symmetric to produced capital – even slaves may vary their effort levels (Leibenstein, 1976). As Morgenstern (1972) scathingly observed, when human factors of production have minds of their own, producers are not fully sovereign; constrained maximization is therefore the wrong math. Still, history is replete with would-be economic dictators who have attempted to minimize consumption in order to commit maximal resources to the accumulation of non-consumption goods, whether civil or military.

Von Neumann systems are idiosyncratic from the viewpoint of standard economics because they maximize what standard economics regards not as results but as inputs. While silent as to ends (Robbins, 1932), neoclassical consumer theory holds that, whatever the ends may be, they are chosen because self-interested human decision-makers happen to prefer them to the available alternatives. Under would-be growth-maximizing dictator's sovereignty, the disenfranchised can assert themselves by playing on the size of the consumption basket.

Like the would-be benevolent welfare maximizer, the would-be growth maximizer requires a great number of socio-technical 'Polanyist facts' in order to carry out his plan. As noted, one such item is what 'in fact' the people regard as the minimum of subsistence. The growth maximizer also needs information on socially necessary Rawlsian 'differences' required for that subsistence to be forthcoming in the most efficient, minimal amount. The need for popular and cadre cooperation in lowerings of the consumption floor explains phenomena such as the continued production (importation) of non-necessities like alcohol, coffee, and tobacco, and lavish celebration of national and religious holidays, under supposed growth maximization. 'Differences' needed to train and motivate cadres shed light on the non-interdiction of elite polytechnics, scholarships for study abroad, chauffeur-driven automobiles, restricted-access shops. If we distort Kuznets with Dr Pangloss, the mushrooming of Committees on State Security in the social frameworks of growth-maximizing dictatorships can be written off to the fact that, well, 'inputs too have inputs'.

Failure to allow for *de facto* input–output relationships likely means that growth of capital stock or of welfare is not 'maximized' but only 'increased'. But if estimates of production coefficients turn out to be 'in fact' seriously wrong, the dictator's policies can produce zero or even 'negative expanded reproduction'. Declines may be temporary, as in Bukharin's 'transition period' (section 6.3) or the Malinowskian yam economy of Chapter 9, or permanent, as in some future Dark Age.

10.6 Intermediates, bads, and the 'most efficacious proportion'

The Senior–Marx 'most efficacious proportion' and Simon Kuznets's 'social framework' are both consistent with the 'sophisticated Classical' view, found in Smith, Say, and Senior, that an optimally retrenched state sector will still have a positive contribution to make to the output of welfare-related goods and services. The 'most efficacious proportion' is not zero but a positive fraction. Government's output may be usefully divided, on that logic, into the part that affects final enjoyment in the manner of Beckerian X-goods, and the part that is better treated as intermediate background. A welfare-related output index might net out defense of automobile plants and repair of port facilities analogously to the netting of grain and flour out of GNP.

In Chapter 7, it was noted with some *Schadenfreude* how Classical–Marxian surplus and transfer writers at opposite poles of the political spectrum railed with similar arguments against the excessive size of the state sector in contemporary mixed economies. Both Left and Right assume the 'most efficacious' proportion to be smaller than the one observed in actual fact. As Marx put it (just for capitalism, of course), '*services* may ... be forced on me – the *services of officials*, etc.' (1905–10, p. 405).

Simon Kuznets approached the problem of the finality of state services out of a general concern to avoid double-counting, to separate gross from net. Unfortunately, the simple split he proposed for government activities (health and education as final and everything else as intermediate), while it leaps with some agility over mode boundaries, fails to do justice to the externality-richness so typical of state goods and services. A stretch of highway may at a given moment convey mining and building equipment, pineapples and cherries, people on their way to work, people on vacation. The same troublesome simultaneity (publicness) characterizes Adam Smith's celebrated trio of intermediates: 'peace, easy taxes and a tolerable administration of justice' (1776, p. lxxx).

Argument over the 'most efficacious proportion' has dominated Western political life for the past quarter-century. The 'archaic' Smithian unproductive-labor debate has been recast as the question of the optimal rôle of the state as producer and consumer. It flourishes in that form despite the near-disappearance from Western economic discourse of the more ton-mentalitarian varieties of materialist fallacy. Service-bashing is now going out of fashion even amongst Marxian economists and socialist planners.

Given the ambiguities behind the notion of 'producing' a given level of confidence and optimism (Keynes's 'animal spirits') from given 'inputs' of monetary and fiscal policy – which requires treating externality-rich public goods in a deterministic input–output framework – it seems presumptuous of economist-observers and politicians to write, as they frequently do, as if the value and composition of the 'most efficacious proportion' were known. In the present state of knowledge, public-goods-augmented input–output tables are a dream, not a reality.

10.7 The 'sole end and purpose of all production'

Late nineteenth-century economics was an intellectual product designed to handle private, marketed, physical, tangible, material goods, of varying durabilities to be sure, but produced mainly under constant returns. Before Keynes, attempts were made to incorporate imperfections of competition and foresight into that neoclassical framework. Since Keynes, the research program of general economics has in large measure consisted of efforts to integrate into the Walrasian framework three major other categories of purposeful human effort. They involve scarce means that have alternative uses and are thought to be sufficiently 'disembedded' in the Polanyi sense as to belong to the economy and to economics. In descending order of obviousness, they are:

(i) the non-storable *services produced in the enterprise sector* and sold (assigned in a Soviet-type system) either to other enterprises as intermediates or else as final X-good services to consumers;
(ii) the non-marketed, storable and non-storable, public and private *goods and services produced in the state sector*; and
(iii) non-marketed *goods and services produced in the household* with store-bought inputs, state inputs, and time.

Private services did not present a very tricky analytical problem even prior to their explicit integration into microeconomics by Say, Walras, Menger, Fisher, and Marshall (section 4.6). Even Smith and Marx at their most literal could be found to include services produced in multi-person firms and profitably sold on markets in annual produce. In the case of private-sector services, the main mote in the economist's eye was extreme tinyness of scale. Unlike single-person (or family) farms, single-person (or family) service firms were harder to recognize as *bona fide* enterprises even when they sold their immaterial outputs for money. (Marx had trouble with the farms, too, because no hired labor meant no exploitation, no surplus-value and no 'capitalism'.)

It was not immediately recognized that private-sector services, with the exception of transportation, might be *bought by enterprises* as intermediate inputs as well as purchased for final enjoyment by consumers, usually rich consumers. The early identification of services with final luxuries remained strong. Say saw through that and introduced into economics the notion of 'intangible' private capital, in the form of trademarks, goodwill, patents. Private services sold to businesses currently represent a sizeable fraction of economic activity in Western mixed economies.

The state sector is now seen as producing goods and services that are both rich and poor in external effects. Defense protects all enterprises and consumers resident in a territorial economy, even those who sympathize with the enemy (Winch, 1973, p. 122). The flows of security that are the collective output of the military effort are especially valued by defense contractors and their employees and stockholders. The defense establishment uses inputs of physical, tangible, and not always durable hardware, software, and human capital. Its output, conceived as the stock from which protection flows, is, like the stock of preservation of the natural environment, difficult to conceptualize (Juster, 1973; section 8.4.3).

Education services are appropriable on an individual basis, and exclusion in their case is technically possible. Primary education is usually regarded as more 'necessary' than is postgraduate education, though the external spinoffs expressed in a Rawlsian difference principle may qualify that beyond recognition. On occasion, expensively-educated people revolutionize the technologies that generate wage goods and services for the poor. The human capital resulting from the efforts of teachers and students ordinarily has a number of external effects: it may be used by the student to earn income; it may at the same time add to the profits of enterprise because of an unfavorable balance of power between boss and employee; acquired knowledge or skill may be treasured by the student for its own sake, because of Veblen's 'instinct of workmanship'. It may yield external 'publick benefits' to society in the spirit of Adam Smith or Heinrich Storch. Literacy and numeracy are thought to reduce information, organizational, policing, and learning costs to society generally, rendering it on balance more flexible, efficient, and creative, though possibly more litigious. The benefits of state dental programs, on the other hand, are probably closer to being genuinely private goods.

The third category, tangible and intangible, mainly private, intermediate and final goods produced in households, violate the factory paradigm in that the outputs (and many of the inputs) have only notional, not market, prices. Still, as we saw in section 8.4, for housework that is susceptible of delegation, imputed prices are readily derived. Here, too, we found evidence of Classical–Marxian bias against immaterial services at the highest level. The United Nations System of National Accounts recommends ambitious programs of imputation for non-market production described as 'primary'. Statisticians are instructed to estimate production and investment of subsistence farmers in poor countries, but are let off the hook when it comes to imputing values for 'non-primary' household services.

Entrepreneurs and workers in atomistic competition probably go about their business little subject to index-number illusion. Their behavior is probably the same (assuming they do not read too many newspapers) whether total output is measured according to the conventions of the Soviet Material Product System, the UN System of National Accounts, Kuznets's 'new version', or Juster et al.'s 'theoretical framework for the measurement of well-being'.

But in our political economy, once an index is decided upon, wages and pensions get linked to it, elections are won and lost over it, legislation promotes it, industries are protected, rivers reversed, to make it grow faster. It takes on a life of its own, 'goading the goaders', inspiring the acts and reporting the effectiveness of state policy in a complex Political Arithmetick.

In theory, any final index of results that avoids input–output error can be defended. As we saw with Ricardo and Polanyi, sovereign researchers can choose their fields of study as idiosyncratically as they wish. But when policies and processes affect real people, index-number illusion has real consequences. That being so, voter-consumers and benevolent dictators might wish to pay careful attention to the criteria used in choosing economic boundaries and computing the value weights that in the end tell us what looks 'net' and what does not. Index-number illusion suggests that economic science may serve humanity best when success indicators are made as welfare-related as is feasible in a world of free-riders.

Delineating a behaviorally-unified domain of production and motivating non-equivalent transfers of its 'surplus' to society's 'non-producers' have challenged even the great economists. Transcription of the archaic, value-laden 'productive/unproductive' dichotomy into concepts that make sense in terms of choosing production boundaries, valuing their products, and establishing unambiguous links between effort, output, and welfare has been a central task of economics for the past two centuries. The job has not yet been completed to anyone's very great satisfaction.

Human agents are presumed to undertake unpleasant work and to sacrifice genuine leisure to engage in politics because these are *means* to their ultimate, unevaluable ends. This is utilitarianism's useful tautology. For Adam Smith, the 'sole end and purpose of all production' is consumption, not production. As a positive bit of analysis, the phrase conveys the logic that, in competitive systems, consumers' sovereignty drives the product mix. It also evokes Smith's preference for such systems over régimes that favor exporters, such as mercantilism, or landlords, like Corn-Law England, or dictators, as in many historical instances, or no flesh and blood human at all, as in von Neumann systems of 'production for production's sake'. If desire for utility is indeed the cause that drives us, it is good science to try to measure the results, not the inputs. Economics' next synthesis may differ from the present one principally in the degree of commitment made to netting such goods and services as are *truly final* out of life's turbulent sea of intermediates and bads.

Note on notes, terms, and translations

The earliest version of this history had 232 pages of notes. *Theories of Surplus and Transfer* has less than one, thanks to Unwin Hyman's innovative house style, which imbeds ordinary citations in parentheses in the text itself. Many of the works cited have been reprinted since they first appeared. In the interests of economy and narrative flow, my in-the-text references give only the *original* dates of such works. The *page numbers* cited in the text, though, refer to the more recent editions that are identified in full against those dates in the Bibliography. Thus (Smith, 1776, p. 315) is a reference to p. 315 of the Modern Library edition of the *Wealth of Nations*.

I have taken the liberty of capitalizing a number of expressions – Classical and Classical-Marxian, but not neoclassical or mercantilist – in order to highlight the former in a somewhat Teutonic way. *Das Kapital* is referred to as such. These conventions are idiosyncratic but I stand by them.

I also attempt to enrich the lexicon of social science with some new, somewhat cumbersome but, I think, readily understandable terms: input-output error, lexicographic modism, economist's sovereignty, pre-public-goods neoclassical, the productive-labor theory of value, the most efficacious proportion, the single-person firm. Users of the future may wish to abbreviate these.

All translations are my own unless the Bibliography lists an English-language edition against the author's name at the relevant date. Thus I am the translator of Strumilin (1926) but not Lenin (1914b), of Garnier (1802) but not Say (1819). In the few instances where I have thought to improve on published translations, a reference to an original-language source is provided. The Russian is transliterated according to the Library of Congress system, except in the case of proper names ending in ii, which are simplified to y.

Bibliography

Abalkin, L. A. (1978), *Konechnye narodno-khoziaistvennye rezul'taty* [*Final Economic Results*] (Moscow: Ekonomika).
Abalkin, L. I. (1988) 'Lekarstva dlia ekonomiki' (Medicines for the economy), *Literaturnaia Gazeta*, 2 November.
Abalkin, L., Medvedev, V. and Ozherel'ev, O. (1988), 'Politicheskaia ekonomika v usloviakh perestroiki' [Political economy in conditions of perestroika], *Voprosy ekonomiki*, no. 3, pp. 1–22.
Abolin, A. (1928a), 'K probleme proizvoditel'nogo i neproizvoditel'nogo truda' [On the problem of productive and unproductive labor], *Planovoe khoziaistvo* [*Planned Economy*], no. 8.
Abolin, A. (1928b), 'Za marksistskoe tolkovanie kategorii proizvoditel'nogo i neproizvoditel'nogo truda' [For a Marxist interpretation of the categories of productive and unproductive labor], *Planovoe khoziaistvo*, no. 10.
Agabab'ian, E. M. (1968), *Ekonomicheskii analiz sfery uslug* [*Economic Analysis of the Service Sphere*] (Moscow: Ekonomika).
Agabab'ian E. M. (1977), *Proizvodstvo i potreblenie uslug v desiatoi piatiletke* [*Production and Consumption of Services in the Tenth Five-year Plan*] (Moscow: Mysl').
Allix, E. (1910), 'J. -B. Say et les origines de l'industrialisme'. *Revue d'Economie Politique*, vol. 24.
Allix, E. (1911), 'La Méthode et la conception de l'économie politique dans l'oeuvre de J. -B. Say', *Revue d'Histoire des Doctrines Economiques et Sociales*, vol. V.
Allix, E. (1912), 'L'Oeuvre économique de Germain Garnier, traducteur d'Adam Smith et disciple de Cantillon', *Revue d'Histoire des Doctrines Economiques et Sociales*, vol. V.
Amonn, A. (1911), *Objekt und Grundbegriffe der theoretischen Nationalökonomie* (Vienna and Leipzig).
Anspach, R. (1976) 'Adam Smith's growth paradigm', *History of Political Economy*, vol. 8, no. 4.
Arrow, K. J. (1962), 'The economic implications of learning by doing', *Review of Economic Studies*, vol. XXIX, June, pp. 155–73.
Arrow, K. J. (1963), *Social Choice and Individual Values*, 2nd edn (1st edn, 1951), Cowles Foundation Monograph 12 (New Haven, CT: Yale University Press).
Arrow, K. J. (1973), 'Some ordinalist-utilitarian notes on Rawls's theory of justice', *The Journal of Philosophy*, vol. LXX, no. 9, 10 May, pp. 245–63.
Arrow, K. J. (1979), 'The division of labor in the economy, the polity and the society', in G. P. O'Driscoll (ed.), *Adam Smith and Modern Political Economy* (Ames, IA: Iowa State University Press), pp. 153–64.
Arrow, K. J. and Debreu, G. (1954), 'Existence of an equilibrium for a competitive economy', *Econometrica*, vol. 22, pp. 265–90.

BIBLIOGRAPHY

Arrow, K. J. and Hahn, F. (1971) *General Competitive Analysis* (San Francisco: Holden Day).
Aslund, A. (1987), 'Gorbachev's economic advisors', *Soviet Economy*, vol. 3, no. 3, pp. 246–69.

Backhouse, R. (1987), *A History of Modern Economic Analysis* (Oxford: Basil Blackwell).
Bacon, R. W. and Eltis, W. A. (1975a), 'How we went wrong', *The Sunday Times*, 2 November.
Bacon, R. W. and Eltis, W. A. (1975b), 'The implications for inflation, employment and growth of a fall in the share of output that is marketed', *Bulletin of the Oxford University Institute of Economics and Statistics*, vol. 37, November.
Bacon, R. W. and Eltis, W. A. (1976), *Britain's Economic Problem: Too Few Producers* (London: Macmillan).
Bacon, R. W. and Eltis, W. A. (1978a), *Britain's Economic Problem: Too Few Producers*, 2nd rev. edn (London: Macmillan).
Bacon, R. W. and Eltis, W. A. (1978b), 'Marketed output – yes; luxuries – no: A reply to Ms. Ietto Gillies', *British Review of Economic Issues*, no. 2, May.
Bacon, R. W. and Eltis, W. A. (1979), 'The measurement of the growth of the non-market sector and its influence: a reply to Hadjimatheou and Skouras', *Economic Journal*, vol. 89, pp. 402–15.
Baran, P. A. (1947), 'National income and product of the USSR in 1940', *Review of Economic Statistics*, November.
Baran, P. A. ([1957] 1966) (1958), *The Political Economy of Growth* (New York: Monthly Review).
Baran, P. A. and Sweezy, P. M. (1968), *Monopoly Capital: An Essay on the American Economic and Social Order* (New York: Monthly Review).
Barkai, H. (1969), 'A formal outline of a Smithian growth model', *Quarterly Journal of Economics*, August.
Barun, M. A. (1930), *Osnovnoi kapital promyshlennosti SSSR [Basic Capital of USSR Industry]* (Moscow: Gosudarstvennoe Izdatel'stvo).
Baster, N. (ed.) (1972), *Measuring Development* (London: Frank Cass).
Baudeau, Abbé N. (1776), *Explication du Tableau Economique*, extracts from *Ephémérides du citoyen* 1767/68 (Paris: Delalain).
Baudeau, Abbé N. (1770), 'Lettre à M. Béardé de l'Abbaye, sur sa critique prétendue de la science économique', *Ephémérides du citoyen*, vol. 7, pp. 80–129.
Baumol, W. J. (1968), *Welfare Economics and the Theory of the State* (Cambridge, MA: Harvard University Press).
Baumol, W. J. (1986), 'Productivity growth, convergence, and welfare: what the long-run data show', *American Economic Review*, vol. 76, no. 5, December, pp. 1072–85.
Baumol, W. J., Blinder, A. S. and Scarth, W. M. (1985), *Economics: Principles and Policy*, Canadian edn (Toronto: Academic Press).
Bazarov, V. A. (1899), *Trud proizvoditel'nyi i trud, obrazuiushchii tsennost'* [*Productive Labor and Labor which Creates Value*] (St Petersburg: Dorvatovskii i Charushnikov).
Becker, A. S. (1969), *Soviet National Income 1958–1964* (Berkeley, CA: University of California Press).
Becker, A. S. (1971), *National Income Accounting in the USSR*, RAND Memo P-4223-2 (Santa Monica, CA: RAND).
Becker, A. S. (1972) 'National income accounting in the USSR', in V. G.

Treml and J. P. Hardt (eds), *Soviet Economic Statistics* (Durham, NC: Duke University Press).

Becker, G. S. (1964), *Human Capital* (New York: Columbia University Press for NBER).

Becker, G. S. (1965), 'A theory of the allocation of time', *Economic Journal*, vol. LXXV, September, pp. 493–517.

Becker, G. S. (1981), *A Treatise on the Family* (Cambridge, MA: Harvard University Press).

Becker, J. F. (1977), *Marxian Political Economy: an Outline* (Cambridge: Cambridge University Press).

Beckerman, W. B. and Bacon, R. W. (1966), 'International comparisons of income levels: A suggested new measure', *Economic Journal*, vol. 76, September.

Beckerman, W. (1974), *In Defence of Economic Growth* (London: Jonathan Cape).

Beer, M. 1938, *Early British Economics: From the XIIIth to the Middle of the XVIIIth Century* (London: Frank Cass 1967).

Beissinger, M. R. (1982), 'The politics of convergence', PhD thesis, Department of Government, Harvard University.

Bell, D. and Kristol, I. (eds) (1981), *The Crisis in Economic Theory* (New York: Basic).

Benjamin, W. 1936, 'The work of art in the age of mechanical reproduction'; reprinted in *Illuminations*, ed. and intro. Hannah Arendt (New York: Schocken Books 1969).

Bentham, J. (1801), 'Defence of a maximum', in *Jeremy Bentham's Economic Writings*, vol. 3, ed. W. Stark (London, 1954).

Bentham, J. (1801–4), 'The Institute of Political Economy', in *Jeremy Bentham's Economic Writings*, vol. 3, ed. W. Stark (London, 1954).

Bentson, M. (1969), 'The political economy of women's liberation', *Monthly Review*, vol. 21, no. 4.

Berdyaev, N. (1937) *The Origins of Russian Communism* trans. R. M. French, 1948) (Ann Arbor, MI: Ann Arbor Paperbacks, University of Michigan Press 1966).

Bergson, A. (1938), 'A reformulation of certain aspects of welfare economics', *Quarterly Journal of Economics*, vol. 52, pp. 310-34.

Bergson, A. 1948, 'Socialist economics', in H. S. Ellis (ed.), *A Survey of Contemporary Economics*, reprinted in *Welfare, Planning and Employment: Selected Essays in Economic Theory* (Cambridge, MA: MIT Press 1982).

Bergson, A. (1949), *National Income of the USSR in 1940: a preliminary report* (Santa Monica, CA: RAND).

Bergson, A. (1953), *Soviet National Income and Product in 1937* (New York: Columbia University Press).

Bergson, A. (1961), *The Real National Income of Soviet Russia since 1928* (Cambridge, MA: Harvard University Press).

Bergson, A. (1963), 'National income', in A. Bergson and S. Kuznets (eds), *Economic Trends in the Soviet Union* (Cambridge, MA: Harvard University Press), pp. 1–37.

Bergson, A. (1964a), *The Economics of Soviet Planning* (Cambridge, MA: Harvard University Press).

Bergson, A. (1964b), *National Income and Welfare*, RAND Memo P-3004, October (Santa Monica, CA: RAND).

Bergson, A. (1978), 'Towards a new growth model', in *Productivity and the Social System - The USSR and the West* (Cambridge, MA: Harvard University

Press).

Bergson, A. (1987), 'Comparative productivity: the USSR, Eastern Europe, and the West', *American Economic Review*, vol. 77, no. 3, June, pp. 342–57.

Bergson, A. and Kuznets, S. (eds) (1963), *Economic Trends in the Soviet Union* (Cambridge, MA: Harvard University Press).

Bergson, A. and Levine, H. S. (eds) (1983), *The Soviet Economy: Toward the Year 2000* (London: Allen & Unwin).

Berle, A. J. and Means, G. C. (1932), *The Modern Corporation and Private Property* (New York: Commerce Clearing House).

Berlin, I. ([1953] 1978), 'The hedgehog and the fox'; reprinted in *Russian Thinkers* (Harmondsworth: Penguin).

Berliner, J. S. (1957), *Factory and Manager in the USSR* (Cambridge, MA: Harvard University Press).

Berliner, J. S. (1964), 'Marxism and the Soviet economy', *Problems of Communism*, vol. 13, no. 5, September–October, pp. 1–11.

Berliner, J. S. (1966), 'The economics of overtaking and surpassing', in H. Rosovsky (ed.), *Industrialization in Two Systems: essays in honor of Alexander Gerschenkron* (New York: John Wiley).

Berliner, J. S. (1976), *The Innovation Decision in Soviet Industry* (Cambridge, MA: MIT Press).

Berliner, J. S. (1983), 'Planning and management', in A. Bergson and H. S. Levine (eds), *The Soviet Economy: toward the Year 2000* (London: Allen & Unwin), pp. 350–90.

Berliner, J. S. (1986), 'Gorbachev and the economic mechanism', mimeo, 28 pp.

Berliner, J. S. (1987), 'Organizational restructuring of the Soviet economy', in US Congress, Joint Economic Committee, *Gorbachev's Economic Plans*, vol. 1 (Washington, DC: USGPO), pp. 70–84.

Bernstein, E. 1899, *Evolutionary Socialism: a criticism and affirmation*; trans. E. C. Harvey, 1909 (New York: Schocken Books 1961).

Berthoud, A. (1974), *Travail productif et productivité du travail chez Marx* (Paris: Maspero).

Bettelheim, C. (1970), *Calcul économique et formes de propriété* (Paris: Maspero).

Bhagwati, J. (1982), 'Directly unproductive, profit-seeking (DUP) activities', *Journal of Political Economy*, vol. 90, October, pp. 988–1002.

Bhagwati, J. (1982), 'DUP Activities and Rent-Seeking', *Kyklos*, vol. 36, pp. 634–7.

Bhagwati, J. (1984), 'Why are services cheaper in poor countries?'; reprinted in *Wealth and Poverty* (Oxford: Blackwell 1985).

Bhagwati, J. and T. N. Srinivasan (1982), 'The welfare consequences of directly-unproductive profit-seeking (DUP) lobbying activities: prices versus quantity distortions', *Journal of International Economics*, vol. 13, pp. 33–44.

Black, R. D. C., Coats, A. W. and Goodwin, C. (eds) (1973), *The Marginal Revolution in Economics* (Durham, NC: Duke University Press).

Blackaby, F. (1978), *De-industrialisation* (London: Heinemann).

Bladen, V. W. (1960), 'Adam Smith on productive and unproductive labour', *Canadian Journal of Economics and Political Science*, November, pp. 625–30.

Bladen, V. W. (1974), *From Adam Smith to Maynard Keynes* (Toronto: University of Toronto Press).

Blades, D. W. (1975), *Activités non-monétaires (subsistance) dans les comptes nationaux des pays en voie de développement* (Paris: OECD).

Blaug, M. (1958), *Ricardian Economics* (New Haven, CT: Yale University Press).

Blaug, M. (1968), *Economic Theory in Retrospect*, 1st edn (Homewood, IL: Irwin).

Blaug, M. (1972), *An Introduction to the Economics of Education* (Harmondsworth: Penguin).
Blaug, M. (1975), 'The economics of education in English classical political economy', in A. S. Skinner and T. Wilson (eds), *Essays on Adam Smith* (Oxford: Clarendon Press).
Blaug, M. (1980a), *The Methodology of Economics* (Cambridge: Cambridge University Press).
Blaug, M. (1980b), *A Methodological Appraisal of Marxian Economics*, De Vries lecture (Amsterdam: North Holland).
Blaug, M. (1988), 'Productive and unproductive consumption', in J. Eatwell, M. Milgate and P. Newman (eds), *The New Palgrave: a dictionary of economics* (New York: Stockton Press), pp. 1007–8.
Bleaney, M. (1976), *Underconsumption Theories: a history and critical analysis* (New York: International Publishers).
Block, H. S. (1979), 'Soviet economic performance in a global context', in US Congress, Joint Economic Committee, *The Soviet Economy in a Time of Change* (Washington DC: USGPO), pp. 110–40.
Blough, R., Muratore, J. and Berk, S. (1987), 'Gorbachev's policy on the private sector: two steps forward, one step backward', in US Congress, Joint Economic Committee, *Gorbachev's Economic Plans*, vol. 2 (Washington, DC: USGPO), pp. 261–70.
Bluestone, B. and Harrison, B. (1982) *The Deindustrialization of America* (New York: Basic).
Blunt, A. (1940), *Artistic Theory in Italy, 1450–1600* (Cambridge: Cambridge University Press).
Boadway, R. W. (1979), *Public Sector Economics* (Cambridge, MA: Winthrop).
Bober, M. M. (1929), 'Academic economics in present Russia: Gelesnoff, *Grundzüge*', *Quarterly Journal of Economics*, vol. 43, no. 2, pp. 352–63.
Bogachev, V. N. (1977), *Natsional'noe bogatstvo v sisteme vosproizvodstvennykh kategorii* [National Wealth in a System of Reproductive Categories] (Moscow: Institut ekonomiki AN).
Bogdanov, A. A. (1897), *Kratkii kurs ekonomicheskoi nauki* [*A Short Course of Economic Science*], 1st edn (4th edn, St Petersburg: Dorvatovskii and Charushnikov, 1904).
Bogdanov, A. A. (1917), *Vvedenie v politicheskuiu ekonomiiu (v voprosakh i otvetakh)* [Introduction to Political Economy in Questions and Answers], 2nd rev. edn (Moscow: Knigoizdatel'stvo pisatelei v Moskve).
Bogdanov, A. A. (1923), *A Short Course of Economic Science*, 2nd edn rev. and suppl. S. M. Dvolaitsky, in conjunction with the author; trans. J. Fineberg (London: Communist Party of Great Britain, 1927).
Bogdanov, A. A. and Stepanov, I. (1910), *Kurs politicheskoi ekonomii* [*Course of Political Economy*] (St Petersburg: Znanie).
Bogomazov, G. G. (1982), 'Spisok literatury po problemam ekonomiki i organizatsii obrazovaniia' [Bibliography on the economics and organization of education], Leningrad University, rotaprint.
Böhm-Bawerk, E. (1884–), *Capital and Interest*; vol. II (Spring Mills PA: Libertarian Press, 1959).
Böhm-Bawerk, E. (1896), *Zum Abschluss des Marx'schen Systems*; trans. in P. Sweezy (ed.), *Karl Marx and the Close of his System* (New York: A. M. Kelley 1966).
Boileau, D. (1811), *An Introduction to the Study of Political Economy: or, elementary view of the manner in which the Wealth of Nations is produced, increased, distributed*

and consumed (London: Cadell and Davies).
Boisguilbert, P. le Pesant de (1696), *Le Détail de la France*; vol. 1 of *Le Détail de la France ... augmenté ... de plusieurs mémoires et traitez [sic] sur la même matière*, 2 vols, 1707; Goldsmith-Kress microfilm no. 4429.
Boisguilbert, P. le Pesant de (1707a), *Dissertation de la nature des richesses, de l'Argent, et des Tributs*, in *Le Détail de la France*, vol. 2; Goldsmith-Kress microfilm no. 4429.
Boisguilbert, P. le Pesant de (1707b), *Traité des grains*, in *Le Détail de la France*, vol. 1; Goldsmith-Kress microfilm no. 4429.
Boisguilbert, P. le Pesant de (1707c), *Le Factum de la France*, in *Le Détail de la France*, vol. 2; Goldsmith-Kress microfilm no. 4429.
Bol'shaia Sovetskaia Entsiklopediia [*Great Soviet Encyclopedia*] (Moscow, 1976).
Bornstein, M. *et al.* (1961), *Soviet National Accounts for 1955* (Ann Arbor, MI: Center for Russian Studies, University of Michigan).
Borodaevsky, A. (1972), 'Uslugi, proizvoditel'nyi trud, natsional'nyi dokhod' [Services, productive labor, national income], *Mirovaia ekonomika i mezhdunarodnye otnosheniia*, no. 7.
Boss, H. (1979), 'Two hundred years of material fallacy', mimeo, Canadian Economic Association conference, Saskatoon, Sask., June.
Boss, H. (1982), 'Productive labour, unproductive labour and the boundary of the economic domain, 1662–1980: history, analysis, applications', PhD thesis, Department of Economics, McGill University.
Boss, H. (1984a), 'Unproductiveness fallacy and material fallacy in the economics of *Das Kapital*: implications for boundaries, value and welfare', Université du Québec à Montréal Department of Economics working paper, February.
Boss, H. (1984b), 'The pre-revolutionary bourgeois economics of socialism', mimeo, New England Slavic Association, March.
Boss, H. (1985), 'Scope, valuation and netness in economics from Petty to Condillac', Université du Québec à Montréal Department of Economics working paper, July.
Boss, H. (1986a), 'Division du travail et travail improductif dans un système de liberté naturelle: le dilemme d'Adam Smith', Université du Québec à Montréal Department of Economics working paper, July.
Boss, H. (1986b), 'A reappraisal of Marxian economics: the productive-labour theory of value and its corollaries', *Historical Reflections/ Réflexions historiques*, vol. 13, nos 2 & 3, pp. 335–75.
Boss, H. (1986c), 'Origins of the Soviet Material Product System', *Canadian Slavonic Papers/ Revue Canadienne des Slavistes*, vol. 28, no. 3, September, pp. 243–65.
Boss, H. (1986d), 'A calculus of present pain', in 'Nikolai Bukharin and the economics of revolution', Université du Québec à Montréal Department of Economics working paper, July.
Boss, H. (1988), 'Problemy proizvoditel'nogo truda i material'nogo produkta v usloviiakh smeshannoi ekonomiki (opyt SSSR)' [Productive labor and material product in a mixed socialist economy: the Soviet case], delivered paper, Learned Council of the USSR Academy of Sciences Institute of Economics, June 19 pp.
Boudin, L. (1907), *The Theoretical System of Karl Marx in the Light of Recent Criticism* (Chicago, IL: Charles Kerr).
Bouvier-Ajam, M. *et al.* (1975), *Dictionnaire économique et sociale*, Centre d'études et de recherches marxistes (Paris: Editions sociales).

Bowles, S., Gordon, D. M. and Weisskopf, T. E. (1984), *Beyond the Waste Land: a democratic alternative to economic decline* (New York: Anchor).

Bowley, M. (1937), *Nassau Senior and Classical Economics* (New York: Octagon, 1967).

Bowley, M. (1975), 'Some aspects of the treatment of capital in *The Wealth of Nations*', in A. S. Skinner and T. Wilson (eds), *Essays on Adam Smith* (Oxford: Clarendon Press).

Braverman, H. (1974), *Labor and Monopoly Capital: the degradation of work in the twentieth century* (New York: Monthly Review Press).

Brenner, Y. S. (1966), *Theories of Economic Development and Growth* (New York: Praeger).

Bronfenbenner, M. (1971), *Income Distribution Theory* (Chicago, IL: Aldine Atherton).

Brus, W. (1975), *Socialist Ownership and Political Systems*, trans. R. A. Clarke (London: Routledge & Kegan Paul).

Brydges, E. (1819), *The Population and Riches of Nations, considered together ...* (Paris, Geneva, London: Triphook).

Buchanan, J. M. (1949), 'The pure theory of public finance: a suggested approach', *Journal of Political Economy*, vol. 57, December, pp. 496–505.

Buchanan, J. M. (1965), 'An economic theory of clubs', *Economica*, vol. 32, February, pp. 1–14.

Buchanan, J. M. (1968), *The Demand and Supply of Public Goods* (Chicago: Rand McNally).

Buchanan, J. M. (1976), 'Public goods and natural liberty', in T. Wilson and A. S. Skinner (eds), *The Market and the State: essays in honour of Adam Smith* (Oxford: Clarendon Press).

Buchanan, J. M. (1978), *The Economics of Politics* (London: IEA).

Buchanan, J. M. (1987), 'The constitution of economic policy', *American Economic Review*, vol. 77, no. 3, June, pp. 243–50.

Buchanan, J. M. (1988), 'The economic theory of politics reborn', *Challenge*, vol. 31, no. 2, pp. 4–10.

Buchanan, J. M. and Tollison, R. D. (eds) (1984), *The Theory of Public Choice* (Ann Arbor, MI: University of Michigan Press).

Buchanan, J. M., Tollison, R. D. and Tullock, G. (eds) (1980), *Toward a Theory of the Rent-Seeking Society* (College Station, TX: Texas A & M University Press).

Buck, T. (1982), *Comparative Industrial Systems* (New York: St Martin's Press).

Bukharin, N. I. (1918), *Mirovoe khoziaistvo i imperializm* [*World Economy and Imperialism*], written 1911–12 (Petrograd: Priboi) New York: International Publishers, 1929).

Bukharin, N. I. (1919), *Politicheskaia ekonomiia rant'e: teoriia tsennosti i pribyli avstriiskoi shkoly* [*The Economic Theory of the Rentier: the theory of value and profit of the Austrian School*] (Moscow: VSNKh); trans. as *The Economic Theory of the Leisure Class* (New York: International Publishers, 1927).

Bukharin, N. I. (1920), *Ekonomika perekhodnogo perioda* [*Economics of the Transition Period*]; trans. as *The Economics of the Transformation Period, with Lenin's Critical Remarks* n.t. (New York: Bergman Publishers, Lyle Stuart, 1971).

Bukharin, N. (1921), *Historical Materialism* (New York: International Publishers, 1925).

Bukharin, N. and Preobrazhensky, E. (1919), *The ABC of Communism: a popular explanation of the program of the Communist Party of Russia*, trans. E. and C. Paul, 1922 (Ann Arbor, MI: University of Michigan Press, 1977).

Burenstam Linder, S. (1970), *The Harried Leisure Class* (New York: Columbia University Press).
Burger, A. (1970), *Economic Problems of Consumers' Services* (Budapest: Akademiai Kiado).
Burns, A. C. and Mitchell, W. C. (1930), *Business Cycles: the problem and its setting* (New York: NBER).
Butel-Dumont, G. M. (1771), *Théorie du Luxe: ou Traité dans lequel on entreprend d'établir que le Luxe est un ressort non seulement utile mais même indispensablement nécessaire à la prospérité des Etats*; Goldsmith-Kress microfilm no. 10707.

Cairncross, A. K. (1958), 'Economic schizophrenia', *Scottish Journal of Political Economy*, February.
Calvez, J.-Y. (1956), *Revenu national en U.R.S.S.: problèmes théoriques et description statistique* (Paris: SEDES).
Campbell, R. W. (1961), 'Marx, Kantorovich and Novozhilov: *stoimost*' versus reality', *Slavic Review*, October, pp. 402–18.
Campbell, R. W. (1974), *The Soviet-Type Economies*, 3rd edn (Boston: Houghton-Mifflin).
Campbell, R. W. (1985), *The Conversion of National Income Data of the U.S.S.R. to Concepts of the System of National Accounts in Dollars and Estimate of Growth Rate*, World Bank paper no. 777 (Washington: World Bank).
Cannan, E. (1904), 'Introduction', notes, marginalia, and enlarged index to Adam Smith, *An Inquiry into the Nature and Causes of the Wealth of Nations* (London).
Cannan, E. (1917), *History of Theories of Production and Distribution in English Political Economy from 1776 to 1848*, 3rd edn (1st edn, 1898) (London: Staples, 1953).
Cannan, E. (1930), *A Review of Economic Theory* (London: P. S. King).
Cantillon, R. (1755), *Essai sur la nature du commerce en général* (Paris: INED, 1952).
Carr, E. H. (1952), *The Bolshevik Revolution, 1917–1923*, vol. II, (New York: Macmillan).
Carr, E. H. and Davies, R. W. (1969), *Foundations of a Planned Economy, 1926–1929*, vol. 1, Part 2 (vol. 8 of *A History of Soviet Russia*) (London: Macmillan).
Central Intelligence Agency (1981), *Handbook of Economic Statistics* (Washington: USGPO).
Chalmers, T. (1832), *On Political Economy, in connexion with the Moral State and Moral Prospects of Society* (Glasgow: Collins).
Chambre, H. (1955), *Le Marxisme en Union Soviétique: idéologie et institutions, leur évolution de 1917 à nos jours* (Paris: Editions du Seuil).
Chapman, J. G. (1963), 'Consumption', in A. Bergson and S. Kuznets, (eds), *Economic Trends in the Soviet Union* (Cambridge, MA: Harvard University Press), pp. 235–82.
Chapman, J. G. (1987), 'Income distribution and social justice in the USSR', rev. edn of paper presented at the National Convention of the American Association for the Advancement of Slavic Studies, November.
Charbonnaud, R. (1907), *Les Idées économiques de Voltaire* (New York: Burt Franklin, 1970).
Chen, N.-R. (1967), *Chinese Economic Statistics: a handbook for mainland China* (Chicago, IL: Aldine Atherton).
Chenery, H. B. (1982), 'Industrialization and growth: the experience of large

countries', World Bank paper no. 537 (Washington, DC: World Bank).
Chenery, H. B. and Syrquin, M. (1975), *Patterns of Development* (Oxford: World Bank).
Chenery, H. B. and Watanabe, T. (1958), 'International comparisons of the structure of production', *Econometrica*, vol. 26, no. 4, October.
Chenery, H. B., Robinson, S. and Syrquin, M. (1986), *Industrialization and Growth: a comparative study* (Oxford: World Bank).
Chenery, H. B., Ahluwalia, M. S., Bell, C. L. G., Duloy, D., and Jolly, R. (1974), *Redistribution with Growth* (Oxford: World Bank).
Chernomordik, D. I. (ed.) (1939), *Narodnyi dokhod SSSR: ego obrazovanie i uchet* [*The National Income of the USSR: its formation and accounting*], Akademiia nauk SSSR, Institut ekonomiki (Moscow–Leningrad: Gosplanizdat).
Chernyshevsky, N. G. (1860), 'Translation and Notes' to the Russian edition of Dzhon Stiuart Mill' [John Stuart Mill], *Osnovaniia politicheskoi ekonomii, s nekotorymi iz ikh primenenii k obshchestvennoi filosofii* [*Principles of Political Economy, with Some of their Applications to Social Philosophy*] St Petersburg: K. Vul'f).
Chukhno, A. A. (1988), *Metodologicheskie problemy politicheskoi ekonomiki sotsializma* [*Methodological Problems of the Political Economy of Socialism*] (Kiev: Golovnoe Izd.).
Chuprov, A. I. (1892), *Istoriia politicheskoi ekonomii* [*History of Political Economy*], 8th edn (Moscow: Izd. Sabashnikovykh, 1915).
Chuprov, A. I. (1902), *Kurs politicheskoi ekonomii* [*Course of Political Economy*] (Moscow: Izd. moskovskogo imperatorskogo universiteta, 1914).
Clark, C. (1939), *The Conditions of Economic Progress* (London: Macmillan).
Clark, C. (1947), 'Russian income and product statistics', *Review of Economic Statistics*, November.
Clark, J. B. (1899), *The Distribution of Wealth* (New York: A. M. Kelley, 1965).
Clark, J. M. et al. (1928), Adam Smith, 1776–1926 (New York: A. M. Kelley, 1966).
Coase, R. H. (1939), 'The nature of the firm', *Economica*, n.s. vol. 4, nos 13–16, pp. 386–405.
Coase, R. H. (1960), 'The problem of social cost', *Journal of Law and Economics*, vol. 3, October, pp. 1-44.
Coats, A. W. (1971), *The Classical Economists and Economic Policy* (London: Methuen).
Cohen, S. F. (1971), *Bukharin and the Bolshevik Revolution: a political biography, 1888–1938* (New York: Vintage, 1973).
Cohn, S. H. (1966), 'Soviet growth retardation: trends in resource availability and efficiency', in US Congress, Joint Economic Committee, *New Directions in the Soviet Economy*, Part II-A (Washington, DC: USGPO).
Cohn, S. H. (1972), 'National income growth statistics', in V. G. Treml and J. P. Hardt (eds), *Soviet Economic Statistics* (Durham, NC: Duke University Press).
Colander, D. C. (ed.) (1985), *Neoclassical Political Economy: the analysis of rent-seeking and DUP activities* (Cambridge, MA: Ballinger).
Colander, D. C. and Klamer, A. (1987), 'The making of an economist', *Journal of Economic Perspectives*, vol. 1, no. 2, fall, pp. 95–111.
Condillac, E. B. de (1776), *Le Commerce et le gouvernement considérés relativement l'un à l'autre*, Amsterdam (Rome: Edizioni Bizzari, 1968).
Coontz, S. H. (1966), *Productive Labor and Effective Demand* (New York: A. M. Kelley).

Cornes, R. and Sandler, T. (1986), *Theory of Externalities, Public Goods and Club Goods* (Cambridge: Cambridge University Press).

Cossa, L. (1893), *An Introduction to the Study of Political Economy* (London: Macmillan, 1980).

Dahrendorf, R. (1979), *Life Chances: an approach to social and political theory* (Chicago, IL: University of Chicago).

Dahrendorf, R. (1981), 'The world-wide shift to the Right', Cummings lecture, McGill University.

Daniels, R. V. (1953), 'The "withering away of the state" in theory and practice', in A. Inkeles and K. Geiger (eds), *Soviet Society: a book of readings* (Boston: Houghton Mifflin, 1961).

Danylyk, J. (1978), 'Towards a reconciliation of Marxist and Western measures of national income' (Washington, DC: CIA, National Foreign Assessment Center).

Davenport, P. (1976), 'Capital accumulation and economic growth', PhD thesis, Department of Political Economy, University of Toronto.

Danziger, S. H. and Weinberg, D. H. (eds) (1986), *Fighting Poverty: what works and what doesn't* (Cambridge, MA: Harvard University Press).

Davies, R. W. (1965), 'Planning for rapid growth in the USSR', *Economics of Planning*, vol. 5, no. 1.

Davies, R. W. (1966), 'The Soviet planning process for rapid industrialisation', *Economics of Planning*, vol. 6, no. 1.

Davydov, I. (1900), 'K voprosu o proizvoditel'nom i neproizvoditel'nom trude' [On the question of productive and unproductive labor], *Nauchnoe obozrenie*, no. 1, pp. 154–63.

De Marchi, N. B. (1972), 'Mill and Cairnes and the emergence of marginalism in England', *History of Political Economy*, vol. 4.

Deane, P. and Cole, W. A. (1967), *British Economic Growth: 1688–1959, trends and structure*, 2nd edn (Cambridge: Cambridge University Press).

Debreu, G. (1959), *Theory of Value: an axiomatic analysis of general equilibrium*, Cowles Foundation monograph 17 (New Haven, CT: Yale University Press).

Dehem, R. (1978), *Précis d'histoire de la théorie économique* (Laval: Presses de l'Université de Laval).

Delaunay, J.-C. (1971), *Essai marxiste sur la comptabilité nationale* (Paris: Editions sociales).

Delofre, F. (1979), 'Notice' to the notes to Voltaire, *L'Homme aux quarante écus*, in Voltaire, *Romans et contes* (Paris: Gallimard, Pléiade).

Denison, E. F. (1962), *The Sources of Economic Growth of the United States and the Alternatives before Us*, Supplementary Paper 13 (New York: Committee for Economic Development).

Denison, E. F. (1967), *Why Growth Rates Differ: postwar experience in nine Western countries* (Washington, DC: Brookings).

Denison, E. F. (1971), 'Welfare measurement and the GNP', *Survey of Current Business*, January.

Denison, E. F. (1974), *Accounting for United States Economic Growth, 1929–1969*, foreword by K. Gordon (Washington, DC: Brookings).

Denison, E. F. (1976), 'The contribution of capital to the the postwar growth of industrial countries', in *US Economic Growth from 1976 to 1986: prospects, problems, and patterns*, Volume 3 – *Capital*, Studies Prepared for the Use of the Joint Economic Committee of the Congress of the United States

(Washington, DC: USGPO).
Dennis, K. (1977), *Competition in the History of Economic Thought* (New York: Arno Press).
Desmars, J. (1900), *Un Précurseur d'Adam Smith en France: J.-J.-L. Graslin, 1727–90* (New York: Burt Franklin, 1973).
Destutt de Tracy, A. L. C. (1817), *A Treatise on Political Economy*, trans. from unpublished ms., intro. Thos. Jefferson (Georgetown, DC: J. Milligan).
Dewey, C. J. (1974), 'The rehabilitation of the peasant proprietor in nineteenth-century economic thought', *History of Political Economy*, vol. 6, no. 1, pp. 17–47.
Dobb, M. (1948), *Soviet Economic Development since 1917*, 1st edn (London: Routledge & Kegan Paul).
Dobb, M. (1973), *Theories of Value and Distribution since Adam Smith: ideology and economic theory* (Cambridge: Cambridge University Press).
Domar, E. D. (1957), 'A Soviet model of growth', in *Essays in the Theory of Economic Growth* (New York: Oxford University Press).
Domar, E. D. (1988), 'The blind man and the elephant', MIT Department of Economics Working Paper no. 473, January.
Dorfman, R., Samuelson, P. A. and Solow, R. M. (1958), *Linear Programming and Economic Analysis* (New York: McGraw-Hill).
Dostaler, G. (1978), *Valeur et prix: histoire d'un débat* (Montreal: Les Presses universitaires de Grenoble, F. Maspero, Les Presses de l'Université du Québec).
Drewnowski, J. (1979), 'The Central Planning Office on trial: an account of the beginnings of Stalinism in Poland', *Soviet Studies*, vol. 21, no. 1, January.
Dubovikov, F. (1923), 'Metody ischisleniia narodnogo dokhoda' [Methods of Calculating National Income], *Vestnik statistiki*, nos 4–6.
Dupont de Nemours, P. S. (1765), 'Préface', *Journal de l'Agriculture*, vol. II.

Eagly, R. V. (1969), 'A Physiocratic model of dynamic equilibrium', *Journal of Political Economy*, vol. XXXVII.
Eagly, R. V. (1974), *The Structure of Classical Economic Theory* (New York: Oxford University Press).
Eckstein, A. (ed.) (1971), *The Comparison of Economic Systems: theoretical and methodological approaches* (Berkeley, CA: University of California Press).
Economic Council of Canada (1979), *One in Three: pensions for Canadians to the year 2030* (Ottawa: Queen's Printer).
Edinburgh Review (1804), 'Review' of Lauderdale, vol. 4, pp. 358–62.
Edwards, I., Hughes, M. and Noren, J. (1979), 'U.S. and U.S.S.R.: comparisons of GNP', US Congress, Joint Economic Committee, *Soviet Economy in a Time of Change*, vol. 1 (Washington, DC: USGPO), pp. 369–401.
Eisner, R. (1988a), 'What's facing the next president?' *Challenge*, vol. 31, no. 4, July–August, pp. 22–31.
Eisner, R. (1988b), 'Extended accounts for national income and product', *Journal of Economic Literature*, vol. 26, no. 4, December, pp. 1611–84.
Ellman, M. (1979), *Socialist Planning* (Cambridge: Cambridge University Press).
Eltis, W. A. (1975a), 'François Quesnay: A reinterpretation, Part One: the Tableau Economique', *Oxford Economic Papers*, vol. 27, no. 2, July.
Eltis, W. A. (1975b), 'François Quesnay: a reinterpretation, Part Two: the theory of economic growth', *Oxford Economic Papers*, vol. 27, no. 3, November.
Eltis, W. A. (1975c), 'Adam Smith's theory of economic growth' in A. S. Skinner and T. Wilson (eds), *Essays on Adam Smith* (Oxford: Clarendon).

Eltis, W. A. (1979), 'Too few producers in Britain and North America', Address to the Empire Club of Canada, 11 January 1979 (Toronto: Canadian Chamber of Commerce).
Eltis, W. A. (1984), *The Classical Theory of Economic Growth* (New York: St Martin's Press).
'The Emaciated Market', review of Bacon and Eltis, *Britain's Economic Problem: Too Few Producers*, The Economist, 24 April 1976.
Erlich, A. (1960), *The Soviet Industrialization Debate: 1924–1928* (Cambridge, MA: Harvard University Press).
Erlich, A. (1971), 'Eastern (Leninist) approaches to a comparative evaluation of economic systems', in A. Eckstein (ed.), *The Comparison of Economic Systems* (Berkeley, CA: University of California Press).
Ezhov, A. I. (ed.) (1965), *Statisticheskii slovar'* [*Dictionary of Statistics*] (Moscow: Statistika).

Falkner-Smit, M. (1929), *La Statistique au pays des Soviets*, 18th session of the Institut international de statistique (Moscow).
Faure-Soulet, J. F. (1964), *Economie politique et progrès au 'siècle des lumières'* (Paris: Gauthier-Villars).
Fei, J. C. and Ranis, G. (1961), 'A theory of economic development', *American Economic Review*, vol. 51, September, pp. 533–65.
Feilbogen, S. (1902), *Smith und Turgot: Ein Beitrag zur Geschichte und Theorie der Nationalökonomie* (Geneva: Slatkine Reprints, 1970).
Feiwel, G. R. (1975), *The Intellectual Capital of Michal Kalecki* (Knoxville, TN: University of Tennessee Press).
Fel'dman, G. A. (1928a,b), 'K teorii tempov narodnogo dokhoda' [On the theory of rates of growth of national income], *Planovoe khoziaistvo*, November and December.
Feldstein, M. S. (1974a), 'Social security, induced retirement, and aggregate capital accumulation', *Journal of Political Economy*, vol. 82, no. 5.
Feldstein, M. S. (1974b), 'The optimal financing of social security', Harvard Institute of Economic Research Discussion Paper no. 388, November.
Feldstein, M. S. (1977), 'Social security and private savings: international evidence in an extended life-cycle model', in M. S. Feldstein and R. P. Inman (eds), *The Economics of Public Services* (London: Macmillan for the International Economic Association).
Ferber, M. (1975), 'Notes on Maurice Weinrobe's "Household Production: an improvement of the record"' *Review of Income and Wealth*, ser. 21.
Feshbach, M. and Rapawy, S. (1976), 'Soviet population and manpower trends and policies', in US Congress, Joint Economic Committee, *The Soviet Economy in a New Perspective* (Washington, DC: USGPO).
Fieldhouse, D. K. (ed.) (1967), *The Theory of Capitalist Imperialism* (London: Longman).
Fine, B. (1983), 'Productive and unproductive labour', in T. Bottomore *et al.* (eds), *A Dictionary of Marxist Thought* (Cambridge, MA: Harvard University Press).
Fink, R. H. (ed.) (1982), *Supply-Side Economics: a critical appraisal* (Frederick, MD: University Publications of America).
Fischer, D. H. (1970), *Historians' Fallacies* (New York: Harper Torchbooks).
Fisher, A. G. B. (1939), 'Production: primary, secondary, and tertiary', *Economic Record*, vol. 15, June.
Fisher, I. (1896), 'What is capital?' *Economic Journal*, vol. VI, December, pp.

509–34.
Forbonnais, F. V. de (1766), *Elémens du commerce* (Leyden and Paris: chez Briasson).
Forbonnais, V. de. (1767), *Principes et observations économiques* (Amsterdam); Goldsmith-Kress microfilm no. 10277.
Fox-Genovese, E. (1976), *The Origins of Physiocracy: economic revolution and social order in eighteenth-century France* (Ithaca, NY: Cornell University Press).
Freeman, R. D. (1969), 'Adam Smith, education and *laissez-faire*', *History of Political Economy*, vol. 1.
Freimundt, E. N. (1960), 'K istorii balansa narodnogo khoziaistva 1917–1928 gg.' [Towards a history of the balance of the national economy, 1917–1928], in Ts.S.U., *Ocherki po istorii statistiki SSSR*, vol. 3 (Moscow: Gosstatizdat).
Friedman, M. with the assistance of R. D. Friedman (1962), *Capitalism and Freedom* (Chicago, IL: University of Chicago Press).
Friedman, M. and Savage, L. J. (1948), 'The utility analysis of choices involving risk', *Journal of Political Economy*, vol. 56.
Fuchs, V. N. (1965), *The Growing Importance of the Service Industries* (New York: NBER).
Fuchs, V. N. (1968), *The Service Economy* (New York: NBER).

Galiani, F. (1751), *De la Monnaie*, trans. and intro. G.-H. Bousquet et J. Cristafulli (Paris: M. Rivère, 1955).
Galiani, F. (1770a), *Dialogue sur le commerce des bleds* (London, 1770); reprinted in *Illuministi Italiani*, tomo VI, vol. 46, *Opere di Ferdinando Galiani*, ed. F. Dias and E. L. Guerci (Milan: R. Ricciardi, n.d. (circa 1970)).
Galiani, F. (1770b), 'Letter to Suard', in E. Ganzoni, *Ferdinando Galiani, ein verkannter Nationalökonom des 18. Jahrhunderts* (Zurich: Girsberger, 1938).
Ganilh, C. (1812), *Inquiry into the Various Systems of Political Economy*, trans. D. Boileau (London: H. Colburn).
Ganzoni, E. (1938) *Ferdinando Galiani: Ein verkannter Nationalökonom des 18. Jahrhunderts* (Zurich: Girsberger).
Garnier, G. (1796), *Abrégé élémentaire des principes de l'économie politique* (Paris: Agasse); Goldsmith-Kress microfilm no. 16892.
Garnier, G. (1802), 'Notes' to his translation of Adam Smith, *Recherches sur la nature et les causes de la Richesse des Nations*, 5 vols (Paris), vol. 5; Goldsmith-Kress microfilm no. 18412.
Garnier, G. (1843), 'Notes' (abridged) to *Recherches sur la nature et les causes de la Richesse des Nations* (Paris: Guillaumin); reprinted (Osnabruck: Otto Zeller, 1966).
Gatovsky, L. M., Kapustin, E. I. et al. (1977), *Ekonomika razvitogo sotsialisticheskogo obshchestva* [*Economics of Developed Socialist Society*], Institut ekonomiki AN USSR (Moscow: Ekonomika).
Geary, R. C. (1973), 'Reflections on national accounting', *Review of Income and Wealth*, ser. 19.
Gerschenkron, A. (1968a) 'The early phases of industrialization in Russia and their relationship to the historical study of economic growth', in B. E. Supple (ed.), *The Experience of Economic Growth* (New York: Random House).
Gerschenkron, A. (1968b), 'Bad economics and shrewd politics', reprinted in *Continuity in History* (Cambridge, MA: Harvard University Press);
Gerschenkron, A. (1969), 'History of economic doctrines and economic theory', R. T. Ely lecture, *American Economic Review Papers and Proceedings*, vol. LIX, no. 2, May, pp. 1–17.

Gershgorn, V. (1921), 'Struktura i sostav glavkov i tsentrov' ('Structure and composition of glavki and centers'), *Narodnoe khoziaistvo*, no. 4, pp. 41–55.
Gide, C. and Rist C. ([1913] 1915), *History of Economic Doctrines*, trans. R. Richards (Boston, MA: D. C. Heath).
Gilbert, M., Jaszi, G., Denison, E. F., Schwartz. C. F. (1948), 'Objectives of national income measurement: a reply to Professor Kuznets', *Review of Economics and Statistics*, vol. 30, no. 3, August.
Gilder, G. (1980), *Wealth and Poverty* (New York: Basic Books).
Gill, L. (1979), *L'Economie capitaliste*, 2 vols (Montreal: Presses socialistes internationales).
Gill, L., (1986), 'Privatisation, dérèglementation, démantelèment du secteur public: pourquoi?' Université du Québec à Montréal Department of Economics Working Paper, July.
Gillman, J. (1957), *The Falling Rate of Profit* (London: Denis Dobson).
Gillman, J. (1965), *Prosperity in Crisis* (New York: Marzani and Munsell).
Godelier, M. (1972), *Rationality and Irrationality in Economics*, trans. B. Pearce (London: New Left Books).
Goldsmith, R. W. (1961), 'The economic growth of tsarist Russia', *Economic Development and Cultural Change*, vol. 9, April.
Gordon, A. S. (1929), *Sistema planovykh organov SSSR* (Moscow: Izd. Komm. akademii).
Gordon, L. A. and Klopov, E. V. (1972), *Man after Work: social problems of daily life and leisure time, based on the surveys of workers' time budgets in major cities of the european part of the USSR*, trans. J. and K. Bushnell (Moscow: Progress 1975).
Gottlieb, M. (1984), *A Theory of Economic Systems* (New York: Academic Press).
Gough, I. (1972), 'Marx's theory of productive and unproductive labour', *New Left Review*, no. 76, November.
Gough, I. and Harrison, J. (1975), 'Unproductive labour and housework again', *Bulletin of the Conference of Socialist Economists*, winter.
Gould, J. D. (1972), *Economic Growth in History* (London: Methuen).
Grandamy, R. (1973), *La Physiocratie: théorie générale du développement économique*, Preface by Jean Fourastié (Paris, La Haye: Mouton).
Graslin, J.-J.-L. (1767), *Essai analytique sur la richesse et sur l'impôt* (London); Goldsmith-Kress microfilm no. 10266.
Graslin, J.-J.-L. and Baudeau, l'Abbé N. (1777), *Correspondence entre M. Graslin ... et ... M. l'Abbé Baudeau ...* (London: Onfroy); Goldsmith-Kress microfilm no. 11543.2.
Gray, S. (1815), *The Happiness of States* (London: Hatchard); Goldsmith-Kress microfilm no. 21102.
Gray, S. (1817), *All Classes Productive of National Wealth; of the theories of M. Quesnai, Dr. Adam Smith, and Mr. Gray, concerning the production of wealth to the community, analysed and examined by George Purves, L.L.D.* (London); Goldsmith-Kress microfilm no. 21714.
Green, D. I. (1894), 'Pain cost and opportunity cost', *Quarterly Journal of Economics*, January.
Gregory, P. R. (1970), *Socialist and Nonsocialist Industrialization Patterns* (New York: Praeger).
Gregory, P. R. (1982), *Russian National Income, 1885–1913* (Cambridge: Cambridge University Press).
Gregory, P. R. and Stuart, R. C. (1986), *Soviet Economic Structure and Performance*, 3rd edn (New York: Harper & Row).

Greider, W. (1978a,b,c), 'Annals of finance (The Fed)', Parts I, II and III, *The New Yorker*, 9, 16 and 23 November.
Griffith, D. F. (1924), *What is Socialism?* (London: Richards).
Groenewegen, P. D. (1969), 'Turgot and Adam Smith', *Scottish Journal of Political Economy*, vol. XVI, no. 3, November.
Groenewegen, P. D. (1977), 'Introduction' to *The Economics of A. R. J. Turgot*, ed. Groenewegen (The Hague: Martinus Nijhoff).
Gromov, E. (1968), 'Ekonomicheskaia rol' sfery uslug' [Economic role of the service sphere], *Mirovaia ekonomika i mezhdunarodnye otnosheniia*, no. 11.
Gronau, R. (1973), 'The measurement of output in the non-market sector: the evaluation of housewives' time', in M. Moss (ed.), *The Measurement of Real Product* (New York: NBER).
Grossman, G. (1973), 'Russia and the Soviet Union', in C. M. Cipolla (ed.), *The Emergence of Industrial Societies*, vol. 4, Part 2 of the *Fontana Economic History of Europe* (London: Collins/Fontana).
Grossman, G. (1977), "The second economy" of the USSR', *Problems of Communism*, vol. 26, September–October, pp. 25–40.
Gur'ev, V. (1967), 'Novaia klassifikatsiia otraslei narodnogo khoziaistva i promyshlennosti' [New classification of the branches of the national economy and of industry], *Vestnik statistiki*, no. 1.
Guroff, G. (1971), 'The legacy of pre-revolutionary economic education: the St Petersburg Polytechnic Institute', *Russian Review*, vol. 31, pp. 272–80.

Hadjimatheou, G. and A. Skouras (1979), 'Britain's economic problem: the growth of the non-market sector?', *Economic Journal*, vol. 89, pp. 392–401.
Hahn, F. (1973), *On the Notion of Equilibrium in Economics: an inaugural lecture* (Cambridge: Cambridge University Press).
Harberger, A. C. (1954), 'Monopoly and resource allocation', *American Economic Review*, vol. 44, May, pp. 77–87.
Harbison, F. (1973), *Human Resources as the Wealth of Nations* (Oxford: Oxford University Press).
Harrison, J. (1973a), 'Productive and unproductive labour in Marx's political economy', *Bulletin of the Conference of Socialist Economists*, autumn.
Harrison, J. (1973b), 'The Political Economy of Housework', *Bulletin of the Conference of Socialist Economists*, winter.
Hartwell, R. M. (1971), *The Industrial Revolution and Economic Growth* (London: Methuen).
Hartwell, R. M. (1973), 'The Services Revolution: the growth of services in the modern economy 1700–1914', in C. M. Cipolla (ed.), *The Industrial Revolution*, vol. 3 of *The Fontana Economic History of Europe* (Glasgow: Fontana/Collins).
Hasbach, W. (1905), 'Germain Garnier als erster Aufsteller der Abstinenztheorie', *Schmoller's Jahrbuch*.
Hawrylyshyn, O. (1976), 'Towards a definition of non-market activities', *Review of Income and Wealth*, ser. 22.
Hawrylyshyn, O. (1977), 'The value of household services: a survey of empirical estimates', *Review of Income and Wealth*, ser. 23.
Hayek, F. A. von (ed.) (1935), *Collectivist Economic Planning* (London: Routledge).
Hayek, F. A. von (1966), 'Dr. Bernard Mandeville', *Proceedings of the British Academy*, vol. 52.
Heckscher, E. F. (1936), *Mercantilism*, trans. M. Shapiro 1936, ed. E. F. Sodelund (London: Allen & Unwin, 1955).

Herlitz, L. (1961), 'The Tableau Economique and the Physiocratic doctrine of sterility', *Scandinavian Economic History Review*, vol. IX, no. 1.
Herlitz, L. (1962), 'Trends in the development of Physiocratic doctrine', *Scandinavian Economic History Review*, vol. IX, no. 2.
Hermann, F. B. W. (1832), *Staatswirtschaftliche Untersuchungen* (Leipzig: Lorenz 1924).
Hicks, J. R. (1932), *The Theory of Wages* (Oxford: Oxford University Press).
Hicks, J. R. (with U. K. Hicks) (1939), 'Public finance in the national income', *Review of Economic Studies*, vol. VI, no. 2, February.
Hicks, J. R. (1940), 'The valuation of the social product', *Economica*, December.
Hicks, J. (1965), *Capital and Growth* (Oxford: Oxford University Press).
Hicks, J. (1969), *A Theory of Economic History* (Oxford: Clarendon Press).
Hilferding, R. (1904), 'Böhm-Bawerks Marx-Kritik', *Marx-Studien*, vol. I, Vienna; trans. in Paul M. Sweezy (ed.), *Karl Marx and the Close of his System* (New York: A. M. Kelley 1966).
Hilferding, R. (1910), *Das Finanzkapital, Marx-Studien*, vol. III, Vienna; excerpted in D. K. Fieldhouse (ed.), *The Theory of Capitalist Imperialism* (London: Longman 1967).
Hill, T. P. (1971), *The Measurement of Real Product: a theoretical and empirical analysis of the growth rates for different countries* (Paris: OECD).
Hill, T. P. (1977), 'On goods and services', *Review of Income and Wealth*, ser. 23, pp. 315–38.
Hirsch, F. M. (1976), *The Social Limits to Growth* (Cambridge, MA: Harvard University Press).
Hirschleifer, J. (1985), 'The expanding domain of economics', *American Economic Review*, vol. 75, no. 6, December, pp. 53–68.
Hirschman, A. O. (1958), *The Strategy of Economic Development* (New Haven: Yale University Press).
Hirschman, A. O. (1970), *Exit, Voice and Loyalty* (Cambridge, MA: Harvard University Press).
Hirschman, A. O. (1977), *The Passions and the Interests: political arguments for capitalism before its triumph* (Princeton, NJ: Princeton University Press).
Hirschman, A. O. (1982), 'Rival interpretations of market society: civilizing, destructive, or feeble?', *Journal of Economic Literature*, vol. XX, no. 4, December, pp. 1463–83.
HMSO (1919), *Monthly Bulletin of Statistics*, year 1, vol. 1, Bulletin 1, July.
Hofmann, W. (1965), *Einkommenstheorie. Vom Merkantilismus bis zur Gegenwart* (Berlin: Duncker und Humblot).
Holesovsky, V. (1961), 'Karl Marx and Soviet national income theory', *American Economic Review*, vol. 51.
Hollander, S. (1973), *The Economics of Adam Smith* (Toronto: University of Toronto Press).
Hollander, S. (1975), 'Attack the best defense', *History of Political Economy*, vol. 6.
Hollander, S. (1976), 'Ricardianism, J. S. Mill and the neo-classical challenge', in J. Robson and M. Laine (eds), *James and John Stuart Mill Centenary Papers* (Toronto: University of Toronto Press).
Hollander, S. (1979), *The Economics of David Ricardo* (Toronto: University of Toronto Press).
Hollander, S. (1984), 'Marx and Malthusianism: Marx's secular path of wages', *American Economic Review*, vol. 74, no. 1, pp. 139–51.

Hollander, S. (1985), *The Economics of John Stuart Mill*, 2 vols (Toronto and Buffalo: University of Toronto Press).
Hollander, S. (1987), *Classical Economics* (Oxford: Blackwell).
Holzman, F. (1956), 'Consumer sovereignty and the rate of economic development', *Economia Internazionale*, vol. XI, no. 2.
Hook, S. (1933), 'Materialism', *Encyclopedia of the Social Sciences*, vol. 10.
Hook, S. (1950), *From Hegel to Marx: Studies in the Intellectual Development of Karl Marx* (Ann Arbor, MI: Ann Arbor Paperbacks, 1971).
Hope, B. F. (1979), 'The concept of productive and unproductive labor in classical economics', PhD thesis, Department of Economics, University of California at Riverside; University microfilm no. 7918249.
Houghton, R. W. (ed.) (1973), *Public Finance*, 2nd edn (Harmondsworth: Penguin).
Howard, M. C. and King, J. E. (eds) (1976), *The Economics of Marx* (Harmondsworth: Penguin).
Howell, P. (1975), 'Once again on productive and unproductive labour', *Revolutionary Communist*, November.
Howey, R. S. (1960), *The Rise of the Marginal Utility School, 1870–1889* (Lawrence, KS: University of Kansas).
Howey, R. S. (1982), *A Bibliography of General Histories of Economics, 1692–1975* (Lawrence, KS: Regents Press of Kansas).
Hunt, E. K. (1979), 'The categories of productive and unproductive labor in Marxist economic theory', *Science and Society*, vol. 43, no. 3, fall.
Hunter, H. (1972), 'Soviet economic statistics: an introduction', in V. G. Treml and J. P. Hardt (eds), *Soviet Economic Statistics* (Durham, NC: Duke University Press).

Ietto Gillies, G. (1978), 'Does the state produce luxuries? A critique of Bacon and Eltis', *British Review of Economic Issues*, no. 2, May, pp. 25–46.
Inman, R. P. (1977), 'Summary record of discussion', in M. S. Feldstein and R. P. Inman (eds), *The Economics of Public Services* (London: Macmillan for IEA).
Institut Marksa-Engel'sa-Lenina-Stalina pri TsK KPSS (1953), *KPSS v rezoliutsiiakh i resheniiakh [Resolutions and Decisions of the Communist Party of the Soviet Union]*, Part II, 7th edn, 1925–1953 (Moscow: Gosizdat politicheskoi literatury).
International Labour Office (1977), *Employment, Growth and Basic Needs: A One-World Problem: the international 'Basic-Needs Strategy' against chronic poverty ... and the decisions of the 1976 World Employment Conference*, intro. J. P. Grant (New York: Praeger for the Overseas Development Council in cooperation with the ILO).
International Labour Office (1979), *Poverty and Basic Needs* (Geneva: ILO).
Isaev, A. A. (1894), *Nachala politicheskoi ekonomiki [Principles of Political Economy]* (St Petersburg: Tsinzerling, 1905).
Ischboldin, B. (1971), *History of the Russian NonMarxian Social-Economic Thought* (New Delhi: New Book Society of India).
Ivanov, G. P. (1987), *Neproizvodstvennaia sfera i sotsialisticheskoe vosproizvodstvo [The Nonproductive Sphere and Socialist Reproduction]* (Moscow: Izd. Moskovskogo Universiteta).
Ivanov, Iu. (1987), 'Possibilities and problems of reconciliation of the SNA and the MPS', *Review of Income and Wealth*, ser. 33, no. 1, pp. 1–18.

Jasny, N. (1972), *Soviet Economists of the Twenties: Names to Be Remembered* (Cam-

bridge: Cambridge University Press).
Jefferson, Th. (1817), 'Introduction' to American edn of A. L. C. Destutt de Tracy, *A Treatise on Political Economy* (Georgetown, DC: J. Milligan).
Jevons, W. S. ([1879] 1965), 'Preface to the second edition', *Theory of Political Economy* (1st edn, 1871) (New York: A. M. Kelley).
John, A. H. and Zauberman, A. (1972), 'Industrialization', in C. D. Kernig (ed.), *Marxism, Communism, and Western Society* (New York: Herder & Herder).
Johnson, E. A. J. (1937), *Predecessors of Adam Smith: The Growth of British Economic Thought* (New York: A. M. Kelley, 1965).
Jones, E. L. (1981), *The European Miracle* (Cambridge: Cambridge University Press).
Jorgensen, D. W. and Griliches, Z. (1967), 'The explanation of productivity change', *Review of Economic Studies*, July.
Juster, F. T. (1973), 'A framework for the measurement of economic and social performance', in M. Moss (ed.), *The Measurement of Economic and Social Performance* (New York: NBER).
Juster, F. T., Courant, P. N. and Dow, G. K. (1981), 'A theoretical framework for the measurement of well-being', *Review of Income and Wealth*, ser. 27, no. 1, March, pp. 1–32.

Kahn, Lord (1977), 'Mr. Eltis and the Keynesians', *Lloyd's Bank Review*, no. 124, April.
Kaldor, N. (1966), *Causes of the Slow Rate of Growth of the United Kingdom: an inaugural lecture* (Cambridge: Cambridge University Press).
Kalecki, M. (1963), 'Introduction to the theory of growth in a socialist economy', trans. Z. Sadowski; reprinted in *Selected Essays on the Economic Growth of the Socialist and Mixed Economy* (Cambridge: Cambridge University Press, 1972).
Kalecki, M. (1967), 'The problem of effective demand with Tugan-Baranovski and Rosa Luxemburg'; reprinted in *Selected Essays on the Dynamics of the Capitalist Economy* (Cambridge: Cambridge University Press, 1971).
Kapeliushnikov, R. I. (1981), 'Kontseptsiia "chelovecheskogo kapitala"' [The concept of 'human capital'], in A. G. Mileitskovskii and I. M. Osadchaia (eds), *Kritika sovremennoi burzhuaznoi politekonomii* [*Critique of Contemporary Bourgeois Political Economy*] (Moscow: Nauka).
Kapustin, E. I. (ed.) (1968), *Sfera obsluzhivaniia pri sotsializme* [*The Service Sphere under Socialism*] (Moscow: Mysl').
Karataev, N. K. (1956), *Ekonomicheskie nauki v moskovskom universitete (1755-1955)* [*Economic Sciences at Moscow University, 1755–1955*] (Moscow: Izd. moskovskogo universiteta).
Karataev, N. K. (1966), *Ekonomiks - burzhuaznaia politekonomiia* [*Economics - Bourgeois Political Economy*] (Moscow: Nauka).
Kaser, M. C. (1966), 'The Soviet ideology of industrialization: a review article', *Journal of Development Studies*, vol. 3, October.
Kaser, M. C. (1970), *Soviet Economics* (New York: McGraw-Hill).
Katsenelinboigen, A. (1977), 'Coloured markets in the Soviet Union', *Soviet Studies*, vol. 29, January.
Katsenelinboigen, A. (1980), *Soviet Economic Thought and Political Power in the USSR* (New York: Pergamon Press).
Katsenelinboigen, A. (1981), 'Jews in Soviet economic science', *Soviet Jewish Affairs*, vol. 11, no. 1.
Kauder, E. (1965), *A History of Marginal Utility Theory* (Princeton, NJ: Princeton

University Press).
Kautsky, K. (1887), *Karl Marx's ökonomische Lehren* I Serie, Band 2 (Stuttgart: Bibliothek Internationale).
Kautsky, K, (1891), *The Class Struggle (The Erfurt Program)*, trans. and abridged W. E. Bohn from 8th edn (1907) (Chicago: Charles Kerr 1910).
Kautsky, K. (1899), *Die Agrarfrage: eine Übersicht über die Tendenzen der modernen Landwirtschaft und die Agrarpolitik der Sozialdemokratie* (Stuttgart: Dietz).
Kautsky, K. (1905), *Ekonomicheskoe uchenie Karla Marksa v izlozhenii K. Kautskago* [*The Economic Teachings of Karl Marx as Set out by K. Kautsky*], 2nd edn (St Petersburg: Sever').
Kautsky, K. (ed.) (1905–10), Karl Marx, *Theorien über den Mehrwert* [*Theories of Surplus-Value*], 3 vols (Stuttgart: Dietz).
Kautsky, K. (1921), *Von der Demokratie zur Staats-sklaverei: Ein Auseinandersetzung mit Trotzki* (Berlin: Freiheit).
Kautsky, K. (1927), *Die materialistische Geschichtsauffassung* (Berlin: Dietz).
Kaye, F. B. (1924), 'Commentary, critical, historical and explanatory', introduction to B. de Mandeville, *The Fable of the Bees: or, Private Vices, Publick Benefits* (Oxford: Clarendon Press).
Kendrick, J. W. (1968), 'National income and product accounts', *International Encyclopedia of the Social Sciences*.
Kendrick, J. W. (1970), 'The historical development of national income accounts' *History of Political Economy*, vol. 2.
Kendrick, J. W. (1971), 'The treatment of intangible resources as capital', paper presented to the Twelfth General Conference of the International Association for Research in Income and Wealth, Ronneby, Sweden, September.
Keynes, J. M. (1926a), *The End of Laissez-Faire* (London: Hogarth).
Keynes, J. M. (1926b), *Laissez-Faire and Communism* (New York: New Republic).
Keynes, J. M. (1933), *Essays in Biography*; in D. Moggridge (ed.), *The Collected Writings of John Maynard Keynes*, vol. X (London: Macmillan, St Martin's Press 1971).
Keynes, J. M. (1936), *The General Theory of Employment, Interest, and Money* (London: Macmillan, St Martin's Press).
Keynes, J. N. (1891), *Scope and Method of Political Economy* (London: Macmillan).
Khavina, S. A. et al. (1975, 1976), *Burzhuaznye i mel'koburzhuaznye ekonomicheskie teorii sotsializma (kriticheskie ocherki)* [*Bourgeois and Petty-Bourgeois Economic Theories of Socialism (Critical Essays)*], vol. II, *1917–1945*, vol. III, *1945–1970* (Moscow: Nauka).
Kidron, M. (1970), *Western Capitalism since the War* (1st edn, 1968) (Harmondsworth: Pelican).
Kidron, M. (1971), 'Capitalism — the latest stage', in N. Harris and J. Palmer (eds), *World Crisis: Essays in Revolutionary Socialism* (London: Hutchinson).
Kidron, M. (1974), *Capitalism and Theory* (London: Pluto Press).
Kindersley, R. (1962), *The First Russian Revisionists* (Oxford: Clarendon Press).
King, G. (1696), 'Natural and Political Observations and Conclusions upon the State and Condition of England'; facsimile reprint in P. Laslett (ed.), *The Earliest Classics: John Graunt ... (and) ... Gregory King ...*, Pioneers of Demography Series (Farnborough: Gregg International Publishers 1973).
Klamer, A. (1983), *Conversations with Economists* (Totowa, NJ: Rowman and Allanheld).
Kneller, G. F. (1968), *Education and Economic Thought* (New York: John Wiley).
Knight, F. H. (1953), 'Is group choice a part of economics? - comment', *Quarterly Journal of Economics*, vol. 67.

Knight, F. H. (1962), 'Capital and interest', *Encyclopaedia Britannica*, vol. 4.
Kofman, B. (1929), *Proizvoditel'nyi trud i metod Marksa* [Productive labor and Marx's Method] (Leningrad: Priboi).
Kolakowski, L. (1974), 'Marxist roots of Stalinism', in R. C. Tucker (ed.), *Stalinism* (New York: Norton).
Kolakowski, L. (1978), *Main Currents of Marxism*, 3 vols (Oxford: Oxford University Press).
Kolakowski, L. and Hampshire, S. (eds) (1974), *The Socialist Idea* (London: Weidenfeld & Nicholson).
Kolganov, M. V. (1959), *Natsional'nyi dokhod* [National Income] (Moscow: Gosizdat politicheskoi literatury).
Koopmans, T. W. (1964), 'Economic growth at a maximal rate'; reprinted in A. K. Sen (ed.), *Growth Economics* (Harmondsworth: Penguin 1970).
Korchagin, V. P. and Sbytova, L. S. (1970), *Sfera uslug i zaniatost' naseleniia* [The Service Sphere and Employment of the Population] (Moscow: Ekonomika).
Koriagin, A. (1968), 'Sfera uslug i problemy proizvoditel'nogo truda' [The service sphere and problems of productive labor], *Mirovaia ekonomika i mezhdunarodnye otnosheniia*, no. 7.
Kornai, J. (1980), *The Economics of Shortage*, 2 vols (Amsterdam: North Holland).
Kornai, J. (1982), 'Adjustment to price and quantity signals in a socialist economy', *Economie appliquée*, vol. XXXV, no. 3, pp. 503–24.
Kovyzhenko, V. (1968), 'Stoimost' uslug: real'nost ili fiktsiia?' [Value of services: reality or fiction?], *Mirovaia ekonomika i mezhdunarodnye otnosheniia*, no. 8.
Koziolek, H. (1957), *Grundfragen der marxistisch-leninistischen Theorie des Nationaleinkommens: Sozialismus* (Berlin: Die Wirtschaft).
Kozlov, G. A. and Pervushin S. P. (eds.) (1958), *Kratkii ekonomicheskii slovar'* [Short Dictionary of Economics] (Moscow: Gospolitizdat).
KPSS (1953), see Institut Marksa-Engel'sa-Lenina-Stalina.
Krasnolobov, I. (1940), *Planirovanie i uchet narodnogo dokhoda* [Planning and Accounting of National Income] (Moscow: TsUNKhU).
Kravis, I. B., Heston, A. and Summers, R. (1982), *Phase III: World Product and Income* (Baltimore, MD: Johns Hopkins for World Bank).
Kravis, I. B., Heston, A. and Summers, R. (1983), 'The share of services in economic growth', in F. F. Adams and B. Hickman (eds), *Global Econometrics* (Cambridge, MA: MIT Press).
Kravis, I. B., Heston, A. and Summers, R. (1986), *Phase IV: World Comparisons of Purchasing Power and Real Product for 1980* (New York: United Nations).
Kronrod, Ja. A. (1948), 'Grundprobleme der marxistisch-leninistischen Theorie von der produktiven und unproduktiven Arbeit in Kapitalismus und Sozialismus', *Sowjetwissenschaft*, vol. 4.
Kronrod, Ya. A. (1947), 'Fundamental questions of Marxist–Leninist teaching on productive labor in capitalism and socialism', *Izvestiia Akademii Nauk SSSR*, Otdelenie ekonomiki i prava, no. 1.
Kronrod, Ya. A. (1958), *Voprosy sotsialisticheskogo vosproizvodstva* [Problems of Socialist Reproduction](Moscow: Akademiia Nauk).
Krueger, A. O. (1974), 'The political economy of the rent-seeking society', *American Economic Review*, vol. 64, June, pp. 291–303.
Krylatykh, E. (1985). 'Sistemnoe razvitie ekonomicheskoi nauki' [The systemic development of economic science], *Voprosy ekonomiki*, no. 10, pp. 119–29.
Kuczynski, M. and Meek, R. L. (eds) (1972), *Quesnay's Tableau Économique* (London: Macmillan).

Kudrova, E. M. (1969), *Statistika natsional'nogo dokhoda sotsialisticheskikh stran* [*National Income Statistics of Socialist Countries*] (Moscow: Statistika).

Kursky, A. (1940), 'Review' of D. I. Chernomordik (ed.), *Narodnyi dokhod SSSR* (1939), *Planovoe khoziaistvo*, no. 1, pp. 104–6.

Kurtzweg, L. (1987), 'Trends in Soviet gross national product', in US Congress, Joint Economic Committee, *Gorbachev's Economic Plans* (Washington, DC: USGPO), pp. 126–65.

Kuznets, S. S. (1934), *National Income 1929–32*, doc. no. 124, 73rd Congress, 2nd sess., 4 January (Washington, DC; USGPO).

Kuznets, S. S. (1937), *National Income and Capital Formation, 1919–1935*, Studies in Income and Wealth, vol. I (New York: NBER).

Kuznets, S. S. (1942), *National Income and its Composition, 1919–1938*, Research Publication no. 40 (New York: NBER).

Kuznets, S. S. (1944), *National Income, a Summary of Findings* (New York: NBER).

Kuznets, S. S. (1946), *National Income and its Composition*, vol. II (New York: NBER).

Kuznets, S. S. (1948), 'National income: a new version', *Review of Economics and Statistics*, vol. 30, no. 3, August.

Kuznets, S. S. (1951), 'Government product and national income', *Income and Wealth*, ed. E. Lundberg, series 1 (Cambridge: Bowes & Bowes).

Kuznets, S. S. (1954), *Economic Change* (London: Heinemann).

Kuznets, S. S. (1963), 'A comparative appraisal', in A. Bergson and S. Kuznets (eds), *Economic Trends in the Soviet Union* (Cambridge, MA: Harvard University Press).

Kuznets, S. S. (1966), *Modern Economic Growth* (New Haven, CT: Yale University Press).

Kuznets, S. S. (1971), *Economic Growth of Nations: Total Output and Production Structure* (Cambridge, MA: Belknap, Harvard University Press).

Kuznets, S. S. (1973), 'Concluding remarks', to M. Moss (ed.), *The Measurement of Economic and Social Performance* (New York: NBER).

Kvasha, Ya. B. (1935), 'Klassifikasiia otraslei promyshlennosti' [Classification of the branches of industry], *Planovoe khoziaistvo*, no. 3.

Kvasha, Ya. B. (1961), 'O granitsakh material'nogo proizvodstva' [On the boundaries of material production], *Uchenye zapiski po statistike*, vol. VI (Moscow: Akademiia nauk SSSR).

Labedz, L. (ed.) (1962), *Revisionism* (London: Allen & Unwin).

Laird, B. D. (1970), *Soviet Communism and Agrarian Revolution* (Harmondsworth: Penguin).

Lal, D. (1983), *The Poverty of Development Economics* (London: IEA).

Lancaster, K. J. (1966), 'A new approach to consumer theory', *Journal of Political Economy*, vol. 74, no. 2, pp. 132–57.

Lancaster, K. J. (1972), *Matematicheskaia ekonomkia*, trans. T. Bereznevaia and D. B. Iudin (Moscow: Sovetskoe Radio).

Lange, O. (1935), 'Marxian economics and modern economic theory', *Review of Economic Studies*, June.

Lange, O. and Taylor, F. M. ([1938] 1964), *On the Economic Theory of Socialism*; ed. and intro. B. Lippincott (New York: McGraw-Hill).

Lange, O. (1963), *Political Economy, volume I: General Problems*, trans. A. H. Walker (New York: Macmillan, Pergamon Press).

Langer, G. F. (1987), *The Coming of Age of Political Economy, 1815–1825* (Westport, CT: Greenwood Press).

Laslett, P. (ed.) (1973), *The Earliest Classics: John Graunt ... (and) ... Gregory King ...,* Pioneers of Demography Series (Farnsborough: Gregg International Publishers).

Latsis, O. R. (1987), 'Individual labor in a modern socialist economy', *Problems of Economics,* August, pp. 37–49; reprinted from *Kommunist,* no. 1, 1987.

Launay, J. (1968), 'Réflexions sur le concept de production', *Economie et Politique,* no. 170, September.

Lauraguais, L. de. (1769), 'Discours sur le commerce', *Journal de l'Argriculture,* November.

Lavergne, L. de (1870), *Les Économistes français du dix-huitième siècle* (Geneva: Slatkine Reprints, 1970).

Lavigne, M. (1979), *Les Économies socialistes soviétique et européennes,* 3rd edn (Paris: Armand Colin).

Lavoie, D. (1985), *National Economic Planning: what is left?* (Cambridge, MA: Ballinger Press).

Lavoie, M. (1987), 'Un Syndical préfère-t-il une théorie monétariste, marxiste ou post-keynésienne du chômage?', paper presented at Keynes colloquium of l'Association d'économie politique, Montreal, January.

Layard, R. (1972), 'Introduction', to R. Layard (ed.), *Cost–Benefit Analysis* (Harmondsworth: Penguin 1977).

Leadbeater, D. (1985), 'The consistency of Marx's categories of productive and unproductive labour', *History of Political Economy,* vol. 17, no. 4, pp. 591–619.

Le Mercier de la Rivière, P. F. J. H. (1767), *L'Ordre essentiel et naturel des sociétés politiques* (published anonymously); (London: Jean Nourse; Paris: Desaint).

League of Nations (1925), *Monthly Bulletin of Statistics* (Geneva), vol. 6, no. 1 January.

Leeman, W. A. (1977), *Centralized and Decentralized Economic Systems* (Chicago, IL: Rand McNally).

Leibenstein, H. (1966), 'Allocative efficiency vs. X-efficiency' *American Economic Review,* vol. 56, June, pp. 392–415.

Leibenstein, H. (1976), *Beyond Economic Man,* 1st edn (Cambridge, MA: Harvard University Press).

Leiss, W. R. (1976), *The Limits to Satisfaction: an essay on the problem of needs and commodities* (Toronto: University of Toronto Press).

Lenin, V. I. (1898), 'Review of Bogdanov, in *Collected Works,* vol. 4 (Moscow: Foreign Languages Publishing House, 1960), pp. 46–54.

Lenin, V. I. (1899), *The Development of Capitalism in Russia: The Process of the Formation of a Home Market for Large-Scale Industry,* in *Collected Works,* vol. 3 (Moscow: Foreign Languages Publishing House, 1960).

Lenin, V. I. (1909), *Materialism and Empiriocriticism: critical comments on a reactionary philosophy;* in *Collected Works,* vol. 14 (Moscow: Foreign Languages Publishing House, 1960).

Lenin, V. I. (1913), 'The three sources and three component parts of Marxism', in *Collected Works,* vol. 19 (Moscow: Foreign Languages Publishing House, 1960).

Lenin, V. I. (1914a), 'Karl Marx', in *Collected Works,* vol. 19 (Moscow: Foreign Languages Publishing House, 1960).

Lenin, V. I. (1914b), 'Socialism demolished again', in *Collected Works,* vol. 20 (Moscow: Foreign Languages Publishing House, 1960).

Lenin, V. I. (1917a), *State and Revolution,* in *Collected Works,* vol. 25 (Moscow: Foreign Languages Publishing House, 1960).

Lenin, V. I. (1917b), 'Can the Bolsheviks retain state power?', in *Collected Works*, vol. 26, (Moscow: Foreign Languages Publishing House, 1960).

Lenin, V. I. (1917c), 'The impending catastrophe and how to combat it', in *Collected Works*, vol. 25 (Moscow: Foreign Languages Publishing House, 1960).

Lenin, V. I. (1919a), 'A great beginning', in *Collected Works*, vol. 29 (Moscow: Foreign Languages Publishing House, 1960).

Lenin, V. I. (1919b), 'The tasks of the working women's movement in the Soviet Republic', in *Collected Works*, vol. 30 (Moscow: Foreign Languages Publishing House, 1960).

Lenin, V. I. (1950), *Sochineniia [Works]* (Leningrad).

Lenin, V. I. (1965), *On the Emancipation of Women* (Moscow: Progress, 1974).

Leont'ev, L. A. (1960), *Nachal'nyi kurs politicheskoi ekonomii [Introductory Course of Political Economy]* (Moscow: Gosizdat politicheskoi literatury).

Leontief, W. W. (1925), 'The balance of the economy of the USSR', *Planovoe khoziaistvo*, no. 12; trans. in N. Spulber (ed.), *Foundations of Soviet Strategy for Economic Growth, Selected Soviet Essays: 1924–1930* (Bloomington, IN: Indiana University Press, 1964).

Leontief, W. W. (1938), 'The significance of Marxian economics for present-day economic theory', *American Economic Review Papers and Proceedings*, vol. 28, no. 1, March.

Leontief, W. W. (1941), *The Structure of the American Economy: 1919–1939* (New York: Oxford University Press).

Leontief, W. W. (1951), *Input–Output Economics* (New York: Oxford University Press, 1966).

Leontief, W. W. (1960), 'The decline and rise of Soviet economic science', *Foreign Affairs*, vol. 38, January.

Leontief, W. W. (1966), *Essays in Economics* (Oxford: Oxford University Press).

Leontyev, L. (L. A. Leont'ev) (1968), *A Short Course of Political Economy*, trans. D. Danemanis (Moscow: Progress).

Lerner, A. P. (1944), *The Economics of Control* (Cambridge, MA: Harvard University Press).

Levine, H. S. (1972), 'Consumption', in C. D. Koernig (ed.), *Marxism, Communism, and Western Society* (New York: Herder & Herder).

Lewin, M. (1966), *Russian Peasants and Soviet Power, a study of collectivization*, trans. I. Nove and J. Biggart, preface by A. Nove (New York: Norton, 1968).

Lewin, M. (1975), *Political Undercurrents in Soviet Economic Debates: from Bukharin to the modern reformers* (London: Pluto Press).

Lewis, R. (1973), *The New Service Society* (London: Longman).

Lewis, W. A. (1954), 'Economic development with unlimited supplies of labour', *The Manchester School*, May 1954; reprinted in A. N. Agarwala and S. P. Singh (eds), *The Economics of Development* (Oxford: Oxford University Press, 1958).

Lewis, W. A. (1978), *The Evolution of the International Economic Order*, Janeway Lecture in Honor of Joseph Schumpeter (Princeton, NJ: Princeton University Press).

Lexis, W. (1899), 'Produktion', *Handwörterbuch der Staatswissenschaft* (Jena: Fischer Verlag).

Liberman, E. (1955), 'Khoziaistvennyi raschet i material'noie pooshchrenie rabotnikov promyshlennosti' [Economic accounting and material stimulation of workers in industry], *Voprosy ekonomiki*, no. 6, pp. 34–44.

Lichtheim, G. (1969), *Marxism: an historical and critical study* (New York: Praeger).

Lifshits, A. L. (1963), 'Proizvoditel'nyi i neproizvoditel'nyi trud v sotsialisticheskom obshchestve' [Productive and unproductive labor in socialist society], in Ya. A. Kronrod (ed.), *Problemy politicheskoi ekonomii sotsializma* (Moscow: Gospolitizdat).
Lindahl, E. (1919), 'Just taxation – a positive solution'; trans. in R. A. Musgrave and A. T. Peacock (eds), *Classics in the Theory of Public Finance* (New York: St Martin's Press, 1958), pp. 168–76.
Lindbeck, A. (1976), 'Stabilization policies in open economies with endogenous politicians', *American Economic Review*, vol. 66, May, L pp. 1–19.
Lindblom, C. E. (1977), *Politics and Markets* (New York: Basic Books).
Lippi, M. (1979), *Value and Naturalism in Marx* (London: NLB).
Liser, F. B. (1979), 'Statistical annexes' to M. McLaughlin (ed.) for Overseas Development Council, *The United States and World Development: agenda 1979* (New York: Praeger).
Litoshenko, L. N. (1925), *Natsional'syi dokhod SSSR* (Moscow: Finansovoe izdatel'stvo).
Litoshenko, L. N. (1926a), 'Natsional'nyi dokhod', *Vestnik finansov*, no. 2.
Litoshenko, L. N. (1926b),'The method of constructing an economic balance', in P. I. Popov (ed.), *Balance of the National Economy of the USSR, 1923–1924*, vol. XXIX of *Works* (Moscow: Works of the Central Statistical Administration) reprinted in N. Spulber (ed.), *Foundations of Soviet Strategy for Economic Growth: Selected Soviet Essays: 1924–1930* (Bloomington, IN: Indiana University Press, 1964).
Longfield, M. (1834), *Lectures on Political Economy* (Dublin: Curry).
Luxemburg, R. (1913), *The Accumulation of Capital*; intro. J. Robinson, trans. A. Schwartschild (New York: Monthly Review, 1968).
Luxemburg, R. and Bukharin, N. (1972), *Imperialism and the Accumulation of Capital*, comp. and trans. R. Wichmann (London: Penguin and Allen Lane).

McCulloch, J. R. (1825), *Principles of Political Economy*, 1st edn; reprint of 1864 edn (New York: A. M. Kelley, 1951).
McCulloch, J. R. (1845) *The Literature of Political Economy* (London: Longman).
McLain, J. L. (1977), *The Economic Writings of Dupont de Nemours* (Newark, DL: University of Delaware Press).
McLellan, D. (1971), *Marx before Marxism* (New York: Harper Torchbooks).
Maddison, A. (1969), *Economic Growth in Japan and the USSR* (New York: Norton).
Maddison, A. (1982), *Phases of Capitalist Development* (Oxford: Oxford University Press).
Maddock, R. and Carter, M. (1982), 'A child's guide to rational expectations', *Journal of Economic Literature*, vol. 20, no. 1, pp. 39–51.
Maitland, J., 8th Earl of Lauderdale (1819), *An Inquiry into the Nature and Origin of Public Wealth: and into the Means and Causes of its Increase*, 2nd edn; 1st edn 1804; M. Paglin (ed.) (New York: A. M. Kelley, 1966).
Makasheva, N. A. (1987), *Konservativnoe napravlenie v sovremennoi burzhuaznoi ekonomicheskoi nauke: neoavstriiskaia shkola* [*The Conservative Current in Contemporary Bourgeois Economics: the neo-Austrian school*] (Moscow: INION AN SSR).
Makasheva, N. A. (1988), *SShA: Konservativnye tendentsii v ekonomicheskoi teorii* [*USA: Conservative Trends in Economic Theory*] (Moscow: Nauka).
Malinowski, B. (1922), *Argonauts of the Western Pacific* (New York: E. P. Dutton 1961).

Malle, S. (1985), *The Economic Organization of War Communism: 1918–1921* (Cambridge: Cambridge University Press).

Malthus, T. R. (1820), *Principles of Political Economy* (London); (New York: A. M. Kelley, 1951).

Malthus, T. R. (1827), *Definitions in Political Economy* (New York: Kelley & Millman, 1954).

Mandel, E. (1962), *Marxist Economic Theory*, trans. B. Pearce (London: Merlin Press, 1968).

Mandel, E. (1967), *The Formation of the Economic Thought of Karl Marx: 1843 to Capital*, trans. B. Pearce (New York: Monthly Review, 1971).

Mandeville, B. de (1705), *The Fable of the Bees: or Private Vices, Publick Benefits (by Bernard Mandeville)*, 2nd edn, 1714; variorum edn. with commentary, Critical, Historical, and Explanatory, by F. B. Kaye, 2 vols (Oxford: Clarendon Press, 1924).

Marcovitch, F. J. (1958), 'Le Problème des services et le revenu national', *Bulletin S.E.D.E.I.S.*, no. 699, 1 June.

Marer, P. (1985), *Dollar GNPs of the U.S.S.R. and Eastern Europe* (Baltimore, MD: Johns Hopkins for World Bank).

Marglin, S. A. (1974–5), 'What do bosses do?' *Review of Radical Political Economy*, Part one, 1974, Part two, 1975.

Marris, R. (1984), 'Comparing the incomes of nations', *Journal of Economic Literature*, vol. 22, no. 1, March, pp. 40–57.

Marshall, A. (1890), *Principles of Economics*, 1st edn; 8th edn, 1920 (London: Macmillan, 1960).

Marx et l'économie politique: essais sur les 'Théories sur la plus-value' (1977), (Paris and Grenoble: Maspero and Les Presses Universitaires de Grenoble).

Marx, K. (1857–8), *Grundrisse: Introduction to the Critique of political Economy*, trans. M. Nicolaus (New York: Vintage, 1973).

Marx, K. (1859), 'Preface' and 'Introduction' to *A Contribution to the Critique of Political Economy* (Peking: Foreign Languages Press, 1976).

Marx, K. (1862), *Resultate der Produktionsprozess* (the 'lost' chapter VI of *Capital*, volume I), in K. Marx, *Capital*, vol. I, intro. E. Mandel, trans. B. Fowkes (New York: Vintage, 1977).

Marx, K. (1867), *Capital: A Critical Analysis of Capitalist Production (Das Kapital)*, 1st edn of vol. I; trans. 1887 from the 3rd German edn of 1883 by S. Moore and E. Aveling (Moscow: Progress, 1974).

Marx, K. (1875), *Critique of the Gotha Programme* (Peking: Foreign Languages Publishing House, 1972).

Marx, K. (1885), *Capital: A Critique of Political Economy*, 1st edn of vol. II, ed. F. Engels; trans. I. Lasker (Moscow: Progress, 1977).

Marx, K. (1894), *Capital: A Critique of Political Economy - the process of capitalist production as a Whole*, 1st edn of vol. III, (ed.) F. Engels; trans. Moscow Institute of Marxism-Leninism (Moscow: Progress, 1974).

Marx, K. (1905–10), *Theories of Surplus-Value* [*Theorien über den Mehrwert*], intended as vol. IV of *Capital*, written 1862–3, published in 3 parts, ed. K. Kautsky (Stuttgart: Dietz); Part 1, trans. E. Burns (Moscow: Progress, 1963).

Marx, K. (1952), *A History of Economic Theories* (New York: International Publishers).

Marx, K. and Engels, F. (1848), *The Communist Manifesto* (Peking: Foreign Languages Publishing House, 1971).

(Marx, K. and) Engels, F. (1878), *Anti-Dühring* (Peking: Foreign Languages

Publishing House, 1974).

Marx, K. and Engels, F. (1956), *Marx-Engels-Werke*, 40 vols (Berlin: Dietz Verlag).

Mattick, P. (1969), *Marx and Keynes: the limits of the mixed economy* (Boston: Porter Sargent).

Meade, J. E. and Stone, R. (1941), 'The construction of tables of national income, expenditure, savings and investment', *Economic Journal*; reprinted in R. Parker and G. C. Harcourt (eds), *Readings in the Concept and Measurement of National Income* (Cambridge: Cambridge University Press, 1969).

Medvedev, V. A. *et al.* (1988a, b, c, d), 'Politicheskaia ekonomiia: uchebnik dlia vysshikh uchebnykh zavedenii' (Political economy: a textbook for institutes of higher education), *Ekonomicheskie nauki*, nos. 7, 8, 9, and 10.

Meek, R. L. (1951), 'Physiocracy and Classicism in Britain', *Economic Journal*, March.

Meek, R. L. (1956a), *Studies in the Labour Theory of Value* (New York: Monthly Review, 1975).

Meek, R. L. (1956b), 'Some notes on the transformation problem', *Economic Journal*, March 1956; reprinted in M. C. Howard and J. E. King (eds), *The Economics of Marx* (Harmondsworth: Penguin, 1976).

Meek, R. L. (1963), *The Economics of Physiocracy: essays and translations* (Cambridge, MA: Harvard University Press).

Meek, R. L. (1967), *Economics and Ideology and Other Essays* (London: Chapman & Hall).

Meek, R. L. (1976), *Social Science and the Ignoble Savage* (Cambridge: Cambridge University Press).

Melman, S. (1970), *Pentagon Capitalism* (New York: McGraw-Hill).

Melman, S. (ed. and intro.) (1970), *The Defense Economy: conversion of industries and occupations to civilian needs* (New York: Praeger).

Melman, S. (ed.) (1971), *The War Economy of the United States* (New York: St Martin's Press).

Melman, S. (1985), *The Permanent War Economy: American capitalism in decline*, rev. edn (New York: Simon & Schuster).

Menger, C. (1874), *Principles of Economics*; trans. J. Dingwall and B. Hoselitz (New York: New York University Press, 1976).

Menger, C. (1883), *Problems of Economics and Sociology*, trans. F. J. Nock, ed. L. Schneider (Urbana, IL: University of Illinois, 1963).

Metzger, J. (1969), 'Le Parti Communiste Français et les ingénieurs, cadres, et techniciens', *Economie et Politique*, no. 175, February.

Meyer, C. (1984), *Die volkswirthschaftliche Gesamtrechnung der DDR: Methodik, Inkonsistenzen, Ideologie* (Munich: V. Florentz).

Mikhailov, A. D. (1939), *Promyshlennaia statistika [Industrial Statistics]* (Moscow/Leningrad: Gosplanizat).

Mill, J. (1966), *Selected Economic Writings* (Chicago, IL: University of Chicago Press).

Mill, J. S. (1844), *Essays on Some Unsettled Questions of Political Economy*, written 1829–30; in *Collected Works of John Stuart Mill*, vol. 4, ed. J. Robson (Toronto: University of Toronto Press, 1963).

Mill, J. S. (1848), *Principles of Political Economy*; in *Collected Works of John Stuart Mill*, vols 2 and 3, ed. J. Robson (Toronto: University of Toronto Press, 1963).

Millar, J. R. (1970), 'Soviet rapid development and the agricultural surplus hypothesis', *Soviet Studies*, vol. XXII, no. 1, July.

Millar, J. R. (1974), 'Mass collectivization and the contribution of agriculture to the first five-year plan: a review article', *Slavic Review*, December.

Miller, J. (1968), 'Marxist economic theory in the USSR', in V. Treml and R. Farrell (eds), *The Development of the Soviet Economy: Plan and Performance* (New York: Praeger).

Mirabeau, le Marquis de (1759), *Sur la necessité des encouragements pour l'agriculture*; reprinted in G. Weulersse (ed.) (1910b), *Les Manuscrits économiques de François Quesnay et du Marquis de Mirabeau* (New York: Burt Franklin, 1968).

Mirabeau, le Marquis de (V. Riquetti) (1763), *La Philosophie rurale, ou économie générale et politique de l'agriculture, réduite à l'ordre immuable des lois physiques et morales qui assurent la prospérité des empires* (Amsterdam); Goldsmith-Kress microfilm no. 9836.

Mirabeau, le Marquis de (1767), *Eléments de la philosophie rurale* (The Hague).

Mishan, E. J. (1960), 'A survey of welfare economics', *Economic Journal*, June.

Mishan, E. J. (1973), *Making the World Safe for Pornography* (Lassalle, IL: Library Press).

Mishan, E. J. (1976), 'Comment' on J. M. Buchanan, 'Public goods and natural liberty', in T. Wilson and A. S. Skinner (eds), *The Market and the State: Essays in Honour of Adam Smith* (Oxford: Clarendon Press).

Mishan, E. J. (1977), *The Economic Growth Debate: an assessment* (London: Allen & Unwin).

Mishan, E. J. (1981), *Economic Efficiency and Social Welfare* (London: Allen & Unwin).

Mizuta, H. (1967), *Adam Smith's Library* (Cambridge: Cambridge University Press).

Molinier, J. (1958), *Les Métamorphoses d'une théorie économique: le revenu national chez Boisguilbert, Quesnay et J.-B. Say* (Paris: SEDES).

Molyneux, M. (1979), 'Beyond the domestic labour debate', *New Left Review*, no. 116, July–August.

Montani, G. (1988), 'Productive and unproductive labour', in J. Eatwell, M. Milgate and P. Newman (eds), *The New Palgrave: a dictionary of economics* (New York: Stockton Press), pp. 1008–9.

Montias, J. M. (1959), 'Planning with material balances in Soviet-type economies', *American Economic Review*, December; reprinted in A. Nove and D. M. Nuti (eds), *Socialist Economics* (Harmondsworth: Penguin, 1974).

Montias, J. M. (1975), 'A classification of communist economic systems', in C. Mesa-Lago and C. Beck (eds), *Comparative Socialist Systems: essays in politics and economics* (Pittsburgh, PA: Pittsburgh University Press).

Moore, J. R. (1975), Mandeville and Defoe', in I. Primer (ed.), *Mandeville Studies, International Archives of the History of Ideas*, vol. 81 (The Hague: Martinus Nijhoff).

Morellet, A. (1769), *Réfutation des Dialogues sur le commerce des blés* (Paris); Goldsmith-Kress microfilm no. 10642.

Morgenstern, O. (1963), *On the Accuracy of Economic Observations*, 2nd edn (Princeton, NJ: Princeton University Press).

Morgenstern, O. (1972), 'Thirteen points in contemporary economic theory: an interpretation', *Journal of Economic Literature*, vol. 9.

Morgenstern, O. and Schams, E. (1933), 'Eine Bibliographie der allgemeinen Lehrgeschichten der Nationalökonomie', *Zeitschrift für Nationalökonomie*, vol. 4, pp. 389–97.

Morishima, M. (1973), *Marx's Economics* (Cambridge: Cambridge University

Press).
Morris, J. (1958), 'Unemployment and unproductive employment', *Science and Society*, vol. 22, no. 3.
Morris, M. D. (1979), *Measuring the Condition of the World's Poor: the Physical Quality of Life Index* (New York: Pergamon for the Overseas Development Council).
Moskvin, P. (1929), 'Narodnyi dokhod i problema proizvoditel'nogo truda' [National income and the problem of productive labor], *Vestnik statistiki*, nos 3–4.
Moskvin, P. (1955), *Voprosy statistiki natsional'nogo dokhoda SSSR* [*Issues in USSR National Income Statistics*] (Moscow: Gosstatizdat).
Moss, M. (ed.) (1973), *The Measurement of Economic and Social Performance* (New York: NBER).
Mueller, D. C. (1976), 'Public choice: a survey', *Journal of Economic Literature*, pp. 395–423.
Mueller, D. C. (ed.) (1983), *The Political Economy of Growth* (New Haven, CT: Yale University Press).
Munro, H. (1975), *The Ambivalence of Bernard Mandeville* (Oxford: Clarendon Press).
Murray, D. (1905), *French Translations of the Wealth of Nations* (Glasgow).
Musgrave, R. A. (1959), *The Thoery of Public Finance* (New York: McGraw-Hill).
Musgrave, R. A. (1985), 'Excess bias and the nature of budget growth', *Journal of Public Economics*, vol. 28, December.
Musgrave, R. A. and Peacock, A. T. (eds) (1958), *Classics in the Theory of Public Finance* (New York: St Martin's Press).
Myint, H. (1943–4), 'The welfare significance of productive labour', *Review of Economic Studies*, vol. XI.
Myint, H. (1948), *Theories of Welfare Economics* (Cambridge, MA: Harvard University Press).

Nagels, J. (1974), *Travail collectif et travail productif dans l'évolution de la pensée marxiste* (Brussels: Editions de l'Université de Bruxelles).
Narodnoe Khoziaistvo Rossii za 1921/22 gg.: statistichesko-ekonomicheskii ezhegodnik [*National Economy of Russia, 1921–22*] (1923), (Moscow: 'Ekonomicheskaia zhizn').
Neumann, J. von (1937), 'A model of general equilibrium', trans. in *Review of Economic Studies*, no. 33, 1945–46.
Nicolaus, M. (1967), 'Proletariat and middle class in Marx', *Studies on the Left*, vol. VII, no. 1, January–February.
Nikitsky, A. (1926), 'Opyty ischisleniia narodnogo dokhoda v SSSR', *Ekonomicheskne obozrenie*, no. 1.
Niskanen, W. F. (1971), *Bureaucracy and Representative Government* (Chicago: Aldine).
Nordhaus, W. D. and Tobin, J. (1973), 'Is growth obsolete?' in M. Moss (ed.), *The Measurement of Economic and Social Performance* (New York: NBER).
Normano, J. F. (1945), *The Spirit of Russian Economics* (New York: Day).
North, D. C. (1977), 'Markets and other allocation systems in history: the challenge of Karl Polanyi', *Journal of European Economic History*, vol. 6, winter.
Notkin, A. I. (1948), *Ocherki teorii sotsialisticheskogo vosproizvodstva* [*Essays on the Theory of Socialist Reproduction*] (Moscow: OGIZ Politicheskoi literatury).

Notkin, A. and Tsagolov, N. A. (1937), 'O teorii i skheme balansa narodnogo khoziaistva SSSR akademika S. Strumilina' [On the theory and balance scheme of the USSR national economy of Academician S. G. Strumilin], *Planovoe khoziaistvo*, no. 4.
Nove, A. (1955), 'Some notes on Soviet national income statistics', *Soviet Studies*, vol. VI, no. 3, January.
Nove, A. (1963), *The Soviet Economy: an introduction*, 2nd edn (New York: Praeger, 1968).
Nove, A. (1964), *Was Stalin Really Necessary?* (London: Allen & Unwin).
Nove, A. (1967), 'Lenin as economist', in L. Shapiro and P. Reddaway (eds), *Lenin the Man, the Theorist, the Leader* (New York: Praeger).
Nove, A. (1969), *An Economic History of the USSR* (Harmondsworth: Penguin, 1970).
Nove, A. (1973), *Efficiency Criteria for Nationalised Industries* (Toronto: University of Toronto Press).
Nove, A. (1977), *The Soviet Economic System*, 1st edn, 2nd edn, 1980 (London: Allen & Unwin, 1982).
Nove, A. (1979), *Political Economy and Soviet Socialism* (London: Allen & Unwin).
Nove, A. (1982), *The Economics of Feasible Socialism* (London: Allen & Unwin).
Nove, A. and Nuti, D. M. (eds) (1974), *Socialist Economics* (Harmondsworth: Penguin).

O'Brien, D. P. (1970), *J. R. McCulloch: a study in classical economics* (London: Allen & Unwin).
O'Brien, D. P. (1975), *The Classical Economists* (Oxford: Clarendon Press).
O'Driscoll, G. P. (ed.) (1979), *Adam Smith and Modern Political Economy: bicentennial essays on the Wealth of Nations* (Ames, IA: Iowa State University Press).
Ofer, G. (1973), *The Service Sector in Soviet Economic Growth: a comparative study* (Cambridge, MA: Harvard University Press).
Ofer, G. (1987), 'Soviet economic growth: 1928–1985', *Journal of Economic Literature*, vol. XXV, no. 4, December, pp. 1767–833.
Okun, A. (1971), 'Should GNP measure social welfare?' *Brookings Bulletin*, summer.
Oldak, P. G. (1966), *Vzaimosviaz' proizvodstva i potrebleniia* [*Interdependence of Production and Consumption*] (Moscow: Ekonomika).
Oldak, P. G. (1970), 'Nakoplennoe i vosproizvodimoe bogatstvo. problema proizvoditel'nogo truda' [Accumulated and reproduced wealth. The problem of productive labor], *Mirovaia ekonomika i mezhdunarodnye otnosheniia*, no. 11.
Olgin, C. (1969), 'Lenin and the economics of socialism', *Studies on the Soviet Union*, no. 1, pp. 105–26.
Ostrovit'ianov, K. V. et al. (eds) (1954), Akademiia nauk SSSR, Institut ekonomiki, *Politicheskaia ekonomiia: uchebnik* [*Political Economy: a textbook*] (Moscow: Gosudarstvennoe izdatel'stvo politicheskoi literatury).

Paglin, M. (1961), *Malthus and Lauderdale: the anti-ricardian tradition* (New York: A. M. Kelley).
Palyi, M. (1928), 'The introduction of Adam Smith on the Continent', in J. M. Clark et al., *Adam Smith, 1776–1926* (New York: A. M. Kelley, 1966).
Paolillo, C. (1977), 'A note on the World Employment Conference', in ILO, *Employment, Growth, and Basic Needs* (New York: Praeger).

Parker, R. and Harcourt, G. C. (eds) (1969), *Readings in the Concept and Measurement of National Income* (Cambridge: Cambridge University Press).
Pashkov, A. I. (1958), *Ekonomicheskii zakon preimushchestvennogo rosta proizvodstva sredstv proizvodstva* [The Economic Law of the Faster Growth of Production of Means of Production] (Moscow: Gosplanizdat).
Pasquier, M. (1903), *Sir William Petty: ses idées économiques* (New York: Burt Franklin, 1971).
Peaker, A. C. (1974), *Economic Growth in Modern Britain* (London: Macmillan).
Pearson, H. W. (1957), 'The economy has no surplus: critique of a theory of development', in K. Polanyi, C. Arensberg, and H. W. Pearson, *Trade and Market in the Early Empires* (Chicago: Henry Regnery, 1971).
Pervushin, A. (1923), 'Narodnyi dokhod' (National income), in *Narodnoe i gosudarstvennoe khoziaistvo Soiuza sovetskikh respublik k seredine 1922–23 gg.* (Moscow: Narkomfin, 1923), pp. 1–10.
Pesek, B. (1961), 'Economic growth and its measurement', *Economic Development and Cultural Change*, vol. 9, no. 3, April.
Peston, M. H. (1972), *Public Goods and the Public Sector* (London: Macmillan).
Petrov, A. I. (1927), 'Teoreticheskie predposylki ischisleniia narodnogo dokhoda' [Theoretical premises of national income calculation] *Planovoe khoziaistvo*, no. 2.
Petrov, A. I. (1931), art. 'Dokhod narodnyi' [National income], vol. 23, *Bol'shaia Sovetskaia Entsiklopediia* (Moscow).
Petrov, A. I. (1954), *Natsional'nyi dokhod SSSR [USSR National Income]* (Moscow: Moskovskii rabochii).
Petrov, A. I. (ed.) (1954), *Kurs ekonomicheskoi statistiki* [Course of Economic Statistics], 2nd edn (Moscow: Gosstatizdat).
Petrov, A. I., Moskvin, P. I. and Morozova, I. D. (1944), 'Svodnyi razdel' [Summary], in Ts.S.U. Gosplana, *Slovar'-spravochnik po sotsial'no-ekonomicheskoi statistike* (Moscow: Gosplanizdat).
Petty, W. (1664), *Verbum Sapienti*, in C. H. Hull (ed.), *The Economic Writings of Sir William Petty*, vol. 1 (Cambridge: Cambridge University Press, 1899).
Petty, Sir W. (1665), *A Treatise of Taxes and Contributions*, in C. H. Hull (ed.), *The Economic Writings of Sir William Petty*, vol. 1 (Cambridge: Cambridge University Press, 1899).
Petty, Sir W. (1671–6?), *Political Arithmetick*, in C. H. Hull (ed.), *The Economic Writings of Sir William Petty*, vol. 1 (Cambridge: Cambridge University Press, 1899).
Pevzner, Ia. A. (1969), 'Povtornogo scheta uslug ne sushchestvuet' [No such thing as double-counting of services], *Mirovaia ekonomika i mezhdunarodnye otnosheniia*, no. 3.
Pevzner, Ia. A. (1987), *Diskussionnye voprosy politicheskoi ekonomiki* [Problems for Debate in Political Economy] (Moscow: IMEMO AN SSSR).
Phelps, E. S. (1985), *Political Economy: an introductory text* (New York: Norton).
Phillips, A. (1955), 'The Tableau économique as a simple Leontief model', *Quarterly Journal of Economics*, vol. LXIX, no. 1, February.
Pigou, A. C. (1932), *The Economics of Welfare*, 4th edn (London: Macmillan).
Pipes, R. (1980), *Struve, Liberal on the Right* (Cambridge, MA: Harvard University Press).
Pitzer, J. (1982), 'GNP of the USSR, 1950–1980', US Congress, Joint Economic Committee, *USSR: measures of economic growth and development, 1950–80* (Washington, DC: USGPO).
Plekhanov, G. V. (1908), *Fundamental Problems of Marxism*, ed. D. Riazanov,

trans. E. and C. Paul (New York: International Publishers, 1929).

Polanyi, K. (1944), *The Great Transformation: the political and economic origins of our time*, intro. R. M. MacIver (Boston: Beacon Press, 1957).

Polanyi, K. (1957a), 'The economy as instituted process', reprinted in *Primitive, Archaic, and Modern Economies: essays of Karl Polanyi*, ed. G. Dalton (Boston: Beacon Press, 1971).

Polanyi, K. (1957b), 'Aristotle discovers the economy', in K. Polanyi, C. M. Arensberg and H. W. Pearson (eds), *Trade and Market in the Early Empires: economies in history and theory* (Chicago: Henry Regnery, 1971).

Polanyi, K., Arensberg, C. M. and Peason, H. W. (1957a), 'The place of economies in societies', version with Appendix reprinted in K. Polanyi, *Primitive, Archaic and Modern Economies* (Boston: Beacon Press, 1971).

Polanyi, K., Arensberg, C. M. and Pearson, H. W. (eds) (1957b), *Trade and Market in the Early Empires: economies in history and theory* (Chicago: Henry Regnery, 1971).

Polanyi, K. (1968), *Primitive, Archaic, and Modern Economies: essays of Karl Polanyi*, ed. G. Dalton (Boston: Beacon Press, 1971).

Polanyi, M. (1960), 'Towards a theory of conspicuous production', *Soviet Survey*, October.

Politicheskaia ekonomiia: uchebnik tom 2, Sotsializm — pervaia faza kommunisticheskogo sposoba proizvodstva [Political Economy: A Textbook, vol. 2, Socialism — The First Phase of the Communist Mode of Production] (1978), (Moscow: Politizdat).

Pollak, R. A. and Wachter, M. L. (1975), 'The relevance of the household production function and its implications for the allocation of time', *Journal of Political Economy*, April.

Ponchaud, F. (1977), *Cambodge: Année zéro* (Paris: Juillard).

Popov, P. I. (1926), 'Introduction' to P. I. Popov (ed.), *Balance of the National Economy of the USSR, 1923/24*, vol. XXIX of *Works* of the Central Statistical Administration (Moscow); reprinted in N. Spulber (ed.), *Foundations of Soviet Strategy for Economic Growth: selected Soviet essays: 1924–1930* (Bloomington, IN: Indiana University Press, 1964).

Popper, K. R. (1947), *The Open Society and its Enemies*, vol. II, *The High Tide of Prophecy, Hegel, Marx and the Aftermath* (London: Routledge).

Popper, K. R. (1963), *Conjectures and Refutations* (London: Routledge & Kegan Paul).

Porat, M. U. (1977), 'The information economy: definitions and measurement', Office of Telecommunications Special Publication 77–12(1), Department of Commerce (Washington, DC: USGPO).

Praderie, M. (1968), *Ni Ouvriers, ni paysans: les tertiaires* (Paris: Seuil).

Pravdin, D. I. (1973), *Neproizvodstvennaia sfera: effektivnost' i stimulirovanie [The Nonproductive Sphere: Efficiency and Incentives]* (Moscow: Mysl').

Pravdin, D. I. (1976), *Razvitie neproizvodstvennoi sfery pri sotsializme [The Development of the Nonproductive Sphere under Socialism]* (Moscow: Mysl').

Prell, M. A. (1986), 'The role of the services sector in Soviet GNP and productivity estimates', unpublished paper, MIT.

Preobrazhensky, E. (1926), *The New Economics*, trans. B. Pearce, intro. A. Nove (Oxford: Clarendon Press, 1964).

Preobrazhensky, E. (1927), 'Economic equilibrium in the system of the USSR', in *Vestnik Kommunisticheskoi Akademii*, no. 22; reprinted in N. Spulber (ed.), *Foundations of Soviet Strategy for Economic Growth* (Bloomington, IN: Indiana University Press, 1964).

Prokopovich, S. N. (1917), *Voina i narodnoe khoziaistvo* [*The War and the Economy*] (Moscow: Efimov and Zheludkova).
Prokopovich, S. N. (1918), *Opyt ischisleniia narodnogo dokhoda 50 gubernii evropeiskoi Rossii v 1900-1913 gg.* [*An Attempt at Calculating the National Income of the Fifty Provinces of European Russia, 1900-1913*] (Moscow: Sovet Vserossiiskikh Kooperativnykh).
Prokopovich, S. N. (1930), *Narodnyi dokhod zapadno-evropeiskikh stran* [*National Income of the Western European Countries*] foreword S. G. Strumilin (Moscow/-Leningrad: Gosizdat).
Prokopovich, S. N. (1931-2), 'National income of the USSR', Birmingham Memorandum of the Bureau of Research on Russian Economic Conditions, no. 3.
Prokopovitch, S. N. (1952), *Histoire économique de l'URSS* (Paris: Flammarion).
Pryme, G. (1816), 'Syllabus of lectures on political economy'; appendix pp. 195-207 of G. F. Langer, *The Coming of Age of Political Economy 1815-25* (Westport, CT: Greenwood, 1987).
Pryor, F. L. (1968), *Public Expenditures in Communist and Capitalist Nations* (London: Allen & Unwin).

Quesnay, F. (1756), 'Fermiers', in *François Quesnay et la Physiocratie*, L. Salleron (ed.), vol. II (Paris: INED, 1958).
Quesnay, F. (1757a), 'Hommes' in *François Quesnay et la Physiocratie*, L. Salleron (ed.), vol. II (Paris: INED, 1958).
Quesnay, F. (1757b), 'Impôts', in *François Quesnay et la Physiocratie*, ed. L. Salleron, vol. II (Paris: INED, 1958).
Quesnay, F. (1758-9), 'Le Tableau Economique', 1st edn in *François Quesnay et la Physiocratie*, L. Salleron (ed.), vol. II (Paris: INED, 1958).
Quesnay, F. (1759), 'Explication du Tableau Economique'; in *François Quesnay et la Physiocratie*, ed. L. Salleron, vol. II (Paris: INED, 1958).
Quesnay, F. (1763), *La Philosophie rurale*, chapitre VII, in *François Quesnay et la Physiocratie*, ed. L. Salleron, vol. II (Paris: INED, 1958).
Quesnay, F. (1766a), 'Observations sur l'intérêt de l'argent', in *François Quesnay et la Physiocratie*, ed. L. Salleron, vol. II (Paris: INED, 1958).
Quesnay, F. (1766), 'Dialogue sur les travaux des artisans'; reprinted in *François Quesnay et la Physiocratie*, L. Salleron (ed.), vol. II (Paris: INED, 1958).
Quesnay, F. (1958), 'Textes annotés', vol. II of *François Quesnay et la Physiocratie*, ed. L. Salleron (Paris: INED).
Quesnay, F. (1972), *Quesnay's Tableau Economique* (1758), trans. and ed. M. Kuczynski and R. L. Meek (London: Macmillan).

Rachkov, P. A. (1958), 'O proizvoditel'nom trude v usloviakh sotsializma' [On productive labor under conditions of socialism], *Voprosy filosofii*, no. 6.
Radkey, O. H. (1955), 'Chernov and agrarian socialism', in E. J. Simmons (ed.), *Continuity and Change in Russian and Soviet Thought* (Cambridge, MA: Harvard University Press), pp. 63-80.
Ramsay, G. (1836), *An Essay on the Distribution of Wealth* (Edinburgh).
Ramsey, F. (1928), 'A mathematical theory of saving', *Economic Journal*, vol. 28.
Rawls, J. (1958), 'Justice as fairness', *Philosophical Review*, vol. 67, no. 164.
Rawls, J. (1967), 'Distributive justice', in P. Laslett and W. G. Runciman (eds), *Philosophy, Politics, and Society* (Oxford: Blackwell), 3rd series; reprinted in E. S. Phelps (ed.), *Economic Justice* (Harmondsworth: Penguin, 1973).

Rawls, J. (1973), *A Theory of Justice* (Cambridge: Belknap Press).
Rehbein, G. (1953), *Zur Marxschen Lehre vom Transport- und Nachrichtenwesen im Gesellschaftlichen Reproduktionsprozess* (Berlin: Die Wirtschaft).
Remington, T. (1987), 'Review' of S. Malle, *The Economic Organization of War Communism: 1918–1921*, *Soviet Studies*, vol. 39, no. 1, pp. 138–9.
Resnick, S. and Wolff, R. D. (1987), *Economics: Marxian versus neoclassical* (Baltimore, MD: Johns Hopkins Press).
Reynolds, L. G. (1983), 'The spread of economic growth to the third world: 1850–1980', *Journal of Economic Literature*, vol. 21, September, pp. 941–80.
Riabushkin, B. T. (1988), 'Valovoi Natsional'nyi Produkt: chto on soboi predstavliaiet i kak ischisliaietsia' [Gross National Product: what it is and how it is calculated], *Ekonomicheskie nauki*, no. 5, pp. 138–41.
Riabushkin, T. V. (1958), *Voprosy ekonomicheskoi statistiki* [*Issues in Economic Statistics*] (Moscow: Statistika).
Ricardo, D. (1951), *Works and Correspondence*, 10 vols, ed. P. Sraffa, with the collaboration of M. Dobb (Cambridge: Cambridge University Press for the Royal Economic Society).
Ricardo, D. (1821), *Principles of Political Economy and Taxation*, 3rd edn, vol. I of *Works and Correspondence*, ed. P. Sraffa with the collaboration of M. Dobb (Cambridge: Cambridge University Press, 1951).
Roberts, P. C. (1971), *Alienation and the Soviet Economy: towards a general theory of Marxian alienation, organizational principles, and the Soviet economy* (Albuquerque, NM: University of New Mexico).
Robbins, L. (1932), *An Essay on the Nature and Significance of Economic Science*, 3rd edn (New York: New York University Press, 1984).
Robbins, L. (1934), *The Great Depression* (London: Macmillan).
Robbins, L. (1970), 'Mill's "Essay on Economics and Society"', in *The Evolution of Modern Economic Theory* (Chicago: Aldine).
Robinson, J. (1934), 'Euler's theorem and the problem of distribution', *Economic Journal*, September, pp. 398–414; reprinted in *Collected Economic Papers*, vol. 1 (Oxford: Oxford University Press, 1951), pp. 1–18.
Robinson, J. (1942), *An Essay on Marxian Economics* (London: Macmillan).
Robinson, J. (1950), 'Review' of E. Böhm-Bawerk, *Karl Marx and the Close of his System*, ed. P. Sweezy (1948) *Economic Journal*, June.
Robinson, J. (1951), 'Introduction' to English edn of R. Luxemburg, *The Accumulation of Capital* (New York: Monthly Review, 1968).
Robinson, J. (1966), *Economics: an awkward corner* (London: Allen & Unwin).
Robson, J. M. and Laine, M. (eds) (1976), *James and John Stuart Mill: papers of the centenary conference* (Toronto: University of Toronto Press).
Roemer, J. (1988), *Free to Lose* (Cambridge, MA: Harvard University Press).
Rogers, J. W. (1971), 'The opposition to the Physiocrats: a study of economic thought and policy in the *ancien régime*', PhD thesis, Johns Hopkins University.
Roll, E. (1956), *A History of Economic Thought*, 3rd edn (Englewood Cliffs, NJ: Prentice-Hall).
Roscher, W. (1854) *Principles of Political Economy*, trans. J. Lalor (Chicago: Callahan, 1882).
Rosdolsky, R. (1968), *The Making of Karl Marx's 'Capital'*, trans. P. Burgess (London: Pluto Press 1977).
Rosenberg, N. (1960), 'Some institutional aspects of the Wealth of Nations', *Journal of Political Economy*, vol. 68.
Rossi, P. (1836–7), *Cours d'économie politique*, 2 vols (Paris: Jouret, 1840–41).

Rostow, W. W. (1960), *The Stages of Economic Growth, a Non-Communist Manifesto* (Cambridge: Cambridge University press).
Rothschild, E. (1981), 'Reagan and the real economy', *New York Review of Books*, vol. XXVIII, no. 1, 5 February.
Rotshtein, A. I. (1932), *Osnovy statistiki sotsialisticheskoi promyshlennosti* [Foundations of the Statistics of Socialist Industry], part 1 (Moscow: Sotsekgiz).
Rubenshtein, K. (1929), 'Metody ischisleniia narodnogo dokhoda v germanskoi literature' [Methods of calculating national income in German literature], *Planovoe khoziaistvo*, no. 8.
Rubin, I. I. (1928), *Ocherki po teorii stoimosti Marksa* [Essays on Marx's Theory of Value], 3rd edn (Moscow: Gosudarstvennoe izdatel'stvo); trans. M. Samardzija and F. Perlman (Montreal: Black Rose 1973).
Rubin, I. I. (1929), *Istoriia ekonomicheskoi mysli* [History of Economic Thought] (Moscow: Gosizdat).
Rubner, A. (1970), *Three Sacred Cows of Economics* (London: MacGibbon & Kee).
Rumer, B. (1981), 'The second agriculture of the USSR', *Soviet Studies*, vol. XXXIII, no. 4, October, pp. 560–72.
Rumiantsev, A. M. et al. (1978), *Politicheskaia Ekonomiia: uchebnik* (Political Economy: a textbook), 2 vols (Moscow: Izd. politicheskoi literatury).
Russell, B. (1920), *The Practice and Theory of Bolshevism*, (London: Allen & Unwin, 1948).
Rutgaizer, V. M. (1975), *Resursy razvitiia neproizvodstvennoi sfery* [Resources for the Development of the Nonproductive Sphere] (Moscow: Mysl').
Rutgaizer, V. M. (1985), 'Interview', in *Izvestiia*, 9 August.
Rutgaizer, V. M. and Sheviakhov, Iu E. (1987), 'Raspredelenie po trudu' [Distribution according to labor], *Ekonomika i organizatisiia promyshlennogo proizvodstva*, no. 3, pp. 3–21.
Rymes, T. K. (1979), 'Money, efficiency, and knowledge', H. A. Innis Lecture, Canadian Economic Association, Saskatoon, 29 May 1979, *The Canadian Journal of Economics*, vol. XII, no. 4, November.

Sahlins, M. (1972), 'The original affluent society', ch. 1 of *Stone Age Economics* (Chicago: Aldine).
Saint-Péravy, J.-N.-M. Guérineau de (1768), *Mémoire sur les effets de l'impôt indirect* (Paris).
Saint-Simon, C.-H. de (1819–20), 'L'Organisateur', vol. IV, pp. 17–26 of Enfantin edn, 1869; reprinted in *Oeuvres de Saint-Simon*, vol. II (Paris: Anthropos, 1966).
Samar, R. N. (1966), 'Ekonomicheskie formy proizvoditel'nogo truda pri sotsializme' [Economic forms of productive labor under socialism], *Vestnik moskovoskogo universiteta*, seriia 7, Ekonomika, no. 2.
Samuels, W. J. and Mercuro, N. (1985), 'A critique of rent-seeking theory', in D. Colander (ed.), *Neoclassical Political Economy: the analysis of rent-seeking and DUP activities* (Cambridge, MA: Ballinger).
Samuelson, P. A. (1954), 'The pure theory of public expenditure', *Review of Economics and Statistics*, vol. 36, pp. 387–9; reprinted in R. W. Houghton (ed.), *Public Finance* (Harmondsworth: Penguin, 1973).
Samuelson, P. A. (1958), 'An exact consumption-loan model of interest with or without the social contrivance of money', *Journal of Political Economy*, vol. 66, pp. 467–82.
Samuelson, P. A. (1971), 'Understanding the Marxian notion of exploitation: a

summary of the so-called transformation problem between Marxian values and competitive prices', *Journal of Economic Literature*, vol. 9, no. 2, June, pp. 399–431.

Sargent, T. W. and Wallace, N. (1976), 'Rational expectations and the theory of economic policy', *Journal of Monetary Economics*, vol. 2, April, pp. 169–84.

Savin, N. (1969), 'Passazhirskii transport i statistika natsional'nogo dokhoda' [Passenger transport and national product statistics] *Vestnik statistiki*, no. 2.

Say, J.-B. (1803), *Traité d'économie politique*, 1st edn (Paris: Degerville).

Say, J.-B. (1819) *Traité d'économie politique*, 4th edn (2nd edn, 1814; 3rd edn, 1817), trans. C. R. Prinsep, *Treatise of Political Economy* (Philadelphia, 1821) (New York: A. M. Kelley, 1964).

Say, J.-B. (1841) *Traité d' économie politique*, 6th edn (5th edn, 1826); ed. H. Say and E. Daire (Paris: Guillaumin, 1852).

Say, J.-B. (1972), *Traité d'économie politique*, preface by G. Tapinos (Paris: Calmann-Lévy).

Say, J.-B. (1828–9), *Cours complet d'économie politique*, 3rd edn with notes by H. Say, 2 vols (Paris: Guillaumin, 1852).

Say, J.-B. (1832), *Treatise of Political Economy*, trans, C. R. Prinsep (Philadelphia: Biddle).

Say, J.-B. (1848), *Oeuvres diverses* (Paris: Guillaumin).

Schroeder, G. (1979), 'The Soviet economy on a treadmill of "reforms"', US Congress, Joint Economic Committee, *Soviet Economy in a Time of Change* (Washington, DC: USGPO).

Schroeder, G. (1987), 'U.S.S.R.: toward the service economy at a snail's pace', US Congress, Joint Economic Committee, *Gorbachev's Economic Plans* (Washington, DC: USGPO), vol. 2, pp. 240–60.

Schroeder, G. E. and Denton, M. E. (1982), 'An index of consumption in the USSR', Congress, Joint Economic Committee, *USSR: Measures of Economic Growth and Development, 1950–80* (Washington, DC: USGPO), Part IV.

Schultz, T. W. (1961), *Investment in Human Capital: The Role of Education and Research* (New York: Free Press).

Schumpeter, J. A. (1912), *Theory of Capitalist Development*, 1st edn, trans. R. Opie of 1926 edn (Cambridge, MA: Harvard University Press, 1934).

Schumpeter, J. A. (1942), *Capitalism, Socialism and Democracy* (New York: Harper & Row, 1962).

Schumpeter, J. A. (1954), *History of Economic Analysis*, ed. E. B. Schumpeter (New York: Oxford University Press, 1968).

Scitovsky, T. (1943), 'A note on profit maximisation and its implications', *Review of Economic Studies*; reprinted in G. Stigler and K. E. Boulding (eds), *Readings in Price Theory* (Homewood, IL: Irwin, 1952).

Seers, D. (1949), 'A note on current Marxist definitions of the national income', *Oxford Economic Papers*, vol. 1.

Seers, D. (1972), 'What are we trying to measure?'. *Journal of Development Studies*, vol. 8, no. 3, pp. 21–36.

Seligman, E. R. A. (1903), 'On some neglected British economists', *Economic Journal*, vol. 13.

Seliunin, V. (1988), 'Istoki' [The sources], *Novyi mir*, no. 5.

Seliunin, V. and Khanin, G. (1987), 'Lukavaia tsifra' [Sneaky figures], *Novyi mir*, no. 2, pp. 181–201.

Sen, A. K. (1981), *Poverty and Famines* (Oxford: Clarendon Press).

Senior, N. W. (1836a) *Outline of the Science of Political Economy* (New York: A. M. Kelley, 1951).
Senior, N. W. (1836b), *Principes fondamentaux de l'économie politique*, tirés de leçons édites et inédites, de M. N. W. Senior,. . .par le Cte Jean Arrivabene (Paris: Aillaud).
Senior, N. W. (1848), 'Review of J. S. Mill's *Unsettled Questions* and *Principles*, *Edinburgh Review*, vol. 88, no. 178, October.
Senior, N. W. (1852), *Four Introductory Lectures on Political Economy* (London: Longman, Brown, Green & Longman).
Seraphim, H.-J. (1925), *Neuere russische Wert- und Kapitalzinstheorien* (Berlin: de Gruyter).
Seton, F. (1957), 'The transformation problem', *Review of Economic Studies*, vol. 24; reprinted in M. C. Howard and J. E. King (eds), *The Economics of Marx* (Harmondsworth: Penguin, 1976).
Shanin, T. (1985), *Russia as a Developing Society: the roots of otherness*, vol. 1 (London: Macmillan).
Sharpe, A. (1982), 'The structure of the Canadian economy, 1961–76: a Marxian input–output analysis', PhD thesis, Department of Economics, McGill University.
Shatalin, S. S. (1971), *Printsipy i problemy optimal'nogo planirovaniia narodnogo khoziaistva* [*Principles and Issues in Optimal Planning of the National Economy*] (Moscow: Obshchestvo Znanie RSFSR).
Shatalin, S. S. (1987a), 'Sovremennoe ekonomicheskoe myshlenie kak faktor intensifikatsii obshchestvennogo proizvodstva' [Contemporary economic thinking as an intensification factor for social production], *Vestnik Leningradskogo Universiteta: seriia Ekonomika*, no. 2, pp. 83–91.
Shatalin, S. S. (1987b), 'Kak izmerit' ekonomicheskii rost' [How to measure economic growth], *Ekonomicheskaia gazeta*, no. 31, July, p. 11.
Shatalin, S. (1987c), 'Strukturnye sootnosheniia ekonomicheskogo rosta' [Structural relationships in economic growth], *Ekonomicheskaia gazeta*, no. 32 August.
Shawcross, W. (1979), *Sideshow: Nixon, Kissinger, and the destruction of Cambodia* (New York: Pocket Books).
Shelp, R. K. (1981), *Beyond Industrialization: the ascendancy of the global service economy* (New York: Praeger).
Shukhov, N. S. (1966), 'Metodologicheskie napravleniia i shkoly burzhuaznoi politicheskoi ekonomii' [Methodological directions and schools of bourgeois political economy], in A. I. Pashkov (ed.), *Istoriia russkoi ekonomicheskoi mysli* [*History of Russian Economic Thought*], vol. III (Moscow: Mysl').
Simon, C. and Witte, A. D. (1982), *Beating the System* (Boston: Auburn House).
Skinner, A. S. and Wilson, T. (eds) (1975), *Essays on Adam Smith* (Oxford: Clarendon Press).
Slovar'-spravochnik po sotsial'no-ekonomicheskoi statistike 1944 [*Dictionary–Handbook on Socioeconomic Statistics*] (Moscow: Gospolitizdat).
Smith, A. (1776), *An Inquiry into the Nature and Causes of the Wealth of Nations*; introduction, notes, marginalia, and enlarged index by E. Cannan (1904) (New York: Modern Library, 1965).
Smolinski, L. (1967), 'Planning without theory', *Survey*, vol. 67, July.
Sohn-Rethel, A. (1972), *Intellectual and Manual Labour*, (London: Macmillan, 1978).
Solodkov, M. V. (1959), 'O proizvoditel'nom trude pri sotsializme' [On productive labor under socialism], *Nauchnye doklady vysshei shkoly* (Ek. nauki),

no. 1.
Solodkov, M. V. (1969), *Metodologiia issledovaniia proizvoditel'nogo i neproizvoditel'nogo truda pri sotsializme* (Methodology for Research on Productive and Unproductive Labor under Socialism) (Moscow: MGU).
Sobol', V. A. (1960), *Ocherki po voprosam balansa narodnogo khoziaistva* [Essays on the Balance of the National Economy] (Moscow: Gosstatizdat).
Solodkov, M. V. (1978) *Neproizvodstvennia sfera pri sotsializme: voprosy teorii i metodologii proizvoditel'nogo truda* [The Nonproductive Sphere under Socialism: theoretical and methodological aspects of productive labor] (Moscow: Mysl').
Solow, R. M. (1957), 'Technical Change and the aggregate production function', *Review of Economics and Statistics*, vol. 39, August.
Sombart, W. (1897), 'Idealen der sozialer Politik', *Brauns Arkhiv für Soziale Gesetzgebung*, vol. 10, no. 1.
Sonin, M. Ya. (1962), 'O kharaktere truda i zaniatosti v domashnem i ichnom podsobnom khoziaistve' (Characteristics of labor and employment in the domestic and private auxiliary economy), *Voprosy narodnogo khoziaistva SSSR: k 85-letiiu ak. S. G. Strumilina*, V. S. Nemchinov et al. (eds) (Moscow: Akademiia nauk).
Sowell, T. R. (1972), *Say's Law* (Princeton, NJ: Princeton University Press).
Sowell, T. R. (1974), *Classical Economics Reconsidered* (Princeton, NJ: Princeton University Press).
Spann, O. (1910), *The History of Economics*, 1st edn; trans. E. and C. Paul of 5th edn, 1919 (New York: A. M. Kelley, 1972).
Speck, W. A. (1975), 'Mandeville and the eutopia seated in the brain', in I. Primer (ed.), *Mandeville Studies, International Archives of the History of Ideas*, vol. 81 (The Hague: Martinus Nijhoff).
Spence, W. (1807), *Britain Independent of Commerce*; reprinted in *Tracts on Political Economy* (London: Longman, Hurst, Rees, Orme, and Brown, 1822).
Spengler, J. J. (1960a), 'Mercantilist and physiocratic growth theory', in B. F. Hoselitz et al., *Theories of Economic Growth* (Glencoe, IL: Free Press).
Spengler, J. J. (1960b), 'John Stuart Mill on economic development', in B. F. Hoselitz et al., *Theories of Economic Growth* (Glencoe, IL: Free Press).
Spengler, J. J. and Allen, W. R. (1960), *Essays in Economic Thought: Aristotle to Marshall* (Chicago, IL: Rand McNally).
Spiegel, H. W. (ed.) (1952), *The Development of Economic Thought* (New York: John Wiley).
Spiegel, H. W. (1983), *The Growth of Economic Thought*, rev. edn (Durham, NC: Duke University Press).
Spulber, N. (1964), *Soviet Strategy for Economic Growth* (Bloomington, IN: University of Indiana Press).
Spulber, N. (1979), *Organizational Alternatives in Soviet-Type Economies* (Cambridge: Cambridge University Press).
Spulber, N. (ed.) (1964), *Foundations of Soviet Strategy for Economic Growth* (Bloomington, IN: University of Indiana Press).
Sraffa, P. (1960), *Production of Commodities by Means of Commodities* (Cambridge: Cambridge University Press).
Stalin, J. V. (1928), 'Industrialization of the country and the right deviation', speech of 24 November; reprinted in N. Spulber (ed.), *Foundations of Soviet Strategy for Economic Growth* (Bloomington, IN: University of Indiana, 1964).
Stalin, J. V. (1933), speech of 7 January, in Institut Marksa-Engel'sa-Lenine-Stalina pri TSK KPSS, *KPSSs v rezoliutsiiakh i resheniiakh*, vol. II (Moscow: Gosizdat politicheskoi literatury, 1953).

Stalin, J. V. (1934), 'Report to the Seventeenth Congress... on the work of the Central Committee', speech of 26 January; reprinted in B. Franklin (ed.), *The Essential Stalin: major theoretical writings, 1905–1952* (Garden City, NY: Anchor Books, 1972).
Stalin, J. V. (1952), *Economic Problems of Socialism in the USSR*; reprinted in B. Franklin (ed.), *The Essential Stalin: major theoretical writings, 1905–1952* (Garden City, NY: Anchor Books, 1972).
Stalin, J. V. (1954), *Works*, vols. 1–11 (Moscow: Foreign Languages Publishing House), vols. 12–14 (Stanford, CA: Hoover Institution).
Stalin, J. V. et al. (1933), *From the First Five-Year Plan to the Second*, English edn (Moscow).
Stanback, T. M. (1979), *Understanding the Service Economy* (Baltimore, MD: Johns Hopkins Press).
Steedman, I. (1978), *Marx after Sraffa* (London: New Left Books).
Stern, J. J. (1975), *Growth and Distribution* (Cambridge, MA: Harvard Institute for International Development for ILO).
Stigler, G. J. (1956), *Trends in Employment in the Service Industries*, ser. 59 (New York: NBER).
Stigler, G. J. (1971a), 'Adam Smith's travels on the ship of state', *History of Political Economy*, vol. 3.
Stigler, G. J. (1971b), 'The Theory of Economic Regulation', *Bell Journal of Economics and Management Science*, vol. 2, spring, pp. 3–21.
Stigler, G. J. (1976), 'The X-istence of X-efficiency', *American Economic Review*, vol. 66, no. 1, March, pp. 213–16.
Stigler, G. and Friedland, C. (1980), *The Year of Economists, 1980–1981*, calendar (Chicago, IL: University of Chicago Press).
Stockman, D. (1986), *The Triumph of Politics: the inside story of the Reagan revolution* (New York: Avon Books).
Stone, R. (1985), 'Foreword' to S. G. Wheatcroft and R. W. Davies, *Materials for a Balance of the Soviet National Economy 1928–30* (Cambridge: Cambridge University Press), pp. ix–xxii.
Storch, H. (1823), *Cours d'économie politique ou exposition des principes qui déterminent la prospérité des nations*, 5 vols, with notes by J.-B Say (Paris: Aillaud, Bossange, Rey et Gravier).
Storch, H. (1824), *Cours d'économie politique... vol. V, Considérations sur la nature du revenu national* (Paris: Bossange).
Streeten, P. (1977), 'Distinctive features of a basic needs approach to development' *International Development Review*, vol. 19, no. 3.
Strumilin, S. G. (1924), 'Khoziaistvennoe znachenie narodnogo obrazovaniia' [The economic significance of public education], *Ekonomicheskaia zhizn'*, pp. 63 ff.
Strumilin, S. G. (1926), 'Narodnyi dokhod SSSR' [The USSR national income], *Planovoe khoziaistvo*, no. 8.
Strumilin, S. G. (1936a), 'K teorii balansa narodnogo khoziaistva' [Towards a theory of the balance of the national economy]', *Planovoe khoziaistvo*, nos 9–10.
Strumilin, S. G. (1936b), in *Ekonomicheskaia zhizn'*, no. 144, 18 October.
Strumilin, S. G. (1950), 'K skheme balansa narodnogo khoziaistva SSR' [Towards a balance scheme for the USSR national economy], lecture, USSR Academy of Sciences; reprinted in S. G. Strumilin, *Statistiko-ekonomicheskie ocherki* [*Statistical and Economic Essays*] (Moscow: Gosstatizdat, 1958).

Strumilin, S. G. (1958a), *Na planovom fronte* [*On the Planning Front*] (Moscow: Gosizdat politicheskoi literatury).
Strumilin, S. G. (1958b), *Statistiko-ekonomicheskie ocherki* (Moscow: Gosstatizdat).
Strumilin, S. G. (1963), *Izbrannye proizvedeniia v piati tomakh* [*Selected Works in Five Volumes*] vols 1–3 (Moscow: Akademiia nauk).
Struve, P. (1913), *Khoziaistvo i tsena* [*Economy and Price*], vol. 1 (St Petersburg: Izd. Riabushinskago).
Studenski, P. (1946), 'Methods of estimating national income in Soviet Russia', NBER, Conference on Research in Income and Wealth, *Studies in Income and Wealth*, vol. VIII (New York: NBER).
Studenski, P. (1961), *The Income of Nations* (1st edn, 1958) (New York: New York University Press).
Studenski, P. (1968), *Dokhod natsii* [*The Income of Nations*] trans. V. M. Kudrov (Moscow: Statistika).
Studenski, P. and Wyler, J. (1947), 'National income estimates of Soviet Russia', in 'The Economy of the USSR', AEA Papers and Proceedings, *American Economic Review*, May.
Sweezy, P. M. (1942), *The Theory of Capitalist Development* (New York: Monthly Review, 1970).
Sweezy, P. M. (ed.) (1948), *Karl Marx and the Close of his System* (1896) by Eugen Böhm-Bawerk and *Böhm-Bawerk's Criticism of Marx* (1904) by Rudolf Hilferding, together with an ... article by Ladislaus von Bortkiewicz... (New York: A. M. Kelley, 1966).
Sweezy, P. M. (1965), 'Paul Alexander Baran, 1910–1964', *Monthly Review*, vol. 17, March.
Swianiewicz, S. (1965), *Forced Labour and Economic Development* (Oxford: Oxford University Press).

Tarbuck, K. J. (comp.) (1972), *Imperialism and the Accumulation of Capital by Rosa Luxemburg and Nikolai Bukharin*, trans. R. Wichmann (London: Allen Lane).
Tawney, R. H. (1929), *Equality*, 1st edn; 4th edn, 1952, intro. R. M. Titmuss (London: Unwin Books, 1964).
'The Teaching of Economics in the Soviet Union' (1944), trans. R. Dunayevskaya, *American Economic Review*, vol. 34, September, pp. 531–7.
Terray, E. (1972), 'Prolétaire, salarié, travailleur productif', *Contradictions*, no. 2, July–December.
Terray, E. (1973), 'Travailleurs productifs et improductifs, leur appartenance de classe', *Contradictions*, no. 3. January–July.
Thurow, L. (1980), *The Zero-Sum Society* (Harmondsworth: Penguin, 1981).
Thurow, L. (1986), 'Who stays up with the sick cow?', review of P. L. Berger, *The Capitalist Revolution: fifty propositions about prosperity, equality and liberty*, *New York Times Book Review*, 6 June.
Tiebout, C. M. (1956), 'A pure theory of local expenditures', *Journal of Political Economy*, vol. 64, October, pp. 416–24.
Timmer, C. P. (1986), *Getting Prices Right: the scope and limits of agricultural price policy* (Ithaca, NY: Cornell University Press).
Todaro, M. P. (1985), *Economic Development in the Third World*, 3rd edn (New York: Longman).
Tollison, R. D. (1982), 'Rent-seeking: a survey', *Kyklos*, vol. 35, Fasc. 4, pp. 575–602.

Treadway, A. B. (1969), 'What is output? Problems of concept and measurement', in V. N. Fuchs (ed.), *Production and Productivity in the Service Industries*, vol. 34 of *Studies in Income and Wealth* (New York: NBER).
Tribe, K. (1988), *Governing Economy: the reformation of German economic discourse 1750–1840* (Cambridge: Cambridge University Press).
Tsagolov, N. A. (ed.) (1969), *Bibliografiia po voprosam politicheskoi ekonomii* [*Bibliography of Issues in Political Economy*] (Moscow: MGU).
Tsagolov, N. A. (1982), *Voprosy Metodologii i Sistemy Politicheskoi Ekonomii* [*Problems of Methodology and Systems of Political Economy*] (Moscow: MGU).
Tsentral'noe Statisticheskoe Upravlenie (TsSU) [Central Statistical Administration] (n.d.), *Statisticheskii spravochnik SSSR 1927* [*Statistical Handbook of the USSR for 1927*] (Moscow: Izd. TsSU).
Tsentral'noe Statisticheskoe Upravlenie (1924), *Narodnoe khoziaistvo Soiuza SSR v tsifrakh, kratkii spravochnik* [*Economy of the Soviet Union in Figures, Short Handbook*] (Moscow: Izd. TsSU).
Tsentral'noe Statisticheskoe Upravlenie (1925), *Narodnoe khoziaistvo Soiuza SSR v tsifrakh . . . – statisticheskii spravochnik* (Moscow: Izd. TsSU).
Tsentral'noe Statisticheskoe Upravlenie (1932), *Materialy po balansu narodnogo khoziaistva SSSR za 1928, 1929, 1930 gg* [*Materials on the Balance of the National Economy of the USSR for 1928. . .*], A. I. Petrov (ed.) (Moscow: Izd. TsSU).
Tsentral'noe Statisticheskoe Upravlenie (1967), *Klassifikatsiia otraslei narodnogo khoziaistva i otraslei promyshlennosti* [*Classification of the Branches of the National Economy and of Industry*] (Moscow: Izd. TsSU).
Tsentral'noe Statisticheskoe Upravlenie (1973), *Narodnoe khoziaistvo SSSR, 1922–1972* [*The USSR Economy, 1922–1972*] (Moscow: Statistika).
Tsentral'noe Statisticheskoe Upravlenie (1979), *Narodnoe khoziaistvo SSSR v 1978 godu* [*Economy of the USSR in 1978*] (Moscow: Statistika).
Tsentral'noe Statisticheskoe Upravlenie, otdel perepisi (1929), *Vsesoiuznaia perepis naseleniia 1926 goda* [*All-Union Census of the Population of 1926*], vol. 18 (Moscow: Izd. TsSU).
Tsentral'noe Upravlenie Narodnokhoziaistvennogo Ucheta (TsUNKhU) [Central Administration of Economic Accounting] (1932a), *Materialy k postroeniiu sistemy pokazatelei ucheta narodnogo khoziaistva SSSR* [*Materials for the Construction of a System of Accounting Indicators for the USSR Economy*] (Moscow: Soiuzorguchet).
Tsentral'noe Upravlenie Narodnokhoziaistvennogo Ucheta (1932b), *Narodnoe khoziaistvo SSSR* [*Economy of the USSR*] (Moscow: Soiuzorguchet).
Tsentral'noe Upravlenie Narodnokhoziaistvennogo Ucheta (1935), *Sotsialisticheskoe stoitel'stvo SSSR* [*Socialist Construction of the USSR*] (Moscow: Soiuzorguchet).
Tsentral'noe Upravlenie Narodnokhoziaistvennogo Ucheta (1936a), *Sotsialisticheskoe stroitel'stvo SSSR* (Moscow: Soiuzorguchet).
Tsentral'noe Upravlenie Narodnokhoziaistvennogo Ucheta (1936b), *Trud v SSSR* [*Labor in the USSR*] (Moscow: Soiuzorguchet).
Tsur, E. (n.d., *circa* 1984a), 'Annotated bibliographical list of Russian original texts concerning the problem of productive labor and national income computations' (Ramat, Israel: EFAL, The Kibbutz Center for Study and Research).
Tsur, E. (n.d., *circa* 1984b) 'Productive and unproductive labor – Marx versus the Soviet material misinterpretation' (Ramat, Israel: EFAL, The Kibbutz Center for Study and Research).
Tsypko, A. (1989), in *Nauka i zhizn'*, nos 1–2.

Tugan-Baranovsky, M. (1894), *Studien zur Theorie und Geschichte der Handelskrisen in England* (Jena: G. Fischer, 1901).

Tugan-Baranovsky, M. (1907), *Ocherki iz noveishei istorii politicheskoi ekonomii i sotsializma* [*Essays on the Recent History of Political Economy and Socialism*], 4th edn (St. Petersburg: Aleksandrov).

Tullock, G. (1974), *The Social Dilemma: economics of war and revolution* (Blacksburg, VA: Center for the Study of Public Choice).

Turgeon, C. (1889), 'Des Prétendues richesses immatérielles', *Revue d'Economie Politique*.

Turgeon, C. and Turgeon, C.-H. (1927), *La Valeur: critique des doctrines anglaises et françaises relatives à la valeur, au prix et à la richesse*, vol. 2 (Paris: Sirey).

Turgot, A. R. J. (1766), 'Reflections on the creation and distribution of wealth', in *The Economics of A. R. J. Turgot*, ed. and trans. P. D. Groenewegen (The Hague: Martinus Nijhoff, 1977).

Twiss, T. (1847), *View of the Progress of Political Economy in Europe since the 16th Century* (Clifton, N.J: A.M. Kelley, 1973).

Ulam, A. B. (1979), *The Unfinished Revolution: Marxism and Communism in the modern world*, 2nd edn (1st edn, 1960) (Boulder, CO: Westview).

United Nations (1947), *Measurement of National Income and the Construction of Social Accounts*, Studies and Reports on Statistical Methods, no. 7 (Geneva: United Nations).

United Nations (1959), Economic Commission for Europe, 'A note on some aspects of national accounting methodology in Eastern Europe and the Soviet Union', *Economic Bulletin for Europe*, vol. XI; reprinted in R. H. Parker and G. C. Harcourt (eds) *Readings in the Concept and Measurement of Income* (Cambridge: Cambridge University Press, 1969).

United Nations (1960), *Studies in Methods*, Doc. No. ST/STAT/ser. F/ no. 2/rev. 1 (New York: United Nations).

United Nations (1964), Department of Economic and Social Affairs, Statistical Office, *A System of National Accounts and Supporting Tables*, Doc. no. ST/STAT/ser. F/no. 2/rev. 2 (New York: United Nations).

United Nations (1968a), *A System of National Accounts*, Doc. no. ST/STAT/ser. F/no. 2/rev. 3 (New York: United Nations).

United Nations (1968b), Statistical Office, *International Standard Industrial Classification of All Economic Activities*, Stat. pap. series M, no. 4, rev. 2 (New York: United Nations).

United Nations (1969a), Economic and Social Council, Statistical Commission, *Conceptual Relationships between the Revised SNA and MPS: Report of the Secretary-General*, Doc. no. E/CN. 3/397 (New York: United Nations, 30 July).

United Nations (1969b), Economic and Social Council, Statistical Commission, *Basic Methodological Rules for the Compilation of the Statistical Balance of the National Economy, 'The Final Version of the System of Material Product Balances (MPS)'*, English trans. of Russian original, Doc. no. E/CN. 3/396 (New York: United Nations, 5 August).

United Nations (1971), Economic and Social Council, Statistical Commission, *Basic Principles of the System of Balances of the National Economy*, ST/STAT/ser. F/no. 17 (New York: United Nations).

United Nations (1977), *Comparisons of the System of National Accounts and the System of Balances of the National Economy*, Part one, *Conceptual relationships*, Studies in Methods, series F, no. 20 (New York: United Nations).

United Nations (1981a), *Statistical Yearbook* (New York: United Nations).
United Nations (1981b), *Comparisons of the System of National Accounts and the System of Balances of the National Economy*, Part two, *Conversion of aggregates of SNA to MPS and vice-versa for selected countries*, Studies in Methods, series F, no. 22, (New York: United Nations).
USSR Gosplan (1922), *Trudy Gosplana* [*Works of Gosplan*] (Moscow).
USSR Gosplan (1927), *Kontrol'nye tsifry narodnogo khoziaistva SSSR na 1926–1927 god* [*Control Figures . . . for 1926–27*] (Moscow: Izd. 'Planovoe khoziaistvo').
USSR Gosplan (1930), *Piatiletnii plan narodno-khoziaistvennogo stroitel'stva SSSR* [*Five-Year Plan of Economic Construction of the USSR*] 2 vols (Moscow: Planovoe khoziaistvo).
USSR Gosplan (1931), *Narodnoe khoziaistvo SSSR na poroge tret'ego goda piatiletki i kontrol'nye tsifry na 1931 god* [*Economy of the USSR on the Eve of the Third Year of the Five-Year Plan and Control Figures for 1931*] (Moscow: Gossotsekizdat).
USSR Gosplan (1934), *Ukazaniia i formy k sostavleniiu narodno-khoziaistvennogo plana na 1935 g* [*Directives and Forms for Compiling the Economic Plan for 1935*] (Moscow: Izd. Gosplana).
USSR Gosplan (1935), *Narodnokhoziaistvennyi plan na 1935 god* [*Economic Plan for 1935*] (Moscow: Izd. Gosplana).
USSR Gosplan (1939), *Tretii piatiletnii plan razvitiia narodnogo khoziaistva Soiuza SSR (1938–1942 gg.)* [*Third Five-Year Plan for the Development of the Economy of the USSR (1938–1942)*] (Moscow: Gosplanizdat).
USSR Gosplan (1969), *Metodicheskie ukazaniia k sostavleniiu gosudarstvennogo plana razvitiia narodnogo khoziaistva SSSR* [*Methodological Instructions for Compiling the State Plan of Development of the National Economy of the USSR*] (Moscow: Statistika).

Vaggi, G. (1987), *The Economics of François Quesnay* (Basingstoke: Macmillan).
Vainshtein, A'lb. L. (1968), 'Introduction' to Pavel' Studenskii (Paul Studenski), *Dokhod natsii*, trans. V. M. Kudrov (Moscow: Statistika).
Vainshtein, A'lb. L. (1969), *Narodnyi dokhod Rossii i SSSR: Istoriia, metodologiia ischisleniia, dinamika* [*National Income of Russia and the USSR: history, calculation methodology, dynamics*] (Moscow: Nauka).
Vaisberg, R. E. (1925a), 'Narodnoe khoziaistvo SSSR kak perekhodnoe' [The economy of the USSR as transitional], *Planovoe khoziaistvo*, no. 9.
Vaisberg, R. E. (1925b), 'Burzhuaznaia ideologiia v ekonomicheskoi literature' [Bourgeois ideology in economic literature], *Planovoe khoziaistvo*, no. 11.
Vaisberg, R. E. (1927a), 'O protsessakh obobshchestvleniia' [On socialization processes], *Planovoe khoziaistvo*, no. 1.
Vaisberg, R. E. (1927b, c), 'Obshchestvennyi produkt pri kapitalizme i v SSSR' [Social product under capitalism and in the USSR], *Planovoe khoziaistvo*, nos 5 and 6.
Val'tukh, K. K. (1965), *Obshchestvennaia poleznost' produktsii i zatraty truda na ee proizvodstvo* [*Social Usefulness of Production and its Cost in Labor*] (Moscow: Mysl').
Valentinov, V. (1971), *The NEP and the Party Crisis after the Death of Lenin: reminiscences of my work at the VSNKh during the NEP* (Palo Alto, CA: Hoover).
Vanous, J. (ed.) (1986), 'Developments in Soviet and East European national income, 1950–85', *PlanEcon Report*, vol. II, nos 50–52, 31 December.
Vanous, J. (ed.) (1987), 'The Soviet information system and its impact on economic reform', *PlanEcon Report*, vol. III, no. 46, 12 November.
Vauban, S. le Prestre de (1707), *Projet d'une dixme royale, qui, supprimant la*

taille... (Paris); Goldsmith-Kress microfilm no. 4431.
Veblen, T. (1899), *The Theory of the Leisure Class* (New York: Modern Library, 1934).
Veblen, T. (1914), *Instinct of Workmanship and the State of the Industrial Arts* (New York: Macmillan).
Viner, J. (1928), 'Adam Smith and laissez-faire,' in J. M. Clark *et al.*, *Adam Smith, 1776–1926* (Chicago: University of Chicago Press).
Viner, J. (1937), *Studies in the Theory of International Trade* (New York: A. M. Kelley, 1965).
Viner, J. (1958), 'Introduction' to Bernard Mandeville, 'A Letter to Dion'; reprinted in Jacob Viner, *The Long View and the Short: studies in economic theory and policy* (Glencoe, IL: Free Press).
Volkov, M. I. *et al.* (eds) (1979), *Politicheskaia ekonomiia: slovar'* [*Political Economy: A Dictionary*] 2nd edn, 1981 (Moscow: Politicheskaia literatura).
Volkov, M. I. *et al.* (eds) (1985), *A Dictionary of Political Economy*, trans. of 2nd edn (Moscow: Progress).
Voltaire (1759), *Candide*; reprinted in *Romans et contes* Frédéric Delofre and Jacques van den Heuvel (eds) (Paris: Gallimard, Pléiade, 1979).
Voltaire (1767), *L'Homme aux quarante écus*; reprinted in *Romans et contes*, Frédéric Delofre and Jacques van den Heuvel (eds) (Paris: Gallimard, Pléiade, 1979).

Walker, K. E. and Gauger, W. H. (1973), 'Time and its dollar value in household work', *Family Economics Review*, fall.
Wallace, M. (1983–4), 'Economic stabilization as a public good: what does it mean?' *Journal of Post Keynesian Economics* vol. 6, no. 2, winter, pp. 295–302.
Walras, L. (1874), *Elements of Pure Economics, or the theory of social wealth*, 1st edn; W. Jaffe trans. of 1926 edn (Philadelphia, PA: Orion, 1984).
Ward, B. N. (1979), *The Conservative Economic World View*, book 3 of *Ideal Worlds of Economics* (New York: Basic Books).
Watson, W. G. (1978), 'Bacon and Eltis on growth, government, and welfare', *Journal of Comparative Economics*, vol. 2.
Weinrobe, M. (1979), 'Household production and national production: an improvement of the record', *Review of Income and Wealth*, ser. 25, March.
Weintraub, E. R. (1977), 'General equilibrium theory', in S. Weintraub (ed.), *Modern Economic Thought* (Philadelphia, PA: University of Pennsylvania Press).
Weldon, J. C. (1973), 'On money as a public good', paper presented to the Canadian Economic Association, Kingston, Ontario, June.
Weldon, J. C. (1977), 'Marx: item no. 10', seminar notes, Department of Economics, McGill University.
Weldon, J. C. (1980), Letter to the author, 1 July.
Weldon, J. C. (1981), 'Pensions are not savings', Canadian Centre for Policy Alternatives, Pension Conference, Université du Québec à Montréal, 22 March.
Weldon, J. C. (1986), 'The classical theory of distribution', mimeo, Department of Economics, McGill University.
West, E. G. (1975a), 'Adam Smith and alienation: wealth increases, men decay?' in A. S. Skinner and T. Wilson (eds), *Essay on Adam Smith* (Oxford: Clarendon Press).
West, E. G. (1975b), *Education and the Industrial Revolution* (London: Batsford).
Weulersse, G. (1910a), *Le Mouvement physiocratique*, 2 vols (Paris: Félix Alcan).

Weulersse, G. (1910b) *Les Manuscrits économiques de François Quesnay et du Marquis de Mirabeau* (New York: Burt Franklin reprint, 1968).

Whately, R. (1826) 'On certain Terms, which are peculiarly Liable to be used ambiguously in Political Economy', appendix to *Elements of Logic* (New York: Harper, 1869).

Wheatcroft, S. G. and Davies, R. W. (eds and intro.) (1985), *Materials for a Balance of the Soviet National Economy 1928–1930*, foreword R. Stone (Cambridge: Cambridge University Press).

Wicksell, K. (1896), 'A new principle of just taxation', in *Finanztheoretische Untersuchungen* (Jena); reprinted and trans. in R. A. Musgrave and A. T. Peacock (eds), *Classics in the Theory of Public Finance* (New York: St Martin's Press, 1958), pp. 72–118.

Wicksell, K. (1898), *Interest and Prices*, trans. R. F. Kahn (New York: A. M. Kelley 1965).

Wieser, F. A. von (1889), *Natural Value* (London: Macmillan, 1893).

Wilber, C. K. (1969), *The Soviet Model and Underdeveloped Countries* (Chapel Hill, NC: University of North Carolina Press).

Wilber, C. K. (1973), 'The human costs of underdevelopment', in C. K. Wilber (ed.), *The Political Economy of Development and Underdevelopment* (New York: Random House).

Wilczynski, J. (1975), 'Cybernetics, automation, and the transition to communism', in C. Mesa-Lago and C. Beck (eds), *Comparative Socialist Systems* (Pittsburgh, PA: University of Pittsburgh Press).

Wilczynski, J. (1977), *The Economics of Socialism*, 3rd edn (London: Allen & Unwin).

Wiles, P. J. D. (1962), *Political Economy of Communism* (Oxford: Blackwell).

Wiles, P. J. D. (1974), *The Distribution of Income: East and West*, De Vries Lectures (Amsterdam: North Holland).

Wiles, P. J. D. (1977), *Economic Institutions Compared* (Oxford: Blackwell).

Wiles, P. and Efrat, M. (1985), *The Economics of Soviet Arms* (London: Suntory-Toyota International Centre, LSE).

Williamson, O. E. (1975), *Markets and Hierarchies* (New York: Free Press).

Williamson, O. E. (1977), 'Firms and markets', in S. Weintraub (ed.), *Modern Economic Thought* (Philadelphia, PA: University of Pennsylvania Press), pp. 185–202.

Wilson, T. and Skinner, A. S. (eds) (1976), *The Market and the State: essays in honour of Adam Smith* (Oxford: Clarendon Press).

Winch, D. M. (1973), *Analytical Welfare Economics* (Harmondsworth: Penguin).

Wolf, H. (1952–3), 'Zu den Grundfragen der marxistischen-leninistischen Theorie der produktiven Arbeit', *Wissenschaftliche Zeitschriften der Universität Leipzig*, no. 4.

Wolff, E. N. (1987), *Growth, Accumulation, and Unproductive Activity: an analysis of the postwar U.S. economy* (Cambridge: Cambridge University Press).

World Bank (1978), *World Development Report 1978* (Oxford and Washington: Oxford University Press for IBRD).

World Bank (1979), *World Development Report 1979* (Oxford and Washington: Oxford University Press for IBRD).

World Bank (1983), *China: Socialist Economic Development*, vol. 1, *Statistical System and Basic Data* (Washington, DC: World Bank).

World Bank (1984), *World Development Report 1984* (Washington, DC: World Bank).

World Bank (1985), *China: Long-Term Development Issues and Options* (Washing-

ton, DC: World Bank).
World Bank (1987), *World Development Report 1987* (Washington, DC: Oxford University Press for World Bank).
World Bank (1988), *World Development Report 1988* (Washington, DC: Oxford University Press for World Bank).
Wyler, J. (1946), 'The national income of Soviet Russia', *Social Research*, December.

Yanovsky, M. (1965), *Social Accounting Systems* (Chicago, IL: Aldine).
Yeh, K. C. (1965), *Soviet and Communist Chinese Industrialization Strategies*, RAND Memo P-3150, May (Santa Monica, CA: RAND).

Zaleski, E. V. (1971), *Planning for Economic Growth in the Soviet Union, 1918–1932*, trans. M.-C. MacAndrew and G. Warren Nutter (Chapel Hill, NC: University of North Carolina Press).
Zaleski, E. V. (1980), *Stalinist Planning for Economic Growth, 1933–1952*, trans. M.-C. MacAndrew and J. H. Moore (Chapel Hill, NC: University of North Carolina Press).
Zaslavskaia, T. I. (1986), 'Chelovecheskii faktor razvitiia ekonomiki i sotsial'naia spravedlivost' (The human factor in economic development and social justice), *Kommunist*, no 13, pp. 61–73.
Zauberman, A. (1960), 'The Soviet debate on the law of value and price formation', in G. Grossman (ed.), *Value and Plan* (Berkeley, CA: University of California Press).
Zauberman, A. (1969), 'Von Neumann's model and Soviet long-term (perspective) planning', *Kyklos*, no. 1.
Zauberman, A. (1971), 'Soviet work related to the von Neumann model and turnpike theories and some ramifications', in G. Bruckmann and W. Weber (eds), *Contributions to the von Neumann Growth Model* (New York: Springer Verlag).
Zauberman, A. (1976), *The Mathematical Revolution in Soviet Economics* (Oxford: Oxford University Press).
Zavlin, P. N., Shcherbakov, A. I. and Iudelevich, M. A. (1971), *Trud v sfere nauki* [*Labor in the Scientific Sphere*] (Novosibirsk: Nauka, sib. otdelenie).
Zeilinger, V. I. and Gukhman, B. A. (1928), 'K metodike postroeniia balansa narodnogo khoziaistva SSSR' [On the method of compiling a balance of the national economy of the USSR], *Planovoe khoziaistvo*, no. 4.
Zhamin, V. A. (1968), 'K voprosu ob ekonomike obrazovaniia' [On the issue of the economics of education], in K. V. Ostrovit'ianov (ed), *Sistema ekonomicheskikh nauk* [*System of Economic Sciences*] (Moscow: Nauka).
Zienkowski, L. (1959), 'Jak oblicza sie dochod narodowy'; cited in United Nations (1959), 'A note on some aspects of national accounting methodology in Eastern Europe and the Soviet Union'; reprinted in R. Parker and G. C. Harcourt (eds), *Readings in the Concept and Measurement of Income* (Cambridge: Cambridge University Press, 1969).
Zoteev, G. (1987), 'Ob otsenke valovogo natsional'nogo produkta' [On the valuation of gross national product], *Ekonomicheskaia gazeta*, no. 42, October, p. 10.

Index

Abalkin, L. I. 175, 180
Abolin, A. 150–1, 227
accounting, national 226, 227, 278
   aggregation in 151, 153, 228
   Kuznets 244–6
   Soviet 151–63, 174–5, 185
   Strumilin's 145
   see also Gross National Product, System of National Accounts; Material Product System
Agabab'ian, E. 159, 173–4
aggregates, in national accounting 228, 231
aggregates in Soviet accounting 153
agriculture
   in Boisguilbert 28, 29
   in Cantillon 29–30
   'exceptionally productive' (Smith) 64
   input requirements of, in Physiocracy 15, 31, 35
   as small in scale 115, 132, 260, 284
Amonn, A. 153, 228
'animal spirits' (Keynes) 10, 222, 283
   in Bacon and Eltis 213
   of farmers in Smith 57
   in Feldstein 218
Arrovian dictatorship 5–6, 117, 210, 221, 276
Arrow, K. J. 10, 117, 202, 219
artisans *see* handicraft production
Austrian school of classical economists 66, 70, 87, 88, 122
   see also Böhm-Bawerk, E.

Bacon, R. and Eltis, W. 69, 207–14, 233
bads
   in GNP 228, 251
   in Mandeville's *Fable* 24
   in neoclassical economics 244
   in Petty 16
   in Smith 57
Baran, P. 192, 193–6, 258
Baran, P. and Sweezy, P. 198, 201
barter 78, 88
   in Smith 58
base/superstructure dichotomy, in Marx 107–9, 118, 124
basic needs
   in development economics 261–4
   see also necessities; Physical Quality of Life Index

Bastiat, F. 72
Baudeau, Abbé Nicolas 35–6
Baumol, W. J. 174
Bazarov, V. A. 99, 124, 127–9, 148
Becker, A. S. non-productive services, in MPS 158, 239
Becker, G. S. 2, 4, 5, 8, 10, 66, 278–9
   and GNP accounting 252
   intermediatization 228
   stocks/flows 75
   time-utilitarianism 205, 248–51
   X-goods 51, 183–4, 186, 248–50, 252, 257, 277, 282
   Z-goods 51, 248–50, 252, 257, 278
Becker, J. F. 192, 201
Bentson, Margaret 204
Bergson, A. 163, 202
Bergsonian social welfare function 202, 257, 274, 278
Berliner, J. S. 178–9
Bernstein, Eduard 125
Bhagwati, J., directly unproductive profit-seeking (DUP) 224
Blaug, M. 59, 73
   general equilibrium 219–20
Bogachev, V. N. 173
Bogdanov, A. A., historical-materialist stage theory 129
Böhm-Bawerk, E. von 88, 122, 126, 137
   see also Austrian school of classical economists
Boileau, Dennis 74–5
Boisguilbert, P. le Pesant de 27–9, 40
boundaries *see* scope/boundaries
Braverman, H. 192, 196–8, 203
Buchanan, James M. 5, 186, 223
Bukharin, Nikolai, economics of revolution 135–42
Burns, A. 153

Cairncross, A. K. 248
Campbell, R. W. problems of international comparison of GNP 167, 242
Cantillon, Richard 29–30
capital
   constant, intermediate services as elements of 158
   human, excluded by Smith 46

THEORIES OF SURPLUS AND TRANSFER

in Marx 95
in Say 70
in SNA 235, 236
in Strumilin 145–6
in von Neumann 280
human in Juster 256
as intermediate good, in Say 71
nature of,
  in 1964 revised SNA 233–4
  in Bacon and Eltis 211
  in Smith 45–50
  in Turgot 38
  variable, in Marx 110
capital formation, and economic growth, in Denison 216
capital-revenue distinction, in Smith 48–9, 51, 106
capitalism, survival of 125–6
capitalist definition of output
  in Baran 195–6
  in Lewis 259–60
  materiality criteria,
    in Marx 93
    in Smith 45
  profit-making criteria 66, 76, 95
    in Marx 93
    in Smith 44, 45, 46, 52
  see also material definitions of output
capitalist mode of production 92
  in Marx 89, 92, 94–6, 107–9, 115, 116, 118
  petty producers beyond, in Marx 105–6
capitalist vs. petty capitalist see Marxian economics
Carlyle, Thomas 58
characteristics, goods as bundle of 83, 174, 177–8, 183–4
Chenery, H. B. 264
Chenery, H. B., Robinson, S. and Syrquin, M. 167, 235, 237
Chenery, H. B. and Syrquin, M. 164–5, 235
Chuprov, A. I. 127
circulation
  in Marx 97–105, 127–8
  in Sweezy 192
  see also production-circulation dichotomy; transportation
Clark, J. B. 219, 223
Classical economics 3, 4, 11, 86–7, 272
  established by Say 67
  growth theory 41, 260
  new, input/output error in 10
  post Keynes 190, 206–19
  revenue-capital distinction 106
  role of materiality criteria 8, 88
  see also Classical-Marxian; Marxian; neoclassical economics
Classical microeconomics 63, 64–78, 76

see also Garnier; Gray; Lauderdale; Say; Storch
Classical-Marxian economics 4, 5, 8–9, 27, 124, 201, 272
  domestic labor as unproductive 206
  see also Classical economics; Marxian economics
Coase, R. H. 112, 205, 254
colonial economics, in Luxemburg 125–6
competition
  beneficial (Smith) 177
  imperfect 2, 7–8, 276
  see also monopoly
  in Marx 91, 116–17
  perfect 178
  under *perestroika* 178, 181–2
competition-monopoly distinction 223
Condillac, E. B. de 39–40, 69, 97
consumers' sovereignty see sovereignty, consumers'
consumers' utility/utility theory 67, 87, 246
consumption
  essential, in Baran 195
  as sole end and purpose of production (Smith) 49, 251, 273–4, 283–7
  denied by Marx 108
consumption-investment distinction 189, 244
  in Bacon and Eltis 209–11
  in Feldstein 215
  in Kuznets 246
  in Malthus 81
  in Smith 43
  in SNA 234, 263
consumption-production distinction, subsistence wage theory 108
copyright, Say on 71, 87

Dahrendorf, R. 178
Davydov, I. 127
Debreu, G. 219
Denison, E. F. 211, 216, 251
development economics 75
  basic needs in 258, 261–6
  in King 23
  in Polanyi 269
dictators, economic 131, 261, 276–7
  see also Arrovian dictatorship; sovereignty, dictator's; taste dictatorship
dictatorships 279–81
directly productive profit-seeking (DPP), Bhagwati's 224–5
directly unproductive profit-seeking (DUP), Bhagwati's 224–5
distribution of income
  equality of 95, 106, 131, 181
  personal vs. functional 37, 68, 181
distribution services

334

as productive 148
as unproductive 19, 22
division of labor/specialization
  between state and private sector 87, 226
  comparative advantage and 66, 82
  and hierarchy,
    in Marx 110
    in Kidron 200
    in McCulloch 66, 82
    in Marx 101–2, 139
    in Polanyi 266–7
    in Senior 83
    in Smith 9, 50, 54, 56, 59–60, 62
    in Smith and Classical economics 39–40, 87
    in Val'tukh 170
domestic labor *see* household activities and housework
domestic servant
  in Garnier 65, 66–7
  in McCulloch 82
  in Marxian economics 80, 107, 203
  in Meade and Stone 230
  in microeconomics 86
  unproductive in Smith 47–9, 51–2
Dupont de Nemours, P. S. 32, 64
durability 16–17, 88, 172
  in Bazarov 128
  in Smith 44–5, 47, 48–9

Eagly, R. V. 81
economic accountability of Soviet state enterprises 179
economic history
  focus on growth of output in 278
  structural change in 79, 272
economics, development *see* development economics
economics of politics 1, 6, 7, 41, 222, 285–6
economists' sovereignty *see* sovereignty, economists'
education 58–9, 70, 85, 169, 171, 285
  in SNA 234, 235
Eisner, R. 255
Eltis, W. *see* Bacon, R. and Eltis, W.
entitlements, in Feldstein 214
entrepreneurs 10, 137–8, 285
  Bacon and Eltis on 213
  in Feldstein 218
  in Marx 93, 99–100, 138
  in Say 70
  in Smith 52, 59–60, 69
equilibrium
  general 11, 85, 88, 219–20
  in Marx 100–1
equilibrium analysis, from exchange of equivalents 72, 88
exchange of equivalents (*quid pro quo*) 7–8, 241, 258, 274

in Bacon and Eltis 210
in Cantillon 29
in Condillac 39–40
equilibrium analysis 11, 88, 220
imperfect 2, 7–8, 77
in Lauderdale 72
in Luxemburg 126
in Marx 91, 97, 100–1, 107
in Quesnay 34, 36
in Say 72, 74, 82
in Smith 44, 51, 60–2
in Val'tukh 170
exchange rates
  in SNA 235–8
  in Soviet GNP 242
exploitation, in Marxian economics 90, 97, 106, 115, 136, 202–3
external effects, quality of being poor or rich
  in 88, 92, 220
  in neoclassical economics of mode 122, 219, 220
  and state services 113, 189, 238, 284

factory paradigm *see* Marxian economics
fallacies of composition, Mandeville 23–4
Feldstein, Martin S. 214–19
feminism
  in Lenin 133
  in Marxism 201–6
  see also household activities and housework
final results of production activity, in Soviet economics 131, 175
final vs. intermediate 3, 7, 274, 275, 282–3
  government activity as, in SNA 229–30, 233
  in Mill 84–5, 87
  in neoclassical economics 244
  in revised SNA 231
  see also netness/finality, welfare relatedness
financial services, as unproductive
  in A.S. Becker 158
  in Baran 196
  in Marx 97, 103
Forbonnais, F. V. de 35, 37
free-rider problem 113, 220, 273, 286
  in Smith 57
Friedman, M. 53

Galiani, Abbé Ferdinando 38
Ganilh, C. 72
Garden of Eden logic 27, 28, 29, 35
Garnier, G. 4. 63, 64–7, 87
  and criticism of Smith 9, 64–7
  microeconomics of immaterial services 64–5
German historicists 122
Gillman, J. 192, 201

335

GNP *see* accounting, national; Gross National Product; material product system; System of National Accounts
goods
 as bundle of characteristics *see* characteristics
 internal (*biens*) (Storch) 75
goods and services *see* services, similarities and differences with goods
goodwill 71, 87, 235, 284
Gorbachev, M.
 and *perestroika* 175, 180–1
 socialist utilitarianism under 176, 177
Gordon, L. A. and Klopov, E. V. 183–4
government activity
 as final,
  in ICP 238
  in Keynes 226, 243
  in Meade and Stone 229
  in SNA 233–4
  in Sweezy 193
 as intermediate,
  in Kuznets 113, 244–6, 283
  in MEW 253
  in Mill 86
  in Studenski/Vainshtein 171
 see also 'most efficacious proportion'; state
Graslin, J.-J.-L. 39
Gray, S. 4, 9, 72–5
Great Depression 189, 191–2
Gross National Product (GNP) 163, 164, 211, 277
 conventions of 228, 231
 deficiencies of 228
 and development economics 264
 dollar exchange-rates in 167
 domestic labor in 206
 improving on 251–7
 King's estimates of 22–3
 netness/finality in 10
 Petty's computation for 15, 16, 17, 22
 welfare-relatedness in 274
 see also accounting, national; Material Product System; System of National Accounts
growth
 by incorrect inclusion of intermediates and bads and exclusion of goods 251
  in Hawrylyshyn 252
  in Juster 255
  in Kuznets 245–6
  in Nordhaus and Tobin 254
 of output insufficient for improvement in welfare 18
  in PQLI 264–6
 of output possibly not related to welfare, due to inclusion of immaterial production,
  in Baran 193, 194, 258
  in Sweezy 193
  in Marx,

due to immiseration 96, 116, 125
 due to lexicographic modism 116–18
 due to low producer utility (alienation) 117–18
of output synonymous with improved welfare 5–6, 275
 problem of international comparison 227, 235, 238, 241–2, 242, 251
 rate of by increase of productive consumption, in Lenin 132–3
 Soviet, without tertiarization 164
 through accumulation, in Smith 46
growth model
 Smithian, in *post* Keynes classicism 207, 258
 von Neumann 280–1
growth theory, Classical 41

handicraft production, as sterile, in Quesnay 32, 33, 38
Harrison, John 204
Hawrylyshyn, O., household services 252, 255
Herlitz, L., on Quesnay 36
hierarchality
 and division of labor 110
 perfect 34, 35, 57–8, 108, 109
  in Marx 109
  in Smith 57–8
Hill, T. P. 75, 252–3
Hirschman, A. O. 10
Hollanderian Classical economics, and interdependence 11
homo economicus 24, 91
 in neoclassical economics 220, 221, 225
homo faber 68, 244
homogeneization of rates of return, prices 178
household activities and housework 8, 269, 285
 in GNP accounting 206, 231–2, 252–5, 256
 as having opportunity cost 251
 in Lenin 133–5
 in Soviet economics 182–5
 in Strumilin 146–7, 182
 see also domestic servant; feminism
households as firms
 in Becker 205, 248–51
 in Marx 108
 in Molyneux 204
 in revised SNA 231, 247
 in Smith 47–9, 52
'humiliating appellation of barren . . .' (Smith) 6, 32, 49–50, 51, 56, 63, 201–6
 and Keynes 78–9

ICP *see* International Comparison Project
immaterial inputs (microeconomics) 63, 67–72

336

immaterial products, in Say 69, 71, 72, 74
immaterial services 8, 64, 65, 86, 88
  in Agabab'ian 173
  excluded from Soviet MPS 151–2
  in Marx 109–10, 111–12
  in Petty 17–18
  planned, excluded from output 159
  in Smith 6, 47, 60
  state as producer of 157–8
  in Strumilin 146
  as unproductive 176
    in Prokopovich 144
  see also material definition of output materiality criteria; material-immaterial
income, national
  real vs. personal 154–6
  in Stalin textbook 161
  see also accounting, national; Gross National Product
income-elasticity, in Boisguilbert 28–9
index-number illusion 257
industrialization
  in Baran 196
  identified with development,
    in Lenin 132–3, 164
    in Lewis 260
industry
  economies of scale, in Bacon and Eltis 212
  factory paradigm, in Marx 90, 114–16
  as producer of material necessities 95, 258
  as productive 80, 132, 137, 190
    in Smith 45, 68
inefficiency, sources of
  in Bacon and Eltis 213–14
  in Petty 17–18
information
  freely available 190
  imperfect 2, 61–2
  scarce,
    as bar to centralized planning 123, 130, 174
    in Smith 61–2
input/output error 6–7, 11, 275
  avoided 10, 158
    by Boileau 74–5
    by Ricardo 77–8, 87
    in Mill 85
  avoided by Keynes 226
  in Bacon and Eltis 211
  in Bukharin 140
  and consumer's sovereignty 257
  in Marx 89, 98, 109, 111, 113
  in Marxist feminism 202
  materialist fallacy 7, 35, 63, 258
    avoided by Bacon and Eltis 208
    avoided in Polayni 268
    in Baran 196
    and domestic mode of production 203

  in Kidron 199, 200, 201
  in Smith 54, 56
  in Soviet economics 174–5
  in Physiocracy 37, 41
  in Say 75
  and scope/boundary, in national accounting 228
  in Smith 41, 53–4, 58, 62
  in Stalin textbook 161–2
  unproductiveness fallacy 7, 19, 24–5
    in Feldstein 214
    in Sweezy 192–3
    in Walras 75
insurance, as luxury, in Kidron 201
integration
  horizontal, in Soviety industry 166
  vertical 34
    in Marx 100, 110, 111
interdependence, in MPS accounting 157–8
interdependence, theories of 11, 63, 258, 273
  basic logic of 1, 2, 9, 90
  in Becker 248–51
  behavioural unity in 273
  in Boisguilbert 27–9
  in Condillac 39–40
  and equilibrium theories 11, 85, 219–20
  in Garnier 64–7
  in Hill 252–3
  and Hollanderian Classical economics 11
  in King 23
  Mandeville's 23–5
  in Marxism 108, 109, 118, 147
  nature of boundaries in 41
  non-market activity, in neoclassicism 122
  in Petty 15–22
  pre-public choice neoclassical 87, 221
  public-goods-augmented neoclassical 9–10, 219–23
  Say's 72
  in socialist utilitarianism 147
intermediate consumption, in SNA 234–5
intermediate goods 6, 25, 159
  investment in, in Bacon and Eltis 211
  in Smith 56
intermediate input, government as
  in Kuznets 10, 228
  in Vainshtein 171
intermediate services 6
  as elements of constant capital 158
  in Marx 111
  public services as 157–8, 283
  in Say 69–70
  transport as, in Kuznets 168
intermediateness 275
intermediateness vs. finality *see* final vs. intermediate; input/output error
intermediatization
  of consumer goods as final (Becker) 228

of government,
  in Mill 86
  in Smith 56–7
  in Kuznets 243–7, 283
  of marketed goods 247–51
  in Mill 84–5, 86
  in Physiocracy 56
  and producers' sovereignty 88
  in Smith 50–1, 56–7
International Comparison Project (ICP) 236–8, 241–2
investment
  in Bacon and Eltis 210, 211
  by government, in Meade and Stone 229–30
  surplus for, in Lenin 131, 178
  see also consumption-investment distinction
investment and savings 80, 122–3, 124, 191, 215–18
Invisible Hand Theorem
  Kidron 200
  in Lewis 259
  in Marx 91, 116
  in Smith 23, 24
  in Soviet economics 182
Isaev, A. A. 126–7

Jevons, W. S. 68, 87, 219
Jorgensen, D. W. 255
Juster, F. T. 75, 145, 222, 279
Juster, F. T., Courant, Paul N. and Dow, G. K. 255–7, 285

Kaldor, N. 212
Kalecki, M. 198
Kautsky, K. 124–5, 140
Kendrick, J. W. 229, 230, 255
Keynes connection, in unproductive labor theory 25–6
Keynes, J. M. 4, 10, 192, 283–4
  and Malthus's analysis of gluts 78–9
  and Mandeville 25
  and market failure 189–90
  and national accounting 163, 228–9
  socialization of investment 122–3
  and sources of inefficiency 18
Keynesian economics 9, 198
  aggregate activity formula 27, 171, 175–6, 231, 243, 244, 251
  creating new problems as it solved old 190
  role of animal spirits in 25, 226
  role of state in 225–6
Kidron, Michael 192, 198–9
King, Gregory 22–3, 40, 229
Klopov, E. V. *see* Gordon, L. A. and Klopov
Kolakowski, L. 122
Kornai, J. 10

Kravis, I. B. 166
Kravis, I. B., Heston, A. and Summers, R. 236, 237, 238, 244
Kronrod, Ia. A. 168
Krueger, A. O. 223–4
Kursky, A. 170
Kuznets connection, in unproductive labor theory 24–5
Kuznets, S. S. 10, 69, 285
  and input/output error 24–5
  intermediateness 113, 175, 228, 244–7, 283
  materiality criteria 56
  and national accounting 229, 285
  re-estimates of Soviet GDP 163, 164
  scope, valuation and netness 3, 6, 15, 153, 228
  social framework 171, 222, 243–7, 282
  and state services 283
  and theory of public choice 55

labor *see* household activities and housework; productive labor; unproductive labor
laissez faire 206, 225, 276
  in Smith 58, 258
  surplus-generation and transfer models in 9, 63, 74, 91
Lancaster, K. J. 174
landlords, in Malthus 81, 87, 91
Lauderdale, Lord 72, 86
law of one price 88, 219
  in pre-public choice neoclassical economics 88, 122
Leibenstein, H. 10, 269
leisure 183–4, 194, 232, 249–50, 252, 254
Lenin, V. I. 131–5, 200
Leontief, W. W. 10, 31, 56, 86, 157–8
Lewis, W. A. 258–60
literacy 265, 285
  see also education
Luxemburg, Rosa 125–6
luxury as final, in Say 71
luxury-necessity distinction 3, 54, 87, 95–6, 260, 274
  in Boisguilbert 27–9
  in Cantillon 29–30
  see also necessary

McCulloch, J. R. 66, 81, 82, 87
Malthus, T. R. 9, 71, 87, 91, 112, 116
  and analysis of glut 64, 78–81
  and unproductive labor 78–81, 112, 126
Mandeville, B. de, *Fable of the Bees* 23–6, 40, 87
marginalism
  Condillac as predecessor of 40
  rise of 8, 76, 88, 122
  Marxian economics survive 9

INDEX

in Russia 126, 145
marginalist post-classical economics *see* marginalism
market failure, and state intervention, in Keynes 79–80, 189–90, 192
market vs. planning, in Bolshevik Marxism 142, 200
marketedness/non-marketedness 52, 55, 178, 191, 273
  in Bacon and Eltis 207–13
  in Smith 9, 44, 45, 48, 51
markets
  imperfect 8
  in Marx 91, 116–17, 181
  as price-making 88
  see also competition; mercantilism
Marshall, A. 11, 87, 88, 126, 168, 189, 219, 274
Marx, Karl
  class analysis 25, 91, 94, 106–7, 114, 115, 125
  Classical economist 9, 10, 89–91, 113
  critique of Smith 91, 93
  as historicist 91–2, 118
  on Malthus 112, 116
  and markets 116–17, 181, 284
  material/capital dilemma 92, 96, 118
  public choice theory 117
  see also Classical-Marxian; Marxian economics; Marxism
Marxian economics 3, 4, 8, 68, 89
  as applied in USSR 9, 142–4, 159–61
  characteristics of,
    base-superstructure analysis 92, 107–9, 118, 124, 143, 201
    'beyond the capitalist mode' 105, 107, 111, 143
    capitalist vs. petty capitalist 97, 105–6, 107, 111, 204
    constant vs. variable capital 109–10, 110, 111–12, 158
    domestic labor theory 203–6
    exploitation 90, 106, 115, 181, 202–3
    factory paradigm 4, 5, 9, 96–7, 114–16, 118, 185, 272
    history vs. microeconomics 97, 101–2, 115, 143
    in Lenin 135
    lexicographic modism 106, 186
    living production machine 90, 109–10, 110, 111
    production-circulation dichotomy 89, 96–103, 114–15
    productive-labor theory of value 89–90, 114–15, 116, 124, 272
    reproduction schemes 98, 100–1, 125
      households 108, 203
    self-exploitation of self-employed 89, 105–7, 232

    social necessity 112
Marxism
  as basis for Soviet state 142–4
  economic *see* Marxian economics
  and feminism 133, 201–6
  Golden Age 123, 124–35
  Old Left *post* Keynes 24, 190, 191–201
  reaction to alienation 202
  revolutionary, War Communism 136, 141
  as social theory 24, 89, 90, 114, 115
  withering-away of state 147, 148, 157
material definitions of output/materiality criteria 8, 64, 197, 258, 261
  in Bazarov 128
  in Garnier 64–5
  in Malthus 79
  in Marx 92, 94–6, 106
  in Mill 84, 85
  in MPS 239–40
  in non-Marxian economics 160
  Petrov's 149–50
  in Petty 17
  in Ricardo 76–7
  in Smith 42, 44–5, 51, 52–3, 65
  Soviet 144, 151, 157
  in Tsur 159, 162
  in Sweezy 192
  Vaisberg's 148–9
  in Val'tukh 170
  see also capitalist definition of output; input/output error; material-immaterial; materiality
Material Product System (MPS) 123, 228, 238–42, 285
  definition of non-material services in 239–40
  household activities in 182
  materiality of 151-2
  of national accounts 151–63
  objections to,
    Oldak 172–3
    Riabushkin 168
  and *perestroika* 163, 185, 242
  scope, valuation and netness in 151, 238–9
  and SNA 162–3, 238–42
material-immaterial distinction 3
  after Ricardo 81–3
  end of 88, 263
  in Say 67
  see also socialist materialism; socialist utilitarianism
materiality
  in Bogdanov 130
  in Bukharin 137–8
  Kronrod, in Soviet economics 168
  in Lenin 131
  in Marx 92–6
  not confined to Bolsheviks 144

in Polanyi 267–8
  in Smith 51
materiality criteria *see* capitalist definitions of output; material definitions of output
Meade, J. and Stone, R. 171, 189, 229–31
measure of economic welfare (MEW) 253–4
Medvedev, V. A. 242
Mensheviks 127, 144, 148, 151, 160
mental labor 148–9, 219
  in Marx 109–10
mercantilism 15, 16, 41, 63, 276
  Keynesian 17
  in neoclassical economics 207
  post Keynes 191
  in Smith 7, 223
  in Soviet economics 176, 178–81
  in Sweezy 192–3
merchants
  in Marx 98, 99, 100
  in Petty 19, 22
microeconomics *see* Classical microeconomics
military expenditure 70, 198, 201, 222–3, 284–5
Mill, J. S. 54–6, 76, 83–6, 87, 88, 128
Mirabeau, Marquis de 32, 33–4
Mishan, E. J. 207
Mitchell, W. C. 153
mixed economies
  capitalist 122, 190
    in Marx 5, 90, 118
    in Say 69
  socialist,
    definition of 122, 148
    see also socialist materialism
  transitional, in Petrov 149–50
mode, modism, mode-mindedness 134, 175, 197, 203, 237, 273
  in Bacon and Eltis 209
  in Bazarov 127
  in Keynes 189–90, 191
  in Kidron 200
  lexicographic 2, 106, 169, 186
  Marxian 9, 10, 92, 105–6, 272
    in Bolshevism 142–3, 160–1
  and Marxian domestic labor theory 203–4
  and mode-neutrality in development economics 263
  in neoclassical theory 221, 223
  in *post* Keynes classicism 206–7
  in Smith 47, 51–2
  in SNA's description of government 233–4
  in Soviet socialism 160–1, 169, 182
  Vaisberg's conservatism 148
  and welfare-relatedness 10
mode of production 1, 5, 76, 86
  domestic,

  in contemporary Marxian economics 201–6
  in Garnier 65
  market, in mixed capitalism 190
  in new neoclassical economics 221–2
  of petty producer 105–6
  see also capitalist mode of production
Molyneux, Maxine 204–6
money
  in macroeconomics 78
  as measuring rod for aggregation 153, 182, 203
  medium of exchange 51, 78, 102, 230, 235–6
  Smith's theory of money profits 43–4
  as store of value 78
monopoly
  'natural' 177
  preferred to competition by producers 181
monopoly-competition distinction, in public-goods-augmented neoclassical 223
Monthly Review 192
Morgenstern, O. 214, 281
Morris, M. D., PQLI 265–6
'most efficacious proportion', of state to private activity 2, 7, 275–6, 277, 282–3
  in Bacon and Eltis 211, 214
  denied in Ricardo 77
  in Marx 112–14, 118
  in Petty 18
  (Senior) 18, 83
  in Smith 57
  as theme of policy debates *post* Keynes 191
  see also government; state
multi-person firms
  in Marx 92, 94, 95, 96, 99–100
  in Smith 56

national character, in Storch 75–6
natural liberty, in Smith 50, 58
nature, forces of, in Marx 101
necessary vs. luxury 3, 54, 95–6, 260, 274
necessities 107, 261
  see also basic needs; luxury
neoclassical economics
  and distribution 19–20, 186
  of mode 219–26, 273
  and producer utility 68
  value theory 76
    in Pigou 153
neoclassical political economy 10, 273, 274
  see also interdependence; neoclassical economics
Net Material Product 10, 162, 277
  in Soviet accounting 170, 172, 175, 183
Net National Product, in Meade and Stone 231

340

netness/finality, welfare-relatedness 6, 63, 76, 273–4, 278–9, 282, 286
  in development economics 261–2
  in GNP accounts 10, 189, 230, 231, 264
  in Hill 252–3
  in ICP 236–8
  in Juster 256
  and Kuznets's social framework 243–7
  and net capital formation 234, 247
  in Nordhaus and Tobin 253–4
  opportunity cost valuations and 243
  in Physiocracy 30, 41
  and PQLI 265
  in pre-Adamites 7, 15
  in pre-public choice neoclassical 225
  in Smith 44, 50–1
  and taste dictatorship 276–7
    in Kidron 200–1
  see also scope
New Economic Policy (NEP) 123, 131, 141, 143–4, 152, 162
  as mixed economy 176
NMP *see* Net Material Product
non-marketed activity
  in interdependence theory 41
  in Polanyi 268
non-productivity
  criticism of 168–9, 176–7
  current status 185–6
  of immaterial services, as fundamental to Soviet economics 158, 176
  of public officials, in Vaisberg 148
  reinterpretation, in Soviet GNP 167–86
  in Stalin textbook 161
  see also immaterial services; unproductive labor
Nordhaus, W. D. and Tobin, J. 228, 253–4
Nove, A. 122, 177–8

Occam's razor used in scientific method 72, 103, 115
Ofer, G. 164–5, 235
Oldak, P. G. 159, 172–3, 184–5
opportunity cost 278
  in Becker 248
  in Garnier 66
  in Hawrylyshyn 254
  of household services 251, 255
  in McCulloch 82
  in Marx 101, 118
  in Smith 51
  in SNA 243
optimal functioning of the economy *see* Study for Optimal Functioning of the Economy (SOFE)
Ostrovit'ianov *see* Stalin textbook
output
  as aggregate activity, in Keynes 27
  as defined in MPS 152
  and welfare 1, 2, 6, 227
  see also capitalist definition of output; material definitions of output

Panglossian argument 5, 8, 37–8, 91, 223, 250, 276, 278
'peace, easy taxes, and tolerable administration of justice' (Smith) 56–7, 258, 283
Pearson, H. 267
pensions *see* investment and savings; retirement and pensions
perestroika
  and Material Product System 163, 167–86, 185, 242
  mercantilism under 176, 178
  mode and matter in 9, 176–82
Petrov, A. I. 147, 148, 149–50, 157
petty producer *see* Marxian economics; single-person firms
Petty, Sir William 2, 15–22, 40, 48
Pevzner, Ia. A. 159
Philip, Prince, taste dictator 207
Physical Quality of Life Index (PQLI) 264–6
Physiocracy 28, 30–7, 64, 278
  demise of 63, 64
  and netness 41
  productive/unproductive labor 2
  Smith's critique of 55–6
  sterility doctrine 31–4, 41
Physiocrats *see* Condillac; Forbonnais; Graslin; Physiocracy; Quesnay; Turgot; Voltaire
Pigou, A. C. 153, 168, 194, 203, 206, 230, 278
planning
  as final luxury 155
  vs. market, in Bolshevik Marxism 121, 139, 142
Pol Pot 19, 278
Polanyi, Karl 266–70, 280, 286
PQLI *see* Physical Quality of Life Index
pre-public-choice neoclassical economics 4, 8, 87–8, 122, 221, 243, 244, 272
  see also material-immaterial; state sector
price/pricing *see* valuation/pricing
private goods and services
  in Soviet economics 160
  in theories of interdependence 76, 284
private sector 209, 213, 215–16, 284
  Gray 74
prodigality 86, 216, 218
  in Smith 49–50, 75
producer utility
  in Becker 10, 256
  and boundary 227
  in Marx 10, 186
  in Say 10, 67–8

producers' sovereignty *see* sovereignty, producers
production
  capitalist mode of *see* capitalist mode of production
  for production's sake 6
    Tugan-Baranovsky 125
    in von Neumann 281–2
    see also sovereignty, consumer's
  'waste' in Kidron 199–200
production-circulation dichotomy
  in Bazarov 129
  boundaries in 127
  in Marx 96, 97–103
production-function logic 6–7, 169
  and domestic labor 205
  in Marx 98, 100, 112
  and mathematical economics 169
  in Polanyi 270
  in Smith 52, 57–9
productive consumption
  in Becker 249–50, 252
  in Hill 252
  in Lenin 132–3
  in Say 68
  in Senior 83
  in Smith 50–1, 58
  in von Neumann 280
productive-labor theory of value 1–2, 169, 272
  Abolin 150–1
  and domestic labor 185, 204–6
  in Garnier 65–6
  in Golden Age Marxism 124
  in Kidron 199–201
  in Lenin 131, 135
  in Marx 89, 92–6, 98–9, 109–10
  in Marxian economics 89–90, 116, 143
  in Marxist feminism 202–3
  and *perestroika* 185, 186
  rejected by Gordon and Klopov 183–4
  in Ricardo 76–8, 89, 90
  in Rubin 151
  in Smith 42, 43–5, 52–3, 89
  in Strumilin 145–7
  in Sweezy 192
productive-nonproductive activity
  in national accounting 157–9
  in Soviet GNP 167–8
productive-unproductive labor 3–5, 9, 213
  in Bogdanov 130
  definitions of 1–2, 130, 271–2
  in Garnier 65–7
  in Lauderdale 72
  in Marx 93–4, 107
  in Physiocracy 2
  in *post* Keynes classicism 201, 206
  in Senior 82–3

  as shorthand for other concepts 1, 3–4, 6, 272, 273
  in Smith 2, 42–3, 44–5, 62
  refuted by Gray 72–4
  see also external effects; final vs. intermediate; necessary vs. luxury
professions
  as anomalies 4, 6, 10, 87
  as immaterial services, in Marx 109, 110
  as productive/unproductive 10, 18, 60, 156, 196
  as single-person firms, in Marx 93–4, 109
  see also immaterial; services; unproductive labor
profit-making criteria *see* capitalist definition of output
profit-seeking 224–5, 273
profit-seeking vs. rent-seeking 3, 223
Prokopovich, S. N. 126, 144, 152, 156, 160
public choice theory 55, 83, 117, 122, 225, 257
public goods augmented neoclassical
  in theories of interdependence 9–10, 273
  unproductive labor theory 223–6
public goods and public services
  in Bacon and Eltis 213–14
  constant-capital costs, in national accounting 157
  externalities as foundation of 189, 191
  as intermediates, in Smith 57
  in Keynesian economics 191, 225
  in Kuznets 24–5
  in Mandeville 25
  in neoclassical economics 186, 219–23
  in Pigou 153
  role of state 87
  in Garnier 65
  in Marx 113–14
  in Say 69–70
  in Smith 54–5, 58–60, 61, 69
  see also 'most efficacious proportion'
  in Soviet economics 157, 160, 186
public sector
  growth of as factor in poor supply 206
  in neoclassical economics 88, 219–23
  see also public goods and public services

Quesnay, François 9, 30–7, 34–6, 44
quid pro quo see exchange of equivalents

rationality of expectations 190, 223
Rawls, J. 10, 25, 71, 202, 262, 279
  'difference principle' 118, 262, 282, 285
rent-seeking 273
  in Krueger 223–4
reproduction schemes *see* Marxian economics
'results, not inputs' 271–86

Kuznets 247, 256
  in PQLI 265
  in Say 69
  see also welfare-relatedness
retirement and pensions, in Feldstein 215–19
revenue-capital distinction
  in Marx 93, 106
  in Smith 48–9, 51, 60–1, 106
revolution
  Bukharin's economics of 135–42
  Marxian socialist, as corollary of lexicographic modism 115
  real costs of, Bukharin on 140–1
Riabushkin, B. T. 168, 242
Ricardo, D. 71, 87, 286
  and input/output error 53, 77–8
  productive labor theory of value 76–8, 89, 90, 95
Robbins, L. 5, 24, 268–9, 281
Robinson, Joan 198
Rossi, P. 9, 91, 107, 111
roundaboutness 51, 87
Rubin, I. I. 128, 151, 192
Russia 126, 132, 136, 141, 258
  Bolshevik economic ideology in 142
Rutgaizer, V. M. 177

Saint-Simon, C.-H. de 70, 71
Samuelson, P. A. 174, 281
Savin, N. 168
Say, J.-B. 10, 27, 63, 67–72, 75–6, 87, 284
  Marx on 91
  production as utility 67–8
  and Smith 9, 54
Say's Law 41, 67, 72, 88, 116
  compatibility with surplus-generation and transfer theory 79
  as joint idea with Mill 67
scarcity of means, in Robbins 269
Schroeder, G. E. and Denton, M. E. 164, 165, 166
Schumpeter, J. A. 3, 39, 70, 72, 76, 271
scientific activity
  in Marx 112
  in Say 70
scientific method 271
  use of Occam's razor 72, 103, 115
scope, valuation and netness (Kuznets) 15, 63, 76, 228, 257, 273, 275, 278, 285–6
  in Becker 250
  in Boisguilbert 27
  in MPS 238–9
  outside Soviet Russia 153
  in pre-public choice neoclassical 243
  in Sweezy 192
scope/boundary 1, 2, 11, 63, 227–8, 271, 273–8, 285
  in Becker 8
  before Smith 7, 15, 40–1
  economists' sovereignty and 2, 5, 6, 128, 257, 277
  in Marx 118
  in Marxist feminism 202
  in material product system (MPS) 152, 154–63
  in mixed Soviet socialism 143, 162
  see also socialist materialism; socialist utilitarianism
  and netness 228, 229, 235, 250
  in Physiocracy 30
  production boundary 41, 126–7, 162
  in Smith 41, 50–1, 62
  in SNA 231
  in Turgot 39
  and value theory 22, 76, 87, 88
  see also scope, valuation and netness
Senior, Nassau 10, 82–3, 85, 87
  and division of labor 9, 54
  Marx on 91, 107, 112
  'most efficacious proportion' 18, 112
servants *see* domestic servants
services
  in Becker 248
  in Hill 253
  'humiliating appellation of barren . . .' (Smith) 6, 32
  as of low productivity per head 88, 160
  in Lewis 259–60
  marketed 7, 147, 156, 207–9
  and Marxian reproduction schemes, in Petrov 150
  as non-productive, criticism of 168–9, 170–1
  private sector 284
  as profitable 87
  proportion of Soviet GDP 164–7, 172
  similarities and differences with goods 23, 86–7, 88, 150
  in Agabab'ian 173–4, 184
  in Bacon and Eltis 208–9
  in Malthus 79, 81
  in Marx 94, 118
  in MPS 151–2, 239–40, 242
  neoclassists 122
  in Oldak 184
  since Keynes 4
  in SNA, not necessarily final 234
  in Soviet economics, reinterpretation of 146, 155, 162, 167–8, 181
  state 7
  see also government activity
  as unproductive 127, 272
  in Baran 195–6
  in Marx 94–6, 105–6, 107
  in Smith 45, 47, 51, 52–3
Seton, Francis 99

single-person firms 2, 87, 97, 284
  agricultural (farms) 9, 60, 179–80
  goods producing 60
  in Marx 94, 96–7, 105–6, 109, 114–15
  service producing 60, 179–80
  in Smith 9, 52, 56, 60
  in SNA 231–2
  see also household activities and housework; professions
Smith, Adam 10, 87, 259, 273, 286
  annual produce 42–3, 55
  critique of physiocracy 41, 55–6
  culture as final 53, 60
  definitions of output, as used by Marx 92
  division of labor 50, 59
  education 58–9
  'humiliating appellation of barren . . .' 49–50, 51
  and immaterial production 41
  Invisible Hand Theorem 23, 24
  mercantilism 7, 9
  monopoly vs. competition 181
  'most efficacious proportion', Marx's comment on 112
  natural liberty 26, 50
  on parsimony, industry and state authorities 9
  'peace, easy taxes and tolerable administration of justice' 56–7, 283
  production-function logic 57–9
  productive labor theories of value 42, 52–3, 56, 63, 192
  productive/unproductive dichotomy 1, 2, 42–3, 44–5, 207
  revenue-capital distinction 106
  single-person firms 9
  surplus-generation and its transfer 9, 44, 51–2, 54
SNA *see* System of National Accounts
social democracy, bureaucratization in (Dahrendorf) 178
social framework (Kuznets) 24–5, 222, 274, 275, 282
  as intermediate 6, 10, 244–7, 270
  in Vainshtein 171
  in Mill 84–5
  in Nordhaus and Tobin 253
  and welfare-relatedness 243, 277
social necessity, in subsistence production 112, 128, 145
social welfare function (Bergsonian) 257, 261–2, 274, 278
socialism
  incomplete 141–2
  Abolin on 150–1
socialist economies, definitions 122–3
socialist materialism
  in Braverman 197

defined 131
Petrov 147, 149–50
in Stalin 161–2
Vaisberg 147–9
vs. socialist utilitarianism 9, 123, 143, 155, 163
socialist utilitarianism
  Abolin 150–1
  in Agabab'ian 173–4
  in Bogachev 173
  defined 131
  and feminism 203
  in Oldak 172–3
  and *perestroika* 176, 185
  and revolution 141
  Rubin 151
  and state control 173
  Strumilin 145–7
  in Studenksi 171
  in Vainshtein 171–2
  in Val'tukh 170
  vs. socialist materialism 9, 123, 143, 155, 163
  see also Mensheviks
socially necessary output, in socialist utilitarianism, Strumilin 145, 147
softness vs. hardness in budgets
  as key to neoclassical modism 222
  in Smith 62
Solow, R. M. 211, 281
Sombart, W. 271
sovereignty
  consumers' 49, 88, 195, 225, 244, 245, 257, 260, 274–6, 286
    denied by Marx 91
    and DUP/DPP 225
    in input/output error 10, 82, 257
    in Keynes–Meade and Stone 244
    and *perestroika* 175, 177, 179
    in Smith 49, 50
  dictator's 282
  economists' 8, 53, 257, 266, 271, 276–7, 285
    and boundary of economy 5, 6, 8, 128, 274–5
    and DUP-DPP 225
    in Polanyi 267–8
  producers' 88, 257, 275
    in Marx 110
    in Mill 85
    in Smith 53, 56
Soviet economics *see* Marxian economics; Material Product System; *perestroika*; socialist materialism
specialization *see* division of labor/specialization
Sraffa, Piero 200, 280
stage theory 142, 198

in Bazarov 127
in Bogdanov 129-31
in Bukharin 138-9, 140-1
Stalin, J. V. 144, 148, 161
Stalin textbook (Ostrovit'ianov) 161-2, 174
state
  economic role of 18, 25, 87, 206-7, 222, 223, 282-3
  in Lenin 135
  as unproductive 8, 9, 65, 74, 77, 113
state authorities
  impertinence of,
    in Smith 49
  incompetence of,
    in Ricardo 77-8
    in Smith 9, 55, 61-2
state intervention in market failure 189-90
state sector 206, 213-14, 282-3
  see also 'most efficacious proportion'
sterility doctrine
  criticised 37-40, 56
  Physiocracy 31-4, 41
stipendiary class, in Turgot 38
Stockman, D. 206
stocks and flows
  in Boisguilbert 28
  in Juster 255, 256, 284-5
  as litmus test of economist (Bogachev) 173
  in Mill 85
  in Oldak 172-3
  in Petty 16-17
  in revised SNA 231
  in Say 72
  in Walras 75, 88, 172
Stone, R. 233
  see also Meade, J. and Stone, R.
Storch, H. 75, 285
Strumilin, S. G. 145-7, 156, 173, 182
Studenski, P. 27, 171, 229, 278
Study for Optimal Functioning of the Economy (SOFE) 170
subsistence wage theory
  consumption-production distinction 108
  in Lewis 259-60
  in von Neumann systems 280-2
  and welfare, in Marx 116
substitution 91, 269
surplus-generation and its transfer, theories of 2-3, 11, 258, 272-3
  in Baran 194-6
  basic logic of 1, 4, 90, 227
  in Boisguilbert 29
  in Bukharin 137
  in Cantillon 30
  Classical 77, 87, 101-2
  as core paradigm in Classical and Marxian economics 9, 75, 90, 155, 169, 190, 271, 283

as core paradigm in New Right 9, 190, 273
  in development economics 266
  and input/output error 9
  in Kidron 199
  in Leontief 158
  in Malthus 78
  in Marx 89, 109, 114
  in Mill 83-6
  motivations for transfers 83, 98, 101
  nature of boundaries in 14
  neoclassical analysis of 122, 219
  in Physiocracy 30, 34
  in Quesnay 34
  in Smith 9, 44, 51-2, 54, 61, 63
  in Turgot 38-9
  value judgements of proponents of 95, 199, 275-6
  see also unproductive labor theory
surplus-generation vs. surplus-absorption 3, 194-5
surplus-value 198, 203
  in Baran 194-5
  in Marx 98, 99-100, 101
  in Sweezy 192
Sweezy, P. 192-3
  see also Baran, P. and Sweezy
Syrquin, M. see Chenery, Robinson and Syrquin; Chenery, and Syrquin
System of National Accounts (UN) (SNA) 162, 228, 243, 285
  conventions of 230-3
  household activities and housework 146, 231-2, 243, 251
  intermediate and final in 228-38
  MPS and 162-3, 238, 241
  non-marketed primary activity in 231, 285
  primary vs. non-primary production 232
  Revised (1968) 233-5
    housework as leisure in 146
    non-marketed primary activity in 231
  see also Gross National Product; Material Product System

target population 277, 279
  in development economics 262
  in Marx 94, 115, 117
  in Marxist socialist utilitarianism 175
  in Rawls 262
  in Vaisberg 149
taste dictatorship 25, 200-1, 207, 277
tertiarization 6, 164, 166, 190, 197
time-utilitarianism, G. S. Becker 205, 248-51, 256
Tobin, J. see Nordhaus, W. D. and Tobin
trade see mercantilism
transport
  freight vs. passenger 150
  public,

as immaterial production in USSR 156
as material service in MPS 168, 239
as non-productive 158, 159, 168, 185
transportation
  in Marx 97, 100
  as productive 102–3, 148
  as unproductive 127, 128
  as material product,
    in Vaisberg 148
  in Petty 19, 22
  in Say 68–9
  see also circulation; production-circulation dichotomy
Tsur, E. 159, 162
Tsypko, A. 176
Tugan-Baranovsky, M. I. 125, 126
Turgeon, C. 87
Turgot, A. R. J. 38–9

United Nations *see* System of National Accounts (UN) (SNA)
unproductive consumption, in Say 68
unproductive labor theory 2, 8–9, 27, 271, 272
  in Baran 195–6
  in Braverman 197–8
  in Bukharin 139–40
  in classical macroeconomics 78–81
  in conservative economics 191
  Crusoe connection 24
  in Feldstein 218
  in Kuznets 244
  Kuznets connection 24–5
  Lewis version 259
  in Malthus 64
  and marginalist revolution 122
  in Marx 93
  in Mill 83–6
  public-goods-augmented neoclassical 223–6
  in Smith 41, 42–3, 56, 60, 258, 261
  and welfare relatedness 190
  see also productive-labor
Ur-primary production 58, 109, 155
  and Polanyi's sorcerer 267–70
utility theory/consumers' utility 67, 76, 86, 87, 172, 227, 277, 279–80

Vainshtein, A'lb. L. 171–2
Vaisberg, R. E. 147–9
Val'tukh, K. K. 170
valuation/pricing 63, 88, 243, 273, 277
  in Bacon and Eltis 213
  in Becker 249, 250–1
  in Condillac 40
  in Kuznets 3
  in Marx 40

in MPS 242
in Say 67
in SNA 235–7
see also netness; scope
value, creation of 40
value theory *see* productive-labor theory of value
Volkov, M. I. 175–6
Voltaire, and Panglossian argument 5, 37–8
von Neumann, John 10, 280
von Neumann systems 6, 108, 118, 246, 277, 280–2, 286

wage, as opportunity cost of time (WOCT) (Hawrylyshyn) 254
wage theory 46–7, 49, 110, 203, 210, 280
Walras, L. 4, 5, 75, 87, 88, 172, 219, 284
War Communism, revolutionary Marxism 136, 138, 141
warehousing 159
  in Bazarov 127
  in Marx 97, 102
waste production, in Kidron 199–201
wealth, nature of 15, 27–8, 82, 94
Wealth of Nations, Adam Smith *see* Smith, Adam
wealth replacement, in Feldstein 215, 217
Weldon, J. C. 103, 219
welfare 1, 2, 8, 131, 203, 257
  measure of economic (MEW) 253–4
welfare-relatedness
  consumers' sovereignty and 10, 225, 243
  and growth 5–6
  in ICP 237, 251
  in Marx 116–18
  and *perestroika* 185
  planned output and SOFE 169–70
  see also growth; netness/finality, welfare-relatedness
Wicksell, K. 189, 220
Wolff, E. N. 192, 201
women *see* feminism; household activities and housework
work, non-work, and leisure, in Becker 249–50

X-goods (Beckerian) 186, 248–50, 252, 257, 277, 282
  in Gordon and Klopov 183–4
  in Smith 50–1
X-inefficiency (Liebenstein) 160, 269

Z-goods (Beckerian) 51, 248–50, 252, 257, 278
Zaslavskaia, T. I. 177